MW01611709

Standard History of Houston, Texas

From a study of the original sources

BENAJAH HARVEY CARROLL

Standard History of Houston, B. J. Carroll
Jazzybee Verlag Jürgen Beck
86450 Altenmünster, Loschberg 9
Deutschland

ISBN: 9783849684815

Publicly available via the Woodson Research Center and the Museum of Houston project through the following Creative Commons attribution license: "You are free: to copy, distribute, display, and perform the work; to make derivative works; to make commercial use of the work. Under the following conditions: By Attribution.

www.jazzybee-verlag.de
admin@jazzybee-verlag.de

Printed by Createspace, North Charleston, SC, USA

CONTENTS:

PREFACE

The Story of Houston has not proved an easy one to write. A city is in many respects a conglomeration of units rather than an aggregate of unities. the units are of character so varying that it is hard to reduce them to a common denominator. Municipal consciousness is vague and much that happens in the development of a city seems to be fortuitous rather than teleological. Yet Houston has in many respects grown to formula and plan and has often responded heartily to conscious effort made at improvement of conditions. The foundations of the past have been used and effort has been often cumulative in results. Undeniably there is a municipal spirit, an esprit du corps of the citizens that argues well for the future of the town.

The plan followed in writing this history has been to outline the beginnings of things, especially in the days of the Republic, in a manner that in so far as possible follows the order in which the events occurred. After Texas entered the Union the growth of the city is incidentally shown in tracing the growth of the several institutions the aggregate of whose history is the history of the city. The last chapter of the book hinges in a manner directly on to the last chapter on the days of the Republic and outlines the various periods in the municipal life, gives pen pictures of the city at intervals of years, and recapitulates briefly the latest era of greatest achievement.

The volume is true history in that an appeal has been made directly to the sources of history. These have been three; newspapers, there have been newspapers in Houston from the earliest times and it began with a newspaper advertisement; the observations of eye-witnesses as they were recounted in books, especially those of travel and adventure, as to conditions in Houston; and the recollections of the citizens themselves. A number of manuscript letters of Sam Houston and others were also used.

Every extant number of the files of the Telegraph, the Morning Star, the Houston Post and the Houston Chronicle was carefully searched for data, an expert spending four months in going over the newspaper files alone. Matter sufficient for the writing of five volumes the size of this one was obtained and the question of the selection of data assumed importance. Many facts and incidents are given as they are recalled in the memories of old citizens who had personal knowledge of the facts or who participated in the events.

A number of the chapters were written by Dr. S. O. Young, whose family belongs to the earliest settlers and who often writes from personal recollections of events occurring within the last half century. Dr. Young was at one time the editor of the Houston Post, was later the managing editor of the Galveston News and has a wide acquaintance with both local and Texas history and is famed as a raconteur.

A number of chapters, including all those of the period of the Republic and the chapter on the Wm. M. Rice Institute, were written entirely by the editor.

Such statistics as are given without reference to their source are those current in the newspapers of their respective dates or such as are given by those in position to possess true information.

This work may fairly lay claim to the following negative merits:

There is not one line of its text that is advertising. Such mention as is made of firms, persons or corporations is absolutely gratuitous and is made because the editor believed that the person, firm or corporation deserved such mention in fairly telling the story of Houston.

There is no conscious or deliberate padding of facts and figures or exaggeration of statement. The editor feels great pride in Houston, but he has made no attempt to show the city in a rosy glow.

There has been a careful avoidance of the valley of dry bones of municipal politics. Dead issues have been left in their moribund condition fully wrapped in their shrouds and vestments. Only when such important matters as the beginning or ending of the carpet bag government or the change from the old ward system of politics to the commission form of government were to be noted have the issues of municipal campaigns been noticed. Much more has there been an avoidance of state and national politics.

In writing this history special prominence has been given to the Rice Institute because this institution seems certain to play a tremendous part in the city's future history. The sketch of William M. Rice is the only one ever written and in preparing it the men who had known him in his lifetime and his business activities were consulted for information in their possession. It is believed to be a faithful portrayal of the man who takes rank as Houston's greatest benefactor.

Growth in the future will be so rapid that unless some measures are taken to preserve the city's early story it might easily be lost.

Such a volume as the present one, despite the care and trouble necessary to prepare it, necessarily appeals to a circle of readers found within the list of the citizens of Houston itself, together with a few outside students of economic or municipal conditions. It is believed, however, that this book will be of interest and value to all lovers of Houston and the editor chiefly deplores that he has found it impossible to even name all the worthy men and women who have contributed to the growth and prosperity of the city, and will be the first to admit that the services of many here unnamed are worthy to take rank along with the highest and best of those capitulated.

The editor cordially acknowledges the aid and assistance rendered by newspaper writers, by musicians, by architects and by others who have given counsel or advice on matters relating to their professions or callings.

The work is submitted as a record of the achievements of a city that is just three quarters of a century old. The record is carried to a date that varies between February 28, 1911 and November 1, 1911, as the chapters went to press at varying dates. It is the wish of the editor that it may prove to be worthy of the friendly consideration of those who love Houston and believe in her future.

Nov. 21, 1911.

THE EDITOR.

CHAPTER I - SETTLEMENT AND PIONEER LIFE

HOUSTON, a Monument to Real Estate Promoters' Art. First Built on Paper and Advertised all over America. Prohibitive Prices of Land at Harrisburg Caused Choice of Houston's Site. Foresight of A. C. and J. K. Allen. The First Steamer up the Bayou. City Mapped and Plotted. Rivalry with Harrisburg. Founding of Harrisburg. Geological Formation of Harris County. Early Social Conditions. Fights and Murders. Civil Officers, Laws and Justice. Building Court House and Jail. First Court Trials, First Wedding, First Divorce. City's Mayors under the Republic. Much Litigation and Many Land Frauds.

Houston is a splendid monument to the success of the real estate promoter's art. Other cities have prospered Topsy wise. They just grew. A lucky place at a cross roads, a river bend or a mountain pass where they might catch the drift from the tides of travel and by the simple process of accretion or the fortuitous concourse of human atoms a city came into being. Not so Houston. Its site was selected by promoters, it was mapped and planned ere ever a house was built, its advantages were touted in the national press and it has performed the singular feat of growing largely according to the plans and specifications originally laid out for its development and has surpassed the most "whopping" predictions as to its growth and prosperity.

All the stage wits and travelling vaudeville artists use Harrisburg as the target for their country village jokes and yet curiously enough it was the prohibitive price of land in Harrisburg that caused Houston to be chosen and built. The promoters recognized the obvious fact that Harrisburg is a better place for a city than Houston and tried to buy there but the owners of the proposed townsite were greedy and hence a site farther up the river was chosen.

By a deed of the date of August 26, 1836, and for a recited consideration of $5,000, two New York speculators, the brothers A. C. and J. K. Allen, purchased of Mrs. T. F. L. Parrott the south half of the lower of the two leagues of land granted to John Austin, near the head of tide water on Buffalo Bayou. It was immediately put on the market as a townsite. The first formal announcement is an advertisement published in the "Columbia Telegraph" of the date of August 30, 1836. It reads:

"The Town of Houston,

"Situated at the head of navigation on the west bank of Buffalo river is now for the first time brought to public notice, because, until now, the properties were not ready to offer to the public, with the advantages of capital and improvements.

"The town of Houston is located at a point on the river which must ever command the trade of the largest and richest portion of Texas. By reference

4

to the map it will be seen that the trade of San Jacinto, Spring Creek, New Kentucky, and the Brazos, above and below Fort Bend, must necessarily come to this place, and will at this time warrant the employment of at least $1,000,000 of capital, and when the rich lands of this country shall be settled, a trade will flow to it, making it, beyond all doubt, the great interior commercial emporium of Texas.

"The town of Houston is distant 15 miles from the Brazos river, 30 miles a little north of east from the San Felipe, 60 miles from Washington, 40 miles from Lake Creek, 30 miles south-west from New Kentucky and 15 miles by water and 8 or 10 by land above Harrisburg.

"Tide water runs to this place and the lowest depth of water is about 6 feet. Vessels from New Orleans to New York can sail without obstacle to this place, and steamboats of the largest class can run down to Galveston Island in 8 or 10 hours in all seasons of the year.

"It is but a few hours sail down the bay, where one may make excursions of pleasure and enjoy the luxuries of fish, fowl, oysters and sea bathing.

"Galveston Harbor, being the only one in which vessels drawing a large draft of water can navigate, must necessarily render the island the great naval and commercial depot of the country.

"The town of Houston must be the place where arms, ammunitions and provisions for the government will be stored, because, situated in the very heart of the country, it combines security and means of easy distribution, and a national armory will no doubt very soon be at this point.

"There is no place in Texas more healthy, having an abundance of excellent spring water, and enjoying the sea breeze in all its freshness.

"No place in Texas possesses so many advantages for building, having fine ash, cedar and oak in inexhaustible quantities, also the tall and beautiful magnolia grows in abundance. In the vicinity are fine quarries of stone.

"Nature appears to have designated this place for the future seat of government. It is handsome and beautifully elevated, salubrious and well watered and now in the very heart or center of population, and will be so for a length of time to come.

"It combines two important advantages—a communication with the coast and foreign countries and with the different portions of the Republic. As the country shall improve, railroads will become in use and will be extended from this point to the Brazos and up the same, and also from this up to the headwaters of San Jacinto, embracing that rich country, and in a few years the whole trade of the upper Brazos will make its way into Galveston Bay through this channel.

"Preparations are now making to erect a water saw mill and a large public house for accommodation will soon be opened. Steamboats now run in this river and will in a short time commence running regularly to the island.

"The proprietors offer the lots for sale on moderate terms to those who desire to improve them, and invite the public to examine for themselves.
Signed A. C. ALLEN, for A. C. & J. K. Allen.
August 30, 1836, 6 m.

"The Commercial Bulletin of New Orleans, Mobile Advertiser, The Globe at Washington, Morning Courier and New York Enquirer, New York Herald and Louisville Public Advertiser are requested to make 3 insertions of this advertisement and forward their bills to this office for payment."

How familiar it all sounds. Houston boosters ever since then have been consciously or unconsciously plagiarizing that model and brilliantly worded advertisement of the unborn city.

Land in Texas was inexhaustible and cheap, and it is startling only to think of the sheer nerve of the Allen Brothers in buying a large segment of a virgin wilderness on the banks of a brush grown bayou and deliberately starting out to make a great city there and to make it the capital of a new nation and then to advertise it all over a foreign country, for the United States was then a foreign country. Not only did the Allen Brothers start out to work this miracle but they actually accomplished it. Within a year's time this city of paper and tents was the capital of Texas and was entertaining distinguished men from many parts of the world.

Like most promoters, the Allens strained the facts a bit, but the facts could stand the strain. Communication with the coast and foreign countries was not of the best. It took four days to traverse the distance from Harrisburg to Houston by boat and only a bridle path traversed the jungle that intervened between the two points by land.

When the new city was first announced, Dr. Pleasant W. Rose of a neighboring town with a party visited the site of the city. They found "one dug out canoe, a bottle gourd of whiskey, a surveyors chain and compass and a grove inhabited by four men camping in tents."

Low hanging trees and snags in the bayou made progress slow by water. Francis R. Lubbock, one of the earliest and most prominent citizens, who was later Governor of Texas, "discovered Houston," in January, 1837. The little steamer on which he came up the bayou required three days to make the trip from Harrisburg, a distance of 12 miles by water. He says: "The slow time was in consequence of the obstructions we were obliged to remove as we progressed. We had to rig what were called Spanish windlasses on the shore, to heave the logs and snags out of our way, the passengers all working faithfully. All hands on board would get out on the shore, and cutting down a tree would make a windlass by boring holes in it and placing it upon a support and throwing a bight of rope around it, secure one end to a tree in the rear, and the other to the snags or fallen trees in the water. Then by means of the capstan bars we would turn the improvised capstan on land and draw from the track of the steamer the obstructions."

The saddest part of it was that even then the passengers came very near not finding the city. A party of them took the yawl to try and find the landing but missed it and passed on until they stuck in the brush in White Oak Bayou and then backed down until they found wagon wheels and footprints in the mud bank at the waters edge and then saw the stakes driven in the ground that indicated that Houston was there.

This steamer was the "Laura" and was the first to ever reach the wharfless landing.

The Allen Brothers had the germ of faith. It could not move mountains and hence the feature of beautiful elevation in the advertisement was a trifle difficult to find, but it could and did build cities.

The original plan of the city and the map of it contemplated only 62 blocks, all on the south side of Buffalo Bayou. Gail Borden, the man who subsequently discovered or invented condensed milk, and T. H. Borden made the survey and map in 1836. The streets were given the names they now hold except that Austin Street was then Homer Street and LaBranch Street was then Milton Street. Homer Street had its name changed within a short time in honor of Stephen F. Austin and Milton Street in honor of Alcee LaBranch Charge d' Affairs from the United States and the first minister to announce the recognition of Texas among the nations of the world. Epic poets of Greece and England were thus forced to give place to American heroes and statesmen:

Another map, made by Girard, of the Texas Army, is now in the possession of John S. Stewart of Houston.

On the original map, block 31, the present site of the court house, was set aside and marked court house, and block 34, the present market square, was marked Congress Square.

John Allen, who selected the site of Houston immediately following the Battle of San Jacinto, called the street now traversed by the Houston and Texas Central Road, Railroad Street, saying, "This is the street which the great Texas railroad will traverse. His foresight was correct and his prophecy came true, but he died before the first locomotive blew its whistle over the right of way. His death occurred in 1838.

On April 7, 1837, the townsite was enlarged and a new map was drawn, extending one tier of blocks beyond Rusk Street on the south, one tier beyond Crawford Street on the east and one tier beyond Clay Street on the west. The square west of the Rice Hotel square on Main Street was originally designated as Capitol Square but when the Capitol building was erected in 1837 it occupied the site now occupied by the Rice Hotel and soon to be occupied by the new 18-story Rice Hotel.

A little group of settlers, among them the promoters of the town, settled in Houston during the year 1836. They lived in tents. On January 1, 1837, the city was still one of tents although Henry Allen had a small log house and several small houses were in course of erection. Logs were being hauled in from the forest for a hotel on Franklin Street at the corner of Travis, now occupied by the Southern Pacific building, where the old Hutchins House stood for many years. Col. Benjamin Fort Smith built the first hotel. He had been Inspector General at the Battle of San Jacinto. All lumber was them sawed by hand and cost from $150 to $200 per thousand feet. There was a saw mill at Harrisburg but some of the earliest houses were built out of lumber that was shipped from Maine by water.

Most of those who came to the new town stayed, possibly because it was practically impossible to get away. The forests that surrounded Houston on every side were filled with abundance of wild game. Bear, deer, antelope, buffalo, wild turkeys in great flocks, and large herds of wild mustang horses roamed within a few miles. On the opposite side of Buffalo Bayou several tribes of wild Indians were accustomed to camp in the splendid forest, a custom which they kept up for several years after the founding of the town.

The streets were broad paths cleared by the axe, and bottomless with mud in wet weather. There were no sidewalks. The tents and huts clustered on the banks of the steam or a few blocks away. The town was still without a hotel, a court house, a jail or a church in December, 1836. Even the saloons occupied large tents. The battle of San Jacinto had been fought and won, but in Houston as elsewhere the inhabitants were without money, without revenue, without credit and without many of the most ordinary necessities of life. Cane brakes were burnt down and corn planted on the charred ground brought forth good crops. Some of the inhabitants had slaves, and cotton was early planted. Harrisburg was still the metropolis because it had a saw mill and its saloons were housed in wood instead of canvas. By December, 1836, the rivalry between the two places was keen, but Houston was pulling for the honor of being selected as the seat of government and aspired to be the capital of the new nation and the city destined to become a nest of sky-scrapers and the most populous city of Texas was fairly launched. One somehow wishes that its valiant yankee promoters could have seen a vision of even the Houston of today with bird men soaring in aeroplanes around the lofty buildings that serrate the city's skyline and give to it for the first time that beautiful elevation of which the initial advertisement spoke.

Under the Mexican government, a short time before the commencement of the Texas revolution in 1833 there had been created the municipality of Harrisburg as a political subdivision.

This included the entire district of which Harris county is only a part. For a short time the island of Galveston also formed a part of Harrisburg County as the municipality was called under the Republic after the Declaration of Independence in march, 1836, and continued to be called for several years.

When Houston was founded this section was sprinkled with settlers in all directions. A Mr. Knight and Mr. Walter C. White at the time of Long's expedition in 1820 had burnt off a canebrake and raised a crop of corn on the San Jacinto near its month, but subsequently moved to Brazoria.

John Henry Brown in an article in the Houston Post of December 17, 1891, gives a detailed account of the first settlers largely from information from Mary J. Briscoe, of Houston, a daughter of the John B. Harris who founded Harrisburg. He settled there in 1824, laid out the town in 1826 and built the first steam saw mill in Texas for which he received as a bounty two leagues of land. He was a merchant, a tanner and the owner of a schooner whose name—"The Rights of Man," reveals something of his religious and political views. This schooner plied between Harrisburg and New Orleans. In 1828, David, a brother of John B., arrived in Harrisburg and in 1830 William P. Harris and "Honest Bob" Wilson arrived, who were followed in 1832 by Samuel Harris, a fourth brother, all coming from Cayuga County, New York.

Mary Jane Harris, a daughter of the first settler, married Captain Andrew Briscoe, a colleague of the great Mexican patriot, Don Lorenzo De Zavala, and was one of the early settlers in Houston. Her daughter. Mrs. Adele B. Looscan, lives in Houston.

Perhaps the honor of being the first settler in Houston should go to a Mrs. Wilkins, who, with her two daughters and a son-in-law, Dr. Phelps, settled, in 1822, in territory now within the city limits of Houston.

Harrisburg was the seat of justice of the new Republic from March 22 to April 13, 1836. On the approach of the Mexican Army it was abandoned and Santa Anna put it to the torch. The first lone star flag made in Texas was improvised at Harrisburg in September, 1835, by a Mrs. Dobson and other ladies. A Miss Troutman, of Georgia, gave a lone star flag to Captain (later Colonel) William Ward, near the same time.

Following the battle of San Jacinto the First Congress of the Republic met in Columbia and on December 15, 1836, selected the new town of Houston as the seat of government to continue until 1840. The seat of government was moved to Houston just prior to May 1, 1837, and soon after—an event that proved to be even more important—the county seat was moved from Harrisburg to Houston. Since that time Harrisburg has been in a state of arrested development, a sleepy little town on the bayou, while Houston has steadily grown until its city limits have been thrust into the very heart of old Harrisburg and the turning basin and ship channel bid fair to give back to that town, now de facto a part of Houston, the dignity and prosperity it enjoyed three quarters of a century ago.

Harris County, in which Houston and Harrisburg are now located has an elevation of from 50 to 75 feet above sea level. Its surface is almost level with an almost imperceptible slope toward the south. One-fifth of the surface is slightly undulating.

A scientific writer in an early newspaper, who appears to know what he is talking about, says that the geological formation is past tertiary and that below the surface there is a layer of clay with streaks of calcareous nodules varying in color from white to gray and yellow to red. In the northern part of the county below the clay there is a stratum of sand, and in the southern part a moderately hard calcareous sandstone in which springs originate. Water is found from a depth of 15 feet upward and contains small quantities of lime, magnesia, chloride of sodium, and other minerals with a trace of organic matter. The surface soil in the north is a sandy earth and in the south a black waxy loam enriched with decomposed organic matter. It is probable that there are large deposits of oil at a considerable depth as oil has been found on nearly all sides of the county.

Most of the stirring events of early Texas history center elsewhere than in Houston, although the actors in those events were often residents of and visitors to the little new town on the bayou. Where these events relate to Texas rather than to Houston history they cannot even be categorized. San Jacinto had been fought before Houston was founded, and the events of the following years were mainly those of frontier growth all over Texas although the country was causing one of the prettiest diplomatic webs to be woven in the history of the American continent and England, France, Germany and other countries soon east covetous eyes upon the new republic. The important years for the new town were from the middle of April, 1837, to the latter part of 1839, during which time it was the seat of government.

The years 1837 and 1838 were the fat years of growth and prosperity for Houston and the year 1839 the lean year of famine, pestilence and backset in Houston as elsewhere.

Government and the administration of justice, occupied much of the time of the settlers in their isolated forest town and, in a community where the key note was independence and where the population was of the rough, hardy, self-reliant, courageous and opinionated sort, neither government nor the administration of justice was easy. Every man had infinite confidence in his own judgment and was always ready to back his opinion with pistol or bowie knife if anybody doubted its correctness. The duello was still an institution and quarrels and fights among the prominent citizens were thoroughly a matter of course.

The army and the legal profession and the government had made titles super-abundant and one could not fire a load of buckshot into any group without crippling a few judges, colonels and majors and as likely as not a general or a member of Congress or some cabinet dignitary.

The cooped up condition, the utter lack of news facilities and outside objects of interest, the sense of military importance and the undeniable fact that a goodly per cent of the population had left its former home moved by other motives than undiluted enthusiasm for Texas and that another portion was far better at a fight than at plowing corn, made for fractiousness and trouble. Government was largely personal, the statesmen all quarrelled with each other outrageously and often without adequate cause and partisanship ran high. All offices, both civil and military, were elective and there was an active demand for rotation in office so that everybody got honored with a few titles sooner or later. The multitude of personal difficulties is illustrated in the following story by Governor Lubbock which recounts conditions that have not entirely ceased in Houston even at this day. "An occurrence at an early day shows how Houston failed to get a carriage factory and lost at least one good immigrant. Charles Hedenberg, of the firm of Hedenberg & Vedder, commission merchants, had induced an uncle of his to come out from New Jersey with the view of establishing a carriage manufactory. Arriving very early in the morning his trunks were taken to the business house. About ten o'clock that day Hedenberg suggested to his uncle that the Congress of the Republic was in session and that if he would go up to the Capitol he might be entertained, and after a while they would go to the house. While the Jersey man was seated in the Senate Chamber rapid firing took place in the hall of the building which caused every one to rush out to see what had occurred. The uncle was just in time to see the body of Senate Clerk Thompson being borne away after having been badly shot up by Senate Clerk Brashear. He had never seen a man shot before and rushed out of the building going down Main Street on the west side. After walking several blocks he was passing the Round Tent saloon when a soldier, who had just been shot by a man named Seevy, rushed out and nearly fell upon him. Now thoroughly frightened he dashed across to the other side of the street and just as he got over in front of John Carlos' saloon, a man rushed out of the saloon door with his bowels protruding from an immense gash inflicted on him by the bowie knife of a discharged soldier. The visitor rushed to the commission store and gasped out an order for his trunks to be put on a dray and sent to the boat for Galveston at once. The nephew remonstrated. 'Why Uncle, you have not had time to look at the town.' The old man replied, 'Charley, I have seen all I ever want to of Texas. Get my trunks.'"

Government, as has been pointed out, was the chief concern of the Texans. Harrisburg County was created by the General Council at San Felice, but was not fully organized until 1837.

Captain Andrew Briscoe, elected chief justice by the first Congress, held elections for precinct and county officers who had their offices at the county seat at Harrisburg. Those elected were: sheriff, John W. Moore; coroner, William Little; clerk of the district court, James S. Holman; clerk of the county court. Dewitt Clinton Harris. By the middle of 1837 Houston had captured the county seat from Harrisburg and the county offices and most of the officials moved there.

The first court house and jail, necessitated by the removal of the county seat, were built in 1837. The jail was a log structure with a kind of upright log palisade as a part of it, but the new court house was a two story frame building. They were built by Dr. Morris S. Birdsall, the contractor with the county. The course of law did not wait for their completion. The first instrument in writing in the Harrisburg or Harris County records is a bond for title from Zadoc Hubbard to Lorenzo Brown to make good and sufficient title to one-half of lot 10, block 21. The instrument is dated February 22, 1837 and is recorded February 27. The site is that of the store later occupied by W. D. Cleveland.

The first grand jury, which met in the shade of some lopped off branches of trees on court house square, had B. F. Smith as foreman and the following members: Edward Ray, B. Stencil, Abraham Roberts, P. W. Rose, William Goodman, M. H. Bundic, William Burnett, John Goodman, Sr., Freeman Wilkerson, Gilbert Brooks, Thomas Hancock, Allen Vince, John Dunnam, John Earls, Elijah Henning, Andrew II. Long and James House, Sr.

Three indictments were brought in at its first session: one against Whitney Britton for assault and battery, one against John T. Beall for murder and a third against James Adams for larceny. The results of the trials suggest with a grim sort of humor the mental attitude of the people toward the several classes of offences. Whitney Britton's case was dismissed as a triviality, the petit jury decided that John T. Beall had done no more than they would have done under the circumstances and brought in a verdict of justifiable homicide, but when the scoundrel James Adams, who had stolen property instead of battering up the human form divine or taking human life, came to trial, he met the full vigor of an outraged justice. He was found guilty of theft, was ordered to make restitution to Lawrence Ramey of $295, and the notes he was charged with having abstracted, and was further sentenced to get 39 lashes on the bare back and be branded with the letter "T" in the right hand. He would thus carry, graven in his palm the insignia that he was a thief, as long as he lived.

The 39 lashes were to be laid on by the sheriff in a public place on Friday, March 31, 1837, and it was so done.

In extenuation of the high value attached to property and the low value set on life it should be remembered that every man went armed and was supposed to be able to take care of himself and that the citizens were living in an almost unproductive wilderness where poverty was attended with great hardships.

The cases cited above were tried at the first district court held in Houston which was presided over by Hon. Benjamin C. Franklin.

All killers did not escape punishment even at that early day however, and the first years of Harris County might show a better record for legal executions for homicide than the last decade. While the courts were yet young, two men were tried for murder. One, a gambler named Quick, had killed a man with whom he was gambling, and the other, named Jones, had killed a fellow soldier, Mandrid Wood, of the New Orleans Grays. Judge J. W. Robinson, who had been lieutenant governor under the provisional government in 1835–6, was on the bench and overruled all motions for a new trial and thwarted all efforts for delay after the men had been tried and convicted of murder. Everything had been done to prevent the sentence and it was finally represented to the court that the jail was very insecure, the weather quite cold and the men forced to wear irons for greater security because of the weakness of the palisade jail. The judge was so touched by the recital that he pronounced sentence that "the prisoners, in consequence of the insecurity of the jail, the extreme cold weather and their uncomfortable situation," be hung on the Friday following, which was done in a clump of timber that long bore the name of hangman's grove.

During 1837, Houston, which had become both the seat of the county government and of the national government became ambitious for yet more government as, counting citizens, state officials and congressmen, there were nearly a thousand people in her environs, and so early in June, Congress was persuaded to incorporate Houston as a city. Organization was delayed several weeks which gave an opportunity for mass meetings and protests which were greatly enjoyed by the citizens.

The first mayor was Francis Moore, Jr., who did not assume office until the first Monday in January, 1838. George W. Lively was mayor in 1839 and George H. Bringhurst was surveyor, an office of importance where land titles and head were rights beginning to assume importance. John D. Andrews became mayor in 1841 and in 1842 was re-elected. In 1843 Francis Moore was re-elected. Horace Baldwin succeeded him in 1844, and in 1845 W. W. Swain assumed the office which he held at the time of annexation.

Among the names of early aldermen are found Captain R. P. Boyce, J. De Cordova, author of the First Handbook of Texas, and Alexander McLewen.

Dr. Moore, the first mayor, was for a long time the editor of the Telegraph, he and his partner, Jacob W. Cruger, having established the first newspaper in Houston by the removal, early in 1837 of the "Telegraph" from Columbia, the newspaper following the seat of Government to Houston. Dr. Moore was afterwards state geologist and held many prominent positions.

The first marriage license signed under the law of the Republic was issued at Houston on July 22, 1837, signed by DeWitt C. Harris, county clerk. It authorized Hugh McCrory to wed Miss Mary Smith. The ceremoney was performed the following day by Rev. H. Matthews, a Methodist minister. Mr. McCrory died within a few months and in 1840, his widow married Dr.

Anson Jones, afterwards the last president of the Republic of Texas and perhaps the greatest diplomat of any man who ever held that office.

Mrs. Jones survived for many years, dying on December 31, 1907, in Houston, and holding at the time of her death the office of President of the Daughters of the Republic of Texas.

In 1905, the writer visited her in Houston and heard from her lips many stories of the early history of Texas. Her son, Judge Anson C. Jones was county judge for a number of years and many relatives of note still live in Houston, among them Judge Charles E. Ashe, of the 11th district court, a grandson.

Not until the 24th of March, 1838, was the first divorce granted at which time the gallant court relieved Susan Williams from the matrimonial fetters that chained her to John Williams.

The court house was the center of city life. At least one of the four pages of the early editions of the newspapers in Houston was entirely given up to advertising sheriffs sales, and other matters that centered around the court house.

On August 6, 1844, the two story frame court house was sold to make room for what was described as a "palatial structure," the second of the seven buildings which have occupied court house square. All of them have been palatial structures however, the last, recently dedicated, costing about a half million dollars.

By December 4, 1839, there were 400 suits on the docket and a bell had been placed on the court house to summons the citizens. Disputed land titles caused most of the suits. All kinds of frauds were practiced by sharpers upon strangers and one green horn, fresh from the States, purchased in good faith a head right to had alleged to have been issued to Peter Ourang Outang. The papers were full of warnings but the sharp practices flourished.

CHAPTER II - EARLY DAY AMUSEMENTS

Hunting, Fishing and Poker. The Jockey Club and Horse Racing. Notable Dances, the San Jacinto Anniversary Ball and Description of Sam Houston and Other Participants. A Festival Meal at Houston's First Hotel. City's First Theatres and their Performances.

Hunting, fishing and fighting were occupations so ordinary among the early inhabitants of Houston that one does not know whether to rank them as amusements or ordinary matters of daily routine.

Worlds of fish and game were to be had and every man was an expert with shot gun and rifle. Wild turkey and prairie chickens were in great favor as game birds but there were so many varieties of the feathered tribe in the forests, including even gaudy paroquets, that the great French naturalist Audobon, the most famous of ornithologists was a visitor to Houston before the town was a year old. An unflattering description of the town in his diary bears the date of May 4, 1837.

The Round Tent and other saloons, mostly under canvas, provided abundance of cheap whiskey and furnished a congregating place for the thirsty and the fractious. Poker, twenty deck poker, faro, stud poker, and several Mexican card games were in full blast. At elections the candidates would each have his open barrel of whiskey, and during the campaign to open up a whiskey barrel and distribute tobacco was the accepted popular method of electioneering.

One of the most wholesome influences of the genesis of Houston was that of Masonry. Holland Lodge No. 1, the mother of Texas lodges was organized in 1837. And by the middle of 1839 Temple Lodge No. 4, was in existence.

Masonry preceded the building of churches in Houston for as late as October 14, 1839, the Morning Star complains editorially that "In a city of 3,000 inhabitants and so much wealth there is no place for public worship and not one resident minister." There had been preaching services prior to that time however and even congregations organized.

Nicholas Nickleby, which was running as a serial in English papers and magazines was attracting wide attention and being eagerly read in Texas, in 1839.

The Jockey Club was established early and held spring and fall meetings at which racing flourished. Jack and Shelby Smith and General Tom Green were breeders of racing stock and were known as sporting men although the most of the horses that contested were the wiry mustang ponies. At one of the meets, in a close finish, General Houston is said to have cheered one of Colonel Green's mustangs on to victory and leaning over the railing cried as the mare swept into the stretch: "A million on the mare." He was never called "Bet-you-a-million Houston" on that account however, and so the title was left for another Texan by adoption, John W. Gates.

Dancing was in vogue and one of the most memorable balls that was ever given occurred at Houston on April 21, 1837, the first anniversary of the battle of San Jacinto, when General Houston, just elected president, and just returned from New Orleans, where he had gone after the battle of San Jacinto that his wound might heal, was the leading figure.

Other distinguished guests were present in Houston and were doubtless present at that festivity which was held just on the eve of the Second Session of the Congress of the Republic and the first that was to be held in Houston.

The day had been made memorable by the arrival of the first sailing vessel that ever reached Houston, the schooner "Rolla," which had taken four days to make the trip from Harrisburg and had brought a crowd of visitors and guests, and by an Indian war dance around the flag pole at the capitol.

General Houston was then a widower, clothed about with all the romance that made him leave his young wife and the governorship of Tennessee for some mysterious reason, and newly crowned with the laurels of San Jacinto. He had a habit of whittling out of bits of soft pine, little hearts, crosses and other emblems and giving them to the ladies as souvenirs. Some of these whittled souvenirs are still cherished in Houston today by descendents of some fair belle of the pioneer days of Texas.

The wierd contrast between the primitive, crude surroundings and the fine apparal and culture of many of the participants gave to the occasion a genre touch that has perhaps never been surpassed. The scene of the festivities was on Main Street. Houston was still a camp in the woods, its dwellers living mostly in white tents or shanties of clapboards and pine poles. A large two story building, half finished, as yet without a floor and without anything to cover the rafters between the first and second story was the place selected for the dance. Pine boughs, vines, creeping plants and clustered foliage were used to conceal the nakedness of the house and give it a roof. This building stood on ground now occupied by the new wing of the First National Bank and that was for many years occupied by the T. W. House bank.

The following account of the ball is signed "Texan," and appears in many early publications including the Ladies' Messenger, the Post, during the first year of its existance, and, in Governor Lubbock's memoirs. It was written by Mrs. Adele B. Loosean, the daughter of Mary Jane Briscoe, nee Harris.

"Chandeliers were suspended from the beams overhead but they resembled the glittering ornaments of today in naught save the use for which they were intended. Made of wood, with sockets to hold the sperm candles and distributed at regular distances, each pendant comprised five or six lights, which shed a dim radiance, but alas, also a liberal splattering of sperm upon the dancers beneath. The floor being twenty feet wide by fifty feet in length, could easily accommodate several cotillions, and although the citizens of Houston were very few, all the space was required for the large number who came from Brazoria, Columbia, San Felipe, Harrisburg, and all the adjacent country. Ladies and gentlemen came in parties on horseback distances of fifty and sixty miles, accompanied by men servants and ladies' maids, who had in charge the elegant ball costumes for the important occasion. From Harrisburg they came in large row boats, that mode of conveyance being preferable to a horseback ride through the thick undergrowth, for at that time there was nothing more than a bridle path to guide the traveller between the two places.

"General Mosely Baker, one of Houston's first citizens was living with his wife and child (now Mrs. Fannie Darden) in a small house built of clapboards. The house comprised one large room, designed to serve as parlor, bedroom and dining room, and a small shedroom at the back. The floor, or rather the lack of floor in the large apartment, was concealed by a carpet, which gave an air of comfort contrasting strangely with the surroundings.

"As the time for going to the ball drew near, which was as soon as convenient after dark, several persons assembled at General Baker's for the purpose of going together. There were General Houston, Frank R. Lubbock, and his wife, John Birdsall, (soon after attorney-general) and Mary Jane Harris, (now the surviving widow of Andrew Briscoe), General Houston was Mrs. Baker's escort, General Baker having gone to see that some lady friends were provided for. When this party approached the ball room, where dancing had already begun, the music, which was rendered by violin, bass viol and fife, immediately struck up 'Hail to the Chief;' the dancers withdrew to each side of the hall, and the whole party, General Houston and Mrs. Baker leading, and maids bringing up the rear, marched to the upper end of the room. Having here laid aside wraps and exchanged black slippers for white ones, for there was no dressing room, they were ready to join in the dance, which was soon resumed. A new cotillion was formed by the party which had just entered. General Houston and Mrs. Baker were partners, Mrs. Lubbock and Mr. George Cruger, and Mr. Lubbock and Miss Harris. Then were the solemn figures of the stately cotillion executed with care and precision, the grave balancing steps, the dos a dos, and others to test the nimbleness and grace of dancers.

"General Houston had just returned from New Orleans, where he had been since the battle of San Jacinto for the purpose of having his wound treated. Being the president-elect, he was, of course, the hero of the day, and his dress on this occasion was unique and somewhat striking. His ruffled shirt, scarlet cassimere waistcoat and suit of black silk velvet, corded with gold, was admirably adapted to set off his fine, tall figure; his boots, with short red tops, were laced and folded down in such a way as to reach but little above the ankles, and were finished at the heels with silver spurs. The spurs were, of course, quite a useless adornment, but they were in those days so commonly worn as to seem almost a part of the boots. The weakness of General Houston's ankle, resulting from the wound he had received in the battle of San Jacinto, was his reason for substituting boots for the slippers then universally worn by the gentlemen for dancing.

"Mrs. Baker's dress of white satin, with black lace overdress, corresponded in elegance with that of her escort, and the dresses of most of the other ladies were likewise rich and tasteful. Some wore white mull with satin trimmings; others were dressed in white and colored satins, but naturally in so large an assembly, gathered from so many different places, there was a great variety in the quality of the costumes. All, however, wore their dresses short, cut low in the neck, sleeves generally short, and all wore ornaments of flowers or feathers in their hair, some flowers of Mexican manufacture, being particularly noticeable on account of their beauty and rarity.

"At about midnight the signal for supper was given, and the dancers marched over to the hotel of Mr. Ben Fort Smith, which stood near the middle of the block, later for so long a time occupied by the Hutchins House. This building consisted of two very large rooms, built of pine poles, laid up like a log house, with a long shed extending the full length of the rooms. Under this shed, quite innocent of floor or carpet, the supper was spread; the tempting turkeys, venison, cakes and other viands displayed in rich profusion; the excellent coffee and sparkling wines invited all to partake freely, and soon the witty toast and hearty laugh went round.

"Returning to the ball room, dancing was resumed with renewed zest, and continued until the energy of the musicians began to flag, and the prompter failed to call out the figures with his accustomed gusto. Then the cotillion gave place to the time honored Virginia Reel and by the time each couple had enjoyed the privilege of 'going down the middle,' daylight began to dawn."

The above description was written some years after the event, but has reproduced its quaintness, dignity and strange charm with great effect and contains vastly more of human interest than the work of the average society editor in writing up latter-day festivities.

Even that memorable ball, however, was not permitted to be without a reminder that Houston was on the frontier. Among the guests present were the Misses Cooper, and while the dance was in progress news came that their brother had been killed by Indians on the Colorado River.

A little over a year later, on May 21, 1838, there was a grand ball at the Jockey Club, at which we are told the ladies' tickets were printed on white satin and Mrs. Briscoe danced successively with Generals Sam Houston, Albert Sidney Johnson and Sidney Sherman.

Before Houston was a year old it had a theatre and before it was three years old it had two. The first theatre was on the site now occupied by

Henke's store between Louisiana and Milam Streets on Congress Avenue. One of the early plays was "The Dumb Girl of Genoa," which was played so badly that one of the actors by the name of Carlos was hung in effigy on the limb of a large pine tree in front of the hall.

Henry Corri was the manager of a company that came from New Orleans to Houston in 1838. It played the "School for Scandal," and other plays. The newspapers at that remote date were cruel enough to sometimes criticise plays harshly and not give mere press agent notices and boosts according to the prevalent custom now. When it was rumored that one of the actors had been bitten by a mad dog the Morning Star said the report was too good to be true, but suggested that in such case the company might produce Hamlet, King Lear or Othello so as to give room for his newly acquired ability in madness. The press agent sometimes got in his work however in thoroughly approved style as witness the following from the Morning Star: "Engagement of April 29, 1839. Unprecedented! Unparalleled! Unheard of Attractions!!!! First night of the 'Ensanguined Shirt.' First appearance of High P. Ranter, who is engaged for six nights only and can not possibly be re-engaged on account of sickness in the family (who was sick or the nature of the illness does not appear) First appearance of Miss F. Ranter since her recovery from the whooping cough. First night of the real earthquake! Grand Fancy Dress Breakdown on a Cellar Door by Miss S. Swipes. This piece has been got up without regard to expense, weather or anything else. An amount of property has been invested in properties which frightens the manager and will astonish the public. Among other things which have been secured especially for this piece are 400 streaks of lightning with thunder to match and 300 alligator skin shields with brass knuckles and knobs."

The press agent apparently had not, like Miss Ranter, recovered from the whooping cough, but the appetite for amusements must be jaded indeed that does not respond with a gustatory quiver to the delights here promised.

Edwin Booth and other great actors are said to have visited Houston at an early date and with dancing, horse-back riding and racing and "swopping," whittling, romancing in Leatherstocking wise of Mexicans and "Injins," and the delights of the theatre and of electing everybody to office, times were not hopelessly dull in the Houston of the days of the Republic.

CHAPTER III - HOUSTON AND THE RED MEN

Sam Houston and the Cherokees. An Indian Dance. Letters from Chiefs John Jolly and Bowles. Houston's Indian Talk. Fate of Cherokees and Comanches.

Untouched by the stain of bloodshed in Indian warfare, Houston stands almost isolated among the cities of Texas. No savage massacre ever occurred in its environs and the inhabitants of the town were never in the frontier days startled by the blood curdling warhoop. Yet Houston, especially that part now known as the fifth ward, was a favorite camping ground of the Indians and the complete immunity from attack was perhaps due first of all to the influence of Sam Houston and second to the fact that Houston occupied a place near the center of the several settlements.

Sam Houston, be it remembered, was an Indian chief, an adopted member of the Cherokee nation. He had won his first wounds and his earliest laurels in bloody Indian warfare, but he had also been a member of the Indian tribes, had lived in the forests and adopted their customs and spoke their tongue. He had been later a commissioner for their interests at Washington, D. C., and to this day there exists in Houston the commission or passport given to "General Sam Houston" by the United States Government in which he is commended to all Indian tribes. That was before he came to Texas but even as president of the new nation he never forgot his friendship for the Indians and his policy was always one of justice and conciliation to all the tribes and especially to the Cherokees.

Early in May, 1837, a day or two after the opening of the Second Congress and within a few days of the time when General Houston, as president elect, arrived in the city named in his honor, we find him in conference with a number of Indians at Houston. The interview is thus reported in the Philadelphia Morning Chronicle of that time, by its Houston correspondent: "Several tribes of Indians being encamped in the splendid forest which covers the undulating ground on the opposite side of Buffalo Bayou, where the city is situated, a 'big talk' was arranged with the president, General Sam Houston, and the cabinet of Texas, at which Mr. Crawford (the special representative of the British Government) was invited to be present.

"The 'talk' was held in the White House of Texas, General Houston's residence, then a long cabin consisting of a passage or hall open at both ends, and a room of very moderate dimensions on each end.

"On the anniversary of the battle of San Jacinto (April 21st, 1837) a lofty flagstaff had been erected on Main street, and on this occasion a splendid silk flag of the new Republic was for the first time displayed from it. Around this flag several hundred Indians and squaws danced a grand war dance. They began moving around the center like so many radii, as is done in the flower dance when represented on the stage, accompanying the movement in a dull and monotonous sort of music of their own voices, which became quicker and quicker until they got into a very rapid motion with occasional shouts and yells, and then all at once stopped and suddenly dispersed.

"After this the chiefs adjourned to the 'talk.' These consisted of some six elderly and very sedate, grave gentlemen, who were seated around a table and communicated through an interpreter. The latter appeared a very intelligent, middle-aged man, and seemed to possess the implicit confidence of the chiefs.

"General Houston acquitted himself with his usual tact on such occasions, and aroused a real enthusiasm by his 'talk' to the red men. But nothing can be done towards treating with Indians without presents, so next comes that most important part of the whole ceremony.

"In the afternoon the presents were delivered and instant distribution began, each carrying away his share. Tobacco seemed, of all the articles they received, to be the most esteemed. Drunkenness then began, and at last General Houston had to send around to the liquor stores to request that no more whiskey be sold, which had the effect of inducing them quietly to retire to their camp, but the woods rang nearly all night with their yells."

Some of these Indians were wild Comanches from the West and on their way back home they killed and scalped several whites. Not only Mr. Crawford, an agent of the British minister to Mexico who had come on a secret mission, but probably also Alcee La Branche, the United States Charge d'affaires, and R. J. Walker of Mississippi, the first mover of Texas independence in the United States Senate, saw that Indian war dance, for both were in Houston at the time.

Among General Houston's private letters the writer found several documents of great interest including a letter from John Jolly, chief of Houston's own tribe of Cherokees, a communication from Chief Bowles, the head of the Texas Cherokees and addressed to "All my White Friends," and one of Houston's famous Indian talks in his own handwriting and with his own signature and written in the stately form of a ceremonial state paper. As the two latter throw direct light on Houston's methods of dealing with the Indians and his attitude toward them, and as they have never, so far as is known, been published, they are here reproduced from the originals in the possession of Hon. Frank Williams, General Houston's grandson in this city. This is an extract from the John Jolly letter:

"Mouth of the Illinoie.
27 March, 1838.
"Dear Friend:

"I wish you would write and give me all the news and the prospects of your country and what disposition your government will make towards the Red People, and if the Cherokees

will have a country set apart for them and be supported in their rights by your government.

Your friend, (Signed) John Jolly."

The "Indian Talk" is dated October, 1838, and is typical of General Houston's methods. In structure and theme it smacks of the Old Testament. Here is the full text of the talk:

"My Brothers:

"There is much talk of war. It is useless. There is no sense in it. I know that my brothers, the Alabamos and Coosatties, will not deceive me. A few bad men may have gone from amongst you and been killed with the enemy. This shall not destroy your band. Remember the words which I have spoken to you.

"The little chiefs of the Texas nation shall not hurt you. My words have been spoken and the winds shall not scatter them. Remember me and be happy with your women and children. Winter is coming and cold weather and you may be unhappy unless with your women and children. Stay with them until the spring comes and you shall receive a talk from the chief of this nation. You must not take up the tomahawk. Nor will I allow other men to raise it against you.

"I send to you wise men to give you counsel. Listen to them and walk in the path they direct. Tell your young men to stay at home that they may not bring your nation into trouble. Old men speak wisdom and young men should pursue their counsel.

"He that stops his ears against instruction is a fool and the wise men of his nation should punish him.

"There is a light from the countenance of the Great spirit upon the good man when he walketh in the straight path. But brush and darkness falleth in the way of him that walketh the path of crookedness.

(Signed) Sam Houston."

The Texas Indians consisted of the wild Indians, the most warlike of which were the Comanches, yet comprising a score of other tribes, and the semi-civilized Indians or the Cherokees and 12 associate tribes who had crossed the Texas border and occupied the territory lying north of the San Antonio road and the Neches and west of Sabine and Angelina. These Cherokees claimed the land they occupied. The Consultation of San Felipe, in 1835, recognized these claims and a resolution was signed by the entire body to secure the Cherokees in these rights and to have their boundaries established.

General Houston, Col. John Forbes and others as commissioners met the Cherokee chiefs, Bowles, Big Mush and others, at the Cherokee village on February 23, 1836, and entered into a boundary treaty with them. This was never ratified by the Texans. The Cherokees felt that they had been treated in bad faith and entered into negotiations with the Mexicans which the Texans discovered and this ultimately led to the expulsion of the Cherokees, the killing of Bowles and the driving of 4,000 Indians from the border. The Texans showing perhaps fully as much cruelty, treachery and bad faith as the Indians.

One of Houston's last acts as president had been to instruct Colonel Alexander Horton to survey this boundary. This was in 1838 and the work was done at least in part.

President Lamar distrusted the Cherokees and all Indians and his policy was one of warfare, a policy that appealed far more to the fighting Texans than the William Penn policy of peace and equity pursued by Houston. Many land speculators coveted the Cherokee lands which Houston tried to save for the state after the Indians had been driven out.

There were atrocities sufficient to justify the whites and Indians alike in feeling that the other side was dangerous and treacherous and the war of extermination was taken up in earnest after Houston left the presidency for the first time, with bloody results on both sides. When a short time later the Comanche chiefs were massacred at San Antonio in the pocket of Chief Muke-warrah was found a copy of Houston's treaty of 1838.

The only part played by the City of Houston in the Indian wars was in furnishing troops, the Milam Guards participating in more than one hard campaign.

The general sentiment of nearly every early Texan was that the only good Indian or good Mexican was a dead one, and they reformed them at every opportunity. These conversions were lasting. Save those negotiations that were conducted from Houston as the capital of the Republic from the spring of 1837 to the fall of 1839, the Indian history of blood and battle belongs to the history of Texas and not to that of Houston.

CHAPTER IV - CAPITAL DAYS
AND ANNEXATION

Houston Chosen as Capital City of New Nation. Erection of Capitol Building. First Newspaper. British Representative, present at Sam Houston's Inaugural Address. Second Congress Meets in Houston—Its Activities. Visit of Admiral Baudin of France. Mirabeau B. Lamar and His Policies as President. England's Refusal to Recognize Independence. Slaves in Houston. Removal of Capital to Austin. Causes of Annexation. The Vote in Harris County.

John Allen's trump card in founding Houston was that he intended to make it the capital of the Republic of Texas. It would seem a large ambition but the Allen brothers not only announced this as a purpose but carried it out within a year from the time the deed was recorded for the site on which the city was to stand.

They had to catch the capital on the wing, as it were, for it seemed to be very fugacious in disposition. Santa Anna had gotten the capital into the habit of jumping and it had never gotten over the habit. San Felipe de Austin, Washington, Harrisburg, Galveston, Velasco, and Columbia had all enjoyed the fleeting honor.

The first Congress of the Republic, on December 15, 1836, selected the new town of Houston as the seat of government. It was intended that it should remain here until 1840, but it only lasted until the fall of 1839.

The capital building was to be erected under the supervision of Col. Thomas W. Ward and was to contain 22 rooms. He commenced it in April, 1837 and in 14 days had it ready for occupancy making a record job as a contractor and architect.

About the first of May, the Congress arrived and the second session of Congress of the Republic was held in Houston. General Houston made a brilliant inaugural address and the town was filled with visitors. The site of the capitol building was that of the Rice Hotel and was then far out on the prairie.

With the capital came, as has been noted, the Telegraph from Columbia, and the Morning Star and the Intelligencer soon followed suit. Houston was provided from the beginning with newspapers enough to represent the several dissonant views of the ambitious political experts and statesmen who controlled her destiny.

General Houston's office was a small log house on Franklin Street and his residence a clapboard house of two rooms built for him by Captain R. P. Boyce, another noted contractor and builder of the day.

The recognition of the independence of Texas by the United States, news of which had recently arrived; the unsatisfactory condition of the finances of the land law; the information that Northern Indians had visited Matamoras and offered Mexico 3,000 warriors if it would resume the war; praise for the army and its general, Albert Sidney Johnston; the need of a navy; and the resources of Texas and her ability to maintain her independence; were emphasized in the inaugural address.

Perhaps in deference to Mr. Crawford, the British representative, who occupied an honored position in the hall, the president commented on the iniquity of the African slave trade and its prohibition by Texas.

In the session that followed, the government of the republic and its various departments were organized and their power defined, a general land office was established, the public debt was consolidated and funded, and all the islands of the Republic, including Galveston, were offered for sale. The western boundary of the Republic was fixed definitely at the Rio Grande and the Cordova rebellion of Mexicans and Indians was suppressed. The Texas Railroad Navigation and Banking Company was incorporated with a capital of $5,000,000 but never went into existence because of the inability to pay into the treasury $25,000 in gold or silver.

Houston pursued a policy of peaceful negotiations with the Indians wherever possible and of diplomatic handling of negotiations to secure recognition from foreign countries. A commercial treaty with England was announced on January 4, 1838, by General Henderson, who had gone to England and France, in 1837, as Envoy Extraordinary with powers plenipotentiary.

M. de Saligny, as the representative of the French government, visited Houston in the spring of 1838, and on May 13, of that year Admiral Baudin with a French fleet, stopped at the ports of Galveston and Velasco. At Galveston, Baudin returned the salute gun for gun until 22 guns, the national salute, had been fired. The Admiral visited Houston and was received with great ceremonies and it was on his report that France soon after acknowledged by treaty the new Republic.

Mirabeau B. Lamar, himself a hero of San Jacinto and a man of brilliant personal traits and no mean degree of statesmanship, succeeded Houston as president, and was installed in office in December, 1838. He was an anti-annexationist and favored close relationships with Great Britain. The failure of the United States to grant annexation when it was first sought had roused the pride of Texas and thenceforth the annexationists had to fight to a certain extent under cover. This pride was so strong that within two years' time Texas ceased all attempts to secure recognition and from then on the overtures came from the United States. Lamar, in his first annual message, said, that "To Great Britain the independence of Texas could not be an indifferent event."

Lamar favored pressing the war against Mexico and a drastic policy toward the Indians. Texas was in a position where Mexico could not successfully attack her and could not hope to regain her lost province but Texas was still less in condition to successfully attack Mexico. Under Lamar the Comanches were severely punished and the Cherokees were expelled from the state.

By an act approved January 4, 1839, actual settlers coming to Texas, under appropriate conditions, were to receive grants of 640 acres each. This offer was to hold until January 1, 1840. It encouraged imigration to Houston as well as elsewhere in Texas.

England refused to acknowledge Texas' independence in 1839, owing somewhat to O'Connell's attack on Texas as a country where slavery was permitted. This inflamed sentiment in Texas against England and the Houston papers fulminated against O'Connell. The Morning Star said editorially: "We shall always oppose any foreign protection or assistance that may be predicated upon the slightest interference with our domestic institutions as they now are."

By an ordinance of April 12, 1839, passed by the city council of Houston slaves found on the streets after 8 o'clock in the evening, were to receive from 10 to 30 lashes. No free negroes were allowed to live in Houston. The government passed rigid laws forbidding any intermarriage between white people and those of African descent, a law which was especially praised by the British consul to Texas, Mr. Ikin, in a booklet called "Texas," published in London in 1841, in which the purity of the Anglo Saxon race is contrasted with that of the Latin races which have become mongrelized in America by intermarriage with negroes and Indians.

On September 25, 1839, Marshal Soult for France, signed with Mr. Henderson the treaty of amity, navigation and commerce, Marshal Soult, who was also Duke of Dalmatia, saying he was proud to be the European god-father of the new Republic.

This was the last event of international importance that occurred while the capital remained in Houston for in the fall of 1839 the archives were loaded on thirty wagons and removed to Austin, the new capital. Houston was greatly aggrieved at the change and President Lamar, who was supposed to favor it, came in for a large share of local criticism. Sam Houston also opposed the change as Austin was then on the Indian frontier and some stirring chapters of Texas history were made by the old General's subsequent attempt to move the archives and the capital away from Austin.

On November 16, 1840, Lord Palmerston, at London, signed with General Henderson, the treaty by which England recognized the independence of Texas and a similar treaty was signed at the Hague about that time.

The Santa Fe expedition in 1841, was participated in by many Houstonians and Mr. Kendall of the New Orleans Picayune, who was one of those making the trip, has a vivid chapter on Houston and her horse market, in which the Milam Guards are greatly praised. Kendall's book was published in 1845. Houstonians also participated in the Mier expedition that followed, but the fate of neither of these can be considered local history.

Whenever there was a threat of a Mexican invasion, Houston promptly supplied her quota of soldiers, furnishing on one occasion two companies of mounted infantry equipped by local merchants.

Great Britain evinced a lively interest in Texas from the first and had planned to control this country either as a colony, a protectorate, or by close treaties. Between 1840 and 1845 England's plans were enlarged to purchase California, and press England's claims to Oregon that would bring that boundary down to within 45 miles of territory claimed by Texas and thus control the entire Pacific slope of the United States.

Some wise men in Texas and in the United States understood her diplomacy. She prevented Mexico's acknowledging the independence of Texas until it was offered as the price of Texas staying out of the American Union. The United States also waked up to the fact that the Monroe doctrine was in danger and the great presidential campaign of 1844 was waged on the democratic platform of "Polk and Dallas, Texas and Oregon 54°, 40' or fight."

With the United States as the suitor, Texas agreed to come into the Union rejecting, at the same convention, the counter proposition from Great Britain of English friendship, and Mexican recognition of her independence.

George Fisher, one of Houston's most noted citizens, diplomats and soldiers, a Hungarian by birth, saw England's plan most clearly and in a letter, dated, Houston, January 2, 1844, and published in the Madisonian at Washington, February 5, he points out the English menace to the Monroe doctrine.

In a dissertation, written in German and published at the University of Berlin in 1902, the editor of this history has discussed at length the plans of England and other countries in regard to Texas. The title of the book is "Die Annexion von Texas, ein Beitrag zur Geschichte der Monroe Doctrin."

As soon as Texas saw that the United States was in deep earnest at last, sentiment for annexation became strong again. An annexation mass meeting was held in Houston with Hon. M. P. Norton, chairman, George H. Bringhurst and A. M. Gentry, secretaries, and the following committee on resolutions: J. W. Henderson, Francis Moore, Jr., W. M. McCraven, F. R. Lubbock, J. Bailey, A. Wynns, J. W. Brashear, T. B. J. Hadley, T. M. Bagby, William M. Rice, C. M. McAnnelly, M. T. Rodgers, M. K. Snell, H. Baldwin, S. S. Tompkins and John H. Brown. The committee resolved: "That in exchanging our present political position for that of a sovereign state of the American Union, we shall indeed be merging the beams of our single star, but only that it may acquire new and increased splendor from the more full and pervading light of a glorious constellation, as certain planets are said to withdraw themselves from view when they become illumined in a group of great stars."

By the time the vote came on annexation and the constitution which occurred on October 13, 1845, the sentiment was so certain that many stayed away from the polls in full confidence as to how the choice would be made. The vote of Harris County was for annexation, 321, of which number 241 votes were cast in Houston; against annexation 50, of which number 44 ballots were cast in Houston; for the Constitution 299, against the Constitution 68. Texas had returned to her father's house. The Harris County delegates to the Constitutional convention of 1845 were Isaac W. Brashear, Alexander McGowen and Francis Moore, Jr. Its first state senator was Isaac W. Brashear and its first representatives Peter W. Gray and J. N. O. Smith. The lone star had yielded to the sweet influences of the Pleides.

CHAPTER V - EARLY RELIGIOUS ORGANIZATIONS

Houston's Pioneer Churches. Methodists, Presbyterians, Baptists and Catholics Early Founded Congregations.

The first evangelistic sermon ever preached in Houston, according to Dr. B. F. Riley, sometime pastor of the First Baptist church of this city, in his "History of Texas Baptists," was by Rev. Z. N. Morrell. Rev. Mr. Morrell and an aged companion, Rev. R. Marsh, reached Texas in 1835 as Baptist missionaries. Both came to Houston shortly after it was founded. In the general rush for Texas many preachers were included some of whom had come for other reasons than the good of the cause. To guard against ministerial frauds and imposters a meeting was held in the office of Dr. Marsh in Houston on May 8, 1837, while the first Congress to meet here was in session and a preachers' vigilance committee was organized. On the committee, besides the two named, were W. W. Hall, a Kentucky Presbyterian, and three Methodists, W. P. Smith, of Tennessee; L. I. Allen, of New York, and H. Matthews, of Louisiana. The committee pledged itself to recognize no preacher coming from the United States or elsewhere, unless he brought with him testimonials of good character.

Rev. Littleton Fowler, a Methodist minister of piety and zeal was among the early ministerial arrivals. He was elected Chaplain of the Senate in the fall of 1837.

Mr. Fowler obtained as a gift from the Allens the title to the half block of ground on Texas Avenue between Travis and Milam Streets formerly occupied by the old Shearn church, but now occupied by the New Majestic Theatre and the Chronicle building. It was deeded in 1837.

Rev. William Y. Allen, a Presbyterian minister, acted as Chaplain of Congress for a time in 1838 and often preached at the capitol during 1838 and 1839.

Rev. Edward Fountain preached to an unorganized Methodist congregation in Houston in 1838.

The first Sunday School was established in Houston in 1838. It seems to have been largely interdenominational as no churches were then organized. This Sunday School had an average attendance of 100.

David G. Burnett was elected president of the Texas Bible Society which was organized in 1838. Mr. Burnett had been the first President of the Republic and was President when Houston was founded.

The first evangelical church formally organized in Houston was of the Presbyterian faith and the organization was effected on the last day of March, 1838, by Rev. William Y. Allen in the Senate chamber of the capitol building.

The following names were signed to the Presbyterian Confession of Faith, and church government, that was then adopted: James Burke, who was the first ruling elder, A. B. Shelby, J. Wilson Copes, Isabella R. Parker, Ed Belden, Marian Shelby, James Bailey, Sarah Woodward, Jennett Smith, Harris G. Avery, and Sophia B. Hodge. Mr. Allen continued as pastor of this church until 1842. The church built by this congregation was not finished until late in 1840. It was located on Main Street, between Texas and Capitol Avenues, and was destroyed by fire in 1862.

On March 16, 1839, Christ church of the Episcopal faith was organized. On April 1, the first board of vestrymen was selected as follows: William F. Gray, John Birdsall, M. Hunt, A. F. Woodward, James Webb, William Pierpont, Tod Robinson, E. S. Perkins, D. W. C. Harris, J. D. Andrews, C. Kessler and George Allen. The first church edifice on the site of the present church was consecrated in 1847 by the Right Reverend George W. Freeman, Missionary Bishop of the West. The site of the Church was donated by the Allens.

In May, 1839, Bishop Leonidas Polk visited Houston on a tour of the Republic.

The First Baptist church in Houston was organized on May 22, 1841, by Rev. James Huckins, who had come to Houston under the auspices of the Home Mission Society of New York. The Baptists had no meeting house of their own until 1847, when the efforts of a few noble women and of Elder Tryon at last secured one.

Mrs. Nathan Fuller, wife of Col. Nathan Fuller, and Mrs. P. L. Hadley were prominent in the group of women who secured the church building.

When Rev. Littleton Fowler, the Methodist minister, preached in the capitol at Houston in 1837 he found in the city "gaming and vice and any number of doggeries," but no churches. Mr. Fowler was an ardent mason and later helped to organize the Grand Lodge of Texas in the Capitol building.

Abel Stevens was appointed to the Galveston and Houston circuit on December 3, 1838, but did not take up the work. During 1839, Rev. L. G. Hoard and Rev. Jesse Strickland preached several times in Houston. On December 4, 1839, Rev. Edward Fountain was appointed preacher in charge for Houston and Galveston, but worked almost exclusively in Houston during the year 1840. On Christmas day, 1840, T. O. Summers was appointed in charge of Houston and Galveston. In Houston he preached in an upper room, over a store, on Capitol Avenue between Milam and Louisiana Streets. In 1841, Rev. Mr. Summer organized the first permanent Methodist church in Houston, for a long time known as Shearn church, but now bearing the name of the First Methodist church. Among the early members were C. Shearn, D. Gregg, A. H. Sharp, Mrs. Campbell, Mrs. Winn, (a daughter of Dr. Ruter,) Mrs. Mixon, E. D. Johnson, John H. Walton, Mosely Baker, Dr.

John L. Bryan, Mrs. Bryan, Mr. and Mrs. Andrew McGowan, H. Tracy, A. Crawford, Francis Moore McCrea, C. Dikeman and G. S. Hardcastle. The history of this church has been well compiled by Mrs. I. M. E. Blandin of Houston.

Abbé Domenech, who was in Houston in July, 1848, makes an ugly little remark in his book, "Missionary Adventures in Texas and Mexico," that has become famous. He says: "Houston is a wretched little town composed of about 20 shops and a hundred huts dispersed here and there among trunks of felled trees. It is infested with Methodists and ants." The only thing the Abbé tells of Houston besides this statement is the story of his fight with the ants, these insects causing him much tribulation.

Many enterprising missionaries and clerics of the Catholic faith visited Houston during the early days and a congregation was early formed. It flourished and erected its first building in 1841. This congregation was and is known as the Church of the Annunciation and has played a large part in the religious history of Houston.

CHAPTER VI - EARLY GROWTH AND THE BAYOU

City of Houston's Early Progress and Poverty. Arrival of Schooner "Rolla." Financial Panic and Yellow Fever Epidemic of 1839. First Book Published in City. Building of Wharves and Organization of Chamber of Commerce. Early Descriptions of the Buffalo River and its Steamboat Life. British Consul Ikin's Description of Houston. Civic Prosperity. Houston Enters Union as Commercial Emporium and Business Capital of the State.

Such an accumulation of individual cells is a town, so gradually does it grow, and by such processes of accretion, and so persistently do the newspapers and periodicals of any period overlook that which is distinctive and of the deepest interest to subsequent generations as being a mere matter of course, that it is difficult to trace the hues of a city's growth.

Here and there however, events are recorded which, if they will not exactly serve as milestones on the highway of progress are at least indications of the direction in which progress was made as the stones and gravel mark the path of vanished glaciers.

When John Allen cut with his bowie knife the coffee bean weeds from what he had marked out as Main Street, a mere muddy pathway that ran down to a muddy bayou's bank, he was tracing a highway that was one day to be a canyon between skyscrapers and both his faith and his works speedily began to be justified.

To his tent town there came, on January 1, 1837, the first steamer, the "Laura," commanded by Captain Grayson, with a full load of settlers and immigrants, some of them men of fame already and others to achieve it in the new country of Texas.

In April, of that year, the capitol was moved and the capitol building was constructed and a kind of gubernatorial hut was erected on Travis Street at the spot now occupied by the Trimble laundry.

On April 21, the schooner "Rolla," after spending four days on the route from Harrisburg to Houston, arrived. This was the first sailing vessel to reach the new town. She had a cargo consigned to Allen Brothers, and was chartered by Messrs Dykeman and Westcott and had made the water voyage from St. Joseph, Florida. Her numerous passengers attended the famous anniversary ball in the Carlos building.

The arrival of the Telegraph from Columbia and the founding of the Morning Star gave Houston two good newspapers. Jack Eldinge, poet and editor was one of the early promoters of the Morning Star, which changed hands often during the first few years of its existence.

In the fall of 1837, the first two-story dwelling house was built in Houston by Judge A. C. Briscoe on the corner of Main Street and Prairie Avenue. Later it was for many years the home of Dr. I. S. Roberts. The only other two-story buildings that year were the court house and the capitol.

In the spring of 1838, one of the papers says that Houston has 400 inhabitants and pine stumps on Main Street. During the year, ice was advertised for sale at the cut rate of fifty cents a pound.

A petition, signed by many voters, appears in the Telegraph of October 11, 1837, asking that something be done to remedy the muddy condition of the streets around the capitol and the President's house.

The year 1839 was in many respects a hard year. During that year New Orleans refused credit to the merchants, the first yellow fever epidemic visited Houston and caused many deaths, and on September 15, of that year, the moving of the capital to Austin was begun.

In May of that year the first regular board of health was appointed by the city council and a short time later a city hospital was created and the cost and upkeep of this hospital was a large item of city expenditure for the year. From July 1 to December 31, 1839, there were 240 deaths in Houston, mostly from yellow fever, out of a population given as 2,000. Yellow fever raged in New Orleans, Galveston and Houston and ravaged the Texas coast. Its mosquito origin was not then known but all early settlers noticed its relation to ditches, filth and bodies of stagnant water. Dr. Ashbel Smith also noted that a fall of temperature checked its spread. A norther, on November 20, when the mercury fell to 40 degrees Farenheit, put an end to the plague.

The fourth of July, of 1839, was celebrated jointly by the Sunday School and the new military company, the Milam Guards. There were 70 in attendance at the Sunday School. Rev. William Y. Allen read Deuteronomy, sixth chapter; J. R. Read spoke for the Sabbath School; J. W. Eldridge read the Declaration of Independence and D. Y. Portiss spoke for the Guards. It was a curious joint celebration of another nation's holiday.

During the year the treasury notes of the Republic, known as "red backs," fell to fifty cents on the dollar. They later fell as low as ten cents on the dollar. Mexico was threatening an invasion but not much heed was paid to this threat by Texas although it fulfilled its intention of hurting the credit of the new nation abroad.

The first flour brought to the new city had sold for $30 a barrel, in gold, but the price had materially fallen although all flour was imported, but now in the depreciated currency a barrel of flour cost $80; a beef, the same; corn meal was $8 a bushel; corn, $4 per hundred ears; sugar, 42 cents a pound, and other prices in proportion. Famine and bankruptcy threatened the town. Some of the early merchants were Dowell and Adams, F. R. Lubbock, William D. Lee, Tom League, T. W. House, Cruger and Moon, and Sam Whitney, also proprietor of the Telegraph. The newspapers published each day lists of current prices and also of New Orleans rates on money.

All the New Orlenas bank notes sold below par but the bank notes of McKinney and Williams, bankers at Galveston, remained at par and furnished a striking tribute to the credit and solidity of a Texas institution.

On December 24, 1839, the newspapers note with pride that some brick sidewalks have made their appearance on Main Street. During the same month they complained of the rotten wooden city bridges and of the effluvia, arising from the neglected market place.

Probably the first book ever published in Houston, and certainly the first book, a copy of which is to be found in the city's library, was published in Houston in 1839. It is called "General Regulations for the Government of the Army of the Republic of Texas," and contains 187 pages and shows creditable press work and also well formulated military regulations. It was published in the office of the Houston Intelligencer. In the next few years advertisements for printers and bookbinders make their appearance in the papers.

In 1840 the tide of prosperity again slowly turned Houston-ward which had suffered severely in temper and resources from the removal of the capital.

On February 3, of that year, the newspapers advocate a line of stages to Austin which was soon after inaugurated. During the month of February a Brazoria man was appointed post master at Houston. This was regarded as the crowning insult and the subject furnished a controversy that lasted for months.

Bids were received in February to construct a wharf from the foot of Main Street to the foot of Fannin Street, and on February 26, there was a curious organization formed known as the "Anti-Rat Society," headed by John W. Eldridge. Its purpose was not to attack the head ornaments of the women but the rodents that swarmed everywhere in the town so as to be a pest.

Houston's first Chamber of Commerce was organized on April 5, with E. S. Perkins as president. An advertisement of that month, notes that 20 barrels of whiskey have been received for sale by one firm and others had large consignments of the same insinuating beverage. The Morning Star complains on April 20, of the rowdies and black legs who make life intolerable by their carouses and fights and two days later dragged these offenders over the coals again in an article beginning "We are informed that some of the black leg gentry took offense at our remarks." The thugs and rowdies were handled without gloves by the paper and during the year a warm campaign in favor of temperance and against the use of whiskey in the Houston climate was waged by it.

A new military company, known as the Dragoons, was organized in April, 1840. On April 23, one of the papers tells of a tall lank stranger who visited the city and wrote after his name the letters P. O. P. S. F. C. The stranger was asked the meaning of the letters and said they were an abbreviation of his title, which, on request he gave as "Professor of Psalmody and School-master from Connecticut." The professor however did not participate in the first concert given in Houston on May 1, by Emil Heerbrugger at which solos were rendered on the piano, the violin and the French horn.

A gentleman by the name of Louis, of France, opened a fencing school but found some difficulty in persauding the citizens to abandon the bowie knife for the rapier as a means of settling difficulties and smoothing out wrinkles in a sensitive honor. News of Filisola's invasion and of Burleson's campaign against the Lipans appeared in the papers.

The papers lament the slow mails. This is a characteristic complaint of the period: "Pleasant—To have the United States Mail lay at Galveston two days after its arrival, to have it put on board the slowest boat that runs on the bayou and to have that boat lay three days on Red Fish Bar."

Shallow water on Cloppers Bar delayed passenger traffic and the mails, and it was suggested that if all the boats would drop bouys along the line of the channel over this bar that boats always passing in the same track would rub a channel deep enough for convenient passage and that the mud thus rubbed up by the boat bottoms would be washed out of the way. It was one of the earliest projects for deepening the ship channel.

Henry Stuart Foote traversed the bayou in 1840, and in his book, published in Philadelphia the following year, tells of a herd of buffalo on Galveston Bay, of the wonders of water bird life, the flaming flamingoes, the giant white pelicans, the rice birds, the white and gray cranes and the eagles. Of the bayou he says: "In view of navigation only, Buffalo Bayou in connection with Galveston Bay is among the most important water courses of Texas. To Houston there is a safe and constant steamboat navigation every day in the year, and for practical purposes this city may be considered the most inland point of navigation of the country. As evidence of this fact the city of Houston is among the most flourishing towns in Texas."

A description of the bayou by the Abbé Domenech a few years later mitigates his offensive description of Houston already quoted. The Abbé says: "We entered the little Buffalo River bordered with reeds and bullrushes in the midst of which herons and cranes and thousands of ducks were disputing. By and by the banks increased in height, approached so near to each other and formed so many narrow tortuous windings that at every instance the boat was caught either by the bow or the stern. At length the high lands appeared, covered with magnolias with their large white flowers and delicious perfumes. Gray and red squirrels leaped from branch to branch, while mocking birds and cardinals imparted life and language to these wonderful solitudes."

A vivid picture of steamboat life on Buffalo Bayou at this period is given by an Englishwoman, Mrs. Houstoun, who accompanied her husband on a yachting voyage and hunting expedition to America. Her style is piquant and her comments are offered without apology. Chapter X of Vol. II of her book, "Yacht Voyage to Texas," published in London in 1844, deals with the trip up the bayou and with the city of Houston. She says:

"It was about 2 o'clock in the afternoon of a bright frosty day that we put ourselves on board the Houston steamer—Captain Kelsey. She was a small vessel, and drew but little water, a circumstance very necessary in these small rivers. The American river steamers differ very much in appearance from those to which an European eye is accustomed. They have the appearance of wooden houses, built upon a large raft; there is a balcony or verandah, and on the roof is what is called the hurricane deck, where gentlemen passengers walk and smoke.

"On the occasion of our taking our passage, both ladies' and gentlemen's cabins were quite full, and I therefore preferred spending the evening in the balcony in spite of the cold. I had kind offers of civility but I could not help being amused at the terms in which some of them were couched. The question addressed to me of 'Do you liquor, ma'am?' was speedily followed by the production of a tumbler of egg-noggy, which seemed in great request, and I cannot deny its excellence. I believe the British Navy claims the merit of its invention, but this is matter of dispute.

"We dined soon after our arrival on board and found everybody very orderly and civil. Certainly there was a strange mixture of ranks, but this made it more amusing to a stranger. The supper consisted of alternate dishes of boiled oysters, and beef steaks, of which there was plenty and the latter disappeared in marvelously quick time between the strong jaws of the Texan gentlemen. I confess to preferring meat which has been kept somewhat more than an hour, especially in frosty weather. On one occasion our dinner was delayed for some time, while the cook went on shore and 'shot a beef.' There was fortunately water enough for us to cross Red Fish Bar, and we were fast steaming up Buffalo River. For a considerable distance from the mouth the shores are low, flat and swampy, but as the stream narrowed there were high banks, and the trees were quite beautiful in spite of the season, which was extremely unfavorable to foliage and woody scenery. Such magnolias—eighty feet in height, and with a girth like huge forest trees,—what must they be when in full blossom! There were also a great number and variety of evergreens, laurel, bay and firs, rhododendrons, cistus and arbutus. It seemed one vast shrubbery. The trees and shrubs grew to a prodigious height, and often met over the steamer, as she wound through the short reaches of this most lovely stream.

"My berth opened out of the state cabin, and as the only partition was a Venetian door, I could not avoid hearing all the conversation that was carried on by my neighbors. Cards and drinking constituted no inconsiderable part of the pleasures of the evening, but with all the excitement of talk, tobacco chewing and brandy, I never heard people more orderly and reasonable.

There was no private scandal, no wit, no literature, no small talk; all was hard, dry, calculating business. One rather important looking gentleman made a stump speech on the expediency of Texas becoming a colony of Great Britian! I do not know the orator's name but General or Colonel he must have been. Military titles are taken and given here with as little ceremony as the title of Count on the Continent. Mr. Houstoun sprang into a General at once.

"There was a Baptist preacher on board, a thin, weary looking man, with a cast in his eye which was very comical. He had fought for his country and though now a man of peace, delighted in displaying his knowledge of military matters. He was going to Houston to establish a school for young gentlemen, while his wife was to superintend the education of their sisters. This, he said, he was induced to do that his boys might not mix with their inferiors. He could not bear, he added, that his sons should be acquainted with vulgar boys, which they were obliged to do at Galveston, but he didn't like it, and now at his school, he could choose the boys! Exclusiveness here! Where shall we look for a country where the real charitable feelings of equality exist? I may remark that my maid was obliged to wait until all these people had done their meals, because, I was told, they did not like her to eat at the same table. At seven o'clock in the morning we arrived at the pretty town of Houston. It is built on high land, and the banks, which are covered with evergreens, rise abruptly from the river."

The lady's book has a frontispiece steel engraving of Houston, evidently made by the artist from the description in this last sentence. It shows a city on the sloping side of a lofty hill with a vista of mountains all about. A beautiful arched viaduct spans the stream just above the wharf where a huge side wheel steamboat lies at anchor. It is a very flattering engraving. Later the lady incidentally gives the information that Houston had only one brick house at this time.

In a newspaper of April 19, 1839, it is stated that a census shows Houston to have 2,073 people, 1,620 males and 453 females, and property assessed worth $2,405,865 with the wharves of a large commercial city and five steamers constantly plying between Houston and Galveston. These figures seem padded somehow and the wharves then were only mud banks and plank platforms at the water's edge, but in 1840, one gets some authoritative information as to the city in a booklet entitled "Texas," by Arthur Ikin, Great Britain's Texas consul, published in London, in 1841. Mr. Ikin says: "Houston, though scarcely five years old, has 5,000 inhabitants; several religious congregations; shops of every kind; daily and weekly newspapers; numerous professional men; a theatre, race course, hotels, cafes, etc., etc., and several steamers running between Galveston and this city which will always be a great depot for the retail trade of the interior."

Mr. Ikin also says that the states which have most largely contributed to the population of Texas are: Alabama, Georgia, Tennessee, Kentucky, the Carolinas, and Virginia. "The warm hearted liberality, intelligence and taste for refinement which have always distinguished the people of these last mentioned states, are characteristics that have not been lost by transmigration across the Sabine."

There is incidental talk of a railroad again in 1840, and on June 8, of that year, the announcement is made that the city schools will again be opened. The early schools of the city were private schools. Hon. Alcee LaBranche, the United States representative was shown marked courtesies in Houston during the year.

W. L. McCalla was in Houston, in 1840, and the next year published a book, "Adventures in Texas." Here is his sole reference to Houston: "I enjoyed for a season the hospitality of the city of Houston. Here, consulting my moderate purse, I purchased and mounted a poor, little, ugly, worthless Indian mare." It is to be hoped that, had his purse been longer, Houston could have offered him a better bargain in horse flesh.

After 1840, Houston grew steadily and quietly. Five years after its foundation the city revenue was, for the year, $4,740, specie value.

From June 1, 1841, to May 5, 1842, there was exported 2,460 bales of cotton, 72,816 feet of lumber, and 1,803 hides and four commercial steamers plied on the bayou. From January, 1842, to January, 1843, the city consumed, according to the market reports, 1,124 beeves, 340 hogs, 165 pigs, 128 calves and 36 sheep.

By a city ordinance of June 8, 1841, the city became known as the port of Houston and put on a wharfmaster and rates of wharfage. By an act of Congress approved January 29, 1842, the city was given the right to remove obstructions from the bayou and to improve navigation.

In the spring of 1844, T. N. Davis brought the first cotton compress to Houston. The paper announced that Mr. Davis could compress 500 pounds of cotton into a space 22 inches square in fifteen minutes by the aid of two hands. The two hands referred to seem to have been hired assistants.

The Morning Star of December 20, 1845, discusses the prospects of Houston, saying: "Notwithstanding the bad state of the roads, large numbers of teams arrive daily from the interior with cotton. Four or five new stores have been opened here within the last month, and we are informed that several merchants expect to open stores as soon as Annexation is consummated. There is not a house in town to rent and several new buildings are going up. The hotels are literally crowded with boarders. The value of real estate in this section of the city has advanced at least 100 per cent within the last two months."

On June 2, 1845, the finance committee made a report to the city council that the amount of assessed and appraised property in the city was $336,559 and at one-half per cent that it would bring in taxes a total of $1,632.79, which sum would be sufficient to make all improvements, pay the debt and leave a surplus in the treasury. As a matter of fact the city's total debt on January 1, 1846, only aggregated $875. Houston, when Texas entered the Union, was practically out of debt, and on an assured basis

of prosperity and the highway to growth and influence. There was published in 1846 a book called "Prairiedom," a story of Texas, written by a "A Southron." Pages 84 and 85 of this volume, mirror Houston in pleasing fashion as an abode of prosperity. The author says: "The city of Houston is a place of active and profitable trade and in its rise and progress is as much a miracle in town making as Rochester or Chicago. Houston is the largest and most flourishing town in the interior, second only to Galveston in commercial importance, and must always maintain its ascendency over any other rival. It has now a population of from 4,000 to 5,000 inhabitants, 40 stores, 3 commodious public houses, several newspapers, a large cotton press, an iron foundry, two extensive stearin, candle, oil, and beef packing establishments, a steam saw and grist mill, various mechanic shops, schools, and four churches, all of which are well attended by an intelligent, industrious and moral population. In 1839, only eight bales of cotton were sent from this point, in 1844, 7,000 bales and in the current year (1845) some twelve or fifteen thousand bales will probably be shipped."

Thus it is manifest that during the Republic, Houston thoroughly established itself as a seaport, as a commercial manufacturing and exporting city, and as the home of a cultivated and substantial people. It had already become the commercial emporium and the business capital of the state when annexation was consummated.

CHAPTER VII - THE CITY GOVERNMENT

Early City Limits. First Market House. "Reconstruction" Administration. First Bridge Across Buffalo Bayou. The First Fire Company. Houston Hook and Ladder Company. The Fire Department of Today. Early Police Officers. Some Old Police Notes. The Police Department Today. City Water Works. Houston Gas Company. Contending with a Big Debt. What Mayor D. C. Smith Accomplished. Mayor Rice and the Commission Form of Government. What the Commission Has Done for Houston.

Although Houston was founded in 1836, and soon became something of a big place, having city boundaries, which were the bayou on the north, Walker Street on the south, Bagby Street on the west and Caroline Street on the east; her affairs were under the control of the county, for the first two years of her existence. However rapid growth and increased importance soon demanded a government of its own, and accordingly an election was held in 1838, and "incorporation" having carried, application was made and granted, for a charter for the city of Houston in 1838. Another election was then held and Dr. Francis Moore was elected the first mayor of the new city. He served but one year, which was the full term of office in the beginning. About the first thing done by the new officials was to extend the city limits, for purposes of taxation, for then, as now, in certain directions, actual settlement had extended far beyond the original limits. The limits of the city were extended so as to form a square, each of the four sides of which should be three miles in length, thus making the area nine square miles, the court house being in the center of the square.

Beyond the fact that the city limits were extended, little in the way of public improvements seems to have been done by the first or second city administrations. In 1836, when the Allens laid out the city, they set aside the ground, known as Market Square, for the purposes for which it has always been used. On a map published as early as 1839 it is designated as "Congress Square," probably because it is skirted by Congress Street, at that time one of the main thoroughfares of the city. This square was used as a public gathering place by the people, and later, traveling circuses pitched their tents there. In 1839, the city had a fine market square but no market house beyond a big shed that had been erected for temporary use. Two Frenchmen, known as the Rosseau Brothers, had a canvas covered frame structure on Preston Street, near the middle of the block, fronting Market Square, where they sold vegetables, game and such things. On the square itself was the big shed spoken of. This was under the control of the city and had a regular market inspector. This first inspector was Thomas F. Gravis, who gave his attention to his duties for one-half the market fees. Afterwards, when he found that one-half was not enough for his support, he asked for and was given all the fees.

September 20, 1840, the city council determined to erect a permanent building, to cost $1,200, and the contract was given to Thomas Standbury & Sons, who completed the structure at a cost of $8,000 to the city. That contract for $1,200 and the final bill for $8,000 read like some of the transactions of the city fathers when the city was under a "reconstruction" mayor and board of aldermen after the war. There was no doubt a vast difference, however, for in 1840, Texas money was far below par in all money markets of the world.

The old market house was a long, single story, frame structure that extended from the middle of the block, facing Preston Street to Congress Street on the other side. At the end facing Congress Street was a two-story building, the upper story being used as a city hall and police court and the lower story as a city jail and in a small structure adjoining, built a few years later, were quarters for the fire department. When the market house was completed, an ordinance was passed by which private, competitive markets were outlawed, and the position of market master became a valuable one, a fact that is attested by there having been ten applicants for the place in 1841. Mr. E. M. Holmes was the successful candidate. In 1845 the duties of market master and those of city marshall were combined and the honors and dignity of the place were borne by Mr. William Smith, better known as "Billy" Smith, for the next three years. After the late forties. Captain R. P. Boyce filled the position for several years.

Among other innovations made by the "reconstruction" administration of Houston, after the war, was one by which the city surrendered all control over the market, leasing the whole thing to private individuals. The first lessee was a Mr. McGregor, who took charge in 1869. In 1871 the old wooden building was torn down to make place for a new brick structure. This new building Mr. McGregor also leased and held until it was destroyed by fire, in 1876. This famous market house should take first place among the historic buildings of Houston, for it was not only the first really substantial building of the kind erected here, but it was the first one, in the construction of which, what has come to be known as "high finance" methods were employed. The history of the construction of the market house reads like the plot for a comic opera. In 1871, Mayor Scanlan signed a contract with Mr. William Brady and the latter's New York associates, for the construction of the building at a total cost to the city of $228,000. To pay for this the city was bonded in the sum of $250,000 at 8 per cent for 25 years. The work of actual construction commenced, but had not progressed far when things began to happen. It was discovered that the plans and specifications did not call for floors in some rooms, nor for plastering and windows in others. No blinds or shades were mentioned at all, and a careful study of the plans and specifications, revealed the fact that they were scarcely more than in skeleton form. As so many changes were necessary the city concluded to make some additional ones, and put in a theatre on the second floor of the building. There were changes and counter changes until finally, when the building was completed, its cost was $470,000 instead of the $228,000 originally counted on. On the morning of July 8, 1876, a fire, which started in the theatre, totally destroyed the building. It was insured for $100,000, but though it had cost the city of Houston nearly half a million dollars, the insurance companies refused to pay even the $100,000, and rebuilt the market house at a cost to themselves of about $80,000. This new building was also destroyed by fire in 1901, and the present magnificent city hall was erected on its site.

Of course it became necessary to issue more bonds to meet the increased cost of the famous market house, and in order to do this it became necessary to increase the city limits so as to have as large a tax area as possible. This was easy and at a stroke of the pen the area of Houston was increased from nine square miles to twenty-five square miles and bonds were issued against the entire territory. Issuing bonds became such a mania with the "reconstructionists" that by the time the Democrats secured control of the state and passed a law firing them all out of office, Houston had a bonded debt approximating $2,000,000 and had, to show for it, an $80,000 market house and a sewer two or three blocks long on Caroline Street. The new mayor and aldermen, appointed first by the governor and then elected by the people, reduced the city limits to the original nine square miles, but to reduce the bonded debt was not so easy. They struggled with it for years. Finally part of the debt was paid on a compromise basis and part by issuing new bonds on the reduced area. This worked a hardship on some of the citizens, for today property owners are taxed to pay interest on loans negotiated against property still a mile beyond the present city limits.

In early days there was little or no necessity for the people of Houston to cross to the north side of the bayou. There was nothing over there to attract them except hunting and fishing, and small foot-bridges answered their purposes for that, so no bridges were built for many years. Those coming to or going from Houston, who had to cross the bayou, did so at a ford, located at a point which is now the foot of Texas Avenue. But the trade of Houston with the interior began to increase, so a suitable bridge became an absolute necessity. In 1843, such a bridge, the first to span the bayou, was completed. In its issue for December 21, 1843, the Morning Star said:—

"The bridge over Buffalo Bayou in this city was completed on Monday. It is 100 feet long and 16 feet wide. The distance between the two piers is 50 feet. The piers are 26 feet high, consisting of four upright posts resting on a mud sill 40 feet long, and supporting a beam 18 feet long. The two outside beams resting on the pier are supported by king posts eight feet high with braces 25 feet long. This bridge, though insignificant in comparison with most of the bridges of the United States, is doubtless the longest and most substantial bridge that has ever been erected in Texas."

The bridge was located on Preston Avenue and stood for ten years, being swept away in 1853, when a great rise in the bayou occurred. It was replaced by a new bridge, known for years as the "Long Bridge." It was in fact a long bridge, for its constructors, bearing in mind the fate of the first one, took steps to guard against a repetition of that disaster, by placing the two ends far beyond the reach of possible high water and elevating the main part of the bridge to what they considered a safe altitude. No definite figures are obtainable, but as the bridge began at a point a little over half way between Smith Street where it crosses Preston Avenue, and the top of the banks of the bayou on the south side, and extended to a point on the north side about half way up the block on that side, it is evident that the bridge was very appropriately named "Long Bridge." This bridge stood for years, and while it was more or less damaged by several floods, it was never swept away. After a great flood in the late seventies it was remodeled. The approaches on both sides were filled in and the present bridge was constructed and has stood there ever since.

There should be a tablet, or monument placed on this Preston Avenue bridge, to mark the place, for while it is not the original structure, it occupies the point over which, for many years, almost the entire commerce of the state passed. Before the Houston and Texas Central Railway was built, the entire cotton crops east of Texas came to Houston in wagons drawn by from eight to twelve pairs of oxen, and all entered the city over that bridge, and all goods shipped to the interior went out the same way. It was no unusual thing as late as 1858–59, to see wagons on the streets of Houston from as far north as Waco. The Houston merchants bought all the crops from and sold all the goods to the interior planters and merchants.

Even before Houston became a city, in name at least, by obtaining a charter, steps were taken to organize a fire company. In 1836, Protection Fire Company No. 1 was organized. That was perhaps the first organization of the kind in Texas. They had no engine nor anything with which to fight fire, except buckets, and their method was a primitive one of forming a line and passing the buckets from hand to hand. As crude as this method was, much good was accomplished, because executed by an organized force rather than an excited mob. Protection Company No. 1 preserved its organization and identity, until the old volunteer department was absorbed by the city and became the present pay department. In the early fifties this company bought its first engine. It was an old fashioned hand engine, but at that day was looked upon as a grand affair. It was a vast improvement on buckets, at any rate, and did a great deal of good work. Houston was growing rapidly at that time and the demand for better fire protection was becoming more apparent each day. The whole city being constructed of wood, and the houses, in the business part of the town, being jumbled close together, the fire risk became very great. The imperative need of better protection was accentuated in 1858–59 by the occurrence of two great fires, one sweeping away the block bounded by Main, Franklin, Travis and Congress Streets and the other, the block bounded by Main, Congress, Travis and Preston Streets. In addition to these there was another big fire that destroyed a number of buildings on both sides of Main Street between Texas Avenue and Capitol Avenue. In 1860, the warehouse of T. W. Whitmarsh, containing 2,100 bales of cotton, was burned. When the first of these great fires occurred, a number of young men met and formed Houston Hook and Ladder Company No. 1. This company was organized April 17, 1858. Its first officers were: Foreman, Frank Fabj; 1st assistant, E. L. Bremond; 2nd assistant, O. J. Conklin; president, Henry Sampson; vice-president, Fred A. Rice; secretary, Wm. M. Thompson; treasurer, S. H. Skiff. The charter members were: J. C. Baldwin, C. A. Darling, Frank H. Bailey, I. C. Stafford, Ed. Riodan, R. W. Dowling, Pete Schwander, Paul Schwander, George A. Peek, W. S. Owens, Charles Nordhausen, John S. Hirshfield, J. L. Talman, R. B. Wilson, J. D. McNulty and John W. Clark.

The company entered at once into active service and accomplished great good through their well-directed and intelligent efforts.

When the great Civil War broke out in 1861, the company became badly disorganized because nearly all of its members entered the Confederate Army. In later years it was the proud boast of the surviving members that there was not a great battle fought from the Potomac to the Rio Grande, that did not have an old member of Hook and Ladder on the field. A great many of them lost their lives during the four bloody years, and, these noble fellows had their names recorded in mourning and filed in the archives of the company, as a slight tribute to their great worth. During the war the organization of Hook and Ladder No. 1 was kept up by those members who, for one reason or another, did not go to the front. The actual work of firefighting was done by negroes under the direction of white officers. After the war was over the returning members took up the work where they had left it, new blood was incorporated, and the company became as active and efficient as ever. The original idea of having none but gentlemen in the company was adhered to. A rigidly enforced set of by-laws demanded character and standing of all applicants for membership. No one being admitted until he had passed a searching investigation, the company preserved its early reputation, and it became known as the best organized and most thoroughly drilled truck company in the South.

Four years after the war, April 17, 1869, the company celebrated the eleventh anniversary of its organization and elected officers. The following roster shows the character of men who formed the membership at that time: Foreman, Frank Bailey; 1st assistant, C. C. Beavens; 2nd assistant, J. W. McAshan; president, S. T. Timpson; vice-president, F. A. G. Gearing;

secretary, Jesse C. Wagner; assistant secretary, L. F. DeLesDenier; treasurer, C. A. Darling; steward, J. D. Johnson. Members:—J. C. Baldwin, H. P. Roberts, O. L. Cochran, C. S. Marston, R.W. Shaw, P. E. Dowling, J. A. Bailey, George W. Gazley, E. L. Bremond, Will Lambert, Isaac Siegel, G. A. Gibbons, H. M. Phillips, Jules Albert, A. Levy, J. M. Tryan, C. Lachman, H. C. McClure, W. B. Bonner, A. J. Rogers, J. B. Cato, R. Cotter, A. Ewing, Taylor McRear and John House. Total, 34.

Soon after the formation of Hook and Ladder, there was another fire company organized, called Liberty Fire Company No. 2. This gave Houston three fire companies and in order to make them all more efficient and useful, Mr. T. W. House, who was mayor in 1862, determined to organize a regular fire department. He combined the three companies into one organization, known as the Houston Fire Department. Mr. E. L. Bremond was made chief engineer, with H. F. Hurd and R. Burns as assistants. The R. Burns mentioned in the foregoing was not Major Robert Burns at one time prominent in the Houston fire department, but who at that time, 1862, was in Virginia with the Texas Troops under Lee. This Houston Fire Department flourished for a little time and then dropped out as a department leaving the individual companies to act as they saw fit. Twelve years later Mr. J. H. B. House, under more favorable conditions, took up the work begun by his father, in 1862, and organized a thoroughly efficient fire department. The department was reorganized in May, 1874. Mr. J. H. B. House was made chief; Mr. Z. T. Hogan, assistant chief and Mr. C. C. Beavens, second assistant.

The following companies composed the department: Protection Fire Company No. 1, engine house on Texas Avenue, between Fannin and San Jacinto Streets; Hook and Ladder Company No. 1, on Prairie and San Jacinto Streets; Liberty Fire Company No. 2, on Franklin, between Milam and Louisiana Streets; Stonewall Fire Company No. 3, on Travis Street, between Prairie and Texas Avenues; Lee Fire Company No. 4; Brooks Fire Company No. 5, engine house near the corner of Liberty and MeKee Streets; Mechanics Fire Company No. 6. Engine house on Washington and Preston Streets. The department, thus organized in 1874, constituted the nucleus of Houseton's capable department of today.

Although the Houston Fire Department was not quite one year old on April 21st, 1875; a point was stretched and the department celebrated its first anniversary on San Jacinto Day, that year, in grand style. There was a great procession, in which, besides the local companies, the fire departments of Dallas, Waco, Calvert, Bryan, Brenham and Hempstead were represented by strong delegations. Col. J. P. Likens was orator of the day. The following local companies were in line:

Protection No. 1. the oldest fire company in the state, organized in 1836. Houston Hook and Ladder No. 1, organized April 17, 1858. Liberty No. 2,

Stonewall No. 3, and Brooks No. 5, all organized in the late sixties. Mechanics No. 6, organized October 28, 1873. Houston's Futures, a company of boys, had been organized but a short time, but appeared in the procession dragging their little hand engine. The following were the officers of the various companies of the department:

Protection No. 1, Charles Wichman, foreman; L. Ollre, first assistant; S. M. McAshan, president; Robert Brewster, secretary; R. Cohen, treasurer. Hook and Ladder No. 1, H. P. Roberts, president; T. L. Blanton, vice-president; William Cameron, secretary; O. L. Cochran, treasurer; Dr. T. Robinson, foreman; J. C. Hart, first assistant; G. W. Gazley, second assistant. Stonewall No. 3, Joseph F. Meyer, foreman; L. M. Jones, first assistant; F. J. Frank, second assistant; W. Long, president; F. Ludke, vice-president; W. E. Smith, secretary. Brooks No. 5, I. C. Lord, foreman; William Alexander, first assistant; J. C. Thomas, Jr., second assistant; J. C. Thomas, Sr., president; I. Snowball, vice-president; S. L. Mateer, secretary; Thomas Milner, treasurer. Eagle No. 7, John Shearn, Jr., foreman; Willie Van Alstyne, first assistant; Ed Mather, second assistant.

During the year Mr. J. H. B. House had resigned as chief of the department but continued to take an active interest in all that concerned it. On his retirement the department heads were arranged as follows: W. Williams, chief; C. C. Beavens, first assistant; Fred Harvey, second assistant. In the parade that day the Silsby, steamer of Protection No. 1, was drawn by four black horses, driven by Mr. J. H. B. House.

In 1876, the Houston fire department had two steamers, one extinguisher engine, two hand wagons and one hook and ladder company. The annual operating expense for the entire department was about $9,000. Its membership was composed of the best and most prominent citizens, all volunteers, and all well trained and effective firemen.

In 1893, the volunteer department was disbanded and the paid fire department was inaugurated. At first it was only a partial pay department, being composed of paid experts, and others who had to be on duty all the time, and of volunteer firemen who gave their services free, whenever a fire was actually burning. However, in 1895, this halfway system proving unsatisfactory, the city took over the whole department and placed it on the pay basis. Its success was assured from the start, and the Houston Fire Department entered at once on its career of usefulness. One or two things have contributed to its success. One is that the department has always been as far removed from politics as possible, even under the old administration conducted under the mayor and board of aldermen. Another is that the chiefs of the department have always been chosen because of their fitness to administer the affairs of their important office; for their executive ability as practical firemen, rather than for their "pull" as practical politicians and popularity among the voters of the city. But perhaps a thing that has contributed most to its success, is the fact that in the performance of its duties it has received the unanimous support and encouragement of the citizens of all classes. Unlike the police department, it has never had to perform duties that created strong animosity in certain quarters. Its progress has been smooth and unobstructed, and today Houston has a good and well organized fire department. In January, 1903, Houston had 59 firemen on the regular list and a number of others on the waiting list. There were at that time 20 pieces of firefighting apparatus. Today there are 104 officers and men employed in the Fire Department of Houston, and there are 30 pieces of firefighting apparatus, of which 9 are modern steamers having a combined capacity of 5,900 gallons of water per minute, and two are chemical engines of the latest design. The Department has 51 horses in active service. The actual cost of maintaining and operating the Department for the year ending February 28, 1911, was $124,443.76.

In early days, when a man's reputation for personal courage, honesty of purpose and a bulldog determination to do his duty was established, he was recognized as fit material out of which to make a peace officer. It was the man's personality, rather than his ability as a business man, or his ability as an executive officer that counted. The only executive ability demanded of him was that he be "quick on the draw" and expert in the use of his pistol. The early peace officer had no regular deputies nor had he a "force." He was the whole thing himself, and on occasions when he needed assistance, he could, and did call on any citizen or citizens to help him. In a newly settled place like Houston in the early days, there were a number of rough and desperate characters. Against such men as these, a weakling or a man who did not have a reputation for coolness and for a bravery vastly superior to their own, would have been worse than useless and would have really added to the criminal record by offering himself up as a sacrifice to the outlaws.

In the very early days police affairs were in the hands of the sheriff, and this condition prevailed for sometime after Houston had become a chartered city. In 1840 or 1841, Captain Newt. Smith, one of the heroes of San Jacinto, was elected city marshal and served as such until 1844, when Captain Billy Williams was elected to succeed him. In the late forties Captain R. C. Boyce was elected city marshal and held office for a number of years. The city marshal's office was no sinecure. From 1840 to 1860, Houston was at times, particularly about election times and on days of public gatherings, what one might call in the vernacular a little "wild and woolly."

On such occasions both the sheriff and marshal had their hands full. There were numerous desperate characters here, whiskey was cheap and plentiful and the wonder is that there were so few tragedies. It is a remarkable fact that none of the three men who served as marshal during that troublesome period ever had to kill a man. It was not because they were not perfectly prepared and willing to do so should occasion arise, and it was possibly a knowledge of that fact, on the part of the desperadoes, that caused them not to offer resistance when the officers went after them. At the close of the war, Mr. I. C. Lord was city marshal and his administration was far more strenuous than any that preceded it. This was due to the generally disrupted condition of society; to the fact that the town was full of returned Confederate soldiers, Federal soldiers, newly freed negroes and worthless white men, known as "scalawags" and "carpet-baggers," who did all in their power to stir up strife between the white people and the negroes. Killings were of frequent occurrence, and the police figured in the large majority of them.

As bits of police history are always interesting the following are given here as characteristic. They are taken from an old book at police headquarters, called the "Time Book," dated 1882. A record on the first page reveals the fact that the police force in 1882, consisted of a chief, a deputy chief and six patrolmen, the latter divided into a night and a day relief. Charles Wichman was chief, or city marshal, and W. W. Glass was deputy chief. W. H. Smith and F. W. McCutchin were the day force, while B. F. Archer, Jack White, James Daily and Nat Davis were the night force. All of these old officers are dead.

From December 23 to 27, 1882, six special policemen were added to the force to guard against trouble during Christmas times. These special officers were Bill Paris, Fred Merald, Louis Williams, Bud Butler, John Kelley, and John Donahue.

On November 1, 1885, officers described as "cow catchers" are spoken of for the first time in the old record book. These were two in number, J. E. Jemison and George W. Penticost. Items of personal interest are: "W. W. Glass, resigned Feb. 19th, 1886." Another "J. Fitzgerald, clerk, June 1, 1886." According to the book, Alex. Erickson was city marshal and B. W. McCarty, clerk, in April, 1892. James H. Pruett was marshal and A. R. Anderson, deputy in 1894. Deputy Chief J. M. Ray filled the same position in January, 1895. Among the old tragedies fatal to peace officers, recorded in the old book is this: "Richard Snow, killed in the fifth ward." Snow was a policeman, but beyond the brief record of the fact that he was killed nothing is said of the tragedy which occurred March 17, 1882.

Under date of February 8, 1886, appears: "Henry Williams killed by Kyle Terry at Market Square."

"March 14, 1891, J. E. Fenn was killed by Henry MeGee." Fenn went into a negro dance hall to make an arrest and was shot down by MeGee, a negro tough.

Captain Jack White, one of the Sabine Pass heroes, and for many years a police officer of Houston, died in 1896 and is thus referred to in the "time book;" "Jack White died September 15, buried with military honors."

Under date September 17, 1893, it was recorded that officer Pat Walsh, alighting from a street car, fell on his revolver discharging it and inflicting a wound from which he died later. In another old book at police headquarters, is recorded the killing of W. A. Weiss by J. T. Vaughn, on the night of July 29, 1901. Vaughn killed Weiss at Congress Avenue and San Jacinto Street and was himself killed the same night. On December 11, 1901, is recorded the killing of J. C. James by Sid Preacher, a gambler. Preacher used a shot gun. No sooner was James down than Preacher turned and killed Herman Youngst, another policeman. While James was dying he managed to get his pistol out and kill Preacher, just as the latter was starting to run away. James died at almost the same moment that his finger pressed the trigger. Every year has seen its tragedy in the police force. In 1910, Assistant Chief Murphy was killed by McFarlane, a discharged officer. Instead of the chief, deputy chief and six policemen that constituted the police force in 1882, Houston now has a chief and assistant chief and a police force of 103 policemen. In place of the two mounted policemen, described as "cow catchers" in 1885, there are now 18 mounted officers and four motorcycle officers. Chief of Police J. M. Ray, for the year ending February 28, 1911, reports the total number of arrests made by his department during the year to have been 5,928, classified as follows:

Violating State Laws	4,525
Violating City Ordinances	716
United States Deserters	2
Suspicious Characters	668
Lunacy	17
Total	5928

During the year there were 1,753 runs, covering 2,691 miles, made by the patrol wagon during the day, and 1,960 runs, covering 3,690 miles, made during the night.

Chief Ray says, in his report: "It gives me great pleasure to report that there has been less crime committed in the city during the past few months than ever before in the history of the city, which is not only gratifying to the public at large but to the officers of the department. Earlier in the year, before Chief Ray and his assistants took charge of the department, conditions quite the reverse of those spoken of by the Chief had prevailed in Houston, and it was this, no doubt, that led Mayor Rice in his annual message to say:

"During the past year, at different times, there has arisen sharp criticism of the police force, on account of crime committed in this city, and as I am the head of the department, I have been censured by some. All crime is deplorable, and no police force is perfect. Whenever I can find any weakness in this or any other department, I shall weed it out; but I want to serve notice in this, my annual message, that I not only stand for law and order; that I am not only going to enforce the law, but that the 'gun toter' and perjured criminal witness in the city, are going to be eradicated, if I have to call upon every law-abiding citizen in the community to assist me."

During the year ending February 28, 1911, the total cost for maintaining the Police Department, was $109,200, while the revenue from fines, costs of court, etc., was $25,202.60.

Duff Voss, who made a record for efficiency and courage as deputy sheriff, is now the Chief of Police of Houston, and conditions have continued to improve. They are not perfect as a policeman was killed by a negro in August, 1911, and earlier in the year, two policemen engaged in a pistol duel on Main Street to settle a private grudge and crimes against life are alarmingly frequent in Harris County, which has one of the bloodiest records in the United States.

A lax public sentiment and sharp criminal practice have made it almost impossible to convict for any kind of homicide. With this exception the laws are well enforced. No public gambling place exists in the city of Houston, the Sunday closing laws are rigidly executed, the social evil is segregated almost entirely and immoral houses are not tolerated in the business and residence sections of the city. All city ordinances are well enforced, property is well protected, and there is a growing sentiment to back the mayor's energetic campaign against "gun toters" and gun users. Citizens are determined that harmless bystanding shall be made a less dangerous occupation and hope to see the time come when ladies may go upon the streets without any risk of being perforated by stay bullets fired in impromptu pistol duels of citizens and officers on crowded thoroughfares.

Until about 1878–79, Houston had but little need for waterworks. To that time water for drinking purposes was obtained from under-ground cisterns and that for fire protection purposes from similar cisterns located at convenient points along Main Street. When a fire occurred in the resident part of town, private cisterns were pressed into service. These cisterns, both public and private, were from twelve to twenty feet deep and from eight to fifteen feet in diameter, and held many thousand gallons of water each. Their construction was simple. A large cistern was first dug of the desired dimensions and its bottom and sides lined with brick, as carefully placed as though a house were being constructed. When the brick work was completed the inner surface, sides and bottom, was plastered over with water-proof cement. As only the water that fell in the winter was caught and preserved, the water was delightfully cool and no one ever needed ice water. But by 1878 Houston had grown beyond the stage of cisterns and the citizens began to realize that they would have to look elsewhere for their water supply.

On January 15, 1878, Mayor James T. Wilson, in a message to the council, drew attention to the growing need for water-works and sewers. On November 30, 1878, the city entered into a contract with Mr. J. M. Loweree and his associates, to supply the city with water. January 11, 1879, an ordinance was passed to amend the ordinance of November 30, 1878, authorizing Loweree and his associates to organize themselves into a corporation to be known as the Houston Waterworks Company.

On April 15, 1879, the Houston Waterworks Company was organized, with Joseph Richardson, of New York, president; T. F. White, of Houston secretary; William Runkle, of New York, treasurer; and Joseph Richardson, Daniel Runkle, William Runkle and W. Steiger, of New York, and E. Pillot and T. F. White, of Houston, as directors. J. M. Loweree was named as superintendent. Books for subscription to the capital stock of the company, were opened at the City Bank.

The company lost no time in getting to work, and the water works were completed in July of that same year. In August, the water committee reported to the city council that the test of the system made by them was satisfactory and recommended that the contract be finally signed. The system was a make-shift affair, and no effort was made to supply the city with suitable drinking water. The water supply was pumped direct from the bayou, and the only use it could possibly be put to was for fire purposes. Still for this it was a great improvement on the old cisterns. In the early nineties it was discovered that an abundant supply of pure artesian water could be obtained anywhere in or near Houston, and the Waterworks Company sank several wells. This gave an abundance of pure drinking water, as well as water for other purposes. However, the company persisted from time to time in pumping bayou water into the mains, which made the whole system very unpopular. The city authorities and the waterworks management were constantly at war. This continued until 1906, when the city of Houston purchased the water plant from its owners, paying $901,000 for it. The city at once increased the water supply from artesian wells and cut out the bayou water entirely. At the time of the purchase, the private corporation was charging 50 cents per thousand, meter rate, and, as already noted, was pumping from the bayou whenever it suited their convenience to do so. The city, so soon as it got control, reduced the rate, and today charges only 15c per thousand gallons, and it is all wholesome artesian water.

Since the waterworks is the only public utility owned and operated by the city it is interesting to compare its administration with that of its predecessor, the private corporation. During the first five months of the commission's management, the city saved in salaries alone, $2,307.88, notwithstanding the fact that the pay of all operatives had been materially increased. During the same period, the city showed a gain in earnings, including hydrant rentals formerly paid by the city, of $10,575.35 and all this with a decreased charge to the consumer for the service. With a decreased consumption of fuel, the average monthly pressure was increased from 53.5 pounds in September, 1906 to 62 pounds in February, 1907. All other public utilities are owned by private corporations, yet they have all put themselves into hearty co-operation with the commission and usually respond promptly to definite popular demands for better and more extended service.

The Houston Gas Company was organized in 1866, by Mr. T. W. House, Sr., captain; N. P. Turner, governor; J. W. Henderson, Robert Brewster and one or two others. This was the first of Houston's public utilities, and while it did not meet with actual opposition of any kind, it did meet with something harder to overcome—an almost fatal indifference on the part of the public. A plant was erected, mains were laid, and then the company had to take up a campaign of education, and, to actually drum for customers. The hotels, restaurants and public places that open at night were the first, and for some time, the only customers. The gradually the merits of the "new" light became apparent and homes and other places became customers. Then the company made a contract with the city to light the streets, and the use of gas became general.

In 1869, the company was well on its feet and was doing a large business. That year Mr. T. W. House, Sr., was elected president; J. W. Henderson, vice-president; S. M. McAshan, secretary and treasurer; and N. P. Turner, superintendent. The company's stock was commanding a premium and it was evident that Houston could and would support such a concern. Perhaps the secret of the success of the company lies in the fact that from the very beginning it has been its aim to give the public fair treatment and to give value received for every dollar collected. Unlike most corporations, the Houston Gas Company has been run in the interest of the public from the day of its organization, hence it has met with no opposition and its course has been free and unobstructed.

When the company first began manufacturing gas it fixed the price at $1.50, and this was never changed, not even when the strong competition of electric lights came about, until in 1910, the price was reduced to $1.10, and on January 1, 1912, it will be reduced to $1.00.

Since 1905 the company has increased its capacity in every way. The mileage of gas mains has been increased from 51 miles, in 1905, to 120 miles in 1911, and during that time the company has spent $528,000 on extensions and mains alone. In 1907 the company purchased three additional lots on Crawford and Magnolia Streets, and made a contract with a Philadelphia concern to build a mammoth gas-holder on this property. This holder is the largest in Texas. It is 100 feet in diameter, 150 feet high and has a capacity of one million cubic feet. It cost about $100,000 to build it. The use of gas for heating and cooking has vastly increased the demand for it.

On January 1, 1846, the city of Houston had a debt of $875, and had to show for this debt, in the way of public improvements, a fine bridge over Buffalo Bayou, a good wooden market house, a block long, and a well-built wooden two-story city hall and city jail combined.

On January 1, 1875, when the "reconstruction" mayor and aldermen had been turned out of office and the people of Houston had been given the management of their own affairs, the city of Houston had a debt of about two million dollars and had, to show for it, an $80,000 brick market house and a sewer about two blocks long on Caroline Street.

Of course it was out of the question to hope for any growth or advancement of Houston with such a debt as it had, hanging over it. With the last possible cent squeezed out of the taxpayers it was impossible to pay the interest on the debt and to pay the necessary, current expenses of the city. There was but one thing to do, compromise the debt that had been so unjustly saddled on the people, and if this could be done, make a new start in life. The very best business men of Houston were placed in office, with the sole purpose of using their business talent and experience in an attempt to solve the trouble. Repeated and varied offers were made to the bondholders but to all of them a deaf ear was turned.

Administration after administration took up the burden, but all were forced to lay it down again. Suits were brought and judgments were obtained against the city, thus increasing the debt all the time. Finally the people became absolutely desperate and began, not only to speak of the repudiation among themselves but to advocate it in the newspapers and advance arguments to prove the justice of taking such a radical step. If the bondholders were frightened by such talk they gave no signs of being so, but remained obdurate, quietly demanding their money. They made it quite plain, too, that it was hard cash and no new bonds that they wanted.

Such were the conditions when, in 1880, after consulting among themselves, a committee of the most prominent business men of Houston, waited on Mr. Wm. R. Baker, one of the great men and successful financiers of Houston, and told him that he had to become mayor of the city and settle that debt. He objected strenuously, but when told that he would be allowed to select his own board of aldermen and that there would be no opposition to the ticket, he consented. He and those whom he had chosen to serve with him were elected by practically a unanimous vote of the people. At the end of the first two years they had accomplished no more than had their predecessors. They were given another trial. When their second term expired, the city debt, so far from being settled was actually about $200,000 greater than when they went into office. The cause of this was quite apparent. Had the bondholders had the framing of the slate, they would have chosen the very men that the people chose, for, with such leading and prominent business men in office, all talk of repudiating any debt of the city became impossible.

Then the people did what proved to be the wisest thing they ever did. They had seen that the great financiers could do nothing so they went to the other extreme and turned the affairs over to what was facetiously called "the short hair" element. This might have proven a fatal error had the people selected another man than Mr. Dan. C. Smith for mayor. At that time he was practically unknown to most of the people, for he had never taken part in public affairs and had never sought office of any kind. He was the right man for the place, as results showed. His co-workers were known as the labor crowd and it was said that the city had been turned over to the labor element. This caused the bond holders to sit up and take notice at once, for they could imagine "repudiation and ruin" written everywhere on the wall. They became both willing and anxious to listen to reason and before Mayor Smith's first term had expired, he had the city debt well under way toward settlement, by compromise; and at the end of his second term, the entire debt was either wiped out or settled on a most advantageous basis.

It must not be presumed that the settlement was made entirely through fear on the part of the bond holders. They sent their representatives here and discovered, what the people of Houston had also discovered, that Mayor Smith was a man possessed of executive ability of the highest order, that he was honest and capable and that it was his intention to do what was just and right and nothing more. They realized that it would be folly to try to "dicker and dillydally" with such a man and they did not try to do so. At the end of four years, Mayor Smith turned the city over to his successor with its affairs in admirable shape. The big debt had been compromised on a basis that was fair and just to both creditor and debtor, and had been placed in such form that the city could pay off the bonds as they fell due and could pay interest on them without cripling itself to such an extent as to interfere with current expenses and needed improvements. He also turned over the city on a cash basis, with little or no floating debt. Succeeding administrations served with more or less credit.

In 1896, H. B. Rice was elected mayor. He was young, and a well-trained business man. As mayor he had brought to his attention, in a practical way, the many defects in a system by which the affairs of a great corporation, such as a city were often turned over to the management of men, many of whom were unfitted through lack of education and training to manage any business at all. He recognized that honesty without ability was quite as harmful, as actual rascality, and that the affairs of the city suffered through the absence of business methods in their management. There was offered no remedy, however. He served for two terms and while his administration was marked by improvements in many departments, there was room for a great many more, which could not be made under the form of government then in vogue.

Government was through a mayor and board of aldermen. Each alderman was elected, not by the whole city, but only by small numbers of voters living in wards and they necessarily represented many local and conflicting interests to the prejudice of the wisest and most economical administration for the city as a whole. Then, too, each alderman was, in a measure, independent of the mayor or of his other fellow aldermen. Having obtained his authority from the votes of his ward only, he recognized no higher authority than the ward and placed its interests above those of the community as a whole. With such methods it was not surprising that but little public good was ever accomplished, even when, as was often the case, honorable and capable men were placed in power. Yet, such were the conditions that existed in every city in this country in 1900.

The great disaster in Galveston, September 8, 1900, forced a change in the form of government in that city, which seems destined to be far-reaching and wide spread in its effects. In their great distress and seemingly hopeless condition, the people abandoned the old mayor and board of aldermen form of government, and the governor, by popular request, appointed a board of commissioners, consisting of five business men to take control of the city's affairs. The form of government was permanently changed, and though the people later elected their commissioners, instead of having them appointed by the state governor, the commission form of government in Galveston is today the same as when it was first inaugurated. Only a few unimportant changes and modifications have been made. The immediate, beneficial effects of the Galveston commission form of government became so apparent that other cities began to study it and soon realized that in it lay the secret of successful municipal government. It seems paradoxical to say that the most dangerous form of government that could possibly be devised, is the safest and best, and yet this so far has proved true. With such power as is given under the commission form of government, bad and dishonest men could ruin and destroy a city in much less time and far more effectually than good and honest men could build it up. But in this self-apparent weakness lies its strength, for while the public is constantly on its guard, there is only the remotest chance of the reins of power falling into undesirable hands.

Four years after its inauguration in Galveston the commission idea was submitted to a vote of the people of Houston, and, on the tenth day of December, 1904, was adopted. A charter, to suit the needs of the new plan, was prepared by a committee composed of members of the city council and leading citizens, and became the present city charter. It was granted by the legislature on March 18, 1905.

The following synopsis of an address delivered by Mayor Rice before the Chicago Commercial Club, December 10, 1910, gives not only the leading features of the commission, but also some of the things that have been accomplished through it. Mr. Rice said: "The essential differences between the commission form and the old form of municipal government are three:

"The substitution of a smaller number of aldermen, elected from the city at large, in place of a large number of aldermen, elected from different wards or subdivisions of the city; vesting of a co-ordinate power in the mayor as in the city council to dismiss any officer of the city government, except the controller, at any time, without cause, and, the essential provisions safeguarding the granting of municipal franchises. Instead of a body of twelve aldermen, elected from different wards or subdivisions of the city, under the Houston system, four aldermen are elected from the body of the city by the votes of all the citizens, in the same way in which the mayor is elected. These four aldermen, together with the mayor, constitute the city council or legislative department of the city government. The executive power is vested in the mayor, but by an ordinance, for the administration of the city's affairs, a large part of executive or administrative power is subdivided into different departments, and a committee is placed over each department, and one of the four aldermen, nominated by the mayor, is what is known as the active chairman.

"The mayor and all four aldermen are members of each committee. The active chairman of the committee practically has control of the administration of the department, unless his views are overruled by the whole committee but by the organization of the committees the active chairman does his work, to a certain extent, under the supervision and direction of the mayor, who is, in the last analysis, the head of each committee and the person in whom the executive power of municipal government ultimately rests.

"Under the old system of government, by which twelve aldermen were elected from as many different precincts of the city, it frequently happened that unfit men came to represent certain wards in the city council. Now, unless a man has sufficient standing and reputation throughout the body of the city as a fit man for the office of alderman, he will not be elected. Again, each alderman under the present system represents the whole city. Under the old system the conduct of public business was continually obstructed by a system of petty log-rolling going on among and between the representatives of the numerous sub-divisions of the city. Then, too, the smallness of the number of aldermen now affords opportunity for the transaction of business.

"An executive session is held previous to each meeting of the city council, at which matters to come before the council are discussed and action determined on. The small number of aldermen enables the city administration to act on all matters of importance as a unit. In other words, the system makes it possible to administer the affairs of the city in a prompt and business-like way.

"This is one of the strongest arguments in favor of the present commission form of government, for with a majority of the aldermen always in session, public business can be, and is, promptly attended to. It is no longer necessary to go before the city council with petitions to have something done. Any citizen who desires to have a street paved, taxes adjusted, a nuisance abated, or anything else, has only to call at the mayor's office and have the matter promptly adjusted. After a hearing, the matter is decided by the council in the presence of the applicant. To illustrate the great difference between this method and the old one the following comparison is made. By the old method a petition was addressed to the council. This was referred to a committee, which acted when convenient. Then a report to the council was made by the committee. After the action of the council it went to the mayor and from him to someone else for execution. The people do not pay their taxes for such treatment. They want their business attended to promptly and that is what is being done under the commission."

Mayor Rice illustrated the promptness with which the public business it attended to by relating the following story:

"A gentleman, a non-resident of Houston, whose home was in a Western state, owned some property in our city and the property had been recently taken into the city limits. Investigating his assessment, he found that his property had been placed at a much higher valuation than that of his neighbor. Being a stranger, he called upon one of Houston's leading attorneys and asked his advice how to proceed for relief. The attorney suggested that they step over to the mayor's office and have the matter corrected. The owner of the property thought it would be wiser for the lawyer to get some of his friends to sign a petition to the council so that it would have some weight with the authorities. The attorney replied that this mode of procedure was entirely unnecessary, as Houston now had a business-like government. They called at my office and stated their mission. I sent for the tax collector, and in an hour the stranger had his tax receipt in his pocket. The owner of the land said that if the case had been in his city it would have taken weeks for adjustment, on account of the red tape in existence."

One of the most striking features of the commission charter is the power that it confers on the mayor. Under its provisions any officer of the city except the aldermen, who are elected for two years, and the controller, who is appointed for a term of two years and subject to removal by the council only for cause, may be removed by the mayor or may be removed from office at any time at the will of the council.

This feature of the charter has been subjected to more adverse criticism than all the others combined, and yet it has proven in practice to be one of the best and most fruitful for good. Because of it, the city attorney does not refuse to collect taxes and say to the city government that he was elected by the people and is responsible to them and that he does not favor collecting taxes. Because of it, the chief of police does not refuse to enforce the criminal ordinances of the city and give the same excuse for declining to do so.

Because of it, the tax collector can not arbitrarily select what persons he is to exempt from the payment of taxes, and inform the government that the people elected him and that he is responsible to the people. The mayor, under the charter is the responsible head of the government. If things are permitted to go wrong, it is his fault, and if any officer of the city refuses to enforce the law, the mayor can remove him in five minutes time. Of course it is imperatively necessary for the people to select a man of good sense and character to be mayor, but when they have done so, they will know that he will not be, as under the old system, a dummy and figure head and a helpless spectator to wanton disregard of law and mal-administration. This so-called, "one-man" feature of the commission embodies its whole aim and intention—a responsible head to the city government, chosen by the people themselves.

When the commission form of government went into effect, July, 1905, the various departments were organized and at the head of each was placed a commissioner. The school board under the commission has been kept out of politics. On this board are democrats, republicans, Israelites and Christians, all working without compensation, for the best interest of the public schools of the city. The labor question has been eliminated also; union labor and non-union labor both work for the city. The only point insisted on is that the laborer shall understand that the city of Houston comes first and his organization second, when he works for the city. If a commissioner discharges an employe in his department, the action is final. An appeal to the mayor will do no good, for so long as the head of the department manages and works conscientiously for the city, the mayor will sustain him and leave him with absolute authority. No alderman can appoint a man on the police force. The mayor selects a chief of police and holds him responsible for the conduct of his men, who are all selected by the chief himself.

The school board is nominated by the mayor and confirmed by the council. It in turn selects a school superintendent. The teachers are selected for their fitness. No commissioner can even suggest the name of a teacher to the board. All the commissioners have to do is to supply the money to support the schools. Their connection with the administration of the schools, begins and ends there.

Another most important change that was made when the commission charter was adopted was that relating to the matter of franchises. Under the new charter no franchise can be granted for a longer period than thirty years unless it be submitted to a vote of the legally qualified voters of the city and approved by them. The expense of this election must be borne by the person applying for the franchise. If a majority of the votes is favorable, the franchise may be granted in the form as submitted, but cannot, in any case, be granted for a period longer than fifty years.

The council may, on its own motion, submit an ordinance granting a franchise to the vote of people of the city.

If a franchise be granted for a period of thirty years or less, the proposed franchise shall be published in the form in which it is finally passed and shall not thereafter be changed, once a week for three consecutive weeks, at the expense of the applicant. And, if at any time within thirty days after its final passage, a written petition is presented to the council, signed by at least 500 legally qualified voters of the city, then such franchise must be submitted to an election of the people to determine whether or not it shall be granted. No franchise in the streets, highways, thoroughfares or property of the city can ever be granted until it has been read at three regular meetings of the council.

No franchise can be granted unless the ordinance granting the same provides for adequate compensation or consideration therefor, to be paid to the city, and in addition to any other form of compensation, the grantees shall pay annually such a fixed charge as may be prescribed in the franchise.

Every grant of a franchise shall provide that on the termination of the grant, the property of the grantee in the streets, avenues or other public places, shall thereupon, without compensation, or upon the payment of a fair valuation therefor, become the property of the city, and in estimating such value, the value derived from the franchise, or the fact that it is or may be a going concern, shall not be considered in determining the value. Every grant of a franchise shall provide, by forfeiture of the grant or otherwise, for efficiency of public service at reasonable rates, and to maintain the property in good order. The city reserves the right to inspect the books and accounts of the grantee of a franchise, which books and accounts shall be kept and reports made in accordance with the forms prescribed by the city council.

The charter reserves the right in the city of Houston to regulate the rates of all public utility corporations. The charter contains a referendum feature by which 500 citizens on petition can secure a vote on any municipal measure or utility.

The foregoing brief summary shows the means placed in the hands of the commissioners by the charter and their methods of enforcing its provisions. Now let us see what have been the results accomplished.

The commission has now been in active control of the city's affairs a little over six years. Inaugurated in July, 1905, the commission found a floating debt of a little over $400,000, an empty treasury and the city without credit. The work of retrenchment and economy was begun at once. Useless and expensive offices were abolished, while others were consolidated. A national bank was made treasurer, allowing a salary of $50 per month for clerk hire, and the bank agreed to pay interest on all balances to the credit of the city.

The city attorney was instructed to file suits against all delinquent tax payers. This alone resulted in the collection of nearly $100,000 in the first eight months and during those first eight months of the commission's life, by the strictest economy, $306,202.47 of the old floating debt was redeemed, besides paying all current expenses promptly at the end of each month.

Since the inauguration of the commission rule the city has wiped out its entire floating debt, and the taxpayers have been given, out of the treasury, without the issuance of a single bond, the following permanent improvements:

City Attorney, Law Library	$ 974.10
Assessor and Collector, Block Book System	10,000.00
City Hall, Furniture and Fixtures	1,123.67
Police Department	4,096.03
Fire Department, Buildings and Equipment	66,150.45
Electrical Department	26,551.21
Health Department	6,168.26
Parks	52,007.53
Streets and Bridges	65,714.10
Asphalt Plant	3,000.00
Auditorium	332,276.02
Ship Channel	98,027.40
Sewers	85,212.18
Paving Streets	179,261.96
Water Department, Extension of Mains and Improvements	247,932.02
Wharves and Ships	33,109.89
School Buildings	340,323.65
Total Improvements	$1,865,757.17

EXTRAORDINARY EXPENSES.

	$ 73,300.00
Storrie Certificates	
Refund Paving Certificates	120,308.70
Sinking Fund	120,220.00
Making a Grand Total of	$2,179,585.87

All of this was paid out of current revenues, besides the elimination of the floating debt of more than $400,000.

All this has created business confidence in the city as a government, and has given it a credit that it never had before. Assessments have been increased in a just and equitable way, while the tax levy has been reduced 30c on the $100 valuation. The tax levy is $1.70 on the $100. The tax roll for 1912 will carry a valuation of $80,000,000.

Moral accomplishments have been in keeping with material feats. Gambling houses have been cleaned out; variety shows have been abolished, pool rooms have been closed, and the saloons have been closed after 12 o'clock every night and all day on Sunday.

Houston's experience demonstrates to the world that the commission form of city government is decidedly a success. The city owns the water works but all other public utilities are under private management and control. They, however, willingly and cheerfully cooperate with the commissioners in all efforts made to extend their usefulness and to increase public comfort and safety. In 1905, when the commission came in power, the price of gas was $1.50, Jan. 1, 1912, it becomes $1.00. The electric light plant has also made a material reduction in its charges, the city having set the example by reducing the cost of water from 50c per thousand gallons to 15c per thousand. City water is supplied from 44 artesian wells with a daily capacity of 16,000,000 gallons. The average daily consumption is 7,800,000 gallons. Fire protection is annually increased—three and one-third per cent in 1910–11. The street car company has reduced its fare for children under 12 years of age to two and one-half cents, and pays annually one per cent on its gross receipts to the city. The salaries of firemen, policemen, and of some of the employees who have worked for years and been faithful and efficient, have been increased. These wonders have been wrought in the short period of six years and it is worthy of attention that most of them were assured facts before the expiration of the first three years of the commission's life. The people have grown to have large confidence in the commission, give it their heartiest support and unite with it in its efforts to build up Houston.

Under the commission the mayor is practically an autocrat. The commissioners are largely secretaries in charge of their functions. In one case a commissioner, who displeased the mayor was deprived of all participation in the city government during the remainder of his term. Not a speech has ever been made in the city council under the commission form of government.

In 1911, the office of Superintendent of Complaints was created as a buffer between the city council and the public service corporations. Any citizen can at once register complaint against any public service or utility corporation and attention is at once paid to them. This office is filled by J. Z. Gaston, formerly city commissioner, who first advocated the commission form of government in a public speech in Houston and who is called here "the father of the commission form of government."

The roster of the present city commission officials, committees department heads and boards is, August, 1911, as follows:

CITY OFFICIALS.
- Mayor, H. B. Rice; Mayor, pro. tem., Jack Kennedy; Commissioners, J. J. Pastoriza, Jack Kennedy, Robert L. Jones, W. J. Kohlhauff; Water Committee, R. L. Jones, Chairman, J. J. Pastoriza, Jack Kennedy, W. J. Kohlhauff; Street and Bridge Committee, Jack Kennedy, Chairman, W. J. Kohlhauff, Robert L. Jones, J. J. Pastoriza; Fire Committee, W. J. Kohlhauff, Chairman, Jack Kennedy, J. J. Pastoriza, Robert L. Jones; Ordinance Committee, Jack Kennedy, Chairman, W. J. Kohlhauff, Robert L. Jones; Board of Appraisement, J. J. Pastoriza, Chairman, W. J. Kohlhauff, James P. Welsh.

HEADS OF DEPARTMENTS.
- T. C. Dunn, Active Vice-President of the Union National Bank, Treasurer
- D. C. Smith, Jr. Controller and Secretary
- Miss Roberta Cotter Assistant Secretary
- Jno. A. Kirlicks Judge Corporation Court
- W. H. Wilson City Attorney
- J. E. Niday Assistant City Attorney
- Frank L. Dormant City Engineer
- James P. Welsh Assessor and Collector
- Dr. Geo. W. Larendon City Health Officer
- Dr. F. J. Slataper Bacteriologist
- Duff Voss Chief of Police
- W. X. Norris Building Inspector
- Nelson Munger Purchasing Agent
- F. J. Ollre Market Master
- C. R. George City Electrician
- R. F. Ollre Chief of the Fire Department
- M. Murphy Wharf Master
- E. R. Parker Fire Marshall

Board of Liquidation: F. A. Reichardt, Ed. H. Harrell, O. T. Holt, B. F. Bonner, H. W. Garrow.

Board of Health: Dr. Joe Stuart, President; Dr. W. A. Archer, Dr. J. W. Scott, Dr. Sidney J. Smith, Dr. J. D. Duckett. Dr. S. H. Hillen.

BOARD OF SCHOOL TRUSTEES.

President, Rufus Cage; vice-president, B. B. Gilmer; secretary, A. S. Cleveland. Finance Committee: G. H. Pendarvis, Sam Swinford, B. B. Gilmer. Teachers Committee: A. S. Cleveland, J. D. Duckett, B. B. Gilmer. Course of Study and Text Books: S. McNeill, A. S. Cleveland, Sam Swinford. School Property, Purchase and Repairs: B. B. Gilmer, G. H. Pendarvis, S. McNeill. Hygiene: J. D. Duckett, G. H. Pendarvis, S. McNeill. School Medical Inspector: Dr. W. W. Ralston. Grievances and Complaints: Sam Swinford, J. D. Duckett, A. S. Cleveland. W. Peine, Business Representative of the Board.

Owing to the fact that the city hall has been destroyed by fire, twice, there are very few official documents in existence relating to the early history of the city. Major Ingham S. Roberts, whose family was a pioneer in Houston, gives a list of the mayors of Houston, compiled from various sources which differs from other lists and the recollections of the "oldest inhabitants" by claiming that Dr. Francis Moore was not the first mayor of Houston, as all historians and writers have given him credit for being. In the Telegraph of September 29, 1837, Major Roberts found a notice of a special election to fill vacancies left by aldermen Hugh McCrory and Leman Kelcy, deceased, which notice was signed by James S. Holman, mayor. On this evidence he transfers to Mr. Holman the honor of having been the first mayor of Houston. Major Roberts may be correct or it may be that in the case of a delayed election, Mr. Holman was an appointed mayor pro tem. The complete list, as prepared by Major Roberts and published by him in The Historical Review, of southeast Texas, of which he was one of the editors, is followed as to order of names here:

1837, James S. Holman; 1838, Francis Moore, Jr.; 1839, George W. Lively; 1840, Charles Biglow; 1841–42, John D. Andrews; 1843, Francis Moore, Jr.; 1844, Horace Baldwin; 1845, W. W. Swain; 1846, James Baily; 1847–48, B. P. Buckner; 1849–52, Francis Moore; 1853–54, Col. Nathan Fuller; 1855–56, James H. Stevens; 1857, Cornelius Ennis; 1858, Alexander McGowan; 1859, W. H. King; 1860, T. W. Whitmarsh; 1861, W. J. Hutchins; 1862, T. W. House, Sr.; 1863-4-5, William Andrews; 1866, H. D. Taylor.

In 1867, Alexander McGowan was elected mayor, but on December 5, of that year, General J. T. Reynolds, commander of this military district, took semi-military control of the city's affairs and left the mayor with only nominal authority. This state of affairs continued until August 8, 1868, when Governor E. J. Davis turned McGowan out of office and appointed J. R. Morris in his place. At the same time he appointed T. H. Scanlan an alderman from the Third ward. In September, Judge B. P. Fuller, the recorder and I. C. Lord, the city marshal, were removed by Davis and their places filled by J. G. Tracy, as recorder, and Capt. A. K. Taylor, as marshal. Captain Taylor became disgusted and quit and was succeeded by Capt. M. E. Davis.

But the governor grew tired of taking merely cherry-bites and, in 1870, made a clean sweep, turning everybody out who had been elected by the people and putting in his own henchmen. He appointed T. H. Scanlan mayor, and made four negro aldermen. That was the beginning of scallawag and carpet-bag rule in Houston.

In 1872, a so-called election was held, and, by importing negroes from the adjoining counties to vote the republican ticket, and obstructing the white voters in every way, Scanlan and his negro associates were declared elected.

At the state election, held in November, 1873, the democrats secured control of the state. In January, 1874, the charter of Houston was amended and under its provisions Governor Richard Coke appointed all the city officials of Houston. T. H. Scanlan and his negroes were ousted and J. T. D. Wilson was appointed mayor and a board of aldermen, consisting of representative citizens, was put in. Soon after that an election was held and Mr. Wilson was elected mayor in regular form. His successors have been:

1875–76, I. C. Lord; 1877–78, J. T. D. Wilson; 1879, A. J. Burke; 1880–84, W. R. Baker; 1886–88, D. C. Smith; 1890, Henry Scherffius; 1892–94, John T. Browne; 1896, H. Baldwin Rice; 1898–1900, Sam H. Brashear; 1902, O. T. Holt; 1904, Andrew L. Jackson; 1905–1911, H. Baldwin Rice, who is still in office.

CHAPTER VIII - THE BENCH AND BAR

High Character of Early Lawyers. First District Court. Early Legal Documents. Great Criminal Lawyers. Ex-Governor Henderson's Butcher Knife. Members of Early Bar. Criminal and District Court Judges. The County Court and Its Judges. Judge Hamblen's Reminiscences. Harris County Bar Association. Houston as a Source of Legal Business.

It is true of every nation's pioneer history that "there were giants in those days." Such names as Campbell, Tankersley, Gray, Palmer, Henderson, Manley, Riley, Thompson, Tompkins and a number of others, who established the high standard for the Houston Bar at the very beginning, are sufficient to prove this true of the Bench and Bar of this city. In the beginning Harris County was known as Harrisburg County, and court has been held here since 1837.

The first record entry of proceedings of the Harrisburg (Harris) County Court shows that the court was thus constituted:

Hon. Andrew Briscoe, chief justice; C. C. Dyre, M. Battle, John Denton, Joel Wheatin, Isaac Batterson, Abram Roberts, and John S. McGahey, commissioners. D. W. Clinton Harris, county clerk. The chief business of the term was granting ferry privileges, but public roads were promoted to some extent. On petition of B. Fort Smith, commissioners were appointed to lay off a road to the county line, towards Washington; others to survey a line for a road to Liberty, via Harrisburg and Lynchburg.

D. W. Clinton Harris belonged to the family that gave the county its name. Judge Andrew Briscoe was the father of Mrs. M. Looscan and of Mrs. M. G. Howe. His widow, Mrs. Marry Briscoe, long survived him.

Several incidents of early justice and the founding of the courts have been recounted in an earlier chapter. The members of the first petit jury were: Berry Beasley, Sam M. Harris, Archie Hodges, J. James Perchouse, D. S. Harbert, Edward Dickinson, John Woodruff, Marsh McKever, Elliot Hodges, Lemar Celcey, John O'Brien and Joseph A. Harris. The jury rendered a verdict of justifiable homicide in the case of Joseph T. Bell, and the prisoner was discharged.

The first judicial act in the municipality of Harrisburg, as Harris County was first called, was in the probate court. Hon. A. Briscoe, judge of that court, on petition of Richard Vince, by the latter's attorney, Thomas J. Gazley, appointed Vince administrator of the estate of Robert Vince, deceased.

The first licenses to practice law in Harris County were issued to N. Bassett, Swift Austin, Francis W. Thornton, Robert Page, Henry Humphrey and James Brown on March 19, 1838, these gentlemen having successfully passed an examination conducted by David G. Burnett, John Birdsall and A. M. Tompkins, a committee of examiners appointed by the court.

One of the earliest cases was that against David S. Kerkernot, who was indicted March 2, 1837, for filching a mule belonging to the Republic of Texas, which act was declared to be "against the peace and dignity of said Republic." Another indictment was returned by the grand jury against the same man in December, 1838, and seems to refer to the same case, for the indictment declares that he took the mule "with force and arms." This man Kerkernot appears to have occupied much of the time of the courts, for in the September term of 1837 he was plaintiff and William Scott, defendant, in a suit where the title to 177 acres of land on the San Jacinto, granted to Stephen F. Austin, was in controversy. One of the early documents relates to a suit brought by the city of Houston against Henry R. and Samuel J. Allen for taxes, amounting to $1,943. The suit was filed in 1839.

There were many able and brilliant members of the early Houston Bar. The large majority of these confined themselves to the practice of civil law but one or two won name and fame as criminal lawyers. This latter field was very exacting, for legal ethics were on a high plane and the lawyer who attempted to win a case by chicanery or doubtful methods was generally reduced to the level of the police court where such men properly belong. In the days of Manley, Henderson, Barziza, Riley, Cook and one or two others, the criminal lawyer used no convenient witness, or fixed juries, but depended entirely on his knowledge of law and his eloquence as a pleader, to win his cases. For a man to have fame as a great criminal lawyer in those days was looked upon as an honor.

Col. John H. Manley was one of the greatest criminal lawyers who has ever practiced at the Houston Bar. His methods were strictly ethical and no man was better equipped mentally than he for the difficult tasks he undertook. He had a thorough and profound knowledge of criminal law and combined with all this he was an eloquent orator and pleader. Members of the bar refer to him as a perfect type for a model lawyer.

In the same category with Colonel Manley, was Captain D. U. Barziza. His history is remarkable in many respects and will bear telling briefly. His father was an Italian nobleman, who had the good, or bad fortune of thinking for himself on many subjects, among them being religion and forms of government. He was a protestant, a Baptist, and a republican. He longed for a freedom that Italy could not offer, so he gave up his estate and title and came to America. Finally he settled in Texas. Captain D. U. Barziza, his youngest son was educated at Baylor University, at Independence, and had just completed his course when the Civil War broke out. He volunteered at once and was made captain of one of the companies that afterwards formed part of Hood's Texas Brigade in the Army of Northern Virginia. His army record was a brilliant one. After the surrender, he came to Houston, and in order to support himself he secured a place as night clerk at the old Rusk Hotel. Here he studied law and looked after the comfort of belated travelers for several months. He had no law practice and, as it seemed, no way of ever getting any. But his opportunity came. Captain John Steel killed Colonel Kirby, apparently in cold blood, in the office of the military commander of the post here. Steel shot Kirby down on sight, without a word. As a matter of fact Steel's provocation had been great and a bitter feud had existed between the two men for years. On its face the case was one of cold-blooded murder. Steel was a prominent and well-known gambler, while Kirby was a man of wealth and great power and influence. Barziza recognized his opportunity and promptly volunteered to defend Steel. His services were accepted. Able and prominent lawyers were employed by Kirby's friends to assist the state's attorney in the prosecution of Steel. Barziza refused all proffers of assistance. The trial lasted for two or three days and by the time it had gotten under way, the lawyers for the prosecution realized that they had a giant to contend against. Barziza's handling of the case excited the admiration of other members of the bar, but his great triumph came when he went before the jury to plead the case. The speech he made that day was spoken of for years afterwards as the most eloquent that had ever been delivered in the Harris County court house. It was so eloquent and his arguments were so convincing that the jury, after the briefest deliberation, returned a verdict of "not guilty," and Steel walked out a free man. Barziza's reputation as a criminal lawyer was established at once.

Another of the great criminal lawyers of Houston was the Hon. Charles Stewart. He was a man of unsullied character and too big in every way for little things. He was of splendid physique and personal appearance and is described one of the most superb orators that ever faced a jury. He handled many of the most famous criminal cases tried in Harris County in the late seventies and eighties, one of the most famous being that of a young man named Grisom, who had killed a doctor for reproving him for swearing in the presence of ladies. The case was a desperate one, and at the first trial Grisom had been sentenced to death, but was granted a new trial because of irregularity on the part of the jury that had condemned him. At the second trial the prosecution was powerful and it is said that but for the eloquence of Colonel Stewart, Grisom would have undoubtedly been hanged. As it was he escaped with a verdict of man-slaughter and a short term in the penitentiary.

The man to whom was assigned the difficult task of facing these grants, was Major Frank Spencer, who for years was the criminal district attorney for the Houston-Galveston district, and who died in Galveston in 1907. He was very eloquent, very bitter and very aggressive. He attacked unceasingly and when a lawyer won a victory over him he deserved all he got.

A connecting link between the famous criminal and civil lawyers of the early days was Governor J. W. Henderson. He did a large and very lucrative practice in both branches and appeared to be as much at home in the one as in the other. Perhaps, though, he was more distinguished as a civil lawyer than as a criminal one. He was a man of fine personal appearance and to some extent a self-made man. He cultivated a brusqueness of manner and was extremely democratic, counting among his friends and adherents people of all conditions and walks of life. He was a natural orator, a deep thinker, and had, what was of the greatest value, good hard common sense and the ability to put it to the best use at the proper moment. His success at the bar was great. Before a jury he was almost irresistable. The Governor was a secessionist and died an unreconstructed rebel. During reconstruction days he was a power of strength to the home people in their struggle for self government, and never lost an opportunity to strike a blow at the usurpers. His zeal and energy in that respect were so well known that he was watched and feared by the republican leaders, more than any other man in Houston. One night, entirely unintentionally on his part, he came near precipitating a riot on Preston Street. The Governor had gone into one of the stores on Main Street and purchased a long carving knife to take home. It was wrapped in brown paper, and being too long to put in his pocket, he carried it under his arm. On his way home he heard that Jack Hamilton was to speak from the balcony of the Dissen House that evening, so the Governor concluded to remain down town and hear him. He arrived rather late, but becoming interested in what Hamilton was saying, he kept getting closer and closer until he was within a few feet of the speaker. Then the Governor and the spectators were amazed and startled, for four or five men jumped on the Governor and held him firmly. There was a terrible uproar and the affair was becoming serious, when someone found the cause of the trouble. In getting through the crowd the paper cover of the carving knife had been torn off, and some of the watchful friends of Hamilton concluded that the Governor was slipping up on the speaker to annihilate him with the carving knife, had seized the Governor and disarmed him. The Governor was furious, but when the crowd learned the cause of the trouble, the laughter broke up the speaking. Governor Jack Hamilton, who, though a republican, was a warm personal friend of Governor Henderson was about as indignant as the latter, when he found what had been done.

Among those who confined their practice to civil law Judges Peter Gray and W. P. Hamblen, both through ability and long service, deserve to be placed at the head of the list. Both were men of the greatest integrity and each had marked ability as a lawyer. Neither was peculiarly remarkable for oratorical power but each was a profound scholar and well versed in the intricacies of the law. They are classed together in this way because they were the nestors of the Harris County Bar and their careers were very similar. Judge Hamblen died in 1911 as judge of the 55th district court, which office he had held for many years.

Among the other distinguished, members of the Bar in early days were: Benjamin Tankersly, E. A. Palmer, A. N. Jordan, S. S. Tompkins, A. P.

Thompson, A. S. Richardson, Charles Jordan and Archibal Wynne. For some years, later, C. B. Sabine was a member of the Harris County Bar. He was after-wards Judge of the U. S. Federal Court in Galveston.

Among the prominent members of the Bar after the war, were: Major W. H. Crank, Captain E. P. Turner, George Golthwaite, the attorney for the Houston and Texas Central Railroad, and known as the "Supreme Court lawyer" of that road, Judge Wilson, Judge James Masterson, Judge C. Anson Jones, youngest son of the last president of the republic of Texas, a brilliant young man who was cut off in the prime of life, W. A. Carrington, J. C. Hutchinson, Judge James Baker, father of Captain James A. Baker and Col. W. B. Botts, all men of probity and honor, of skill and power, of learning and eloquence, of old fashioned courtesy and chivalrous consideration, of chaste diction and faultless bearing, who gave the Bar of Harris County its high standards, its legal ambitions and its lofty ethics and who have preserved the good name of the bar without shame and without reproach.

When the first amended constitution of Texas was adopted by the people, it created a criminal district court for Harris and Galveston Counties and Judge Gustave Cook was appointed Judge and occupied that position for 14 years. In addition to his great learning as a lawyer he had attributes of character that rendered him a most lovable person and enjoyable companion. He was light-hearted, a lover of jokes and pranks, was famous as a raconteur, and so free and generous with his money that he was always "broke," and was finally driven to resign from the bench and go back to the practice of law to make a living. His successors on the bench have been, in the order named: C. L. Cleveland, E. D. Cavin, J. K. P. Gillespie, E. R. Campbell and C. W. Robinson. R. G. Maury is the present criminal district attorney.

The following were the officers of the Eleventh District Court from its organization to the present day:

- From 1837 to 1842—Benjamin C. Franklin, Judge; James S. Holman, Clerk; John W. Moore, Sheriff.
- From 1842 to 1849—Richard Morris, Judge; F. R. Lubbock, Clerk; M. T. Rodgers, Sheriff.
- From 1849 to 1854—C. W. Buckley, Judge; F. R. Lubbock, Clerk. David Russel, Sheriff.
- From 1854 to 1862—Peter W. Gray, Judge.
- From 1862 to 1866—James A. Baker, Judge; W. B. Walker, Clerk; B. P. Lanham, Sheriff.

For the period from 1866 to 1869, there were no elections held and the Bar selected the following named to act as judge of the court: Geo. R. Scott, C. B. Sabin and P. W. Gray.

- From 1869 to 1870—Geo. R. Scott, Judge.
- From 1870 to 1892—James R. Masterton, Judge.
- From 1892 to 1896—S. H. Brashear, Judge.
- From 1896 to 1900—John G. Tod, Judge.
- From 1900 to date—Charles E. Ashe, Judge.

The Fifty-first District Court was organized in 1897, and since that time, has had but three presiding judges, as follows:

- From 1897 to 1902—Judge Wm. H. Wilson.
- From 1902 to 1911—Judge W. P. Hamblen.
- From 1911 to date—Judge Wm. Masterson. Judge Masterson was appointed by Governor Colquitt following the death of Judge Hamblen.
-

The Sixty-first District Court was organized in February, 1903, and has had only one presiding judge since it organization, Judge Norman G. Kittrell.

The act creating Harris County Court was passed by the Legislature in February, 1867. Judge John Brashear was elected judge and served until 1869. Judge M. N. Brewster succeeded Judge Brashear and served until 1876, or during the time the republicans had control of the county. Judge C. Anson Jones was elected, and took charge of the office at the July term of the court in 1876. He served until 1882, when, on his death, Judge E. P. Hamblen was elected and took office November 24, 1882. After rather a sharp campaign, Judge W. C. Andrews was elected and assumed the duties of his office at the November term in 1884. Judge Andrews was a candidate for re-election, but just before the election he died (November 1, 1892) and Judge John G. Tod was elected and took office at the November term of the court, 1892. Judge Tod remained in office for two terms and was succeeded by Judge W. N. Shaw at the November term in 1896. Judge E. H. Vasmer was elected in 1898, and held office for four years, being succeeded by Judge Blake Dupree in 1902. Judge Dupree also held office for two terms and was followed by the popular present incumbent, Judge A. E. Amerman in 1906, who is now filling his third term. George Jones has been County Clerk for many years.

The act creating the Corporation Court for Houston was passed by the Legislature in 1899. Before then the duties of the judge of this court, or rather of its predecessor, the city court, were performed, sometimes by the mayor, sometimes by a city recorder and sometimes by a justice of the peace. It was more or less haphazard and methods were undergoing constant change. At the first election, Judge A. R. Railey was elected and served until 1902, when he was defeated after a sharp contest, by Judge Marmion. Judge Marmion was elected one of the city commissioners when the form of city government was changed, and Judge John H. Kirlicks was appointed to fill his unexpired term, and has held office ever since.

This is one of the busiest courts in the city and may be said to be in session every day in the year, except Sundays and holidays. A morning session of the court is held at 9 a. m., and an afternoon session at 4 p. m. It has jurisdiction over city and police cases only.

An idea of the character of men that laid the foundation of the Harris County Bar, can be formed from reading the following extracts from an address delivered by Judge W. P. Hamblen at a banquet of the Houston Bar Association, held January 20, 1910. Judge Hamblen, as the oldest member of the Bar, was the best source for its history. He said:

"I came to the Bar when Judge Peter W. Gray was judge of the court. He was the distinguished uncle of Judge W. G. Sears, whose nephew is now a member of this Bar, and he admitted me to the rights of our profession. He was one of the chiefest among the intelligencers of that day. He was accomplished, educated in all the refinements as well as in all the substantials of the profession; so discriminating, so penetrating, that no proposition of law was presented to him that he did not seize; so absolutely honest that his reputation could stand among a million without a scar. And moreover I was fortunate enough to be a favorite of his and was appointed by him district attorney of this district at that very term of his court, because of the absence of the district attorney. My relations with him were, I might say, those of a child and its father. In those days an admission to the bar was not as it is today, the formal appearance before a committee almost as a school boy at a spelling match, but it was a procession of young men to the Bar of the court, summoned by a committee appointed by the judge who participated in the examination. When the examination was through the judge descended from the bench and taking the hand of each applicant spoke words of encouragement.

"I remember when some youngsters from the country on Cypress were brought before him because they had gone to the house of a poor old German and his wife and made the old couple cook a supper and dance for them. They were presented before Judge Gray and a fine was imposed, and the boys asked for mercy. One of them was the son of his most particular friend, one of all others whom it would have been his pleasure to please. His lecture to these young men from the bench can never be forgotten by anyone who heard it. That lecture to those young men and especially to the son of his friend was so touching that no heart could be unmoved, and every youngster who received the admonition went away feeling that he had done a wrong which was not expiated by the punishment.

"I can briefly mention men who were honorable members of our Bar at the time I was admitted in 1855. There was E. A. Palmer who was afterwards Judge of the District Court of Harris County, and A. N. Jordan, both from

Virginia, ranking high in their profession. The former died in 1864, and in 1866, the eyes of the latter I closed in death. Governor J. W. Henderson, from Tennessee, once lieutenant governor of our state and for six years its governor. He was the author of the verse:

'Here is our old friend, John Doe; We have laid him down to sleep, Together with his companion, Richard Roe, In one common, lonely heap, With none so bold as dare a vigil keep.'

"He passed away in 1886. Judge Algernon P. Thompson, an Englishman, a most scholarly gentleman, who once declared that the author of the phrase 'to-wit' should be burned alive. Benjamin F. Tankersley, from Mississippi, I believe, father of our distinguished townsman, Marshal Tankersley, a most highly esteemed and worthy lawyer who died during the Civil War. C. B. Sabin, long a practitioner in this city, who died in 1890, while occuping the bench of the United States district court. Judge George Goldthwaite, so widely known for his erudition and legal acumen that he was considered competent to write a book on continuations without a ground. He died about 1886. Col. J. T. Brady, from Maryland, once prominent and foremost in all that upbuilds a state, once a senator from this district in our state legislature, died about 1891. * * * Hon. James H. Masterson, for more than twenty years distinguished on the bench of the district court; Judge E. P. Hamblen, my worthy relative, who once graced the county court bench—the two latter being now dwellers with us. Judge A. R. Masterson, who has the proud distinction of having surrendered with Lee at Appomattox. * * * We will not forget that old commoner, Charles Stewart, so long your representative in Congress, a powerful democratic expounder and able advocate. He located in Marlin and returned here after the war. His 'praises have been sung by loftier harps than mine.'

"Those who have gone before stood in the front of the battle for judicial propriety and integrity, and for a construction of laws that preserved the constitutional liberties without flaw or blemish. R. K. Cage, father of our worthy citizen, Rufus Cage, and grand-father of Elliott Cage, died a few years ago. That soul of wit, John Manley, a son of North Carolina, died in 1874."

The Houston Bar Association was organized in November, 1870. Judge Peter W. Gray was president, George Golthwaite, vice-president; J. T. Whitfield, recording secretary; N. P. Turner, corresponding secretary, and W. C. Watson, treasurer. The objects of the association were the elevation of the legal profession in Houston and to take proper steps looking towards the purchase of a law library. As its organization the association was not strong numerically but it was composed of some of the best men in the legal profession. Today the association will compare favorably, numerically, mentally, or in any other way with like associations found anywhere in this country. The following named gentlemen compose the association today:

L. R. Bryan, president; Thomas H. Botts, secretary; Chester H. Bryan, treasurer.

ROLL OF MEMBERS.

Amerman, C. A.; Anderson, W. W.; Andrews, Jesse; Ayres, L. C.; Amerman, C. H. C.; Autrey, James L.; Andrews, Frank; Ashe, Chas. E.; Baker, James A.; Barbee, Will S.; Botts, Thos. H.; Bryan, Chester H.; Beatty, L.; Burns, Waller, T.; Breaker, George H.; Beard, Stanley A.; Britton, Thos. G.; Branch, E. T.; Baldwin, J. C.; Ball, Thos. H.; Borden, Henry L.; Brashear, S. H.; Bryan, L.; Lewis, R.; Bailey, Edward H.; Breeding, Jas. A.; Barkley, K. C.; Burns, Coke K.; Bailey, W. S.; Blankenbecker, L. E.; Campbell, E. R.; Campbell, J. W.; Carter, C. L.; Cage, Elliott; Colgin, J. F.; Cole, J. F.; Cole, Robert L.; Chew, E. T.; Dannenbaum, H. J.; Dabney, S. B.; Dupree, Blake; Dunn, T. L.; Dickson, Raymond; Eagle, Joe H.; Ewing, Presley K.; Ford, T. W.; Ford, T. C.; Fisher, Henry F.; Franklin, R. W.; Graves, Geo. W.; Garwood, H. M.; Green, Jno. E.; Garrett, D. E.; Garrison, John T.; Guynes, Chas. O.; Gill, W. H.; Hamblen, E. P.; Hamblen, W. P., Jr.; Hamblen, Otis K.; Hamblen, A. R.; Harris, John Charles; Holt, O. T.; Hume, F. Charles; Harralson, E. M.; Hardy, D. H.; Hutcheson, J. C., Jr.; Hume, D. E.; Highsmith, C. C.; Hume, F. Charles, Jr.; Huggins, W. O.; Holmes, H.; Hunt, W. S.; John, Robert A.; Johnson, W. T.; Jones, Frank C.; Jones, Murray B.; Jones, Homer. (San Antonio); Kittrell, Norman G.; Kittrell, Norman G., Jr.; Kirlicks, John A.; Kelley, R. H.; Kennerly, T. M.; Lane, Jonathan; Louis, B. F.; Lockett, J. W; Lewis, T. B.; Logue, John G.; Lewis, John W.; Love, W. G.; Matthews, J. C.; Monteith, W. E.; Myer, Sewall F.; Maury, R. C.; Montgomery, H. F.; McRae, Chas. C.; McCarthy, Ed., Jr.; McLeans, John L.; Niday, J. E.; Parker, E. B.; Phelps, Ed. S.; Peterson, Samuel; Price, J. A.; Pleasants, A. W.; Pendarvis, G. H.; Phelps, Lewis C.; Parker, J. W.; Read, John Archer; Robertson, Robert L.; Robinson, C. W.; Roberts, I. S.; Sewall, Cleveland; Standifer, I. M.; Streetman, Sam; Stewart, John S.; Simmons, D. E.; Stewart, Minor; Storey, Jas. L.; Stone, T. H.; Sears, G. D.; Shands, H. A.; Smith, Lamar; Tarver, W. F.; Taylor, C. H.; Townes, J. C., Jr.; Townes, E. W., Jr.; Taub, Otto; Tallichet, J. H.; Tharp, G. W.; Tod, John G.; Teat, G. L.; Teagle, C. A.; Taliaferro, S.; Vann, Andral; Van Velzer, A. C.; Warnken, C. A.; Wharton, C. R.; Wilson, A. B.; Wilson, Earl; Wolters, Jake F.; Wagner, Meyer C.; Ward, W. H.; Whitehead, R. L.; Wilson, W. H.; Wood, Chas. B.; Wrenn, Clerk C.; Warren, John B.; Wharton, Earl.

Owing to the vast business interests, lumber, cotton, rice, oil, manufacturing, railroad and lands, represented in Houston there has arisen a demand for high-grade, highly-paid lawyers and the city's brilliant bar has always responded to this demand, which has also caused many eminent lawyers to move to Houston. The largest law firm south of New York is located in Houston, that of Baker, Botts, Parker & Garwood. A former member of this firm, Judge R. S. Lovett, is at the head of Southern Pacific and Union Pacific, and those roads generally known as the Harriman system. Hon. Tom Ball resigned his position in Congress to practice law in Houston and is a member of the noted firm of Andrews, Ball & Streetman.

Governor Stephen S. Hogg, after his two terms of office had expired, moved to Houston and practiced law here until his death. Judge W. H. Gill, chief justice of the court of criminal appeals at Galveston, resigned his position to practice law in Houston as a member of the same firm to which Governor Hogg had belonged. Judge Gill is recognized as one of the most brilliant lawyers in the state. More recent acquisitions are Hon. John M. Duncan, of Tyler, and Hon. Monta Moore, of Cameron.

The list of men who have achieved notable success at the Houston bar is a long one and would be in many respects identical with that of the Bar Association.

Two members of the Houston Bar were chosen to head the respective forces of the prohibitionists and anti-prohibitionists in the great campaign for a change in the Texas constitution that was fought out in the summer of 1911 and resulted in a scant and Phyrric victory for the antis. One of the two is Hon. Tom Ball, already referred to; the other is the Hon. Jake Wolters, formerly an officer of the First Texas Volunteer Cavalry in the War with Spain and at present a member of the law firm of Lane, Wolters and Storey. Both leaders rendered brilliant service and both are talked of by their admirers as desirable candidates for United States Senator.

CHAPTER IX - MEDICAL HISTORY

Pioneer Physicians and Their Labors. First Houston Medical Association. Organization of the State Medical Association. Railroad Surgeons Association. Harris County Medical Association. Houston's Modern Hospitals. Story of Early Epidemics. The Doctors and the Newspapers.

The most casual reader of these pages must be impressed by the fact that the history of the growth and development of Houston is in many respects, the history of the growth and development of Texas. This could scarcely have been otherwise, since the men who laid the foundation for the future metropolis of Texas were the same whose wisdom, power and influence were directed toward the upbuilding of the state. Under such conditions as these it is not strange that many movements, commercial, financial, scientific, and educational, that tended towards intelligent growth and expansion, should have either originated in Houston or originated through Houston influence.

Perhaps the most lasting and beneficial work done by the early settlers, aside from that of those whose efforts were directly in the interest of purely material enterprises, was that of the medical men. Their labor was scientific and largely unselfish, since it aimed at the prevention of disease rather than at its cure, and therefore had about it elements, antagonistic to their selfish interests. Texas was new, Houston was new and society was much disorganized.

Fortunately the practice of medicine was placed in safe hands at the very beginning and as early as 1836 a standard was fixed by such men as Ashbel Smith, who was physician, surgeon, scientist, statesman and scholar; by Alexander Ewing, who was chief surgeon of the Texas army, a skilled physician and a profound student; by Phillip Anderson, chief surgeon of the Texas Navy who was, with the exception of Dr. Ashbel Smith, the most learned man in Texas at that time, and by Dr. McAnally, who, in addition to his skill as a physician and surgeon, was a great scientist. Merely calling over these names is sufficient to show on what a high plane the practice of medicine was placed at the very outset in Houston.

During the period from 1840 to 1850 the medical profession in Houston was much strengthened by the addition of several young physicians who came from the older states. These young men were graduates from the best literary and medical colleges in the land and were all men of culture and refinement. Among them were Dr. S. O. Young, Sr., Dr. Wm. McCraven, Dr. W. D. Robinson, Dr. Wm. H. Howard, and Dr. L. A. Bryan.

No effort looking towards an organization of the medical profession seems to have been made prior to March 11, 1857, at which time the Houston Medical Association was organized by Dr. J. S. Duval, Dr. Wm. H. Howard,

Dr. Greenville Dowell, Dr. R. H. Boxley, and Dr. H. W. Waters. Dr. Duval was elected president, Dr. Waters, vice-president, and Dr. Boxley, secretary. The avowed objects of the association were: "To cultivate the science of medicine and all its collateral branches; to cherish and sustain medical character; to encourage medical etiquette and to promote mutual improvement, social intercourse and good feeling among members of the medical profession." At that day Osteopaths, Electro-Magnetic, and Christian Science healers were unknown. There were but two schools of medicine, the allopaths, or regulars, and the homeopaths.

There was as much feeling against the Homeopaths on the part of the regular physicians at that time, as there is today, as the following shows. It is the first resolution adopted by the Houston Medical Association after its organization, and is presented as characteristic of the feelings of that body at the time:

"Whereas—The scientific medical world has proven Homeopathy to be a species of empiricism, too flagrant to merit the confidence of rational men, and too fabulous to deserve even the passing notice of an educated physician, and as we are convinced that it is a delusion, far surpassing any other ism known to the world, witch-craft not excepted, therefore we will not recognize, professionally or privately, any man who professes to cure diseases through the agency of Hahnemanic teachings.

"Be it Resolved—That as a diploma from a regularly organized medical school is the only evidence of qualification which our community can obtain in regard to the doctors in their midst, we respectfully recommend to the citizens of this flourishing city that they demand of every man who assumes the responsibility of a physician to their families, their diplomas as certificates of their worthiness of patronage, and that they see to it that they are not imposed on by a diploma from a medical society or a certificate of qualification as a dresser in a hospital."

Notwithstanding this opposition, qualified Homeopaths came to Houston and flourished. It is probable that the Houston Medical Association continued in active operation for some time, for two years later, in 1859, a call was issued by Houston physicians inviting the physicians from other points in the state to assemble in Houston for the purpose of organizing a State Medical Association. Unfortunately there is no local record of this meeting, but that it was held, and an organization perfected, is attested by the fact that when the Houston physicians, in 1869, issued another call for the purpose of forming the present State Association, it was spoken of as the "re-organization" of the State Association.

Some time in March, 1869, the physicians of Houston issued a circular letter addressed to the physicians of Texas requesting them to assemble in Houston on April 15, for the purpose of re-organizing the State Medical Association. This letter was not only sent through the mails, but was published in the papers of the state, so it had a wide distribution. In response to this call twenty-eight physicians, mostly from Houston, Galveston and nearby-points, assembled in the west parlor of the Hutchins House on April 15, and organized, or re-organized The Texas State Medical Association. The first officers elected were:

Dr. T. J. Heard, of Galveston, president; Dr. R. H. Jones, of Washington County, first vice-president; Dr. D. R. Wallace, of Waco, second vice-president; Dr. A. A. Connell, Jr., of Houston, recording secretary; Dr. W. P. Riddell, of Houston, corresponding secretary, and Dr. F. Hassenberg, of Houston, treasurer.

A two days' session was held, but beyond perfecting a thorough organization, little was done.

The second meeting of the association was also held in Houston. At that meeting the following officers were elected:

Dr. R. T. Flewellen, of Houston, president; Dr. D. R. Wallace, of Waco, first vice-president; Dr. A. A. Connell, of Houston, recording secretary; Dr. S. O. Young, of Houston, corresponding secretary, and Dr. W. P. Riddell, of Houston, treasurer.

The attendance was rather disappointing, being practically the same as at the first meeting. Only one or two new members, all from near-by points, were admitted.

On April 15, 1871, the association held its third session in Houston. There was a better attendance and increased interest was shown. At the election, Dr. D. R. Wallace, of Waco, was elected president and all the other officers were re-elected. Doctor Wallace was a man of fine executive ability and his influence for good was felt at once. At his suggestion the State Association was brought into closer relation with the American Medical Association and Dr. S. O. Young was chosen as the first delegate from Texas to that association. Various committees on special subjects were appointed to whom were assigned topics to be reported on for discussion at the next meeting.

The fourth annual meeting was held in Houston, April 15, 1872. At the election of officers, Dr. D. F. Stuart, of Houston, was elected president. Doctors Connell and Riddell having died, some changes in other offices were necessary. Dr. S. O. Young was elected recording secretary, and Dr. J. Larendon, also of Houston, was elected treasurer, an office he held for over a quarter of a century.

At that meeting it was determined to abandon the idea of making Houston the permanent headquarters of the association, and to hold future meetings at various points in the state, so Waco was chosen as the next meeting place.

The organization of the Texas Medical Association has been dwelt on at some length for a twofold reason. First, because it was a Houston idea, conceived and carried out by Houston men, and next, because this

Association has been instrumental in accomplishing much good for the people of Texas, that could have been accomplished by no other means. Before the Texas Medical Association came into being the state was literally overrun by medical quacks and imposters of every character. There were no laws to restrain these people and none to protect the public against them. Among the first acts of the Texas Medical Association were those looking to the curbing and restraint of frauds and the protection of reputable physicians.

As early as 1871 the Association began the crusade for the regulation by law of the practice of medicine in Texas. Results were rather meager at first. The opening wedge was placed when the Legislature passed a law requiring all physicians to file a statement of where, when and at what schools they had been graduated, and to also register their diplomas. This shut out some of the imposters but not all, for there are bogus medical schools as well as bogus graduates. The work was continued, however, and has resulted in such laws as that requiring a state board of medical examiners before which every physician who desires to practice medicine in Texas has to appear and stand an examination, even though he be a recent graduate from the Texas Medical College. Another great thing accomplished was the passage of a law creating the State Board of Health.

In all these movements Houston physicians were prominent and either conceived the original idea or were largely instrumental in putting it into execution. From the first they were leaders in all that promised for uplifting the medical profession, or for safeguarding their fellow citizens against preventable diseases and epidemics and quack cure-alls and fake panaceas. Today the medical profession in Texas is well organized. The state is divided into divisions, such as the East Texas Medical Association, and the West Texas Medical Association, and each of these has sub-divisions. Nearly every county in the state has its County Association. Then, too, special interests have their own organizations, a notable one being the Railroad Surgeons Association, which had its inception in Houston. An idea of its strength and importance may be formed from the following:

On January 21, 1896, the Railroad Surgeons of Texas held a meeting at Houston. The following were elected officers: Dr. M. D. Knox, president; Dr. T. J. Wagley, first vice-president; Dr. J. C. King, second vice-president; Dr. W. H. Monday, third vice-president; Dr. Clay Johnson, secretary, and Dr. A. A. Bailey, treasurer.

The following named surgeons were present and took part in the deliberations: Drs. J. M. Richmond, J. H. Reuss, A. B. Gardner, M. D. Knox, W. W. Lum, C. C. Nash, J. H. Jenkins, C. T. Hughes, P. M. Raynor, F. O. Norris, Van. B. Thornton, A. D. Epperson, A. A. Thompson, W. T. Harris, T. A. Pope, A. L. O'Brien, W. H. Monday, J. C. Mayfield, F. B. Seyman, J. W. Cox, Sam B. McLeary, W. M. Garrett, James Byars, H. L. Fountain, J. C. Loggins, C. A. Smith, Clay Johnson, A. C. Scott, A. A. Bailey, J. M. Blair, S.

C. Red, R. T. Morris, L. H. Lamkin, D. F. Steuart, Joseph R. Steuart, T. J. Boyles, F. B. King, G. D. Parker, O. C. Norsworthy, W. E. Drisdale, N. J. Phoenix, T. M. Reeves, and M. J. T. Jones.

Although there were a number of able and prominent members of the medical profession in Houston and Harris County, no attempt was ever made to form a county medical association until in December, 1868.

In 1868, several Houston physicians met and organized the Harris County Medical Association. There were not many present at that meeting, and, with the exception of Dr. Ashbel Smith, who resided in the lower part of the county on Galveston Bay, they were all residents of Houston.

Before then the formation of both a city and county medical association had been discussed, but neither had ever advanced beyond the stage of suggestion and talk, and it is doubtful if the organization of the association of 1868 could have been accomplished had it not been for the fact that it was considered imperatively necessary to have a local medical association to form the nucleus for the State Medical Association.

On December 8th, 1868, the following named physicians met in the parlors of the Hutchins House, for the purpose of forming a county medical association: L. A. Bryan, W. H. Howard, J. Larendon, D. C. Stuart, T. J. Poulson, R. W. Lunday, Alva Connell, Sr., Alva Connell, Jr., G. H. McDonald, W. D. Robinson, T. J. Devereaux, J. M. Morris, and W. P. Riddell.

Aside from issuing an address to the physicians of Texas, inviting them to meet in Houston on April 15th, for the purpose of organizing a State Medical Association, the Harris County Association, after that first meeting never held another, and was allowed to die a natural death. In late years, however, physicians have been more active and since 1904 have a county association that compares favorably with any similar association in the country. It has a large membership and has accomplished much for the advancement of medical science, and for the creation of closer fraternal and professional relations between its members. The association holds weekly meetings, and the attendance is always large, and interest in its aims and objects is never allowed to flag. The following named are its officers and members:

President, Dr. E. F. Cooke; vice-president, Dr. J. H. Hulen; secretary, Dr. L. Allen. The members of the board of censors are J. E. Hodges, H. C. Moore and E. M. Arnold. The committee on public health and legislation is: W. M. Wier, J. A. Kyle and J. H. Foster. The delegates to the State Association in 1911 were O. L. Norsworthy and J. H. Foster. A full list of the members is as follows: L. Allen, N. N. Allen, W. C. Archer, W. A. Archer, E. M. Armstrong, E. M. Arnold, D. L. Akehurst, C. M. Aves, J. M. Blair, C. C. Barrell, F. M. Bourland, J. G. Boyd, J. M. Boyles, I. Braun, H. E. Brown, C. E. Bruhl, W. M. Brumby, San Antonio, J. M. Burditt, E. F. Cooke, I. E. Cottingham, R. L. Cox, P. H. Cronin, E. P. Daviss, J. B. DuBose, Humble, J.

D. Duckett, J. C. A. Eckhardt, Austin, W. R. Eckhardt, Wm. Ehrhardt, Westfield, F. G. Eidman, B. V. Ellis, Houston Heights, H. A. Englehardt, B. C. Eskridge, H. C. Feagan, J. H. Florence, F. C. Ford, J. H. Foster, W. A. Garrett, J. P. Gibbs, C. E. Gray, E. E. Grant, Cypress, E. N. Gray, A. E. Greer, C. C. Green, E. L. Goar, H. R. Gilliam, G. W. Griffith, LaPorte, W. A. Haley, G. P. Hall, Gavin Hamilton, E. G. Hamilton, J. A. Hill, C. W. Hoeflich, J. E. Hodges, A. P. Howard, R. H. Harrison, J. A. James, F. B. King, R. W. Knox, A. Krause, J. A. Kyle, G. W. Larendon, J. W. Lane, E. H. Lancaster, Z. F. Lillard, S. M. Lister, W. H. Martin, G. H. Meyer, K. N. Miller, G. S. Milnes, R. H. Moers, H. C. Moore, J. T. Moore, S. H. Moore, R. T. Morris, J. A. Mullen, E. C. Murray, A. J. Mynatt, C. W. Nelson, F. H. Neuhaus, O. L. Norsworthy, S. G. Northrup, C. F. Payne, G. D. Parker, W. G. Priester, I. E. Pritchett, Wallace Ralston, S. C. Red, G. J. Robinson, W. L. Rogers, F. R. Ross, J. W. Sandlin, Humble, P. H. Scardino, J. W. Scott, R. T. Scott, W. N. Shaw, T. W. Shearer, J. L. Short, E. S. Silbernagel, F. B. Smith, P. L. Smith, S. J. Smith, F. J. Slataper, J. R. Stuart, M. B. Stokes, C. O. Terrell, W. B. Thorning, R. H. Towles, Houston Heights, S. V. Wagner, C. A. Wallace, C. D. Warren, A. E. White, R. D. Wilson, M. A. Wood, W. M. Wier, E. A. Wright, F. B. Wilkes and J. B. York.

All of the physicians live in Houston except those whose residence is designated. The association has been very active and has favored preventive measures against disease. Among the men who have been prominent as its presidents have been Drs. E. N. Gray, J. P. Gibbs, W. M. Wier, W. W. Ralston, J. H. Foster, J. T. Moore, and E. F. Cooke.

In 1911 the association began the publication of a bulletin containing the discussions at the meetings and giving matters of medical news to the physicians.

The city of Houston has a thoroughly organized health department. The city administration has taken especial pains to guard the public health, and while the indigent sick are carefully treated and nursed, the principal efforts of the health department are directed towards the prevention, rather than the cure of disease. In this great work the department has been materially aided by the wisdom of the commission in obtaining an abundant supply of pure water and in extending the water main, so as to furnish the citizens pure and wholesome water for all purposes. The great benefit of this is shown by the decreased death rate from year to year, which decrease keeps pace with the extension of the water mains. Then, too, the department retains the services of a skilled pathologist and bacteriologist, who carries on investigations relating to the purity of milk, water, foods, etc., as well as diagnosing and locating transmissible diseases.

An idea of the extent of the work carried on by the health department may be formed from the statement that during the municipal year ending February 28th, last, there were 4,000 patients treated at the city dispensary,

550 at the hospital and 36 at the pest camp. The department also vaccinated 2,000 school children; fumigated 783 rooms, 2 automobiles and 7 box cars for the following diseases

Tuberculosis	349 rooms
Diphtheria	157 rooms
Smallpox	147 rooms
Scarlet Fever	54 rooms
Typhoid Fever	49 rooms
Pneumonia	5 rooms
Scabes	2 rooms
Causes not specified	100 rooms
Cerebro-spinal Meningitis	16 rooms
Smallpox	7 Box Cars
Scarlet Fever	2 automobiles

During the year 1910 there occurred in the city of Houston 1,386 deaths, of which 822 were whites and 564 negroes. The death rate was 13.5 per thousand, that for the whites being 10.7 per thousand and for the negroes 22.1 per thousand. There were 1,654 births reported; 1,312 white and 342 negro.

The pathological laboratory under the management of Dr. F. J. Slataper, has been no less busily engaged. During the year 1,781 chemical and microscopical examinations were made. These cover a wide range from the simple testing of milk to the most complicated investigation of disease germs. The list of examinations shows the scope of the department activity.

Cultures examined for diptheria	45
Specimens of sputum examined for tuberculosis	209
Tuberculin test in human	1
Specimens of blood examined for typhoid fever	48
Specimens of blood smear examined for malaria	38
Feces examined for ova of intestinal parasites	23
Specimens of urine examined—chemically	316
Specimens of urine examined—microscopically	168
Samples of food examined	53
Samples of milk collected and examined	322
Samples of milk brought to the laboratory and examined	113

Total samples of milk examined	435
Samples of city water collected and examined	9
Stomach contents examined	4

A city hospital was established in 1838 but only lasted a few years. About 1868, the city having obtained ownership of the block between McKinney and Lamar Avenues and Carolina and Austin Streets, decided to establish a city hospital there. An arrangement was made, whereby the county should have the right to use the hospital also, by paying a fixed amount for each patient sent there, but should have nothing to do with the control or management of the institution. Houston had a regular city physician and the county had its physician also, but neither of these had anything to do with the hospital, which was under the control of a physician who took it under contract, receiving a fixed amount, based on the number of patients under treatment, and paying all the expenses of the institution himself. Dr. Charles Owens was the first physician to take charge of the hospital under the contract system and continued at the head of the institution, until his death in 1874. Soon after that a new lease or contract was made with Dr. T. J. Boyles and Dr. D. F. Stuart and the location of the hospital was changed. The McKinney property was disposed of and the hospital was removed to the old Brashear home, located on the, then, city limit line, on the Houston and Texas Central Railroad opposite Glenwood Cemetery. The hospital remained at that location for several years and Drs. Stuart and Boyles introduced many new methods and improvements.

Prosperity necessitated the purchasing of a site near where the Grand Central depot stands, and erecting a commodious hospital building on it. They still retained their contract with the city and county, but established pay wards and private rooms, possibly the first thing of the kind in Texas. They also contracted with the Houston and Texas Central Railroad to treat the sick and injured employees of that road and also with other railroads for similar service. This hospital was known as the railroad hospital until the erection of the Southern Pacific Hospital began in 1910. It is still in operation as a private hospital.

Not barring even the famed Charity Hospital of New Orleans it is safe to claim that in the Southern Pacific Hospital, completed in 1911, Houston has the finest railroad hospital in the South and the equal of any in the country. No expense has been spared in constructing the building and its equipment is all that scientific knowledge could make it. As everyone familiar with the subject knows, the building and equipping of a hospital is only one item of cost, for the successful and proper conducting of such an institution costs far more than all else. This money comes from the voluntary contributions of the employees of the various roads of that great system. These contributions are very small for each individual but in the aggregate, amount to a large sum monthly.

The location of the hospital is ideal. It is far removed from the noise and bustle of the city, and though within easy reach of the heart of the city, is as far as possible in the country. It is in the Fifth ward, on the sloping bank of White Oak Bayou and the site, being somewhat elevated, gives a good view of the woods and stream on the one side and of the city on the other side. On the staff of the hospital are: Dr. R. W. Knox, chief surgeon; Dr. E. J. Hamilton, assistant surgeon; Dr. O. S. Moore, interne; Dr. J. E. Greene, interne; Miss M. F. McMasters, superintendent.

The building is steam heated, cleaned by vacuum cleaners, lighted by electricity and gas, has numerous bathrooms on each floor but only one or two bath tubs in the whole building, these being done away with as far as possible and the shower and needle baths substituted. There is an abundant supply of both hot and cold water at all times, and on each floor is a good supply of sterilized water for use in special cases. The wards are large and each is furnished plainly but very attractively and comfortably. The beds are the ordinary hospital iron frames with absolutely luxurious mattresses and snow white linen. The chairs and tables are dark oak and rose wood, while on the walls are attractive pictures. One of the most striking features of each ward and private room is the lighting. No electric light is visible, the lighting being done by reflection and diffusion. This does away with all glare and makes the light very pleasing to the eye.

There are several operating rooms, each completely furnished with operating tables and equipped with all aseptic accessories and a complete equipment of instruments. On the ground, or basement floor there is an emergency operating room, equipped in every way as the others are and always ready for instant use.

The X-ray laboratory is complete in every way and is constantly used in determining the extent of injury to bones. One feature of its use that has been very beneficial to the men who have gone there for treatment for supposed fractures, has been the demonstration through the X-ray that the injuries have been to the ligaments and sinews and not to the bones, thus enabling them to avoid long delays for observation and consequent loss of time on their part.

The laboratory of clinical pathology is very complete. Every facility for making a rapid and proper diagnosis of obscure diseases is furnished the surgeons. Only graduated trained nurses are employed in the hospital.

The Baptist Sanitarium, located on the corner of Lamar Avenue and Smith Street, is one of the most complete institutions of its kind in the South. Every arrangement has been made for the treatment and comfort of its patrons and its fixtures and appliances are all modern and of the latest models. The building is steam heated and both electricity and gas are used in lighting. It is four stories high and has a capacity for fifty patients. The wards and private rooms are arranged so as to secure the greatest comfort, and everything is done for the welfare of the patients. The operating room is located on the fourth floor and is modern in every way. It is large, well lighted and thoroughly equipped with everything that goes with a first-class operating room.

Graduated trained nurses are employed and there is also a school for nurses in connection with the sanitarium. Dr. D. R. Pevato is the superintendant in charge and is personally responsible for many of the modern improvements installed.

Today no city of its size in the United States is better equipped with hospitals and private infirmaries than Houston. These are modern and up-to-date in every way, the strictest aseptic rules having been adhered to in their construction and every precaution taken against contagion and infection. Before the discoveries of modern medicine and surgery, hospitals were regarded, with much truth and justice, as hot-beds of contagion and infection, particularly the latter. Today it can be truthfully asserted that the modern hospital is freer from the danger of contracting disease than any other place in a community, for contagious and infectious diseases are not only intelligently treated, but their spread and propagation are effectually stamped out by scientific methods. Houston has a number of such institutions, which measure up to the highest standard of usefulness and comfort.

The best known of the private hospitals is the Norsworthy hospital.

The Norsworthy hospital is located on the northeast corner of San Jacinto Street and Rosalie Avenue and is in the quietest and most attractive resident part of the city. It is a large three-story brick building with a spacious over-ground basement. The top floor is arranged for an operating room and its accessories and adjuncts, and on this floor are the rooms for the nurses. The second and third floors are for patients alone, and these rooms are so arranged that one can have a ward bed, a single room with or without a private bath or two connecting rooms with or without a private bath.

The whole building is heated by hot water radiation; cleaned by automatic electric vacuum cleaners; plumbed for gas and wired for electric lights, call buzzers, private telephones and fans. An electric elevator and dumb waiter are parts of the equipment.

All the floors are doubled with deadening felt between them. The exposed flooring is of especially selected rift lumber. The entire building is plastered. The walls are in various oil tints, so as to add cheerfulness to each room. The interior finish is according to strict aseptic rules throughout, rounded corners and smooth wood with enamel finish. The operating room has all the accessories of a modern aseptic hospital. The floor and wainscoting are of Terrazo, and the walls and ceiling are white enamel. It has a complete equipment of instruments and an aseptic operating table. The room is excellently lighted for both day and night work. Adjoining the operating room is a sterilizing room for instruments and dressings, a dressing and sterilizing room for surgeons, and an anesthetic room.

The X-ray laboratory is equipped with the Scheidel Western X-ray Company's special hospital outfit, complete for radiograph work, and a dark room equipped with photographic apparatus for quick developing. The laboratory of clinical pathology has a complete equipment of instruments and apparatus necessary for all bacteriological and pathological work; embracing blood, urine, stomach contents, sputum, feces, tumors, tissues, vaccine therapy, milk and water analysis. This laboratory is under the direct charge of Dr. E. H. Lancaster, the house surgeon and pathologist, who was formerly pathologist for the State Board of Health. Only graduated nurses are employed in this hospital. Dr. O. L. Norsworthy is surgeon-in-chief and is assisted by two house surgeons, Dr. J. P. Gibbs and Dr. E. H. Lancaster.

With little or no knowledge of the laws of sanitation or hygiene it is not surprising that the early settlers were the victims of frequent and fatal epidemics. Their mode of life and surroundings were conducive to disease, and being, necessarily, ignorant of the causes of many of the most fatal diseases, a statement which applies with equal force to the physicians of that day in spite of their great learning, proper preventive measures were seldom ever adopted and all that was done, or could be done, was to cope with the disease after it had developed and secured a foothold.

The result was that Houston was frequently swept by epidemics of cholera and yellow fever. In 1839 there was a severe epidemic of yellow fever. A number of planters and farmers from the older states had settled in or near Houston, bringing their slaves with them, thus supplying abundant material for the ravages of the fever when it appeared. It is a well known fact that negroes are more or less immune from yellow fever, but the epidemic of 1838 seems to have been an exception to this rule for the mortality among the negroes was very great. It is interesting to note the fact that the fever appeared in Galveston before coming to Houston and that its appearance here followed the arrival of a man who had been sick in Galveston, but had recovered and come here.

In 1843 there was another great epidemic of yellow fever during which the mortality was very great. There was lack of proper food, and but few nurses and physicians to care for the sick so that the mortality that year was spoken of ever after when making comparison with subsequent epidemics. The disease appears to have been peculiarly fatal that year, whole families being swept away.

In 1845 or 1846 Houston had its first epidemic of cholera. The negroes seem to have been the principal victims, though many whites were attacked also. There is no record of the mortality although, according to tradition, it was rather heavy and confined almost exclusively to the negroes.

From 1843 to 1847 there was no yellow fever in Houston. During these four years the population had increased and the town had taken on quite respectable proportions. Thus there was an abundance of new material for the disease when it made its appearance late in the summer of 1847. That year resembled 1843 in the number of fatal cases, and a great number of physicians were among the very first victims. It is said that in proportion to the population, more physicians lost their lives during the epidemic of 1847 than in any other of those that followed. This fact may in a measure account for the great mortality among the people.

In 1853 and again in 1858 and 1859 Houston was scourged by yellow fever. The epidemic of 1858 was marked by great mortality. Houston's population at that time was between 8,000 and 10,000, and while there is no official record of the fact, it was estimated that the deaths that year were close to 1,800.

From 1859 to 1863, Houston appears to have escaped the visitations of yellow-fever, but in 1863 there was an epidemic though by no means a severe one compared with those which had preceded it. This is all the more remarkable when it is remembered that at that time there were thousands of soldiers here, very few of whom had ever been exposed to the fever.

In 1866, Houston had its second epidemic of cholera. The disease was confined exclusively to the negro population. Conditions were very favorable among them for its propagation. They had only recently been freed and had not yet learned even the first principles of how to care for themselves. They were congregated in huts and hovels and made not even a pretence of living clean and sanitary lives. There were not so many fatal cases as might be supposed and after a month or so of intelligent effort on the part of the health authorities, the disease was stamped out.

The next year, 1867, occurred one of the greatest yellow fever epidemics that ever cursed Houston. The first cases occurred early in August and the plague lasted until late in December, the last deaths occurring two days after Christmas. Everything was very favorable for the spread of the disease. The town was full of strangers, new comers, and in addition to these, there was the army of occupation, consisting of several thousand Federal troops, few of whom had ever been exposed to the fever. When the presence of the fever was announced there was something of a panic, and as many as could do so got away from the city. There were a number of physicians here, including some army surgeons. With the exception of some of the older physicians none of these doctors had ever seen yellow fever, but, be it said to their glory, not one deserted; every man remained at his post, though a great many of them paid the penalty of their lives by doing so. The mortality was frightful, due in a large measure to lack of proper nourishment, proper nursing and medical attention. The physicians were absolutely worked down and while they did all that they could, it was physically impossible for them to attend to hundreds who might have been saved could they have reached them. The Federal soldiers died like sheep. There were about 2,500 of them and of these over 700 men and officers died.

The mortality among the citizens, while not so great, was very heavy. On one day alone, September 26, there were 29 deaths in the city exclusive of those which occurred among the soldiers.

The epidemic of 1867 was the last that Houston has had, for though from time to time there have been epidemics of yellow fever at other Texas cities, notably that at Calvert in 1873, Houston has escaped. In 1897 it was reported that there was yellow fever in Houston and Dr. Guiteras, a government expert was sent here to investigate. He pronounced it yellow fever and Houston was promptly quarantined against by all Texas towns. The cases were then investigated by such yellow fever experts as Dr. D. F. Steuart and Dr. R. H. Harrison, who had gone through a number of yellow fever epidemics, and they, without hesitation, pronounced the disease dengue fever and all quarantine was promptly raised. The people knew them and had perfect confidence in their judgment and experience.

Before closing this brief history of the medical profession in Houston and of some of the things that have been accomplished by it, it may not be inappropriate to speak of the attitude the doctors have always maintained towards quacks and those who adopt the methods of the charlatan. They have always been consistent in this and their antagonism at times has been so bitter that it has almost defeated itself by creating sympathy for those whom they have attacked. This has been particularly true in those cases where the attacks have been based only on the fact that the sinning doctor advertised in the newspapers. The attitude of the Houston physicians and also that of the Houston newspapers towards the advertising doctor is well shown in the following instance:

During January, 1910, the South Texas District Medical Association held a session in Houston. During the session a banquet was given which was attended by all the doctors and some of the Houston editors. Speeches were made, the principal topic discussed being "Quackery in Houston." Dr. John T. Moore, president of the Harris County Medical Association, spoke at some length saying that Houston was a hot-bed for quacks and charlatans. He described them as "criminals" posing as physicians for the people. Many such, he declared, had been run out of Dallas, San Antonio and other Texas cities, but Houston was still their Mecca. Here they established resplendent suites of offices and extorted from the ignorant, large sums of money for which they gave no legitimate professional return. He denounced them as "swindlers" and "confidence men" and declared that the newspapers were solely responsible for their criminal success. The newspapers were the intermediary between them and their dupes, whose money they sought. The newspapers by opening their advertising columns to them became not only their solicitors but their sponsors. If the newspapers would close their columns to these men and refuse to print their glowing and deceptive advertisements, these fellows would be forced to seek other fields. Doctors Norsworthy and Parker indorsed all that Doctor Moore had said and declared that if the newspapers would assist the doctors these monsters who prey on the sick and afflicted would soon be run out of town.

Mr. M. E. Foster, president of the Houston Chronicle Publishing Company, entered a strong protest against the attitude taken by the physicians towards the press. He admitted that fraudulent and deceptive advertisements, claiming to cure incurable diseases, should be rigidly excluded from the newspapers. But he claimed it was difficult, if not impossible for a layman to determine just what was fraudulent and what was legitimate.

He cited the fact that the mosquito theory of the propagation of yellow fever had been denounced as a fraud by the medical profession and that many other discoveries of real merit now accepted universally had been at first ridiculed by the doctors. He also pointed out that the newspapers were always ready to co-operate in measures for the public health. Thousands of columns of space have been freely given by the newspapers in the campaign of education against tuberculosis, the typhoid fly, the yellow fever and malarial fever mosquito, small-pox, cholera and other diseases although the physicians still retain an antiquated and inexcusable prejudice against publicity and advertising.

CHAPTER X - CHURCH HISTORY

Founding of the Evangelical Churches in Houston. Organization of the Baptists, Methodists, Presbyterians, and Episcopalians. German Lutheran Churches, Disciples and Christian Scientists. The Roman Catholic Institutions in Houston. Congregation Beth Israel and Hebrew Synagogues. The Houston Y. M. C. A.

Under the spreading branches of a large oak tree, that stood on Market Square, was held the first religious service in Houston. The minister was a transient Methodist preacher, whose name, unfortunately, has not been handed down to posterity. Thus in the open air, seated on planks laid over convenient logs, the early Houstonians, in 1837, hears the gospel. The good man's audience was composed of christians of all denominations and beliefs, for at that time the Baptists, Methodists, Presbyterians and Episcopalians, had not formed themselves into local church organizations, as they did soon after.

In 1838 or 1839, the Allens donated two or three lots, on the northwest corner of Main and Capitol Streets, to the churches of Houston. It was a gift specified to no denomination, but was for the use of all. There was a small house erected on this property and it was used by all donominations except the Methodist, who used the Capitol, a block further down Main Street. The Presbyterians finally fell heirs to this property, when the other denominations secured locations of their own.

On April 10, 1841, the first church meeting of what is now the First Baptist Church, was held and is thus recorded in the old minutes:

"Convened at the usual place of worship, April 10, A. D., 1841, in the City of Houston, County of Harris, Republic of Texas, members of Baptist churches from different parts of the United States and of the Republic, for the purpose of forming an Evangelical Church of Christ of the regular Baptist order.

"On motion of Brother S. P. Andrews, Brother Huckins was called to the chair, and Brother Gardner Smith was chosen secretary of the meeting * * * *. On motion of Brother Bigalow, Brother S. P. Andrews was elected to serve as deacon.

"Constituent Members: Barnabas Hascall, Martha Mulryne, Obedience Smith, Gardner Smith, Benjamin M. George, Abigail Hascall, Louisa Jane Schroder, Charlotte M. Fuller, Israel B. Bigalow, Elizabeth C. Wilson, S. P. Andrews, Elizabeth Anisworth, Mary George, Mary H. Bigalow, John Lawrence, Mary A. Andrews, Piety L. Hadley, Sarah L. Robinson, Hannah Town, Charlotte Beach, Kitty Mulryne, (colored), Melvina Gray, (colored), Grace League, (colored), Inda Schroder, (colored)."

The usual place of worship spoken of in the minutes, was the general meeting house, corner of Main and Capitol Streets. Reverend James Huckins, of Galveston, who presided at the organization of the church became its first pastor and continued as such until the latter part of 1845.

After the organization of the church, two devoted and zealous Christian women, Mrs. Piety L. Hadley and Mrs. Charlotte M. Fuller determined through their own exertions, to build a church edifice. They did not meet with much encouragement, not even from members of their own families but they were not discouraged. Someone, as a joke, made them a present of a mule. They fattened this animal up and sold it, thus securing the nucleus for the church fund. They organized a sewing society, made useful things, gave a church fair and sold them. The sale of the mule and the goods at the fair netted the ladies $450. They gave another fair which earned $900. With this money they purchased the lots, corner of Travis Street and Texas Avenue, where the first church stood for so many years. In all their labors and trials these ladies had the untiring aid and support of a good old Christian, "Brother Pilgrim."

After the purchase of the lots the ladies wrote to Rev. William M. Tryan, then a missionary in Washington County, asking him to come to Houston and take charge of the church. Dr. Tryan accepted the call, and, on February 1, 1846, took charge of the First Baptist Church then numbering 17 members. He was reputed to be a highly educated gentleman, a sincere christian and an earnest worker, and soon commanded the respect and love of the whole community. Under his charge the membership grew rapidly, many of the best and leading citizens joining the church.

He at once began securing funds to erect a suitable church building. Owing to the financial weakness of his church and the community at large, he had to look elsewhere for assistance, and obtained the greater part of the money from those of the faith in other states. He received material assistance in his good work from Mr. W. R. Baker, Mr. T. W. House and Mr. B. A. Shepard, none of whom was a member of the Baptist Church, but all except Mr. House being inclined towards that denomination. The building was completed and dedicated by Dr. Tryan, just four months before his death from yellow fever in November, 1847. Before the building was completed, Mrs. Hadley and other ladies had organized a Sunday School.

According to the minutes dated June 6, 1846, "on motion of Brother E. B. Noble, it was resolved that Elder William M. Tryan, Brother T. B. J. Hadley, Messrs B. A. Shepard, C. W., Buckley, N. Fuller and William R. Baker be appointed a board of trustees for the First Baptist Church of Houston, and that Brothers Tryan and Hadley be authorized and requested to take the legal steps for the incorporation of said church."

At another conference meeting about that time, Brother Bowers was authorized to buy a box of candles for the church and it was arranged that each member should pay his or her share of the expense of the transaction. The church building stood on the corner of Travis Street and Texas Avenue, and was quite an imposing structure for that day. It had gothic windows and a high steeple and was considered by some of the old fashioned members to be too gaudy for the purposes to which it was dedicated. The indignation of these good brothers over the gothic windows and steeple was as nothing to that which was shown when a melodeon was installed and a choir was organized. One of the most zealous of the objectors went to the length of slipping into the church one night, stealing the melodeon and throwing it into the bayou, where it remained for a long time until scooped out by a dredge-boat.

A fine bell was presented to the church in November, 1850, and for years was hung in the steeple, that a few years before had excited so much antagonism. The donor was Mr. William McMahan, one of the members, who had been one of the principal objectors to the style put on by the builders of the church, but who seems to have changed his views. Mr. B. A. Shepard generously assisted the church in a financial way all through its early experience as did also Mr. W. R. Baker. Later, when the gas works were built, Mr. T. W. House presented the church with gas fixtures.

On the death of Dr. Tryan, the church called Rev. R. C. Burleson, then of Kentucky, as pastor of the church. He proved to be a worthy successor of the lamented Tryan, and under his charge the church grew and prospered. He remained with the church for a little more than three years, and was succeeded by Rev. Thomas Chilton of Alabama. Mr. Chilton had been a prominent lawyer and a member of the United States Congress for some years but had relinquished all earthly honors and glory to take up the work of a humble minister of Christ. He was a fine orator, a thorough christian and a zealous worker and many accessions to the church marked his pastorate.

Of Mr. Chilton's immediate successors the church records furnish little definite information. The frequent removals together with the Civil War troubles greatly damaged the church work. Rev. Mr. Tucker was pastor when the war broke out and promptly laid down the cross and took up the sword. He raised a company, was elected its captain, and commanded it during the war. Then came Rev. F. M. Law, followed by Rev. J. B. Link, who had also been a Confederate soldier during the war but who took charge of the church after the war was over. Rev. J. T. Zealy became pastor September 16, 1869, and served the church for six years. During his ministry two chapels, one in the Fourth and the other in the Fifth ward, were built and mission Sunday schools were established. In addition to that the property at the corner of Rusk Avenue and Fannin Street was purchased. Following Mr. Zealy, Rev. Dr. Horace Clark occupied the pulpit until April 1, 1877, when Rev. Dr. J. M. C. Breaker assumed charge. In 1883, the church property on Texas

Avenue and Travis Street was sold and it was determined to erect a new building on the property owned by the church, on Rusk Avenue and Fannin Street. The cornerstone of the new church was laid July 23, 1883, with imposing ceremony, and the new church, though not quite completed, was opened the first time for services, Sunday, January 27, 1884, Dr. Breaker, the pastor, preaching an appropriate sermon to a large congregation.

When the great storm of 1900, swept over the gulf coast the Baptist church on Rusk and Fannin was so badly damaged that it had to be torn down. It was then determined to abandon that site and erect a new church one block further south on the corner of Fannin Street and Walker Avenue. The new building was completed in 1903, and is one of the handsomest churches of Houston. It is of gothic architecture and the materials used in its construction are stone, brick, and concrete. It extends 75 feet on Fannin Street and 111 feet on Walker Avenue. At the corner is a tower of moderate height which adds much to the beauty of the building. The windows are all of stained glass. Dr. J. B. Riley an eminent scholar and historian, was pastor at the time.

Rev. Dr. J. L. Gross became pastor of the First Baptist Church, November 1, 1905, and has remained with the church ever since. He had come to Houston a few weeks before and had delivered one or two sermons which so pleased the members that they made a successful effort to retain him permanently as their pastor, and they have never had reason to regret doing so. He was called to take charge by a unanimous vote of the church. He is recognized as one of the strong men of the Baptist church and his influence for good has been very great. Like the Rev. Dr. Chilton, Rev. Dr. Gross was engaged in the practice of law before entering the ministry. Born in Georgia, he was graduated from the University of Georgia, with the degree of Bachelor of Arts and Bachelor of Law, and later took a course in the Southern Baptist Theological Seminary at Louisville, Ky. His first church work was at Washington, Ga. He then accepted a call to Griffin, Ga., and from there went to Selma. Alabama, whence he came to Houston.

In 1905, Rev. H. C. Smith organized the First Baptist Church of Houston Heights and under his ministry a beautiful house of worship was built.

The Baptist Temple was organized June 21st, 1908, in Houston Heights, with a constituent membership of 20. The Rev. F. Huhns presided at the organization and was elected pastor. He is a graduate of the Rochester Theological Seminary and of the Southern Baptist Theological Seminary at Louisville, Ky. He had been engaged in missionary work in Philadelphia, Chicago and other large Eastern and Northern cities, and, for three years before coming to Houston, had been missionary evangelist of the Union Baptist Association, Rev. Evander Ammons is now in charge, Mr. Huhns having resigned to take charge of a church in Pittsburg, Pa.

The following are some of the Baptist churches and Baptist missions in Houston, today: First German Baptist Church, Rev. F. Severs, pastor: First Baptist Church, Houston

Heights, Yale Street, between Ninth and Tenth Streets, Rev. C. A. Earl, pastor; Lee Avenue Baptist Church, Houston Heights; Brunner Baptist Church, Rev. W. P. Grow, pastor; Liberty Avenue Baptist Church, Rev. Robert Carrol, pastor; Calvary Baptist Church, Preston Avenue and Sampson Street, Rev. J. E. Treloar, pastor; Tuam Avenue Baptist Church, corner Tuam Avenue and Fannin Street, Rev. J. W. Loving, pastor. This is the South End Church.

Bishop Street Baptist Church, corner Bishop and Fletcher Streets, Fifth ward, Rev. Thornton A. Payne, pastor; The Emanuel Baptist Church, Brook Smith Addition, Rev. George H. Lee, pastor; Tabernacle Baptist, Rev. D. C. Freeman, pastor.

All of these churches have church homes, some of them very handsome. They have been served by capable and consecrated pastors.

There are many negro Baptist churches in Houston, the number of negro Baptist in the city being greater than that of the whites. They have several handsome churches.

The organization of the Methodist church in Houston was unique in one way. While the preliminary steps in the formation of each of the other denominations were taken by at least two or three zealous Christian men and women, the foundation of the Methodist church was the act of a single individual,—Mr. Charles Shearn. Mr. Shearn was an Englishman, having been born in England, October 30, 1794. He died in Houston, November 12, 1871. He came to Texas in 1834, and settled in west Texas. When General Urrea marched from San Patricio to Goliad, he captured Mr. Shearn, who was a member of a small company of Texans, and would have shot him but for the fact that Mr. Shearn was an Englishman and claimed to be an English subject. Mexico respected and feared England too much to ill-treat one of her subjects, and that fact saved Charles Shearn.

He removed to Houston in 1837, the year following San Jacinto, and spent his life here, leaving behind him the respect, love and admiration of the whole community. Mr. Shearn began life in Houston as a merchant and prospered. The first year of his residence here he induced a Methodist missionary to come here from the states, and took him to his home, as his personal guest. This was a Mr. Sommers, and it was perhaps he who held the first religious service in Houston, under the old tree on Market Square, referred to elsewhere. Mr. Shearn kept Mr. Sommers as his guest and together they succeeded in gathering a sufficient number of sympathizers, to form a Methodist class. In 1842, they determined to build a church, and Mr. Shearn was made chairman of the building committee. The Morning Star, in 1843, had this notice of the proposed church:

"The Morning Star has been informed that the Methodist Society of this city has obtained, chiefly through the liberality of the brethren in the United States, sufficient funds to erect a large and commodious church. It has been planned to lay the corner-stone of the building, March 2, the anniversary of Texas independence. The building is to be of brick, about 60 feet by 35 feet. Most of the material has been bought and paid for and the construction of the building will be hastened as rapidly as possible."

The corner-stone of the brick building was laid, March 2, 1843, according to program, local Masons, Odd Fellows and a military company assisting at the ceremonies. Col. James Riley, one of the most eloquent members of the Houston Bar, delivered an address that was long remembered. Mr. Shearn was superintendent of construction and had the building completed and ready for occupancy, the following May.

On May 7, 1844, the following notice was published:

"The new Methodist Episcopal Church in this city will be open for Divine service on next Saturday evening. On Sunday morning the dedication sermon will be preached by the Rev. Mr. Richardson, president of Ruterville College. Several clergymen from the county will be in attendance.

(Signed) A. Applewhite, C. Shearn, Building Committee."

Among those citizens who contributed largely towards the success of the church, were Mr. T. W. House, Sr., who was Mr. Shearn's son-in-law, Mr. Gregg, Mr. McGowan and Mr. Hardcastle. The church was in constant use from 1844, until 1861, when it was blown down by a storm.

A large wooden building, unceiled, and but crudely finished, was constructed on the site at Milam Street and Texas Avenue, and in this building for several years the Methodists held their meetings. The war, lasting from 1861 to 1865, followed by political troubles and the terrible epidemic of yellow-fever in 1867, caused much delay in building a new church. Then, too, there was great poverty among the members and as these seemed satisfied with the old wooden church, it was not until 1871, that a serious effort was made to erect a suitable building. That year Mr. Shearn saw the possibilities of building a new church, and Messrs. House, Gregg, McGowan and Hardcastle again came to his assistance, with the result that what was known as Shearn Church was erected on the old site of the first building. Credit for building Shearn Church is due almost entirely to Mr. Shearn who paid the greater part of the cost of constructing it. The Methodists clung to the old location on Texas Avenue and Milam Street until 1907, when it was abandoned and a new church, which was called the First Methodist Church, was erected at Clay Avenue and Main Street. The new church fronts 125 feet on Main and runs back 175 feet on Clay Avenue. It is constructed of Bedford gray granite, Powhatan pressed gray brick and pearl-tint terra cotta. It is one of the finest and most costly structures of its kind in the South. Rev. Dr. W. P. Packard is the present pastor.

St. Paul's Methodist Episcopal Church was organized, January 1, 1906, with a membership of 130, seventy-six from other churches, fifty-four by letter and profession of faith. In 1907, it had 475 members and a Sunday school of 450 pupils, a Home Missionary Society of forty members and a Young Ladies' Society of sixty-five members.

Before the contract for the erection of its house of worship had been let, $130,000 was raised. Bishop Seth Ward turned the first spade-full of earth. Bishop Key named the building and selected an organizer and builder to take charge of the whole matter. The plans called for an expenditure of $175,000. The corner-stone was laid with religious and Masonic ceremonies June 24, 1907, and until the building was ready for occupancy, the congregation met in a small chapel nearby. The lot on the corner of McGowan Avenue and Milam Street, was the gift of Mrs. J. O. Ross, and the official board of the church, the Women's Societies and other auxiliaries were organized at her nearby residence.

The first pastor was Rev. Dr. George S. Sexton, formerly chaplain of the First Texas Infantry, U. S. V. Dr. Sexton has held many important charges and was a remarkably gifted man to whom the greatest credit for the classic edifice is due. A set of chimes was given by Mrs. M. T. Jones. The church has art windows, the subjects of which are: Portraits of John and Charles Wesley; "Christ the Consoler"; "Christ and the Doctors"; "Ruth, the Gleaner"; "Christ in Gethsemane"; "Mary at the Tomb"; "The Ascension"; "Moses and the Law". In the Sunday School room special windows represent the flight of angels through the heavens on the night of the birth of Christ, proclaiming "Peace on earth, Good Will towards men." This is one of the most artistic and beautifully finished buildings to be found anywhere in this country. Its exterior is of classic and Byzantine lines, the building being in an architectural class all its own. The method of getting plans for the building was novel. No competitive plans were submitted, the architects simply developing plans to meet the requirements of the building committee. A committee visited the notable churches in the larger cities of America and adopted the best features of some and rejected the bad features of all of them. The result was the present building. Rev. Dr. Sam. R. Hay is at present pastor of St. Paul's, and under his charge the church continues to grow and extend its good influence.

In addition to Shearn Church, now called the First M. E. Church, South, and St. Paul's, there are several churches and chapels of the denomination doing good work in various parts of Houston. The following is a list of them: First Methodist Episcopal Church, Tenth and Harvard Streets, Houston Heights, Rev. C. L. Elliott, pastor; Trinity Methodist Church, corner Loraine and Gano Streets, Rev. F. G. Clark, pastor; Tabernacle Methodist Church, corner Polk and Caroline Streets, Rev. W. W. Watts, pastor; Epworth Methodist Church; Brunner Avenue Methodist Church, Rev. W. W. Sherill, pastor; Grace Methodist Church, Houston Heights, Rev. T. M. Brownlee, pastor; Harrisburg Methodist Episcopal Church, South, Rev. R. C. George, pastor; McAsham Methodist Church, Rev. A. P. Bradford, pastor; Washington Avenue Methodist Church, Washington Avenue between Houston Avenue and Trinity Street, Rev. H. M. Timmons, pastor; McKee Street Methodist Church, corner Conti and McKee Streets, Rev. H. M. Walling, pastor; Ebenezer Methodist Church, corner Harrington and Chestnut Streets, C. H. Beneke, pastor; Bering Memorial Church, corner Milam Street and McKinney Avenue, Rev. E. A. Konken, pastor.

There are many colored Methodists in Houston and the negroes have several substantial churches with large congregations.

The Methodists are the strongest in number and influence of the Evangelical churches in Houston and have exerted from the earliest days a wide influence for good.

Of all the early Houston churches the Presbyterians had the easiest time establishing themselves. They did not have to worry about a building site and then about a building to put on it. They had all these at the very beginning, for the city founders, the Allens, being members of the Presbyterian Church themselves, set aside two or three lots on Main Street and Capitol Avenue, for church purposes and gave it to the Presbyterians, stipulating only that all denominations should have the use of the small building, they placed on it, until they could secure churches or meeting places of their own. This was faithfully carried out, and for several years Baptist, Methodist, and other denominations made as free use of the building as did the Presbyterians themselves. In the early part of 1843, several members of the church began an active canvass for funds with which to erect a suitable church building. They were successful and a large building was erected near the northwest corner of Capitol Avenue and Main Street, facing Main Street. The building was completed in 1842, and services were held in it regularly. This structure had a church bell, the first one ever rung in Houston. In its issue of February 11th, 1843, the Morning Star, said:

"We are requested to mention that the bell of the Presbyterian church will be rung regularly on Sunday mornings at 9 o'clock for Sunday School and again half an hour before meeting, and will be tolled ten minutes before service begins."

Many of the leading and most influential citizens of Houston were members of the Presbyterian church, among them being Mr. M. D. Conklin, Mr. A. S. Burke, Mr. T. M. Bagby, Mr. Horace Taylor, Mr. E. H. Cushing, Mr. Geo. W. Kidd, Sr., Mr. Lillie, and Dr. Cowling, all men of the highest standing. All these were not Houstonians at the very earliest stages of the city's beginning, but all were so early on the scene that it is not unjust to class them all together. At whatever stage they enlisted they did such valiant work in the cause of religion in Houston that no discrimination should be made in awarding credit for what has been accomplished. They have all, long ago passed to their rewards from a higher than earthly court.

The large wooden edifice stood for many years on its original site, and was destroyed by fire one September night in 1859. The fire started in Baker and Thompson's saw-mill, which stood on the southwest corner of Texas Avenue and Main Street. The fire consumed all the buildings facing Main Street, on both sides of the street between Texas Avenue and Capitol Avenue.

The years 1858 and 1859, were sorrowful ones for the Presbyterian church in Houston. In September, 1858, one of their most beloved and universally popular pastors, Rev. Mr. Ruthvan, was lost at sea. He took passage from Galveston for New Orleans on the ill-fated steamer Nautilus, which went down during a great hurricane which swept over the gulf. Only one person, a negro, who clung to some wreckage, was saved, of all the passengers and crew. By a singular coincidence, another pastor of that church was lost at sea, eight years later. This was Rev. Dr. Castelton, who with his wife, sailed out of Galveston harbor on a sailing vessel in 1866. Not a trace of the vessel nor of any of her passengers or crew has ever been found.

The wooden church which had been burned, was replaced by a brick building, which was placed further back on the property, facing Capitol Avenue. Services were held in this house for many years, until, in 1879, it began to crack and was condemned as unsafe. The building was practically torn down and made safe. While this was being done services were held in Pillott's Opera House. In May, 1880, the congregation moved back to their own church and the first sermon was preached by Rev. Dr. E. D. Junkin, who had just accepted a call to the church. Dr. Junkin was a very able man and a profound scholar, but above even these he had qualities of heart that soon endeared him, not only to his own congregation, but to the citizens of Houston at large, so that his influence for good was very great. He was the son of Rev. George Junkin, the founder of Lafayette College at Easton, Pennsylvania, and was born at Miller, Pennsylvania, February 3, 1829. He was graduated from Lafayette College and received his D. D. degree from Washington and Jefferson College. In 1854, he was graduated from Princeton College, and in 1855, was licensed to preach. After pastoral service in North Carolina and Virginia he came to Houston and remained in charge of the First Presbyterian Church until his death which occurred at Johnson City, Tenn., on July 31, 1891, while on his way to Virginia to visit old friends.

Dr. Junkin's successor was Rev. Dr. Wm. Hayne Leavell, who was also a great scholar and pulpit orator. The church was fortunate in getting such a man as he to follow Dr. Junkin. Under his administration some of the best work of the church was done. He remained with the church until February, 1906, when he resigned and was succeeded by Rev. Dr. William States Jacobs, the present pastor, who took charge and preached his first sermon March 4, 1906.

Dr. Jacobs is easily one of the most popular men and preachers Houston has ever known. He always commands large congregations and has taken a virile part in the city's vital and material development. The Chamber of Commerce, the real estate men and the music lovers of Houston have found a great helper in Dr. Jacobs and he has brought many high grade lyceum entertainments to Houston as well as the Russian Symphony Orchestra. Dr. Jacobs is the author of the great descriptive phrase that is Houston's motto "Where 17 railroads meet the sea." He holds many scholarly degrees and is a popular platform orator.

At a congregational meeting, October 30, 1893, it was resolved that "the building committee be, and they are hereby, authorized to negotiate the sale, and the trustees to execute the necessary papers, for the transfer of the property now owned by the First Presbyterian Church of Houston, on the corner of Main Street and Capitol Avenue; provided that there can be realized a sufficient amount to secure the half block on Main Street and McKinney Avenue, known as the House property, and, in addition, not less than $20,000 in cash."

The building committee was thus constituted: Rev. Dr. W. M. Hayne Leavell, pastor; R. F. George, representing the board of elders; O. C. Drew, representing the board of deacons; Dr. D. F. Steuart, representing the members of the church; and Charles Dillingham, representing those members of the congregation not members of the church.

The church property brought $45,000 and the committee paid $22,500, and the cost of paving for the other property, bringing the cost to between $24,000 and $25,000.

Work on the new church was begun at once, and when completed it was pronounced by competent judges, to be very nearly architecturally perfect. Its exterior is strikingly beautiful and its interior finish is fully in keeping with the exterior.

The Presbyterian Church in Houston long ago outgrew the capacity of the mother church and also that of its strongest off-shoots, and now there are nearly a dozen Presbyterian congregations in and near the city, all flourishing and prospering. The following of these all have their own houses of worship:

Woodland Heights Presbyterian Church, Beauchamp Avenue and Hooker Street, Rev. George W. Martin, pastor; First Presbyterian Church of Houston Heights, corner of Rutland and Eighteenth Street, Rev. R. D. Wear, pastor; Oak Lawn Presbyterian Church, corner of Stiles and Sherman Streets, Rev. A. N. Wylie, pastor; Hardy Street Presbyterian Church, Rev. Granville

T. Story, pastor; Second Presbyterian Church, Main Street and Denis Avenue, Rev. Frank E. Fincher, pastor. This is one of the handsomest churches in the city. Third Presbyterian Church, corner of Bingham and Johnson Streets, Rev. J. M. Gaul, pastor; Central Presbyterian Church, corner of Fannin Street and Pease Avenue, Rev. A. B. Buchanan, pastor; Westminster Presbyterian Church, Washington and Boulevard, Rev. E. Sinclair Smith, pastor. The new edifice of this congregation is very modern, and Dr. Smith, one of the most highly honored of the city's pastors.

The chapels of the Second Presbyterian Church, are Park Street Chapel, Market Street Chapel, Hutchins Street Chapel, Hyde Park Chapel, and Blodgett Mission Sunday School. Rev. Stanley White is superintendent in charge of missions.

On March 16, 1839, while the city of Houston was still in its swaddling clothes, 39 earnest churchmen met and organized "the Protestant Episcopal Church of Houston, Republic of Texas." Isolated from the older parts of the country, with no means of communication, save by water or by ox or horse-drawn vehicles, over almost impassable roads, this handful of earnest Christians laid the foundation for a church which was destined to become the first in wealth, influence and power of its denomination in Texas. At the beginning they had only such services as itinerant ministers and missionaries could give them. Bishop George W. Freeman, Missionary Bishop of Louisiana took great interest in the struggling church, and in all ways in his power contributed to its advancement.

The church adopted a constitution and took the name of Christ Church, May 12, 1845. Measures were taken to build a chapel to cost $2,500. Its corner-stone was laid in 1846, and it was consecrated by Bishop Freeman, May 9, 1847. Houston was then a most uninviting field for clergymen and for some years there was no regular minister in charge. However, the membership increased so rapidly that before the first ten years had elapsed a large house of worship was demanded. The corner-stone of a new building was laid in 1859, and within two years the building was completed at a cost of $16,000. This building was used for years, but in 1876, a third church was erected, and in 1893, the corner-stone of the present beautiful building was laid.

Of the fifteen rectors of Christ Church before 1892, few remained longer than two or three years, while others remained but a short time. In 1892, Rev. Henry V. Aves, then in charge of St. John's Church at Cleveland, Ohio, where he had served seven years, accepted a call here. He was confronted with a church debt of $30,000, and found only one society for work connected with the church, that of the Ladies' Parish Association. In less than ten years the debt had been wiped out and several helping societies had been organized and were working effectually. The Sheltering Arms, a home for indigent women; the Woman's Auxiliary, a power in the missionary field; a sewing school; the Girls' Friendly Society, the Altar Society, the Choir Chapter, the Young Women's Guild, Christ Church Grammar School and several working bodies connected with the three mission chapels, were all the results of Rev. Dr. Aves' personal efforts. The building used for the Sheltering Arms had been erected and paid for and an infirmary and operating room were projected, before his first ten years expired.

Rev. Dr. Aves received most valuable support and assistance in all he did from R. M. Elgin, father of the Vestry, who had grown gray in the service of the church before the arrival of Dr. Aves, and also from A. S. Richardson, W. D. Cleveland, W. V. R. Watson, Presley K. Ewing, William M. Mitchell and Sam McIlhenny.

Christ Church building is one of the handsomest and most imposing churches in Houston. A rectory which cost $10,000, was erected in 1902, and a parish school was opened the same year as a memorial to Judge Peter Gray and his wife.

When Dr. Aves was elected Bishop of Mexico, and decided to accept the position, he communicated his decision to the rectory of Christ Church. The regret of that body is embodied in a letter and accompanying resolutions from which the following is a quotation:

"We admire, love and esteem you, and some of us lean on you as the strong staff of our religious life. Your beautiful Christian character has been, through these many years, a beacon for us in God's watch-tower. You have never, during this long time, preached a sermon, though some have necessarily been better than others, that would not have honored any pulpit; not one that would not have been a means of grace to any Christian. You have here, at the baptismal fount, tenderly held our little ones and signed them with the sign of the cross. You have here, at the marriage altar, pronounced the words of holy wedlock and blessed with your benediction the plighted troth. You have here, at the open grave and in the hidden sanctuaries of sorrow, ministered comfort with a heart as boundless as human love and as tender. It is hard, recalling your ministry, to give you up. We feel that in your departure 'a beacon light will be blown out above us, a buoy bell stilled upon the sea.' We feel that taking you all in all, we shall long wait to look upon your like again. But we cannot, will not speak to you words of parting. Adieu—to God—there safe we leave you. Our trembling lips do speak, but ah, how faintly do they shadow forth the tremor of our hearts. Precious memories of your past, prayerful hope for your future—let this be our sentiment.

Faithfully and Affectionately, Your Rectory: Robert M. Elgin, Senior Warden; W. D. Cleveland, Junior Warden; Wm. V. Watson; Presley K. Ewing; Sam McNeil; M. H. Westcott; R. T. Morris; Frank Cargill; Joseph Towlis."

After the departure of Rev. Henry Aves, who is still Bishop of Mexico, Rev. Dr. Peter Gray Sears was called to the pastorate of Christ Church, and has proven himself a worthy successor. Dr. Sears is one of the most profound scholars and pulpit orators in the South, and, like Bishop Aves, he is a tireless worker. He has not only continued the work, but has added to the usefulness of Christ Church in the moral upbuilding of the city and community.

In addition to the mother church, there are the following Episcopal churches and chapels in Houston today: Trinity Church, corner Main Street and Holman Avenue, Rev. Robert Lee Craig, rector; St. John's Church, corner Leeland Avenue and Velasco Street, O. M. Longnecker, superintendent; St. Marry's Episcopal Church, Rev. G. W. R. Cadman, rector; Clemens Memorial Church, corner Bingham and Sabine Streets, Rev. T. J. Windham, minister in charge; St. Andrew's Mission, 230 West Seventeenth Street, Houston Heights, Rev. Mr. Cadman, minister in charge.

The first German Lutheran Church erected in Houston was quite an imposing wooden structure that for years stood on the southwest corner of the block of which The Daily Post now stands. The church owned a quarter of the block, but utilized only the corner on Texas Avenue and Milam Street. Rev. Mr. Braun was the first and only pastor of the church while it occupied that location. In connection with the church was a school patronized by the German citizens of Houston and by many of the Americans who desired to have their children taught the German language, hence it was generally crowded to its full capacity. There were a number of Lutherans in Houston, and as the city grew the needs of their church grew also, and soon it became necessary to build other houses of worship. The first of these was one on Louisiana Street between Preston and Prairie Avenues. But the demands of commerce seem to have been greater than those of the church, and both the Texas Avenue and the Louisiana Street properties were sold and the churches moved elsewhere. At present the Lutherans have two large and flourishing churches, one on Caroline and Texas Avenue and the other on Washington Avenue and Young Street. In both churches the sermons are in the German language, but both English and German are used in their Sunday Schools.

The Christians in the past fifteen years have come to prominence and the Central Christian Church, on the corner of Main Street and Bell Avenue is one of the handsomest of Houston's many handsome churches. It was completed in 1907. The Second Christian Church is located at the corner of Hogan and Common Streets.

In the last ten years, the Christian Scientists have made great gains in Houston. There are now two churches of this faith and the first church of the city is erecting a beautiful classic church building with a Greek front, on Main Street.

All church statistics are difficult to get, but the many beautiful buildings erected by the various denominations within the past decade is evidence of their flourishing condition.

The first Catholic church in Houston was built on three lots on the northeast corner of the block on Franklin Avenue and Caroline Street. There was a large gully running up Caroline Street and the little church was built on the very edge of this. Behind the church, and running east and west, was a long, single-story building used as a home for the priest and also as a parish school. Both the church and the school house were wooden structures. Father Querat had charge of both the church and school for many years, and was one of the best known and universally respected men in the city. He was a Frenchman, as his name implies, and was an accomplished scholar, and was almost as popular with the Protestants as he was with the members of his own faith. For about a quarter of a century that little church was the only place of worship the Catholics had in Houston. In 1868 or 9, the church sold the old church property and purchased the block on Texas Avenue and Crawford Street, and in 1870, began the erection of a large brick building on it. This building, the Church of the Annunciation, was completed in 1871, and remains today one of the handsomest church edifices in the city. It occupies about one quarter of the block, the remainder being occupied by a handsome home for the priests and a large and commodious school, all constructed of brick, and of attractive architectural design. Father Hennessy has had pastoral charge of this church for over thirty years, and, is looked up to with love and veneration by the members of his congregation, and by all Houstonians who know the sterling and lovable qualities of the man.

The growth of the church exceeded that of the city and became necessary early in the eighties to build other edifices. One was built on Washington Avenue, another in the Fifth ward and others steadily followed, until Houston has a number of Catholic Churches, a number of them handsome and imposing buildings.

In addition to what may be called the parent church. The Annunciation, the following are prominent: St. Joseph's Church, Father Banfield, pastor; Church of the Blessed Sacrament, on Sherman Avenue, Brady addition; St. Patrick's Church, Father Haughran, pastor; and Sacred Heart Church, on Pierce Avenue and San Jacinto Street. The parishes are large and growing so rapidly that constant additions to the number of churches and chapels have to be made.

The Roman Catholic Church in Houston has among its institutions, seven churches, four of them fine structures that would be ornaments to a city twice the size of Houston, a fine infirmary and several first-class schools. The infirmary and the schools are not under the church control except spiritual and are managed by the sisters of religious orders who have devoted their lives to that work. They have absolute control of all temporal matters. The hospital is the St. Joseph's Infirmary, one of the oldest and best patronized institutions of its kind in the state. St. Agnes' Academy is one of the schools and it is one of the leading educational institutions of the city. Its patronage is large, and though only five years old it is already placed in the front ranks of denominational institutions of learning in Texas.

The picturesque school building, located in the south end on Fannin Street, combines beauty and comfort in its ample accommodations.

There are, in round numbers, 10,000 communicants of the Catholic church in Houston, and the property of the church is valued at very nearly half a million dollars.

Houston will soon be known as the city of churches for every creed and variation of a creed seems to have its representatives here. In addition to the leading denominations enumerated in the foregoing pages there are the following named churches and religious associations in Houston:

Clark Street Mission, Apostolic Faith; Brunner Tabernacle, Apostolic Faith; Houston Heights Assembly, Apostolic Faith; International Bible Students Association; Congregational Church, corner Caroline Street and McKinney Avenue; Unitarian Church, Carnegie Library; Theosophical Society, Odd Fellows Hall; Oriental Textile Chapel, corner of Twenty-fourth and Lawrence Streets, Houston Heights; Balfour Mission, 210 San Jacinto Street; and the Star of Hope Mission, 714 Franklin Avenue, which holds services every night in the year.

In the very early days the leading representative of the Hebrews in Houston, was the venerable Rabbi Levy. No man stood higher in this community than he and none enjoyed the respect and esteem of all classes of citizens more than he. He was known among the people as "Father" Levy and his whole life was such as to warrant this love and confidence. He was an old man, had a long white beard and was the living picture of an old Patriarch. For many years he administered to the spiritual needs of his people and when he passed away, in the late fifties, he was mourned by the whole community.

During the war the Hebrew congregation in Houston preserved its organization.

That the congregation was kept in existence was due to the fact that in April, 1860, there came to Houston a family that has played a prominent part in its history. Its head was the Rev. Samuel Raphael, and the voyage from England took 10 weeks and was made in a full rigged ship, "The National Guard." Captain Gates, embarking at Liverpool and landing at Galveston. The ship was a merchantman and not a passenger vessel, and the Raphael family which included the Rabbi, his wife, Hannah, and six children, Joseph, Rebecca, Emanuel, Moses, Sarah and Julia, were the only passengers. Three members of this family still survive, E. Raphael, Mrs. Rebecca Nussbaum and Miss Julia Raphael.

Rabbi Raphael, took charge of the Congregation Beth Israel whose membership was only fifteen or twenty. Among them were Sam Meyer, Sol. Hohenthal, Isaac Elsasser, Joe Rosenfield, G. Gerson, Henry S. Fox, Sr., and Isaac Colman. Only one member of the original congregation still survives, Henry S. Fox, Sr., president of the Houston National Exchange Bank.

Rabbi Raphael labored faithfully, and it was mainly through his efforts that the Congregation Beth Israel was held together, and in the end converted into a virile force. He was a man of great scholarship, an eloquent speaker and possessed of much personal magnetism.

Owing to the troubled and disquieting days following the close of the war, nothing was done towards erecting a suitable house of worship by the members of Congregation Beth Israel, until about 1869. That year, however, Benjamin and Mose Raphael, sons of the Rabbi, I. Elsassor, A. Harris, A. S. Fox, J. Harris, M. E. Stern and some others, went quietly to work, raised sufficient funds, purchased a building site on Franklin Avenue, and announced that they would erect a suitable temple. On June 11, 1870, the Telegraph announced that everything was in readiness and that the corner-stone would be laid in a few days by Rev. Henry S. Jacobs, chief Rabbi of the New Orleans Portuguese Synagogue. About 4 o'clock, Thursday, June 16, a procession of fully 1,000 persons, consisting of Civil and Jewish organizations, formed on Main Street, near the Masonic Temple, and led by Schmidt's Band, marched to the site of the synagogue. The corner-stone, a large block of marble, was swinging on a tripod. A Divine blessing was asked by Rabbi Jacobs, after which he informed the Grand Master of one of Houston's Masonic organizations, the he was deputed by the Congregation Beth Israel to request that the corner-stone of its temple of worship should be laid with Masonic honors. The stone, set in the northeast corner of the foundation, was made the receptacle of the following articles: A record of the corner-stone itself; some coins of different countries of different denominations; some currency of different values and countries; a roll of members of the congregation of Beth Israel; a scroll of the Hebrew law; copies of the local newspapers; a photograph and souvenir of Gerson Kursheedt, a member of the congregation who had gone from Texas on a mission to Palestine and had died there.

This Hebrew congregation in 1908, completed a handsome new temple building that is one of the most modern church structures in Houston. It was dedicated with elaborate ceremonies. Dr. Henry Barnstein is Rabbi and has won fame in musical as well as religious circles. The new temple Beth Israel is located at the corner of Crawford and Lamar Street.

The Congregation Adath Geshurun worships in a handsome synagogue located at the corner of Jackson Street and Walker Avenue.

The first public meeting, in the interest of the Young Men's Christian Association, in Houston was held one Sunday afternoon, April, 1886, in

Pillott's Opera House. There was a large attendance of members of all the various denominations in Houston, thus giving evidence that the people of Houston were willing and ready to support such an institution. Many pledges of support and membership were promptly given in response to an invitation.

The following named gentlemen were chosen as a board of directors: Col. Charles Stewart, Capt. W. D. Cleveland,

E. L. Dennis, John Kay, J. F. Dumble, Conrad Bering, Ed. Smallwood, W. V. R. Watson, C. W. Alsworth, Dr. J. M. Arnold, Rufus Cage, Y. M. Langdon.

The sum of $2,000, was raised easily within a few days, and a permanent organization was effected and rooms were secured in the Brown Building, corner of Main Street and Texas Avenue, which were opened to the public on May 13, 1886. There was a reading room and a gymnasium, the latter under the direction of Captain E. B. H. Schnider. It was also announced that the parlor and lecture room would soon be ready for occupancy and that members' tickets were being prepared by the treasurer, Mr. J. F. Dumble.

The following named representative men were chosen as officers to serve for the first two years: William D. Cleveland, president; Y. M. Langdon, vice-president; James F. Dumble, treasurer; Rufus Cage, recording secretary; J. W. Goodhue, general secretary.

The following were chosen as a board of Directors: Charles Stewart, Dr. James M. Arnold, Conrad Bering, William Christian, W. V. R. Watson, E. L. Dennis, John Kay, C. W. Alsworth, Ed Smallwood.

It was made the duty of the General Secretary, under the direction of the board, to plan and carry out the objects of the association.

The association occupied very humble and very inadequate quarters for about twenty years, but in the latter part of 1906, the needs of the association for larger and more convenient quarters became so apparent, that an organized movement was inaugurated to raise $200,000, with which to build the association a home of its own. The movement met with popular favor at once. The city was aroused and subscriptions poured in from citizens of every class until the full amount was in hand. A site was purchased at the corner of Fannin Street and McKinney Avenue, and the following building committee was appointed: W. A. Wilson, chairman; S. F. Carter, treasurer; E. W. Taylor, secretary; Capt. James A. Baker, Jr., W. D. Cleveland, Sr., J. V. Dealy, and J. B. Bowles.

Work was begun at once, and on October 17, 1907, the corner-stone of the edifice was laid with impressive ceremony. Secretary Scott, acting for the directors, arranged a programme for the event.

First there was held a meeting at the old hall, after which a procession was formed and the march taken up to the new building, along Fannin Street. The ceremonies were semi-religious but non-sectarian. The main feature was the laying of the corner-stone by Captain Richmond Pearson Hobson. The members of the building committee had actual charge of the exercises. Mayor Rice represented the city, while Captain W. D. Cleveland, who was the first president of the association, acted as chairman.

On the evening of June 21, 1908, the formal opening exercises of the Young Men's Christian Association took place in the gymnasium of their new building. There was prayer, scripture reading, music and eloquent addresses. The speakers were: Hon. H. M. Garwood and Rev. Peter Gray Sears.

The building is five stories high and is beautifully finished throughout. On the first floor are located the loby, or reception room, a spacious reading room, the gymnasium, swimming pool, hand ball court, bowling alley, dressing rooms, each equipped with rockers and every arrangement for the convenience and comfort of the members.

The assembly room, the lecture rooms, the study and class rooms are on the second and part of the third floors, while the rest of the building is devoted to apartments for roomers. There are ninety-one rooms in all. All are of uniform size, and neatly furnished.

CHAPTER XI - EDUCATION AND FREE SCHOOLS

Houston's Earliest Schools were Private Enterprises. Lack of Proper School Facilities. The Houston Academy. Congressional Appropriations for Public Schools. Free Schools Flourished only after Civil War. Arguments Against the System. Houston First City to Take Control of Her Schools. City School Superintendents. Opening of Public Schools in October, 1877. Comparative Growth from 1877 to 1909. Scientific Features in City's Schools. Superintendent Horn's Summary of Decade from 1901 to 1911. Private School Enterprises.

The early Texans, and those of Houston particularly, placed the cause of education far to the fore while planning for the upbuilding of the new republic. Scarcely a public meeting was held, where questions of public policy were discussed, that the cause of education was not brought prominently forward. After San Jacinto, and while the new Republic was largely in the formative stages, nothing very tangible nor practical in the way of concerted action by the people could be accomplished, but, even at that time, successful efforts were being made to establish private schools in Houston.

Unfortunately there is no record preserved of these very early pioneers in the cause of education. Only a stray remark or a chance allusion, here and there, go to show that soon after Texas independence had been won, the school-master had taken up the task of preserving and perpetuating it. The first reference to a school in Houston is that of Mrs. Dilne Harris, who says, in her reminiscences: "The second anniversary of the battle of San Jacinto ad come and gone and mother said she hoped there would be nothing else to distract us from our studies, as the school would close in June. But there was another sensation.

One Monday morning in May, on our arrival at the school house, we found the town covered with bills. A theatrical company had arrived and would give the first performance Friday night, June 11. This was the first theatrical company to come to Texas. It not only ran the young people wild, but old people were not much better."

Professor H. F. Gillett announced in the Morning Star in 1844 that he had opened his Houston Academy, in the building of the Telegraph, at Main and Preston Streets. Terms per month for tuition in reading, writing and orthography, $2, par funds; arithmetic, grammar and geography, $3; Latin, Greek, mathematics, science and the higher branches of English education, $4. He promised to teach all branches necessary to enter any college in the United States.

The same year Professor W. J. Thurbur announced that he had opened a school in the front room, second story, of Mr. Dibble's building, corner of Main and Franklin Streets, where he would teach geography, arithmetic, English grammar, natural philosophy, orthoepy, orthography, history and composition and that he would open in the same room a night school in which English grammar would receive especial attention.

These two schools are the only early ones of which definite information is obtainable. They were, as their advertisements indicate, private schools. Two years later, however, something more definite in the way of public action was taken. In pursuance to notices in the public prints, there assembled in the Methodist church in Houston, January 2, 1846, a number of teachers and friends of education. The meeting was opened by prayer, by Rev. C. Gillett. Rev. C. Richardson was chosen president of the convention and Peter W. Gray, secretary. Rev. C. Gillett, Rev. C. Richardson, Gen. Hugh McLeod, John H. Walton, John Sayles and James Bailey were constituted a committee to consider and report to the convention, means to further its ends and promote the cause of education.

A few evenings later another meeting was held at which this committee made its report. It favored the adoption of uniform text-books by the private and public schools of Texas a memorial to be addressed to the legislature of the state at its first session; the establishment of a monthly journal to be devoted to the cause of education; the appointment of a standing committee to which persons desiring to make teaching their business might apply for positions and to which committee communities needing teachers might look for supplies; the appointment of six committees to report at the next meeting; measures for a permanent organization and to make suggestions along different lines on subjects of interest to the body; and the appointment of suitable persons to deliver addresses on the subject of education at the next meeting. Many of these ideas have been since carried out but little was accomplished at the time.

In March, 1853, the Houston Academy was opened by Messrs. A. W. Boyd and H. Moore, A. B., who brought to Houston high testimonials as to their character and ability as teachers. They announced that in the academy, pupils would be "instructed in all the branches of science that are taught in the first academies in the Union."

The annual examination and exhibition of the Houston Male and Female Academy was held about the middle of September, 1857, by James Alexander Bolinger, principal. The Scholastic year for 1858 began February 1. Early in that year Professor M. B. Franklin and Mrs. Franklin, from Kentucky, became associated with Professor Bolinger in the management of the Academy.

In October, 1857, there were ten schools in successful operation in Houston. They were those of Mr. Bolinger, Mrs. Styles, Mrs. Green, Miss Maher, Mr. and Mrs. Cunningham. Rev. C. Braun, Professor Ruter and sister, Miss Kate Van Alstyne, Miss K. Payne and Mrs. H. X. Cotton. Yet in spite of the large number of schools there was not sufficient room for the children of the city. Most of the schools were very small affairs, the pupils being huddled together in one small room. The citizens of Houston long suffered for schools adequate to the needs of the community and for this reason alone many children were sent away to obtain an education that should have been obtained at home.

Perhaps the greatest disadvantage was the lack of suitable quarters adapted to the requirements of different departments of educational work. There was no building capable of accommodating not only the primary schools, but advanced schools as well—schools in which everything from the rudiments to the higher branches could be taught. Attempts were made from time to time to meet this demand. In 1857 there were a number of good schools, all well patronized, but all of them in rooms not at all adapted to their needs. The best of these was in Masonic Hall, corner of Main and Capitol Streets and while there were fewer than 100 pupils in attendance it was crowded. All the other rooms in Houston, devoted to school purposes, would accommodate less than 200 pupils and it was estimated that there were 600 children of school age in Houston at that time. Mr. James H. Stevens had willed to the city $5,000 to be devoted to the building of an academy, whenever $10,000 should be contributed by the citizens for that purpose. Including this amount $17,000 was available at the end of 1856, for the establishment of such a school, which sum it was proposed to increase to $20,000. Some time before this the block on which the present High School Stands, had been purchased, and some steps toward the erection of a building had been taken. It had been planned that the proposed building should cost perhaps $15,000 and that the remaining $5,000 of the proposed fund should be held available for a library and for astronomical apparatus.

A meeting of prominent citizens was held; the necessary funds to complete the amount needed were subscribed at once and on September 17, 1857, the corner stone of the Houston Academy was laid. It was made a big event by the people of Houston.

The Houston Academy was completed early in the summer of 1858. It was a brick structure, 64 x 84 feet, of composite architecture, with a large open cupola with Ionic columns, which was surmounted by a gilded globe. Its height from base to cornice was 45 feet. The entire cost of the building was $21,000.

The Houston Academy was not a public school, though it was under the management of a board of directors, consisting of several leading citizens interested in the cause of education. Col. Wm. J. Hutchins was chairman of this board and it was through his influence that Dr. Asbel Smith was induced to act as principal of the school when it began its first session.

When Professor Partridge expressed a willingness to take charge of the school, Doctor Smith retired. Professor Partridge resigned as principal of the Academy about 1859 and was succeeded by Reverend Doctor Hutcherson who had been professor of Latin and Greek at the Oxford University in

Mississippi. Doctor Hutcherson remained in charge of the Academy until about 1863 or '64, when owing to failing health, he resigned, and his work was taken up by Prof. W. J. Hancock, a ripe scholar and an experienced educator. Professor Hancock remained in charge of the school for several years. He was succeeded by Professor Fitzgerald, who had formerly occupied a chair in Baylor University, when that institution was located at Independence, Washington County. Under Professor Fitzgerald's management the Academy grew in popular favor and the attendance became very large. However the Academy was a pay institution, so, when, in the early seventies, the first free-schools were opened, the attendance dropped off to such an extent that the Academy, after a desultory existence, was forced to the wall. Then the Academy association got in financial difficulties and the school was closed until, when the city took charge of its own schools, its doors were thrown open and it became the High School.

The constitution adopted by Mexico, in 1824, made it the imperative duty of the government to educate the masses. When Texas and Coahuila became a state of the Mexican Republic, its constitution declared that public schools were necessary to the life and development of a free people. Yet, under Mexico, little was actually done towards the advancement of public education, beyond the enactment of school laws and setting aside portions of land for the support of schools that were not established, and when Texas declared her independence, one of the most serious of her many grievances was that the mother country had failed to establish a system of public education for the people.

In 1839, the Texas Congress set aside three leagues (13,284 acres) of public land as school lands, in each county, the proceeds to be devoted to the establishment of a permanent school fund. In 1840, another league for each county was added to this appropriation, but the population was so sparse and public money so scarce that nothing practical was accomplished. In 1845, when Texas was admitted to the Union, her state constitution set aside one-tenth of the revenue derived from taxation for a permanent school fund. In five years Texas had 349 public schools, 360 teachers and 7,964 pupils. In 1854 the state system was improved and the school fund received a donation of two million dollars in United States bonds. The school revenue in 1860 was $80,984.

It was not until after the Civil War that free schools became active and vital forces. Being so admirably equipped and having such material resources for the successful inauguration of a permanent school system, it is amazing that the state should have delayed so long in adopting a plan. The true explanation of the delay probably lies in the fact that conditions existing in Texas before the war, were such as existed nowhere else. While there was no aristocracy in one sense of the word, yet there was an aristocracy in another sense. The people were divided into two classes, the rich and the poor, just as they are today, with this difference, that the rich were slave owners and were either planters, lawyers, doctors, or professional men, while the poor were small farmers, tradesmen, laborers, or men of no calling whatever. Social lines were not tightly drawn, it is true, still they were drawn, with the result that there was no unity of purpose or opinion on any subject that involved such close social intercourse as it was thought the public school would bring about. The well-to-do were able and did educate their own children, and thought it unfair, having done this duty to themselves and state, that they should be taxed further for the education of the children of others. On the other side, the poorer classes resented the idea of having their children educated at a charitable institution as they believed the public school to be. Thus it is seen that there was much work in the way of educating the people, of both classes, to a proper understanding of the real meaning and scope of a public school, before the wishes and intentions of the founders of the Republic could be put in practical operation.

During the continuation of the great war, all public schools were practically suspended and the school fund was expended for other purposes than education. In 1866, the office of State Superintendent of Education was created and a State Board of Education, consisting of the Governor, the Comptroller and the State Superintendent of Education was established. Those were "reconstruction days" however. The Governor and other State officials were outsiders who had been appointed to their offices by the United States Government, and were considered interlopers. They were all what was known as "Black Republicans" and necessarily had but little influence with the great mass of Texans, who regarded their every act with suspicion and distrust. Under conditions such as these it is not surprising that very little was accomplished in the way of establishing schools on a safe and proper basis until nearly a decade later.

The constitution of the state required that the public schools should be open for six months each year. As this was impossible with no other funds than that derived from the school fund, provision was made for levying a special school tax in each school district. Such school districts were given authority, in addition to levying the special school tax, to build school houses, employ competent instructors and to put the schools under professional superintendents who were held responsible for their good conduct and advancement. In 1876 only two districts in the state had taken advantage of this law and assumed control of their schools, but in 1906 their were 389 independent districts and 2217 common school districts levying local taxes. These results were obtained largely through assistance given by the Peabody fund, by the aid of which also the Sam Houston State Normal School was established.

Houston was practically the first city to take charge of its public schools. At a public meeting, held March 1, 1870, after some discussion, a petition and bill, prepared by the School Committee, were voted on and adopted, and it was determined to submit a memorial to the voters of the city for signatures. If this memorial were well indorsed, as it was believed it would be, it was hoped that when the legislature convened Houston would have the management of her public educational institutions placed in her own hands.

The committee having the matter in hand, were surprised to meet with the strongest opposition when they circulated the petition for signatures. This opposition came from several sources. The opposition used the old argument that a public school must necessarily be a charity school. This idea being dispelled they claimed that such institutions were undesirable because of the mixed social conditions they would bring about. Such arguments as these were easily refuted but there were others not so easily overcome.

At that time strong sectional and political feeling existed. Not only the people who opposed the schools but the politicians, who cared little or nothing about the schools themselves, as schools, but who saw in their proposed establishment a powerful political weapon, attacked the idea vigorously. These gentlemen argued that books, many of them of undesirable political complexion, would be forced on the public; that teachers, all chosen from one political party, would conduct the schools for partisan ends, and that a large part of the taxes levied would go for the support of some hungry politician as superintendent. In reply to these arguments it was pointed out that suitable books could be selected by a convention of experienced and reputable educators, and that a good board of school directors would select teachers, not because of their political beliefs but because of their qualifications as educators and their ability to teach. It was shown that if a board of school directors so far forgot themselves as to select ignoramuses or political hacks for teachers, such directors could be easily kicked out and good men put in their places.

Those on both sides of the question were sincere in the position they took, and both were united on one thing, which was a desire and determination to remove the schools and the cause of education out of politics. The friends of the measure believed that the only thing to do was to establish the schools.

Mistakes and blunders could be corrected as they were discovered. If for any reason the system should fail, wholly or in part, then the people, having had experience in such matters, would be in position to put in operation a better system; under a republican form of government public education was imperative and no obstacle should be placed in the way of any movement looking to its establishment.

The petition received the indorsement of the people, was forwarded to Austin, and the authority was given Houston to assume the management and control of her public schools. But there was too much opposition to the plan and nothing practical was accomplished. There were public schools here but they were controlled and largely managed by the State Superintendent at Austin, who, it was claimed, furnished the local opposition with a strong argument, by appointing his political friends to the better positions.

The public schools of Houston thus remained in an unorganized condition until December 5, 1877, when by a vote of the people, the city took charge of the schools. The schools were thoroughly organized the following year. The first superintendent of the public schools of Houston was Professor H. H. Smith, who served from 1877 to 1879, when he resigned to take charge of the State Normal School at Huntsville. Professor E. N. Clopper was elected superintendent, when Professor Smith retired, and died while in office in 1880. The Board selected Professor F. E. Burnet as Professor Clopper's successor, but difficulties arose and Professor Burnet resigned. He was followed by Professor Foute, who served from 1882 until 1884 when he was forced to resign on account of failing health, dying soon after. Professor J. E. Dow then became superintendent, serving from 1885 until 1887. Professor W. S. Sutton, a noted educator, served from 1887 until 1902. In 1903, Professor P. W. Horn was elected superintendent and has held the office ever since.

There have been many chairmen of the school board since the organization of the Houston schools, but perhaps the greatest credit for the success of the schools belongs to the first chairman, Captain E. W. Taylor, who served from 1876 to 1886, and who was superintendent, pro tem, several times. Doctor Sears, agent for the Peabody trustees, was largely instrumental in getting the people of Houston to take charge of their public schools and secured from that fund a yearly appropriation of $2,000 for the schools. Mr. Charles E. Shearn, during his service as alderman inaugurated the movement to build better school buildings and in other ways further the cause of education.

The public schools opened October 1st, 1877, under the present system and the following extract from the Houston Age, of October 2, describes the occasion under the heading. "Opening of the Houston Public Schools." The Age says: "Yesterday morning might have been seen bright eyed little boys and girls, satchels and baskets in hand, wending their way through every portion of the city, seeking different routes to their respectively assigned schools. At an early hour an Age reporter sought Professor Smith, and with him made the rounds. There are fourteen public schools in different parts of the city, which, adapted to different wards, are necessarily situated some distance apart, consequently want of time prevented us from visiting the entire number. Eight, however, were visited and we found the teachers of these highly elated with their most promising beginning, and speaking in the most flattering terms of their newly formed young acquaintances.

"We can candidly say that, despite all that has been urged to the contrary, we have never witnessed a more refined and intelligent-looking class of pupils than we found yesterday in our public schools.

"The schools are patronized by our best and most prominent citizens and are conducted by some of the most intelligent ladies in Houston. In short, the public schools of Houston are pervaded throughout with a spirit of refinement seldom found in institutions of a like character.

"In our most pleasant journey with Professor Smith, we found that gentleman fully alive to the onerous labors attending his highly responsible position. * * * * *

"Our first visit was paid to the white school of the Third ward, where we found Miss C. G. Forshey, who as principal, was assisted by Mrs. M. T. Reddish. They were busily engaged in assigning the many pupils to the various grades and classes. Miss Forshey was much pleased with her school. She had under her charge fifty girls and fifty boys, ranging from the first to the sixth grades. In cleanliness, good appearance and polite deportment Miss Forshey's school would be hard to surpass. We may here mention that the pupils are graded according to their mathematical proficiency, the first grades being most primary.

"After leaving the Third we visited the Fourth ward, in which, confining ourselves to this side of the bayou, we found five public schools. The first on our way was that conducted by Mrs. Z. M. Noble, as principal, assisted by Miss Becky Hillyard. In this Noble, as principal, assisted by Miss Becky Hillyard. In this school were 63 pupils, 39 in the second grade and 24 in the first grade. This school house is beautifully situated on Dallas Street, with a large play-ground and other modern school conveniences. The pupils are bright, intelligent children who gave marked attention to the preliminary instruction of Professor Smith, who greeted all the teachers and pupils with encouraging speeches.

"The school of Mrs. M. H. Wynne, in the same ward, numbered 21 pupils, all in the sixth grade and taught by Mrs. Wynne herself. This is the only school confined to one grade and that an advanced one. Here Professor Smith made an examination which reflected great credit on Mrs. Wynne.

"Mrs. Kate de Pelchin, also in the Fourth ward, has under her efficient charge 13 boys and 18 girls, in the fourth and fifth grades.

"In the Second ward, near the Union Depot, is situated the school for that district. It is under the able supervision of Miss Annie Jones, assisted by Mrs. W. M. Roper. These ladies have a new building for their school which has 50 in the first grade and 24 in the second.

"In the same neighborhood is the colored school for the Second ward. There are 72 pupils in this school, ranging from the first to the fourth grade. Mrs. C. E. Johnson is principal. She is assisted by Mrs. J. T. McGee.

"The Third ward colored school is taught by Mrs. L. C. Fisher and H. Dibble, both colored, the former acting as principal and the latter as assistant. They have 89 pupils ranging from the first to the fourth grades.

"Gregory Institute is the colored school for the Fourth ward, the largest school in the city. H. C. Hardy, principal; A. Osborn and Miss Brinkley, assistants; all colored. The pupils number 170, ranging from the first to the seventh grades."

No details of the teachers or enrollment for the other schools were given by the Age, but at a meeting of the teachers and school officials, held October the 13th, Professor Smith made the following report:

"First ward—whites attending, 78; Second ward, 110; Third ward, 118; Fourth ward, 146; Fourth ward south of the bayou—195, making the total of white pupils 617. The number last Saturday was a total of 512, thus showing an increase of more than 100 during the week. The total number of pupils attending the colored schools is 618, an increase of one over the whites. This makes the grand total 1,235 attending our public schools, increasing the number nearly 300 since the opening."

At that meeting Superintendent Smith expressed himself as greatly pleased with such results and expressed confidence in the successful future of the great work that had been placed in his hands. At that meeting the Board of School Trustees issued the following notice:

"Editors of the Age:—The public schools of Houston are now in operation and working in a satisfactory manner, and the Board of Trustees report with pleasure that the number of pupils is daily increasing.

"In view of the fact that there is a large number of children in attendance who are under eight years of age and over fourteen years, the trustees would call the attention of parents and guardians to section 7 of an ordinance to establish and provide for public schools in Houston, which reads as follows: 'All children between the ages of eight and fourteen years, living in the city, shall be entitled to the benefits of the available school fund of the city under this ordinance, without regard to race or color. No child shall be admitted to the public schools of the city who does not reside in the city, and white and colored children shall, in all cases, be taught in separate schools.' signed, E. W. Taylor, B. C. Simpson, R. Cotter, Board of Trustees."

The public schools having been successfully inaugurated, and the people having perfect confidence in the gentlemen who had control of them, all opposition ceased and since then the course of the schools has ever been upward. Many changes have been made and improvements introduced, but the fundamental basis of the system is today the same as that adopted in 1877. The growth of the schools has kept pace with the growth of the city of Houston. In 1877 the schools opened with an attendance of 1,235. During the first week of the session 1885–86, there was an enrollment of 1,725, and this enrollment had grown to 3,604 in 1891. The following facts, taken from an address made by Prof. P. W. Horn, superintendent of the Houston Schools, shows how phenomenal had been the growth of the scholastic population of Houston and of the schools under his charge up to the close of 1909:

"The city schools furnish perhaps the best means of indicating the real growth of the city. While the United States Government takes a census of all the people every ten years, the state of Texas counts her school children every year. In this way the school census, most of the time, furnishes later information than the government census. For instance the government census of 1900 made Houston the second city in the state, the school census of 1909 indicated that Houston was the first city in the state, though she was surpassed a year later by San Antonio, according to the government count. Houston had 17,115 children of the school age, while no other city in the state had as much as 17,000. If you would trace the growth of the city it may be done by reference to the school census of different years. For instance, in 1900 the school census was 8,492, or less than half of what it was in 1909. This shows that our population had more than doubled in nine years. In 1891, on the other hand, we had 6,330 children of school age. In eighteen years the population had almost multiplied by 3. Back in 1881 there were 2,861 children of school age on the census roll. This means that in 28 years to 1909 Houston's school population was more than multiplied by six. In 1880 the government census gave the total population of Houston as 16,664. In other words there were in 1880 fewer people, of all ages in Houston than there were school children in 1909. In 1881 there were actually enrolled in school 1,010 white and 786 colored children, 1,796 in all. In 1908 there were actually enrolled in school 10,631 children. There were in 1909 more children in the high school building and the Fannin building together, than there were, white and colored, in all the schools in Houston in 1881. In 1881 there were 19 white and 11 colored teachers—30 in all—employed in the city schools. In 1909 there were more than 30 employed in the high school alone. The session of that year employed 202 white and 62 colored teachers, 264 in all. The next session demanded the services of approximately 300 teachers. Of the teachers employed in 1881, only one, Professor G. Duvernoy, remained with the faculty in 1909.

"In 1881 the entire expenditure of the city school system for maintenance was $15,369.24. In 1909 it amounted to $231,636.56. In 1881 the average salary of teachers was $43.53 a month. In 1909 it approximated $65. In 1881, there were 7 school buildings for whites and 5 for colored children. In 1909 there were 16 for whites and 10 for colored children. The average number of rooms to the building had greatly increased also. In 1903–04 there were 8,811 children enrolled; in the session of 1908–09, there were 10,651. The actual increase in enrollment was 1,840. In 1903–04, there were 147 white and 53 colored teachers employed, making 200 in all. The 266 teachers of 1908 showed a growth of the teaching force of nearly one-third. In the matter of school buildings there was even a greater degree of progress within the five years ending 1909. Within that period the city had erected 5 new brick buildings, for white children—the Allen, Reagan, Lubbock, Lamar and Travis school buildings—and 3 substantial frame buildings for colored children—those of the Douglass, Luckie and Dunbar schools. It gave in the same period, additional rooms at the Jones, Dow, Taylor, Hawthorne, Austin and Longfellow schools for white, and at the Gregory school for colored children. At the end of the period there was in course of erection an annex to the high school building that would add 30 per cent to its capacity. The high school annex was completed in 1910 and the additional enrollment for that year was about 1,200 pupils.

"Without entering upon the discussion of a political question, it is but justice to call attention to the dates given in the foregoing, which show that all these great improvements have been made since the adoption of the commission form of government. For some years previous to the adoption of that form of government, the schools had received only perfunctory attention; had, in a measure, been permitted to languish, and but little or no advance had been made. So soon as the commission form was adopted, the schools were given that intelligent attention their great importance demanded and wonderful changes were wrought. In carrying out their liberal and progressive policy towards the schools, the commissioners have frequently had to discount the future and anticipate the growth of the city. This has not always met with the approval and indorsement of even some of the best friends of the schools, but results have shown the wisdom of the city fathers. A notable example of this was when the Fannin school was located on its present site. It was considered to be away out in the suburbs and some of the best citizens asked the school board why they did not locate the school in Galveston at once and be done with it. The school was located as originally planned, however, and by 1909, it was one of the most crowded schools in the city. The Allen school now divides the district which the Fannin at first had to serve, and there is a growing demand for a third school in the same district. In 1896 there were only six rooms in the Sidney Sherman school in the Fifth ward. In 1909 there was a 12-room building and another 12-room building and an 8-room building in the same old district.

"The opposition spoken of did not spring from enmity to the schools or to those in charge of them, but was due entirely to a failure on the part of a large number of the most intelligent citizens, to realize the phenomenal growth and expansion of Houston. They desired to be conservative, that was all. As already noted they objected to the Fannin school, but that objection was as peaceful acquiescence compared to the storm of indignation that broke out when the present high school was erected. The school board was accused of stupendous extravagance in erecting a high school building larger than the city would need in a hundred years. In fourteen years the building was not only full, but an annex had to be added increasing its capacity one-third, despite which, it is now painfully crowded An idea of the rapid growth of the school population of Houston may be formed from the statement that the schools opened with 1,300 pupils more in 1908–9 than on the opening day of the previous session. This indicates that the later growth is the larger growth in the city schools.

"All that has been said in the foregoing refers solely to what may be termed the material side of the schools. The real value of an educational system cannot be shown by an array of figures nor estimated by the outlay of dollars and cents. There is a higher and better standard of measurement—the intellectual and practical development of the system. In this regard the people of Houston have every reason to take pride in their schools, for it has been the constant aim of those schools to minister more and more largely to the practical necessities as well as to the intellectual development of the pupils who attend them. It is aimed to give to each boy and girl that which will best fit him or her to meet the actual duties of practical life. With this end in view manual training and domestic science have been installed in the schools. The boys are taught to use their hands, for most of them will have to use their hands when it comes to a question of earning a living, and all of them will have to use their hands to some extent. The boys are taught practical work in regular workshops. Wood work, carpentry, blacksmith and machine work; in fact everything that will tend to make them practical workers when the time comes for them to face the serious problems of life. The girls are taught domestic science. The teaching is not theoretical but intensely practical. Classes of girls are actually at work learning not only the value of food, but how to prepare and cook it. Sewing is also taught and thus the girls turned out by the Houston schools are more thoroughly equipped for life's duties. The business course at the high school is another feature of great practical value. It affords boys and girls an opportunity to obtain a knowledge of bookkeeping, stenography and typewriting. Many who have taken that course are holding responsible positions and filling them well. The night school is another valuable feature of the Houston schools. This, too, is a development of recent years. Every pupil enrolled has to furnish evidence that he is employed in the daytime. No pupil under twelve years of age is admitted. Many pupils over school age have been admitted, some grown men in business. Most of the latter are foreigners anxious to learn the English language. Young women, employed in the daytime, have been taught to cook and sew. Young men, at work in shops in the daytime, have been taught mechanical drawing and other technical things essential to their progress as artisans. Many boys and girls employed in stores come at night for education that will add to their efficiency as workers.

"At the Rusk school in the Second ward, particular effort is made to adopt the work to special needs. At this school there is manual training work, domestic science work and kindergarten work. There is a special room for exceptional and subnormal pupils, one of the few in the Southern States.

"In 1909 there were four kindergartens connected with the Houston public school system; one each at the following schools; Allen, Rusk, Reagan and Travis. The expense of maintaining these kindergarten schools is borne by organizations outside the regular schools.

"The organization of 'a mothers' club' for active work at each school has been of inestimable assistance and benefit. Most of these clubs have been in existence only since 1907 and in 1908 and 1909, they expended in money, $21,548.18, besides the great amount of personal attention and work given by the members. These sums and efforts increase in amounts each year."

The Mothers Clubs and the Art League have aided the progressive scientific movements in the Houston schools. Hygienic lunches, at all the schools, trained nurses at some of them, the examination of the eyes of all the children by the school oculist Dr. W. W. Ralston and medical lectures by specialists and physicians, all of these things have marked the distinctive progressive spirit of the Houston schools under Superintendent Horn, the ablest public school educator in the state, who combines scholarship with rare executive and practical ability.

The teachers and principals of the schools are still miserably underpaid and that fact constitutes the shame of the city in connection with its public schools. That so capable a corps of educators can be recruited for so ridiculously small a remuneration as is paid them, is one of the civic mysteries. Visitors and committees from many cities are wont to come to Houston to study the advanced methods and equipment of the public schools here.

Professor P. W. Horn, superintendent of Houston's public schools, thus summarizes the history of the schools for the decade ending October 1, 1911:

"Ten years ago Houston had just heard the returns from the federal census and was proud to know that her population was given as 44,633. Now she has just learned that the census gives her 78,800 people, and she is disappointed even at that figure.

"At that time the streets of Houston were practically all unpaved and the highest business buildings were only a few stories high. Now she has miles of paving of various kinds, with numbers of office buildings from 10 to 16 stories high.

"The schools have grown as much in the ten years as has the city itself. At that time the scholastic census said that there were 8,492 children of school age. Now the census says that we have 19,112. It is a fact that the former census was based on the ages from 8 to 17 and that the present census has added a year and counts children from 7 to 17. The addition of this year accounts for the fact that the school census has grown so much more rapidly than the federal census indicates.

"Ten years ago there were actually in school 7,253 children. Last year there were 12,868.

"Ten years ago we had 16 school buildings, with 107 school rooms. Last year we had 26 school buildings and 299 school rooms.

"Ten years ago we had 147 teachers. Now we have 325.

"The enrollment in the high school has increased even more rapidly than that in the school systems as a whole. Ten years ago there were 544 pupils enrolled in the white high school building. Last year there were 1,018. While the schools as a whole have increased 77 per cent, the pupils in the high school have increased 87 per cent.

"Ten years ago the total value of all the school property of the city was $430,250. Last year it was $1,000,000.

"Ten years ago, of the ten buildings for white children, five were brick and five were frame. Of the six buildings for colored pupils, one was brick and five were frame.

"Probably the most striking of the things that have been added to the schools during the past ten years are the subjects of manual training and domestic science. These departments are the growth of the last five years and are probably among the most popular features of the schools.

"In the domestic science department work of similar practical value is done for girls. They are taught to cook and to sew. Their cooking is not confined to desserts, or to fancy dishes but includes those things which the average girl is likely to need to know how to cook in the home of her parents, or in her own. The sewing which the girls learn is the kind which they will need in their actual every-day lives.

"Ten years ago there was little or no special attention given to the physical development or welfare of the school children. Now we have a physical director who looks after the physical development of all the school children, and also a woman who gives all of her time to the physical development of the girls of the high school. Not only is there formal gymnastic training in the gymnasium of the high school, and in the outdoor gymnasiums at a number of the ward schools, but there are schedules of games and of contests between the various schools.

"Ten years ago all the children in the schools were using the community drinking cups. Now in most of the buildings, hygienic drinking fountains have been installed so that the children drink without touching their lips to a vessel of any kind, and thus avoid one fruitful source of the transmission of germs of contagious diseases.

"Even up to three years ago there was no medical inspection for the school children. If a teacher thought that a child had measles or smallpox, or that his eyes looked as if they might be contagiously sore, she acted on her own judgment and sent the pupil home. Now we have a paid medical inspector who examines all of the children once a year, and examines special cases at any time they may be sent to him. He excludes from school, children whose physical condition is such that their presence in the room might endanger the health of the other children. There is also a school nurse who goes into the homes of the people when it may be necessary and assists with her advice, seeing to it that the suggestions of the doctor are carried out. This work has done at great deal. Not only for the welfare of the children who were directly affected, but also for the others, by keeping them from the danger of contagion.

"In most of our buildings today there are rest rooms, or emergency hospital rooms fitted up for use by teacher or pupil in case of sickness or accident. Many of them are of such nature that they would be a credit even in a modern hospital.

"Ten years ago it is probable that there was not a piano in any one of the public school buildings of Houston. Now there is at least one in every school building for white children. Some buildings have two or three pianos. A number of the colored schools possess pianos. The influence of the piano in giving instruction to the pupils and in the more matter of coming into and out of the building is greater than one would at first suppose.

"At several of the school buildings now there are also graphophones, with records of classical music for the benefit of the children. At a number of these same buildings there are stereopticons and stereoscopes with views to be used in illustrating the work in history and geography. The stereopticon is one of the strong factors in the work of a good modern school. In many instances the stereopticon, the phonograph and the piano have not cost the board anything, but were purchased by the Mothers' Club at the building.

"This brings us to one of the most vital of all the improvements made in the past ten years, namely, the Mothers' Clubs. Ten years ago there were no mothers' clubs in our schools. Now there is one at every building for white children and at several of the buildings for colored children. During the past five years these clubs have raised and have expended for the schools the sum of $38,070.67. This has, for the most part, been expended for things the board could not at the time have secured.

"However, this sum of money gives only a faint idea of the real greatness of the work of the Mothers' Club.

"Ten years ago there were no night schools connected with our city system. During last year there were such schools with an enrollment of 524 boys and girls, men and women. There is no age limit in the night schools. In some instances men of 40 to 50 years of age attend. The schools are intended for people who must work during the daytime, but who still are desirous of obtaining more education. An effort is made to teach the simplest and most practical things, which the students will put to the greatest use in

121

actual life. For instance, there are classes in reading, writing, arithmetic and spelling. There are also classes in cabinet making, mechanical drawing and forging for the boys. There are classes in cooking and sewing for the girls. There are classes in bookkeeping, in typewriting and in stenography. There are special classes for foreigners who desire to learn to speak and read and write the English language. These classes are held three nights in the week, on Monday, Wednesday and Friday. They are making it possible for the man or woman past school age, or for the child of school age who must help support the family, to obtain the education that will be of the greatest practical use.

"In recent years also there has been a marked movement in favor of the socialization of our school buildings and the widest possible use of our school plants. The present idea is that the schools are for the education not of the children alone, but of the community as a whole. Organizations that have for their object the betterment of the community are welcomed to the use of the building. Improvement clubs hold meetings and lectures are given in the school building. The health of the community is considered and lectures on matters of hygiene are given from time to time.

"There has also been a distinct change in the standards of school buildings to be erected. Years ago, the city stopped putting up frame buildings for the white school children. During the past year it has been definitely adopted as a policy that no school buildings will in the future be erected that are not fire-proof. It was also decided that all school buildings to be erected in the future should be constructed along the most modern ideas as to heating, lighting and ventilation; should have auditoriums and should be so constructed as to be capable of the widest possible use by the community.

"The first of these new buildings to be built will doubtless be the one to take the place of the old Rusk school, which burned last year. The plans that have been drawn for this building are such as to mark a new epoch in the history of school house construction in Texas. When the proceeds of the bond issue of $500,000 voted by the people last May, shall become available, all of the wooden buildings for white school children in the city will be torn down and will be replaced with modern buildings of the kind indicated above. This will mark the last of the old regime, so far as school buildings in Houston are concerned.

"The handling of the financial details of the schools has also been revolutionized in recent years. They are now in the hands of the business representatives of the school board. He looks after such matters as the purchase of supplies, the making of repairs, the keeping of accounts. By giving all his time to the work, he is able, with the help of an assistant, to keep matters in systematic order. He can tell at a moment's notice how much has been spent for a given purpose up to a given time and how much of the year's appropriation for that purpose remains unspent.

"It may be interesting in conclusion to speculate as to the progress of the next ten years. If the same ratio of increase is kept up, which prevailed during the past ten years, Houston will have a population of 138,688, without making any allowance for territorial expansions. There will be 22,776 pupils enrolled in the schools, which is 10,000 more than we have today. There will be 42 school buildings instead of 26. There will be 2,083 pupils in the white high school alone."

TABLE OF COMPARATIVE FIGURES.

	1900–01	1910–11
Total population, census 1900	44,633	78,800
Children in scholastic census	8,492	19,112
Children enrolled in city schools	7,253	12,868
Number of school buildings	16	26
Number of school rooms	107	299
Number of teachers	147	325
Pupils in white high school	544	1,018
Value of all school property	$430,250	$1,000,000

In addition to its splendid public schools Houston has a number of denominational and private schools. The Academy of the Sacred Heart and St. Agnes Academy, both owned and controlled by the Catholics are high-grade preparatory schools and have been mentioned elsewhere in this volume. The Barnett school is a first-class academy for boys, and the Misses Waldo have built up in Westmoreland a select school for girls that is in high repute. There are other private schools of repute and the Y. M. C. A. teaches night classes in many subjects that are giving valuable training to those unable or unqualified to attend the public schools. Two business colleges, Draughan's and Massey's colleges do a flourishing business and there is a dental school that gives special training in dental surgery and confers the degree of D. D. S., on its graduates.

At the several hospitals and the bacteriological department of the city hall laboratory work and studies in microscopy are carried on. Nothing more is attempted in this work in regard to the private schools than to mention several of the more prominent of them. The greatest educational enterprise in Houston, the Rice Institute is unique in history and character and will be treated in a separate chapter.

The district schools of Harris County were organized in 1884 under the jurisdiction and management of the county judge and commissioners court, composed of Hon. E. P. Hamblen, Frank S. Burke, Robert Blalock, H. C.

Throckmorton and George Ellis. The county was divided into 30 school districts which number has been increased to 52.

L. F. Smith was the first superintendent. Henry B. Cline and B. L. James also served prior to the election of Professor L. L. Pugh, who has served for the past nine years, and under his jurisdiction the county schools have reached their present high plane as indicated by the following statistics taken from his annual report of August 3, 1911:

There were then 161 teachers employed, 10 male and 151 female, and the scholastic population was 6,177. There were 82 school buildings for white schools and 31 for colored, of which 18 were brick and 95 frame, with a total valuation of $262,000. The amount paid to teachers was $60,530. W. G. Smiley, J. S. Deady, R. L. Robinson, Dr. L. C. Hanna and Dr. E. E. Grant compose the present Harris County Board of Education.

CHAPTER XII - THE RICE INSTITUTE

Houston's Inheritance Through a Tragedy. The Story of a Famous Crime. A Princely Gift. A Biography of William M. Rice. The Initial Donation. A Continuating Benevolence. The Monument to the Childless Man. William M. Rice as Philanthropist and Business Man. Dr. Edgar Odell Lovett elected President of the Institute. Laying the Corner Stone. The City's Dominant Institution.

Inheriting through a tragedy, on Sunday evening, September 23, 1900, at 7:30 o'clock, the people of the city of Houston became the legal heir of a kind, old man, and as the beneficiaries of his bounty became rightfully entitled to about $4,000,000 which had been set aside for educational purposes, to be administered by trustees in behalf of Houston's white citizens and their children.

The donor, dying at that hour at the hand of his trusted body servant, was truly the victim of his generosity to the people of Houston and sealed his gift with his own blood, for the knowledge that the gift had been made, led, according to testimony credited by the highest courts, to one of the most gigantic conspiracies in modern criminology's annals, having as its purpose the spoilation of the city of its inheritance and of the aged man of his life.

The life of the giver was lost, and that the gift was not lost to its beneficiaries was due to one of those strange chapters of coincidences that form the romance of the history of crime and appal the stoutest hearts with the conviction that there is some strange mechanism of fate, providence or chance that uncovers the skillfully concealed traces of felony and by the seeming accident of insignificant detail exposes one of the joined links of the chain of crime by which its whole buried length is dragged out to the garish light of day.

The omission of a single letter in a proper name written on a check, cost the owner of that name a fortune of millions, branded him as a murderer, and incarcerated him under sentence of death in a grim New York penitentiary. Because the letter "I" was left out of the given name of Albert T. Patrick, a suspicion was aroused that developed into a legal certainty and put the owner of that name behind the bars, under sentence for murder, and, as a corollary, permitted Houston to inherit a school endowment whose assets are now nearly ten million dollars.

The man who died under a chloroform soaked sponge, held in a towel cone over his sleeping face, was William M. Rice, and he was 84 years old when he was murdered in his bed at the Berkshire apartments at 500 Madison Avenue, New York City by his only companion, his valet, Charles Jones. While the aged man was dying two old ladies, his friends, were ringing the bell at the door of his apartments where they had come with gifts of cake and wine for their sick friend. Inside the ante-room the murderer crouched, uncertain in his own mind whether it was the door bell that was clamoring or whether it was the loud alarm of his frightened conscience that called him to remove the death dealing cone from the face of his dying master.

It is not the purpose to tell here the story of that crime. Its details make it one of the causes celebre of criminal history. With the possible exception of the Thaw case the crime has attracted more publicity and been given more newspaper space than any other that ever happened in America where the victim was only a private citizen. The valet, Jones, who actually committed the act of murder according to his own tale, was allowed to go free of justice, and the lawyer, Albert T. Patrick, accused of planning it, after a sensational trial and a brilliant defense conducted before the higher courts by himself, was convicted of murder and is today a life prisoner at Sing-Sing, the death penalty having been commuted by executive clemency. There is hardly a detail of that trial that is not in dispute, but the jury that convicted and the courts that affirmed accepted the following as true facts:

That Patrick was personally unknown to W. M. Rice, and that he was hated by the latter because of hostile litigation in which Patrick had been engaged.

That Patrick met and corrupted Jones, and through Jones learned of the habits of the old man, of his few friends, of his break with his relatives, and of the fact that he had by a will of 1896 donated the bulk of his property to the William M. Rice Institute of Houston, Texas.

That Patrick conspired with Jones to forge a will of later date increasing the legacies to all the beneficiaries of the old will, and leaving legacies to every person with a claim on the estate but leaving the bulk of the fortune to Patrick instead of the Houston Institute. The old will was to be left in existence to prevent relatives trying to break the new one as all inherited more largely under the bogus than the true will. Patrick was made administrator of the will and forged a power of attorney, bogus checks for sums in banks aggregating some $250,000, and all papers necessary to enable him to enter into complete and immediate possession of the fortune of William M. Rice on the death of the latter. All these papers together with a series of letters from Rice to Patrick in which Patrick was made to appear as a trusted legal counsellor, were in evidence to show motive for the crime.

Particularly damning in its effect was a letter purporting to be from Rice to Patrick asking that the body of the writer be cremated immediately on death and expressing a horror of burial and embalming. This letter gave opportunity for immediate disposition of the body.

On Sunday, September 16, 1900, the plant of the merchants and Planters Oil Company at Houston was destroyed by fire. W. M. Rice owned 75 per cent of the stock and letters came during the week asking that he furnish $250,000 to rebuild. This would utilize the supply of ready cash in the banks and the expressed intention of W. M. Rice to send all or a part of this money on Monday, September 24, is believed to have forced his death on Sunday.

Following that death, and before announcing it, Patrick and Jones took possession of all the papers of the dead man including both wills, the alleged forgery bearing date of June 3, 1900. Some of the checks were cashed and attempts to cash another caused the discovery of the misspelled name. By chance, if chance it be, this check was shown to Walter H. Wetherbee, a clerk in Swensen's private bank and the man who was one of the witnesses to the will of 1896. Wetherbee remembered that Patrick had suggested to him, in tentative fashion at least, a proposition for a bogus will, signed by the original witnesses, and at once suspected that W. M. Rice was dead. Jones, on being telephoned to, said that the check, which was for $25,000, was all right, but admitted that Mr. Rice was dead and that he had notified the doctor and Mr. Patrick.

Telegrams from Houston, signed by Attorney James A. Baker and Mr. F. A. Rice, a brother to the dead man, forced a delay in the cremation of the body which Patrick then ordered embalmed. Later an autopsy was held and a congested condition of the lungs discovered such as would result from chloroform.

When Messrs. Baker and Rice arrived from Texas, Patrick weakened gradually and finally, after offering to give the Rice Institute $3,000,000 or $5,000,000 or any sum Mr. Baker might name, relinquished all control of the papers of William M. Rice and agreed to the probate of the will of 1896. Later he was tried and convicted of murder, on the corroborative circumstantial evidence and the confession of Jones who swore the crime was instigated by Patrick.

In the American Magazine of May, 1907, Hon. Arthur Train, then assistant district attorney of New York County, tells in strikingly dramatic fashion the story of the discovery of the links of circumstantial evidence and graphically presents the case of the state in narrative form.

Patrick has constantly maintained his innocence and insists that a thrice perjured, self-confessed murderer such as valet Jones, is unworthy of any credence. The conviction of Patrick and the setting aside as forgeries of the alleged will of June 30, 1900, giving the estate to Patrick, left the Rice estate to the people of Houston.

The manner of the death of William M. Rice and the dramatic litigation that followed it, have absorbed public attention to the exclusion of the study of the character of the reserved, quiet and solitary man whose generosity is to bear such rich and abundant fruit.

William Marsh Rice, as the donor of a fund for the establishment of an institute for the advancement of literature, science and art, for a public library and a great polytechnic school, stands without a rival as Houston's greatest philanthropist. The institute now being built will take the form of a great university with emphasis on the practical arts and sciences. The endowment gifts of William Marsh Rice aggregate at present $9,450,000 at cautious and conservative estimates made in September, 1911, by the board of trustees. The great, distinctive school the endowment will create will be without alliance with or dependence on either church or state.

The man who gave this princely gift in perpetuity to the white citizens of Houston and their children, was one of the earliest inhabitants of the city.

Family records would indicate that he came to Houston in 1838, when the city was little more than a year old. He was a native of Springfield, Massachusetts, and was born in 1819, coming from Springfield to Texas as a young man with a load of merchandise on a sailing vessel. He was defrauded of most of his stock by a sharper on reaching Galveston and wrote to his father about the occurrence. The father urged him to come home but the young man proudly replied that he would never return until he brought back with him more money than he took away.

In Houston he conducted a merchandise business on Main Street near the site of the Houston Land and Trust Company's office building. His first store was a tent. His early stock of goods is said to have been largely brogan shoes and bandana handkerchiefs. When he had built a little store he was accustomed to cook his own meals, work all day in the store and sleep on the counter at night. Constantly he invested his earnings and savings in Houston and Texas property.

When the Civil War broke out his sympathies were with the North and he went to Mexico, remaining there until the conclusion of the struggle, when he returned to Houston where his opinions were known and respected. After the war he became a director and the financial agent of the H. & T. C. Railroad, with headquarters in New York City for convenience in making purchases. Thereafter his home was in the North but it was his habit to come to Houston every year and spend the winter months here. He was always deeply interested in Houston affairs and invested in its enterprises, being one of the stockholders in the first electric light company ever formed here, but he did not like to hold corporate offices of any kind. Those living who knew him, knew him as young men know old men. They describe him as a man very quiet, dignified and reserved, chary of speech but stimulating deep interest by the remarks he made, a close student of men whom he sometimes embarrassed by his pointed scrutiny, but making few friends and few acquaintances.

In manner he was cold, icy, unapproachable, but the few men to whom he gave his friendship discovered that he would go his full length in their behalf and that there was no exhausting his friendship. One of these friends was Sam Houston. On the occasion of a political campaign in which Houston was interested he was shown the list of subscribers and said: "Billy Rice's name ought to be here."

"General, he will not give anything."

"Oh, yes he will; he will give $100." General Houston then went to see his friend, finding him in the store. The conversation was very stately: "Good morning, William, good morning; are you very busy this morning?"

"Well, General, we always find something to do, always find something to do."

"William, we are going to have a very interesting campaign this fall and we shall need some money."

"Well, General, you know business has been very dull, and collections have been very bad, quite bad, General."

"Yes, William, but I have put you down on the list for $100."

"Well, General, I could not possibly pay any more than that, certainly not any more than that; but, General, if you feel you need that much I shall have to spare it to you."

Owing to Houston's friendship Mr. Rice is said to have secured a contract to carry the mails between Houston and Austin, which mail route was one of his early enterprises.

So unapproachable was the manner of Wm. M. Rice that men were often afraid to solicit contributions from him. On one occasion a carpet was needed for a church and the committee asked him for a contribution to help buy the carpet. He refused to help, but after the committee had gone, sent a clerk, had the church measured and as his own gift sent a beautiful carpet and one more costly than they had hoped to buy.

The first intimation of an intention to give Houston a library and school was made in similar fashion. In 1890 Houston was in great need of school facilities. Some of the citizens conceived the plan of securing subscriptions to aggregate $100,000 to build a high school.

Mr. E. Raphael, then a member of the city school board, who had known Mr. Rice since 1868, approached him for a subscription. He told him the Houston Academy was falling down, that the city had no money and that a school was needed. In a manner almost curt Mr. Rice said abruptly: "I will not give a cent. It is the city's business to build its schools, not that of private individuals. But I am going to establish an educational institute to be built after my death. I will give my note for $200,000 to start it and I want you to be one of the trustees." This bolt from the blue was the first intimation to anyone that Mr. Rice had any such idea. He asked Mr. Raphael to notify other trustees. They were not selected all at once but one name at a time with an interval of perhaps a week or a month between each selection. The original board of trustees was William M. Rice of New York City, and F. A. Rice, James A. Baker, Jr., E. Raphael, C. Lombardi, J. E. McAshan and A. S. Richardson, all of Houston.

Of this number William M. Rice, F. A. Rice and A. S. Richardson are dead and have been succeeded by William M. Rice, Jr., B. B. Rice, and Dr. E. O. Lovett.

The initial gift of $200,000 was made in the form of a note, dated May 13, 1891, bearing interest at the rate of 2 1/2 per cent annually, and payable at the death of the donor. This was given to the trustees who were selected for life and given power to elect members to fill vacancies as they might occur. These trustees were given plenary power over the fund with such additions as might be made to it, with instructions to do nothing except care for the money so long as Mr. Rice himself might be alive. He was himself one of the trustees and his dietum as to an investment of the fund or disposition of it in a business way was conclusive.

It became the habit of Mr. Rice to make some additional donation to this endowment fund each year. In 1892 he gave 10,000 acres of agricultural land in Jones County, and the following year he gave 50,000 acres of pine timber lands in Louisiana. The timber rights on these pine lands were sold by the trustees in 1911 for a sum aggregating over $4,000,000, while the title to the land itself was retained.

In 1894, Mr. Rice deeded to the fund the Rice Hotel property and a tract of land on Louisiana Street of about 12 acres, known as the Rice Institute tract. At that time both the donor and the trustees expected that the buildings of the institute would be erected on this tract of land. Other gifts followed, so that at the time of his death property then estimated in value at $1,500,000, had been donated to the institute.

By bequest of his true will the institute was named as residuary legatee of his entire fortune although bequests to his relatives and others aggregated several hundred thousand dollars. The property going to his estate at his death was variously estimated at from $3,000,000 to $4,000,000. This endowment, according to the estimate made by the trustees in the fall of 1911, is now worth $9,450,000. These figures are regarded as being very conservative.

To Mr. Raphael and to other members of the trustees and to relatives, Mr. Rice several times remarked that he had made his fortune in Houston and that he wanted to leave the institution as a monument, the endowment to go on for all time to come as a perpetual supply fund for its needs. At one time he thought of making the gift to Dunellen, New Jersey, where he owned a home, but patriotism and memories of the early days in Houston, the days of hardship and struggle, the days of his youth and his ambition and his hope, fixed his choice on the town to which he had come as a pioneer in almost the first year of its existence.

When the announcement was first made in Houston that the institute was to be given, the citizens were enthusiastic in their praise. J. S. Rice, a nephew, then a young man, said: "Uncle William, the people are saying lots of nice things about you and your gift." The old man hesitated, then said "Jo, your father has a monument in his boys. I have no children." It was the warm yearning in the heart of the childless man that men called cold, to be remembered in his home town, and the children of his fellow citizens will, for countless generations, perchance, drink at the fountain of learning that the childless man left as a monument.

William M. Rice was not himself a well-educated man, but he was profoundly imbued with a sense of education's value and desired that the children of the brave pioneer generation should not lack the best and most effective sort of education.

He had very decided ideas as to what constituted an education and wanted those things taught most that would not leave the graduate with a feeling of being helpless and stranded with no trade, occupation or craft. He believed in educating the hand as much as the head and wanted the students at the school he gave to be in position to exploit the resources of their state, and to stand at the head of its crafts as well as professions, to be able to get, with capable, trained hands and heads, the treasures from mines, forests and prairies, and hence the polytechnic feature of the school will always be emphasized in accordance with the wish of its founder, although its scope has already grown beyond the fondest dreams of the founder, and its character and work will give it full university rank among the educational institutions of America.

So the heart of William M. Rice remained in Houston until his death, yes and will remain here in active benevolence for as long as one may dare to look into the future or to prophesy as to its happenings.

Among other gifts to the institute was an art collection, now insured for $50,000, which was made by Mr. Rice and by friends at his instance. Art, it will be noted, was one of the things that was to be "advanced" by the institute. The pictures in the collection are well chosen and some of them are of rare artistic merit. William M. Rice had an eye for the beautiful, and the charter, that sets out the scope of the institution on which he collaborated when it was drawn up, mentions Art together with Literature and Science as one of the things in which education is to be given.

To the personal characteristics of William M. Rice, that have been noted should be added the fact that he enjoyed exceptionally good health, was a student of hygienics, advocated open air exercises and a careful diet, drank nothing alcoholic and abstained even from tea and coffee, as well as from all greasy foods. He lived largely on cereals and fruit, ate very little meat and did not use tobacco in any form. He was a close trader and did not take undue advantage but made close contracts in good faith, was scrupulous to live up to them, and rigidly demanded that others do the same. Mr. Rice was regarded as a hard man but Mr. Arthur B. Cohn, who was his secretary for many years, and has been the business manager of the Rice Institute since

Mr. Rice's death, says that Mr. Rice gave much to poor people where it was found they merited it, and that he never refused to furnish the amount necessary to erect independent school houses in the county, and that he often helped young men of ambition to secure an education. He detested notoriety in connection with any charity and absolute secrecy was enjoined on his secretary and on the recipients of all his gifts. He was not a society man, and only in business developed any sociability. He was not a church member but was a subscriber to the Christ Church and to other congregations. The story of his early business life is one of struggle during which he occupied humble positions. He never squandered money and never sold property that came into his possession, save under extraordinary circumstances. After he made a business success he financed the H. E. & W. T. Railroad and was one of its largest stockholders. He was one of the organizers of the H. & T. C. stage line to Hempstead that preceded the railroad. He was one of the original organizers of the Townsite Development Company that built and developed towns along the line of the H. & T. C. road between Houston and Dallas. He financed various lumber mills and was one of the first promoters of brick manufacturing in Houston. He was the partner of H. B. Rice in the ownership of the Rice ranch of 9,500 acres about 6 to 9 miles west of Houston, today known as Westmoreland Farms and Bellaire. He engaged in soap manufacturing in Houston in the early 90's. He was one of the main stockholders and largely financed the Merchants and Planters Oil Mill and was a heavy stockholder in Houston's early banks. His estate is one of the largest individual stockholders in the South Texas National Bank, this stock being one of the assets of the institute. It is also a stockholder in the Houston Land and Trust Company. In 1881 and 1882, Mr. Rice financed the building of the Rice Hotel which he described as "a wild pig" of an enterprise. Mr. Rice's early residence was located in the present post-office block.

Having once invested he never looked backward. If any investment he made proved to be a loss, he never complained, never even referred to the matter. He had great personal courage and a high sense of honor and admired these traits in other men. It was his courage that caused him to live alone in New York with his valet, against the remonstrances his friends. During the latter years of his life the reticence and self-sufficiency of William Marsh Rice had caused, to some extent, an estrangement with relatives, but it was an estrangement almost without bitterness.

The first wife of W. M. Rice was Maggie Bremond, eldest daughter of Paul Bremond and his second wife was Elizabeth Baldwin of the famous family of first settlers. His brother, F. A. Rice, married Charlotte Baldwin of the same family. W. M. Rice had several sisters and other relatives in his birthplace in Springfield, Massachusetts. One of these sisters, Mrs. McKee, survived him, but died a few years ago.

The ashes of William M. Rice are in Houston in the vault of the Institute in the Commercial Bank Building. They will be transferred to a place of honor in the Administration Building of the Institute when it is completed.

Portraits of William M. Rice and of Elizabeth Baldwin Rice, painted by Boris Bernhardt Gordon, will also occupy places of honor in the institute he founded.

In 1907, Edgar Odell Lovett, M.A., Ph.D., LL.D., a professor of astronomy at Princeton was chosen president of the institute. Doctor Lovett, who is a noted scholar, toured the world studying the educational institutions in all lands preparatory to making plans for the Rice Institute.

Work on the Administration Building and two laboratories was begun in 1910. The site of the institute is on the Main Street road about three miles from the city. The tract chosen covers more than 300 acres and will be greatly beautified.

The corner-stone of the Administration Building was laid by the trustees at noon on March 2, 1911, the 75th anniversary of Texas independence. The seven members of the board were present. The ceremonies were of the simplest kind. Captain James Baker, president of the board, set the huge stone in place, using a silver trowel made in Houston, and thus inscribed:

"With this trowel the trustees of the William M. Rice Institute laid the corner-stone of the institute on the second day of March, 1911. J. A. Baker, W. M. Rice, Jr., J. E. McAshan, B. B. Rice, C. Lombardi, E. Raphael, and E. O. Lovett."

E. Raphael, secretary of the board, deposited in the receptacle in the stone certain records of interest to Houston and to the institute. These records were sealed in a copper box, on the face of which was the following legend engraved in script:

"This box was deposited in the corner-stone of the Administration Building of the William M. Rice Institute on the second day of March, 1911, the day of the laying of the stone."

Within the box were placed a copy of the Old and New Testament Scriptures of the King James translation; the charter of the Institute, transcribed on parchment, and a brief biography of William M. Rice, the founder of the Institute and short sketches of the careers of the several gentlemen who have served as trustees of the foundation; a photograph, mounted on linen, of the plans for developing the site and buildings of the institute, prepared by the architects; a copy of the Houston Chronicle of January 12, 1911, and a copy of the Houston Daily Post of January 18, 1911. The several sketches referred to include notices of the late F. A. Rice and A. S. Richardson, who, with the founder and Messrs. Baker, McAshan, Lombardi and Raphael, were charter members of the board of trustees of the institute. The carving of the inscription on the stone was deferred until after the settling of the stone in its place. It is a quotation from the Praeparatio

Evangelica of Enselbius Pamphili, the earliest historian of the church. Rendered into English, it reads: "'Rather,' said Demeritus, 'would I discover the causes of one fact than become king of the Persians.'" A declaration made by the Greek philosopher at a time when to be king of the Persians was to rule the world.

In appropriating this expression of the spirit of science from a representative philosopher of that people who originated the highest standards in letters and in art, the trustees of the institute sought to express that devotion to both science and humanism which the founder desired when he dedicated this institute to the advancement of literature, science and art.

A description of the architecture of the proposed institute will be found in the chapter on Architecture and Building. Dr. Lovett and the trustees have not yet announced the personnel of the faculty of the new university but it is announced that it will be open for students at the beginning of the fall term of 1912. The cost of the first group of buildings will be about $1,000,000 and about half of that amount has been spent in further beautifying the grounds by landscape architecture and gardening.

The future of Houston will be dominated to a great degree by the Rice Institute and it will give to the city the academic charm and tone that is greatly needed to relieve the strident commercialism that is now its chief characteristic.

CHAPTER XIII - HOUSTON NEWSPAPERS

Story of First Newspaper in Texas and its Removal to Houston. The Telegraph and Register. The Morning Star. Flood of Newspaper Enterprises Following Civil War. Special Interest and Trade Periodicals in Houston. The Houston Telegram. The Houston Post Organized and Suspended. The New Post. The Houston Herald. The Chronicle and Its Makers. Some Famous Newspaper Men. Some Early and Late Authors and Writers. Organization of Texas State Press Association.

In the winter of 1834, Launcelott Abbotts, a young Englishman, who was a printer, stopping in New Orleans, became acquainted with Mr. T. F. McKinney, a merchant of Valasco and a Mr. Fletcher, a merchant of San Felipe, who advised him to locate in Texas. They praised the climate and soil and dwelt on the generosity of the government in giving to each immigrant a good lot of land. Those portions of Mexico then known as Coahuila and Texas constituted, for governmental purposes, one state, having one legislature and its citizens were called Coahuila-Texanos. Mr. Abbotts having superintended the printing of Mrs. Holley's small book on Texas, published in Baltimore, had a pretty good knowledge of the territory, its people, its resources and of its possibilities, so he took their advice and embarked on a small schooner for the mouth of the Brazos where he arrived about Christmas. He was prevented from landing for a day or two by adverse winds that kept the schooner from crossing the bar at the mouth of the river. Having landed he at once made his way to San Felipe, then the capital of the state. Here he made the acquaintance of two men who were destined to have great influence over his career. One of these was Gail Borden, then known as Gail Borden, Jr., who afterwards became famous as the inventor and manufacturer of condensed milk and as the head of the great Borden Dairy Company. The other was Joseph Baker, who afterwards also became prominent and influential in Texas. These men were contemplating the establishment of a newspaper in San Felipe, and, so soon as they learned that Mr. Abbotts was a practical printer, they made a contract with him to assist in its production. At that time there were no mails or post offices in Texas, so Mr. Abbotts was forced to return to Velasco, a hundred miles distant, to dispatch an order to New York for a mechanical outfit for the proposed paper. On his way back he stopped at Brazoria, then a small village on the bank of the Brazos, where there was a small printing plant of doubtful value owned by a Mr. Gray. This plant was nearly useless, but was capable of being used in a pinch. There was a well-worn press with a sheep skin ink-ball (composition rollers being unknown at that time) a few fonts of old type, some leads and some wood "furniture," and that was all. Mr. Abbotts wanted the proprietor of this outfit to print him 100 copies of a prospectus for the paper he proposed issuing and which it had been decided was to be called the "Telegraph and Register." This the proprietor refused to do, but finally allowed Mr. Abbotts to do the work himself, using the material at hand, for a consideration of ten dollars. There was also an extra charge for the paper used in printing the circulars.

Before the press and type arrived from New York the prospectus had been circulated and a small list of subscribers had been secured. J. L. Hill, of Fayette County was, perhaps, the first subscriber. He has a place in Texas history as the husband of the woman who plotted the escape of Santa Anna when he was a prisoner of war in the hands of the Texans at Columbia. The first number of the Telegraph and Register appeared October 10, 1836, the same day on which the Texans stormed and took the fort at Goliad. It should be noted that no other newspaper was published in Texas at that time or at any time during the Texans' struggle for independence. Before then Mr. Gray, already spoken of, had published a paper spasmodically, and a little sheet had been published for a short time at Nacogdoches. The appearance of The Telegraph and Register was of the greatest value and assistance to those engaged in the work of establishing and maintaining the new republic, since it enabled them to create and concentrate public thought and opinion, which could have been done in no other way than through the medium of a newspaper.

The pathway of the new paper was not strewn with flowers, however, and it had many obstacles to overcome. Soon after its establishment, Mr. Baker, the senior editor, left to join Sam Houston's army. Then Mr. Abbotts grew patriotic and did the same thing. This left the entire responsibility of getting out the paper on the shoulders of a printer from Philadelphia. Probably 22 numbers of the paper had been issued when the Mexicans invaded Texas. Then the printer, alarmed by the approach of Santa Anna and his army, abandoned his post, and, not having the patriotism of Mr. Baker and Mr. Abbotts, instead of joining the Texas army, fled to the United States.

When General Houston retreated from the Colorado River, Thomas H. Borden and his father, Gail Borden, Sr., put the printing material across the Brazos at San Felipe with much difficulty, for it was heavy and transportation facilities were poor, and conveyed it to Harrisburg. There they secured the help of a Frenchman, named Bertrand, and a printer from New York who set up an issue of the paper and had it on the press ready to publish, when Santa Anna's men surprised and captured them. The Mexicans threw the press, forms, type and everything else movable, into the bayou and then proceeded to burn the town, the printing office included. In the general conflagration the homes of Gail and Thos. Borden were destroyed. Instead of being discouraged and disheartened, the Bordens at once ordered new material for their paper from Cincinnati, and sometime in August, 1836, the first number of the paper printed after the war was issued at Columbia, where the first Congress of the Republic of Texas met. The paper bore at its mast head the names of Gail and Thomas Borden, editors and proprietors.

Congress decided to locate the capitol of Texas at Houston and the Bordens moved their printing plant here also, in the spring of 1837.

Houston at that time was only a city in name for there were only a few wooden shanties and most of these were incomplete. Gail Borden having been appointed collector of customs at Galveston and Thomas Borden wishing to retire from the newspaper field, they concluded to dispose of their newspaper plant and sold it to Mr. Jacob Cruger and Dr. Francis Moore. These gentlemen at once revived the Telegraph, publishing it at Houston, first as a weekly, then as a tri-weekly and then as a daily.

In the first issue of the Telegraph and Texas Register, published in Houston, May 2, 1837, was the following: "The City of Houston.—This place is as yet merely a city in embryo, but the industry, enterprise and amount of capital which are now ministering to its greatness, will soon elevate it to a prominent rank among the cities of the older countries. Its situation is remarkably healthy, being upon an elevated and dry prairie, partly in the skirts of the timbered margin of Buffalo Bayou. The principal objection to the place is the difficulty of access by water, the bayou above Harrisburg being so narrow, so serpentine and so blocked with snags and overhanging trees that immense improvements will be required to render navigation convenient for large steamboats."

Though the Telegraph was the first newspaper published in Houston of which definite record has been left, a gentleman named Thomas Wilson announced through the columns of the Telegraph, while that paper was still published at Columbia, that he would begin the publication of a paper at Houston to be known as the Texian, on April 21, the anniversary of the battle of San Jacinto. If the Texian was ever published no record of that fact is now preserved. Probably it never passed the stage of the prospective.

"The history of the Telegraph and Register is intimately connected with the history of Texas," declared the Texas Wesleyan Banner in 1858. "Dr. Francis Moore has been its editor and part proprietor ever since its establishment in Houston. It is the oldest paper in Texas and for years has nobly battled with the various popular vices peculiar to a new country, such as dueling, gambling and drinking. Dr. Moore, its veteran editor, is now its independent proprietor, and intends devoting its columns in future principally to commercial and agricultural intelligence. His past eminent service in the cause of Texan liberty and his intimate alliance with all the various interests of the state, together with his long experience in the chair editorial, entitle him to a liberal patronage."

In 1853, Mr. Harry H. Allen became the editor and proprietor of the Telegraph and continued as such until 1856, when the plant was sold to Mr. E. H. Cushing, one of the best and most gifted newspaper men in the country. He managed and edited the Telegraph for ten years. Mr. Cushing had exceptional opportunity for the exercise of his executive ability and the display of his talent as an editor, for during his administration the great Civil War occurred, which taxed to the limit the resources at hand. Two great difficulties confronted Mr. Cushing. One was to get the news, for there were no mails or telegraph lines to transmit it; the other was to get the paper on which to print the news when it was gathered. The first was overcome by establishing a pony express between Houston and points on the Mississippi River, and the second by using common wrapping paper, wall paper or any other paper that could be procured. One issue of the Telegraph would be brown, another green, to be followed in turn by others representing all the colors of the rainbow. Sometimes the paper could be printed on one side only, because the flowers and vines of the wall-paper on the other side precluded its being used.

Until they were destroyed by fire in the early 80's, Mr. E. B. Cushing, of Houston, son of Mr. E. H. Cushing, had in his possession complete files of the Telegraph for the four years of the war. These were probably the most valuable newspaper files ever owned in the South. Those files contained historical matter and news items of inestimable value. Mr. Cushing loaned these files to President Jefferson Davis to use in the compilation of his history of the Lost Cause. Mr. Davis found in them many things that were new and important to him, and when he returned the files to their owner he said that they contained many things that would have been of great value to him had he known them while he was president of the Confederate States.

In 1866, Mr. Cushing sold the Telegraph to Col. C. C. Gillespie, who was a man of great ability as a writer. He secured the services of James E. Carnes as editorial writer, and between the two the Telegraph was soon made one of the best literary papers in the land. However, too much attention was paid to fine writing and too little to news, and general interest soon waned and the paper was almost dead when Colonel Gillespie sold it to General Webb. General Webb continued to issue the paper regularly until the great financial panic of 1873 occurred, when it was forced to suspend. The old paper was not to remain dead, however. The next year Mr. A. C. Gray revived it. In an editorial of April 16, 1874, Mr. Gray, the new editor and proprietor, said: "The Houston Telegraph is an old and familiar friend to very many in and out of Texas who will hail its reappearance as the return of a much loved and greatly lamented companion. Founded in the days of the Republic, it was true to the government and to the people, and by its efforts accomplished, perhaps, as much as any other instrumentality in calling attention to and developing the resources of this great commonwealth. Under the control and guidance of such men as Gail Borden, Dr. Francis Moore, Harry Allen, E. H. Cushing and others, it has reared for itself an imperishable monument, by its fidelity to law, good government and general progress. Its pages contain an epitome of the history of the Lone Star State, and reflect the progress she has made in her march to greatness * * * * It is with no ordinary satisfaction and, we trust, a pardonable pride, that the present managing editor and proprietor refers to his past connection with and present relation to the office of the Telegraph. Twenty-eight years ago, when a mere boy, he entered it as an apprentice. By patient toil and proper pride in his chosen profession he became its business manager during its most prosperous period. And when, under the financial panic of 1873, it was forced to suspend and ceased to make its daily appearance he mourned as if a friend had fallen. Since then it has been his ambition to call the slumbering Ajax to the field again and bid it battle with renewed energy for constitutional government, Democratic principles and the general weal."

Mr. Gray made good his promises for under his administration and guidance the Telegraph soon became one of the most influential papers in Texas as well as in Houston. It continued to be the leading paper in Houston until 1878. At that time the method of gathering news had become so expensive that a much larger sum than the Telegraph could hope to earn without the most extensive and costly improvements and expansion, was an absolute necessity, and the Telegraph was forced to a final suspension of publication.

In the foregoing pages much space has been given to the Telegraph, because of its long and remarkable record. It must not be supposed that Houston had no other papers during the existence of the Telegraph. There were many others and some quite good ones, too.

In 1891, Mr. J. R. Irion, of Denton, gave the Houston Post a copy of the National Banner for July 13, 1838 and a copy of the Daily Times for April 16, 1840. Mr. Irion was the son of Hon. R. A. Irion, who was secretary of state of the Republic of Texas, under President Houston.

The Banner was a four column paper but the columns were wide. The first page was devoted to miscellany and poetry, the second page was an editorial, strongly urging the Republic to declare war against Mexico. The other pages were filled with interesting news items and advertisements. President Houston published a proclamation offering a reward of $200 for the capture of James Aldridge, accused of killing "Billy," a Choctaw Indian, late of Nacogdoches, and Thomas M. League, postmaster of Houston, published a two-column list of unclaimed letters. Niles & Company were proprietors of the National Banner.

The Daily Times was edited by A. M. Lampkins. An early item of police court news told of the fining of an Indian for riding his horse violently through the streets, and another was the recital of the "cussedness" and the consequent trouble of one "Jawbone" Morris, who had to pay $5 for indulging in disorderly conduct.

The Morning Star, was a tri-weekly paper, first edited by James F. Cruger. It was very influential in the days of the Republic but changed editors often. A valuable but incomplete file of this paper is in the Carnegie City Library. It was extensively used in preparing the earlier chapters of this book.

In the early fifties the fight between the Democrats and Know-Nothings was very bitter. Lines were drawn sharply and city and county campaigns were lively affairs. The Democrats had the great advantage of having the Telegraph on their side, while the Know-Nothings had to disseminate their doctrine by word of mouth alone. The following communication to the Telegraph, published October 19th, 1855, incidentally refers to the strife between the two parties, while it gives, in a nut shell, the whole local history of one journalistic venture in Houston:

"A New Way to Start a Newspaper.—Messrs. Editors—A few short weeks ago there was ushered into and circulated about our city, a sheet bearing the respectable name of the 'Bayou City News,' and on the front in bold letters the motto 'Open to All—Controlled by None.' There being but one secular paper in our city, it was well received and many of our citizens congratulated themselves upon its appearance, expecting of course, from the promises and inducements held out, that it would be a source of pleasure to its readers and reflect credit on its publishers. It was a neutral paper in politics and religion and would advance the great commercial and agricultural interests of our country. It puffed every calling, trade and profession in our midst; pro-pounded more interrogations in one of its issues than could have been answered in half a dozen; and lo and behold! we got up one morning inquiring how the Bayou City News was getting along, and were shocked by the intelligence that, without waiting long enough to have their interrogations answered, they had sold themselves to Know-Nothingism and were about to move up to Washington on the Brazos, where, it is said, an association of gentlemen will christen it the 'Washington American,' and advocate Know-Nothingism in a dignified manner, that is, more dignified than the other Know-Nothing papers. Verily, Messrs. Editors, that was an artful dodge. Gentlemen get up in our city a newspaper, solicit subscriptions among our merchants, mechanics, etc.,—they subscribe, looking on it as an enterprise likely to benefit our city and people; and lo and behold! in about three weeks they find themselves all transferred to an association of Know-Nothings away up in Washington on the Brazos and are very respectfully asked to allow their names and advertisements to be retained. As an inducement for the retention of the latter, we are told that the paper already has a circulation of 1,500, a number which could have been easily increased to 5,000 with the same dash of the pen. I have known, Messrs. Editors, papers like other property, to change hands, and the subscribers to receive the paper for the period subscribed for, but this is the first time I have known of a paper changing owners, location, name, politics and religion and calling on its subscribers, after an existence of three weeks, to sustain it; and I really believe that nothing but the anxiety to get up a Know-Nothing paper could have induced the gentlemen to make so modest a request. —(Signed) Houstonian."

At the close of the Civil War there appears to have been a perfect mania for starting newspapers in Houston. Quite a number were established and there was something like rapid fire change in editors. The following papers were established after 1865 and had all become defunct by 1880:

Daily Evening Star—Editors: R. H. Purdom, W. H. Crank, and W. P. Cole; Daily and Weekly Journal—Editors: R. H. Purdom, Dudley W. Jones, J. J. Diamond, George W. Diamond, and J. W. Diamond; Daily Tri-Weekly and Weekly Union—Editors: J. G. Tracy, E. H. Quick, C. C. Gillespie, James E. Carnes, J. H. Baker, Will Lambert, and J. H. Caldwell; Sunday Gazette— Editors: Charles Bickley, Will Lambert; Gillespies Daily Telegraph—Editors: C. C. Gillespie, Jr., Crawford Gillespie, and H. P. Gillespie; Ku Klux Vidette—Editors and Proprietors: H. P. Gillespie and B. F. King; Daily and Weekly Times—Editors: Sommers Kinney, E. P. Claudon, W. F. Schott, F. Fauntleroy, J. W. Colvin, N. A. Taylor, W. Duesenberry, and Will Lambert; Daily Courier—Hon. Ashbel Smith, Editor; Daily Commercial—Editors: H. Lehman, and N. A. Taylor; Daily Mercury—Editors: J. H. Baker, Sam W. Small, and C. L. Martin; Masonic Mirror and Family Visitor—Editor: B. T. Kavanaugh; Houston Weekly Argus and The Houston Weekly Chronicle also enjoyed a brief existence in this period; The Houston Telegraph—established in 1836, suspended publication during the financial panic of 1873, revived by Mr. A. C. Gray in 1874, and died in 1878. During its long and brilliant career it was edited by the following named gentlemen: Gail Borden, Dr. Francis Moore, C. J. Cruger, Harry H. Allen, C. J. Cruger, E. H. Cushing, C. C. Gillespie, General Webb, A. C. Gray, J. Noble, W. P. Doran, H. P. Gillespie, W. P. Hamblin, N. P. Turner, Charles Bickley, Horace Cone, Sr., T. E. Davis, George W. Kidd, Will Lambert, and C. L. Martin; Houston Nut-Shell— Bottler and Brown, editors and proprietors; Monthly Union Land Register— C. C. Vogel, editor and proprietor; Texas Sun (removed to San Antonio)— A. W. Gifford, editor; Evening News— Editors: D. D. Bryan, and J. P. Farrell; Houston Evening Age—Editors: D. L. McGarey, Charles Bickley, Gustave Cook, F. F. Chew, C. L. Martin, Sam W. Small, Judge J. K. P. Gallaspie, B. F. Hardcastle, A. A. McBride, R. D. Westcott, Ed Smallwood, George King and H. C. Stevens.

The initial number of the Texas Staats Zeitung, a German newspaper, Berger and Leonhardt, publishers, appeared December 11, 1868. The first number of the Texas Gazette, a small daily, appeared December 31, 1875. At that date the Zeitung was merged with the Gazette. The Peoples Advocate, a Greenback organ, C. B. Kitteringham, publisher, appeared in 1878.

Many publications in Houston are designed to foster special commercial interests. Most of these are issued weekly, but several are monthly and of magazine rank.

The Texas Bankers Journal, owned and edited by W. W. Dexter, is a monthly magazine devoted to the interest of banks and bankers, that reflects credit on its editor and the city. It is well gotten up and presents a neat appearance. The Texas Magazine, published by the Texas Magazine Publishing Company, under the management of Mr. Nelson F. Johnson, and edited by Harry Van DeMark, is now safely launched on the magazine sea. Its aim is to exploit the natural, commercial and literary resources of Texas and to develop home talent in magazine writing, though its field for contributions is not restricted to Houston or Texas by any means.

The Vagabond, a monthly, owned, edited and published by Everett Lloyd, was recently resurrected in Houston. It jousts a tilt at everything that "is." The editor calls it "The Diamond of Free-lance Journalism," "A Literary Melting Pot," and says "It skins Vesuvius for size and spunk." The Vagabond bristles with interest and bids fair to prove a success.

The Deutsche Zeitung, is edited and published by Mr. A. Haxthausen, and appears as a weekly. The Houston Labor Journal, is a weekly devoted to the interests of labor and of working men. It is neat in appearance and is well edited by its proprietor, Mr. Max Andrews, whose sanity, fairness and conservatism have put it on a firm basis. The Jewish Herald, a weekly publication, devoted to matters of interest to the Hebrew citizens of Houston, is edited and published by Mr. E. Goldberg. The Texas Realty Journal, a monthly publication as its name implies in the interest of real estate, is published by Mr. C. C. Buckingham, as is also The Texas Tradesman, a journal devoted largely to the lumber interest. The Texas Word is a weekly publication owned and edited by Mrs. R. B. Palmer.

The Houston Telegram, published by the Houston Telegram Publishing Company, made it appearance in 1878, and continued publication as a daily paper for about two years. This was really the old Telegraph under a slightly changed name.

In 1880, Mr. Gail Johnson, grandson of Gail Borden, the founder of the old Telegraph, announced that he would establish a daily newspaper in Houston, to be known as the Houston Post. There was some delay in receiving the press, type, and other material from New York and, Mr. Johnson, having a thoroughly organized editorial staff, grew impatient and determined to issue the Post for a short time as an afternoon paper, having it printed by Mr. W. H. Coyle. This he did and the Post made its appearance on February 19, 1880. Colonel Bartow was leading editor; Dr. S. O. Young, associate editor; Mr. D. D. Bryan, city editor and Mr. Joe Abbey was paragrapher and writer of special articles and humorous sketches. He was the first newspaper man in the South to engage exclusively in such special work.

He afterwards gained something of a national reputation as a humorist. Mr. Johnson was general manager and had supervision over both the editorial and business departments. The Post was first edited in an office on the second floor at 61 Main Street, but on March 11, it moved into new quarters, over the old Cushing Book Store on Franklin Street, opposite the Hutchins House. The press and printing material having arrived, the Post was issued as a morning paper on March 30, 1880, under the new heading, "The Houston Daily Post."

On February 21, 1881, the paper was moved to the Larendon Building on Commerce Street, opposite the Court House, where the Telegram had been located before its suspension. The Post was favorably received by the people of Houston and had quite a good circulation throughout the state. Colonel Bartow had resigned as editor and his place had been filled by Prof. T. J. Girardeau, a polished writer, and the paper was gaining ground rapidly in popular favor when the political campaign of 1882 began. Judge J. W. Johnson, the father of Mr. Gail Johnson, was a staunch Republican, and insisted on having the Post support Hon. Wash Jones, a brave Confederate soldier, for governor against Hon. John Ireland, the regular Democratic nominee. This was done against the protest of Mr. Gail Johnson. The campaign was a very bitter one and resulted not only in the election of Ireland but in the obliteration of the Post. The paper lost ground so rapidly that Judge Johnson who had become sole owner through the retirement of Mr. Gail Johnson in 1883, was glad to dispose of it to a number of Houston capitalists who wanted to have a real Democratic paper. These gentlemen started with the intention of making the Post a first-class paper and they did so. They secured the services of Mr. Hardenbrook, an experienced newspaper man, and gave him free hand to do as he thought best, and, what was more to the point, they gave him practically an unlimited supply of money. The paper had superb backing and loyal support. The Post advanced rapidly in public favor and became at once one of the leading state papers. Mr. Tobe Mitchel was brought here from St. Louis and placed in charge of the editorial department. Hardenbrook gave Mitchel as free a hand as the backers of the paper had given him. No expense was spared in gathering the news and the Post soon became the best and newsiest paper published in the South. This continued for eight or ten months. Then the capitalists realized that while it had cost a small fortune to put the Post in first place among newspapers, it was going to cost another to keep it there, and they threw up the sponge and quit. The Post collapsed.

The suspension of the Post left Houston without a morning paper, but this was not to be for long. When the Post suspended, in addition to the first-class printing plant, there was a large supply of white paper on hand. Mr. Wm. R. Baker turned over all this to Dr. S. O. Young, allowed him the free use of the plant and allowed him to use the paper, paying for what was used

143

and when it was used, at actual cost. Dr. Young at once organized a company and on March 14, the first copy of the Houston Chronicle was issued. The Chronicle was run strictly on the pay-as-you-go principle. It was not a brilliant newspaper, judged by the standard of today, but it was a clean, newsy sheet and while its existence was largely a hand-to-mouth business, it ended its first year with a fair patronage and not a dollar of debt.

Mr. J. W. Watson and Prof. T. J. Girardeau were at that time publishing an afternoon paper called the Herald. After some negotiation these gentlemen and Doctor Young, who had now secured sole control of the Chronicle, determined to merge the two papers. This was done and on April 5, 1885, the Chronicle and Herald were consolidated under the name of the Houston Post. In its first issue the Post said editorially: "Thousands throughout Texas will be surprised to see the above caption, which looks like the materialization of a great but moral enterprise. The revival of the Post is not to be regarded as an assumption of the obligations of that paper, but an authorized use of a name made honorable throughout the state, and the parties, who have adopted the name after mature deliberation, feel an assurance of popular sympathy on that point. The late Post made a brilliant record for itself. * * * * The proprietors of the new Post emphatically announce as the keynote of their enterprise the principle of restricting all expenditures within the limits of income. This may be laughed at, but solid business men will understand and appreciate this honest position assumed by the proprietors of the Post."

The proprietors, Messrs. Girardeau, Young and Watson, the latter being Mr. J. W. Watson, the business manager of the Post, "felt a natural confidence in appealing to the community for its support. They took up the enterprise, not as capitalists nor as adventurers, but as men known and sized up by their fellow citizens in a fair and honorable business which must stand or fall according to the ability displayed and patronage extended." The proprietors of the Post had a hard fight to keep their heads above water. First, Professor Girardeau became discouraged and disposed of his interest to his two partners. However, they were so fortunate as to get Col. R. M. Johnson, one of the best and most practical newspaper men in the country, to take his place. In September, Doctor Young accepted a flattering offer to become one of the editorial writers on the Galveston News. This left as sole proprietors of the Post, Mr. Watson, who was great as a business manager and Colonel Johnson a most capable editor. They were dreadfully hampered by the want of money, so in 1886, they reorganized the Post, turning it into a stock company. The company became "The Houston Post, Houston Printing Company, proprietors." Its officers were: E. P. Hill, president; T. W. House, vice-president; A. F. Sittig, secretary; R. M. Johnson, managing editor; J. W. Watson, business manager. The following named gentlemen were chosen as the first executive committee of the Company: E. P. Hill, T. W.

House, W. R. Baker, Z. T. Hogan, H. F. Macgregor, and S. Taliaferro. For a few years the fight was all uphill, but finally the ability of Colonel Johnson as an editorial writer and manager, backed by the genius of Mr. Watson as a business manager, told and the Post became what it is today, a paper which has the admiration of many people in Texas and a source of pride to Houston. It won its greatest state popularity by espousing the cause of J. S. Hogg, in the great Hogg-Clark campaign.

In 1882, on November 1, the Houston Daily Sun made its appearance. It was a small afternoon paper and had but a short existence.

In April, 1883, The Texas Journal of Education was removed from San Antonio to Houston. This was a monthly publication devoted, as its name indicates, to educational matters. It was in charge of the Public School Superintendents and was edited through a directory, of which Mr. Wilkens was president. The great bulk of its contents was supplied by the superintendents of the different public schools of the State.

The Texas Scrap Book, an eight page, 48 column weekly began publication March 10, 1886, H. R. Zintgraff & Co., publishers. It soon suspended publication, but was revived, February 1887, by Spencer Hutchins & Co., who had bought the title and subscription list, and who assumed all liabilities.

Mr. W. E. Bailey, in 1884, began the publication of the Houston Herald, an afternoon paper. Mr. Bailey, though quite a young man, was a good and experienced newspaper worker and a forcible writer. He had ideas of his own, among them being that no man's financial or social position should shield him from publicity if he deviated in the slightest from the straight and narrow path. The Herald soon began creating almost daily sensations. It claimed that it told nothing but the truth, and intimated that all those who felt aggrieved could obtain satisfaction either through the courts or by calling at the Herald office and interviewing the editor personally. One or two adopted the latter method but they found Mr. Bailey as ready with his hardware as he was with his pen, and in every case the aggrieved ones came off more aggrieved than ever. Of course, the Herald became immensely popular and unpopular, but both added to its circulation, and soon this circulation increased to large proportions. The advertisements poured in, too, and in a few months the Herald was firmly established. The Herald continued its live-wire existence for several years and then, its founder having amassed a small fortune, became more conservative. The Herald became less caustic and prosy and the public to some extent lost interest in it. In 1902, the Herald, though still a good paper, had lost ground and Mr. Bailey was glad to dispose of it to Mr. M. E. Foster, who had organized the Houston Chronicle, and who offered to buy the plant and good will of the Herald. On October 14th, 1902, the publication of the Houston Chronicle was begun as an afternoon paper. That date marks a red letter day in the history of afternoon Journalism in Texas, for from its first issue the Chronicle became the leading and best afternoon paper in the South. Mr. Foster has rare talent as an organizer and he also has executive ability of high order. Every detail had been thought out and arranged in advance, with the result that when the Chronicle made its appearance, it was on a plane that would have consumed months to attain, had ordinary, time-worn methods been followed. The success of the Chronicle has been phenomenal from its first issue and today it stands a monument to the wisdom and ability of its founder, Mr. M. E. Foster. On October 16, the Chronicle began the publication of a Sunday morning edition. The circulation of both the afternoon daily and the Sunday morning editions is very large and extends over the whole state. The paper has made itself very popular by its advocacy of measures for the suppression of gambling, the "pistol toters," mob violence, and, of the officers of the law who shoot fleeing prisoners to prevent their escape. February 28th, 1910, the Chronicle moved into its new 10-story skyscraper on Travis Street and Texas Avenue and celebrated the occasion by coming out in a new dress.

Marcellus E. Foster was an expert newspaper man when he established the Chronicle. He had risen to the position of managing editor of the Houston Daily Post and had inaugurated on that paper some of its most lasting and popular features such as the Happyhammer Page. It was the policy of the Chronicle to put a premium on newspaper excellence in newsgathering and story writing and Mr. Foster surrounded himself with a brilliant staff of specialists. C. B. Gillespie became managing editor. He combined brilliance with a genius for hard work and with kindliness and tact. The men on the Chronicle always do team work. Among those who have added to their reputation and that of the paper, are W. S. Gard, Frank Putnam, B. H. Carroll, Jr., C. H. Abbott, George E. Kepple, O. O. Ballard, Billie Mayfield, John Regan, Chester Colby and the jolly crew of newsgatherers that are still connected with the paper.

The Chronicle has the largest sworn circulation of any paper in the state and with the exception of the Dallas News has the largest list of subscribers of any daily paper in Texas. Its home is the best equipped newspaper plant South of New York and the Chronicle plant is one of the show sites of the city. The Chronicle has successfully conducted a number of crusades against social and political evils and has always been on the side of cleanness and political honesty.

The Galveston News, which has a strong following and a large circulation in Houston was represented here for many years by Colonel Hamp Cook, the dean of the newspaper fraternity of the city. In June, 1907, Mr. J. R. Montgomery took charge of the news end of the Houston office and has been brilliantly successful. A. P. Vaughn is the local business manager.

Many men of natural reputation in journalism are now or have been connected with the Houston press. Besides several of those just named on the Chronicle, George Bailey of "red-headed widows" and "heavenly Houston," fame, of the Post, and Judd Mortimer Lewis, the sweet singer of the South are here now. W. C. Brann, the pyrotechnic writer and founder of the Iconoclast once worked in Houston, and all unrecognized O. Henry, the most famous American writer of short stories, once worked as a newsgatherer in Houston for $16 per week. Karl Crow went to China from Houston; J. C. Dionne has achieved reputation as a special writer on lumber, and the honor roll of Houston journalists is a long one and filled with the record of worthy achievement.

The first Houston author was a Mr. Kerr who wrote a book of poems, which he published at his own expense, about 1837.

It is doubtful if there is a copy of this wonderful book in existence today, for forty years ago it was so rare that Judge John Brashear paid $200 for a copy, part of which was torn off. The book was made up of personal and descriptive poems and was on the order of the poem written and dedicated to General Braxton Bragg by the late Doctor Cooper, the well-remembered horse doctor of Houston, which began:

"There's General Bragg, the noble stag, Who made the Yankee soldiers wag At Chic-a-magua."

Kerr's poems were just that kind and he described Galveston as follows:

"Galveston Island, long and low,
Devoid of trees and shruberee;
Small vessels there can safely go,
And find safety and securitee."

The book contained about fifty "poems," all on the order of the sample given. The poem is not in any way a representative sample of the literary efforts of the early Houstonians. It is given place here merely because it was the earliest effort of which any record exists.

One of the earliest prose writers who published his books was Mr. Cyrus S. Oberly. He was a man of education and considerable literary ability. He published three stories, each based largely on his own experience as a Texas ranger during the Cortina raids and during the Comanche and Apache troubles. He was for nearly three years with the rangers on the Texas frontier, and, of course, had a large fund of personal experience from which to draw in the construction of his stories. He sold the copyrights to a New York publishing house, and in consequence, his books had a much wider circulation in the East than they did at home. He wrote charming newspaper verse and was a regular contributor to the New Orleans Sunday Picayune which, at that time, had a regular literary department. But for his excessive modesty and his proneness to hide his light under a bushel, Mr. Oberly would have attained a much wider reputation as a literary man than he had at the time of his death, and to which he was entitled by his really fine literary productions.

The year 1885 seems to have been one in which the literary talent of Houston shone with peculiar brilliancy. During that year, Mrs. Ella Stewart, now Mrs. Seybrook Sydnor, published "Gems from a Texas Quarry," a compilation of the writings of Texas authors, a book which found a safe place in Texas literature. Mr. James Everett McAshan was brought into prominence that year by the publication of a paper on "The Jew," which was a scholarly production and would have established his reputation as a thinker and writer had he published nothing more. He became a regular contributor to Texas Siftings and wrote many charming short stories, which were widely reproduced. Mrs. Lee C. Harby was a writer of both prose and verse. She was a regular contributor to the leading magazines and as a short story writer, she had few equals.

Miss Claudia M. Girardeau laid the foundation of her literary reputation in Houston. Many of her earlier poems and stories appeared in the Post and in other local publications. Her short stories, won for her a wide reputation. Like Mrs. Harby, she seemed equally at ease either in prose or verse.

Miss Willa Lloyd was another of the writers of 1885. She wrote verses but her chief strength lay in writing sketches and short stories of domestic life.

Mrs. Paul Bremond was the author of a libretto which made quite a reputation for her, both here and in New York. She also wrote salable descriptive articles on travel and some meritorious short stories.

Judge Norman G. Kittrell is one of the most prolific writers Houston has ever had. His writings have been confined to no particular field. He is equally at home in law, art, music, literature, or whatever he chooses to attempt. He has written a novel, a school text book and essays and special articles on innumerable subjects. His novel, "Ned Nigger and Gentleman" was dramatized for a time and had great success. In 1909, he published a valuable text book called by him "A Primer of the Government of Texas."

The Texas State Press Association had its birth in Houston. In response to a call that had been published in the papers over the state, a number of Texas editors assembled in the parlors of the Hutchins House on Franklin Avenue, May 18, 1880, for the purpose of organizing the Texas Press Association. Major E. W. Cave, an old printer, but at that time one of the general officers of the Houston and Texas Central Railroad, welcomed the visitors in an eloquent address, which was responded to by Hon. Hall Gosling, of the Castroville Quill. After the speech-making was over, the editors settled down to work and perfected a complete organization by the adoption of a constitution and by-laws, and the election of officers. At night a banquet was given in honor of the visiting editors by the Houston Cotton Exchange and Houston merchants. Little beyond organization was done at that meeting.

The association met in Houston the following year. Col. Geo. H. Sweet of the Galveston Journal of Commerce, was the orator and a poem was read by Miss Florence M. Gerald of Waco. The session lasted for three days and much good work was done by the association during that time. The association held the two following annual sessions in Houston and then determined, as the Medical Association had done, that it would be more conducing to the growth and health of the association to meet at a different point in the state each year. Houston has not been forgotten by the editors, however, and it has had the honor of entertaining them once or twice since they determined to abandon this city as their permanent headquarters.

CHAPTER XIV - TRANSPORTATION
AND COMMUNICATION

Early Transportation Difficulties. An Early Monopoly Proposed. The First Railroad. Other Early Roads. The G. H. & H. Road. Beginning of Texas and New Orleans Line. Railroads During War and Reconstruction Days. Systems Center in Houston. The Plank Road Company. The Ox-Wagon Trade. Paul Bremond's Enterprise. Growing Need for Roads. Houston as Terminus for Seventeen Roads. Houston's Railroad Trackage, Trains and Headquarters. Sunset Central System. Katy and Sap Terminals. Santa Fe and Frisco Lines. Bayou Navigation. The Wharfage Fight. Charles Morgan and the Ship Channel. The Government and the Channel. Deepening the Channel. Bayou Traffic. Houston Terminal Company. First Street Car Company. Extending Street Railways. Operation Under Stone-Webster Syndicate. Trackage and Pay Roll. Houston Galveston Interurban. Earliest Telegraph Service. Beginnings of Telephone Service. Present Telegraph Service in Houston. Southwestern Telegraph and Telephone Company. Automatic Telephone Company. Wireless Telegraphy.

In the very early days, the question of transportation was the most serious that confronted the pioneer. Except at and near La Bahia, now Goliad; Bexar, now San Antonio, and Nacogodoches, the whole country was a wilderness. These were small but very important Spanish settlements. The early settler had difficulties to overcome in getting into Texas and greater ones in reaching outside markets for his products, after he established himself here. His choice of transportation was limited to scarcely navigable streams, and to the slow and tedious ox-wagons over dangerous and almost impassable trails.

Under such conditions, it is not surprising that so soon as the city of Houston was located, its natural advantages were recognized and it became the center of growth, commerce and trade of the new Republic. The founders of Houston were not slow in appreciating their advantageous position as the natural connecting link between land and water transportation, and as early as 1838 four steamboats were carrying cotton and other Texas products from Houston to New Orleans.

In 1839, the Republic of Texas appropriated $315,000 for the improvement of Texas rivers and harbors, but strange to say no one seems to have been wide awake enough to have attempted to have any part of the appropriation used for the improvement of Buffalo Bayou. Doubtless such action was deemed unnecessary, for the main transportation difficulties were encountered on land and not on water. Stage-coach lines and freight wagons were organized and put in operation, and for years, these and ox-wagons were the only means of communication between Houston and the interior.

Such means were not only very expensive but were absolutely dangerous because of the hostile and blood-thirsty Indians and thieving Mexicans.

These difficulties and costs of communication were thus referred to by President Houston in 1840, when speaking of the removal of the seat of government from Houston to Austin: "During the last year the expense to the government for transportation to Austin, over and above what it would have been to any point on the seaboard, exceeded $70,000, and the extra cost of the mails, aside from all other inconveniences attending its remote and detached situation, amounted to many thousands of dollars more." He explained these facts by reference to the dangers to life and property from attacks by Indians and from frequent raids on the Mexican frontier.

By the late forties, Houston was recognized not only as the most important connecting link between the outside world and the interior of Texas, but as the nexus between the older states and the Pacific Coast. As a result a great many men entered the transportation business and it assumed important proportions. It was expensive to shippers and travelers, but it must not be supposed that it was all clear profit to its operators. It cost one passenger $200 to ride 1,400 miles and it took 30 days to make the trip. It cost a shipper one dollar to ship 100 pounds of freight 100 miles.

Unquestionably this lack of transportation delayed the settlement of the state and as late as 1850 only 16 counties in the whole state had a tax valuation of as much as a million dollars. Harris County with its water and land transportation had reached a valuation of more than a million and a half at that time. Houston at the head of navigation, was the wholesale center and the chief commercial and financial city in Texas and was, in consequence, a center of some importance.

There were schemes and schemers even in the very first days of the Republic. The first of these was the "Texas Railroad and Navigation Company," whose promoters sought to have a monopoly of and control of the transportation facilities and banking of the new Republic. The charter, dated 1836, authorized the company to connect the waters of the Sabine and Rio Grande Rivers by means of railroads, canals and rivers, grouped under the name of "internal navigation and railroads." There was a banking side, too. The promoters had the right of eminent domain and a gratuity of half a mile of land on either side of their right-of-way, and they had begun a campaign of education among the people to teach them how much they were going to do for them when the whole thing was knocked on the head by timely legislation, which took all the life out of the enterprise. The plan, as a whole, was the initial step in the transportation and navigation question which was put before the people of Texas year after year for many years. It was revived in improved form a few years ago by those who desire to incorporate it in a great national inter-costal waterway.

While the commerce of the state was carried on by such crude means as wagons drawn by oxen and horses, as late as 1850, it must not be supposed that the question of railroads was neglected. As a matter of fact railroad building had actually begun ten years before then. In 1840 the Harrisburg and Brazos Valley people let a contract for 3,000 ties and engaged a force of negroes to do grading. The road, later to become the Galveston, Harrisburg and San Antonio Railway, was not yet incorporated. Its directing genius was A. Brisco. The Houston Morning Star in May, 1840, announced that many laborers were "throwing up the track and preparing it for the rails at an early season," and that more would soon be so employed. In 1841, the men controlling the enterprise were incorporated under the name of the Harrisburg Railroad and Trading Company. But they soon abandoned their enterprise, and nothing was accomplished until some years later. It was not until 1847 that it again showed signs of life, this time under the name of the Buffalo Bayou, Brazos and Colorado Railroad. Columbia and Alleyton were the terminal points first determined on.

In 1847, General Sidney Sherman acquired control of the road, bought most of the lots at Harrisburg, gained the assistance of Northern capitalists and got a charter for the road. His local fellow incorporators were: Hugh McLeod, John G. Todd, John Angier, Jonathan F. Barrett, E. A. Allen, W. M. Rice, W. A. Van Alstyne, James H. Stevens, B. A. Shepherd, and W. J. Hutchins. These men were all prominently identified with Houston and Galveston. The spring of 1851 saw the beginning of the survey westward, and the beginning of actual construction, though it was not until late in the next year that rails were laid. At that time the first locomotive ever in Texas arrived. It was named the "General Sherman."

The road was finished in 1852 as far as the Brazos, 32 miles from Harrisburg and in 1860, nine years after it had been begun, it was constructed to Alleyton, 42 miles farther. The intention had been to put this line through to Austin, but San Antonio eventually became its logical objective point.

In 1858 the Columbus, San Antonio and Rio Grande Railroad Company was incorporated. Its object was to construct a line from Columbus, via Gonzales to San Antonio. It was planned to connect this road with the Buffalo Bayou, Brazos and Colorado road at Alleyton by the Columbus Tap road, but work was stopped by the war and was not resumed for several years. But the progressive citizens of Houston were not content with only one railroad, and it reaching out towards the West. They recognized the existence of a large and rapidly expanding territory to the North and Northeast and took steps to provide for its need.

The Houston and Texas Central Railroad (though not by that name) was organized in 1848 and was called the Galveston and Red River Railroad. Under its first charter Galveston was to have been its Southern terminus. Its charter was amended, in 1852, and this also was superseded by a new charter, in 1856, by which the line was given the name it bears today. Grading was begun at Houston, in 1853. There were only two miles of road completed when the first locomotive was put on. With the locomotive came two men, one of whom was destined to become one of the most progressive and able railroad managers in Texas. This was C. A. Burton, who was the first engineer and ran the first locomotive for the Houston and Texas Central Railroad, and who afterwards became the general superintendent of the road. The other was a young man named Dawson, who was the first fireman. He died of yellow fever during the epidemic that occurred soon after his arrival. Twenty-five miles of road was completed by 1856 and ten miles more by May, 1857. It was extended to Hempstead by 1858, and to Millican in 1860. This was eighty miles of road, just about the same as that of the Buffalo Bayou, Brazos and Colorado road. By the completion of these roads Houston established its claim to be considered the great distributing point.

During the period from 1857 to 1860, the Washington County Railroad, a branch of the Houston and Texas Central, was built, as an independent enterprise, from Hempstead to Brenham, 21 miles. Brenham was then one of the most important points in Texas.

The Galveston, Houston and Henderson Railroad, built as an outlet to the Gulf, via Galveston, for lines centering in Houston was begun at Virginia Point opposite Galveston, in 1854, and was finished to Houston in 1858. Its length was 42 miles, and in many respects it was and is one of the most important bits of railroad ever constructed in Texas. Until the summer of 1859 passengers and freight were ferried from Virginia Point to the Island, but a bridge across the bay was then constructed and in 1860 Houston had direct connection with Galveston by rail.

Houston began, in 1856, the construction of the Houston Tap and Brazoria Railroad, seven miles in length, to connect with the Buffalo Bayou, Brazos and Colorado Railroad at Pierce Junction. The Houston Tap and Brazoria Railroad Company was later organized to take over the Buffalo Bayou, Brazos and Colorado road, which it did and in 1861, extended it to Columbia, on the Brazos River, a distance of fifty miles from Houston. That line is now a part of the International and Great Northern system.

The Texas and New Orleans road, now of the Southern Pacific system, was originally chartered under the name of the Sabine and Galveston Bay Railroad and Lumber Company. It was intended to build a line from Madison to Orange, via Beaumont to tide water on Galveston Bay. The Company was chartered in 1859 as the Texas and New Orleans Railroad, the plans of its projectors having been changed and a new charter becoming necessary. By this charter the company was organized to accept an act passed by the Louisiana legislature legalizing the construction of the Louisiana part of the line; and that part in Texas was to be known as the Texas division.

Actual construction of the road was begun at Houston, in 1858, and it was completed to Liberty, 40 miles, by 1860. In January, 1861, it had been completed to Orange, on the Sabine River, 111 miles distant from Houston. The strategic importance of this road became apparent so soon as the Civil

War broke out, for its value would be inestimable in case of the blockade of Texas ports, and the people of Louisiana were urged to complete the link between the Texas border and New Orleans. However, nothing was done and the road remained in its unfinished state until long after the war. The Civil War paralyzed railroad building as it did other industries. At the close of the war, Houston had 371 miles of railroad centering here.

- (1)—Buffalo Bayou, Brazos and Colorado, Harrisburg to Alleyton, 80 miles.
- (2)—Houston and Texas Central, Houston to Millican, 80 miles.
- (3)—Galveston, Houston and Henderson, Galveston to Houston, 50 miles.
- (4)—Houston Tap and Brazoria, Houston to Columbia, 50 miles.
- (5)—Texas and New Orleans, Houston to Orange, 111 miles.
-

The Texas railroads suffered more than almost all other interests combined, during the war. The State Comptroller in a report after the war, said that the railways had been so crippled and disorganized as a result of the four years struggle, that most of the lines had ceased to be anything more than names. Train service over the Houston Tap and Brazoria Railroad was abandoned in the early sixties, and at the comptroller's office, in 1865, it was not known definitely if the Texas and New Orleans road was in operation or not, so meager were the details. It had been reported as in bad condition and unfit for use. The Buffalo Bayou, Brazos and Colorado road was without rolling stock, road bed, bridges or anything else and had been abandoned. The Houston and Texas Central was in a dilapidated condition and unsafe.

During the reconstruction period some of the roads were forced to organize, others to completely reorganize while others were sold outright by the state. By 1870 practically every road in the state was in new hands. Then systems of lines began to take shape. Outside roads began pushing towards the Texas border and Houston became the center of a system as important as any in the South, and more pregnant with future greatness than any other railway center in the South or West.

Today Houston is the center of several great railway systems in Texas.

The Southern Pacific, usually known as the Harriman lines, entering Houston, are the Galveston, Harrisburg and San Antonio; Houston and Texas Central; Texas and New Orleans; and the Houston East and West Texas. The San Antonio and Arkansas Pass road, formerly of the system, was separated from it by the railway commission and is now listed as an independent road.

Chief of the Gould group is the International and Great Northern, 1,106 miles in length, with its headquarters in Houston. This is the only line crossing the state from northeast to southwest. The next in importance is the

Galveston, Houston and Henderson. The Houston Tap and Brazoria road, formerly an independent line is now part of the International and is known as the Columbia Tap. The mileage of the Gould group of roads is 2,923 miles, and there are more roads belonging to it than to any other system in the state.

In the early eighties it was of relatively more importance than it is now, and controlled the Missouri Pacific and the Missouri Kansas and Texas roads. The Missouri Pacific divided the International and Great Northern into two branches, one from Longview to Houston via Palestine; the other from St. Louis to Houston, via the Iron Mountain road to Texarkana, and the International and Great Northern to Houston, and from the Texas and Pacific to Longview. By a lease of the track of the Galveston, Houston and Henderson road for 99 years, an outlet for the International and Great Northern to Galveston was secured.

Down to June, 1907, the Santa Fe lines in Texas aggregated 1,776 miles. Many miles have been built since, nearly all in west Texas. The main line to Galveston was not originally the property of the Atchison, Topeka and Santa Fe Company. Galveston had suffered so much from having Houston quarantine against her every time there was a yellow-fever scare that she determined to build a railroad of her own which would be independent of Houston and reach the interior without coming to or through Houston at all. With this object in view the Santa Fe was built past Houston, but eventually built into Houston from Alvin.

The Katy, or Missouri, Kansas and Texas system, entering Houston from the northwest, is one of the most important freight and passenger lines in Texas. It is made up of numerous small lines, bought and consolidated to form one strong system. From 0 to 1888, the Missouri Pacific Company operated under a lease. For a time, as already noted, the Katy controlled the International and Great Northern, but now it controls less than 1,000 miles in Texas.

The Rock Island system is generally regarded as being allied with the Colorado and Southern system. Of this system the Trinity and Brazos Valley line was formerly the mainstay and the outlet to Houston and the Gulf. That line maintains general offices in Houston. The Rock Island people, operating largely in Oklahoma and Kansas, wanted a direct line for shipment of grain to the Gulf, and the Trinity and Brazos Valley trackage was the most desirable of any that was available. When the Frisco separated from the Rock Island, it built a Gulf connecting line through Louisiana to Houston, completed in 1909, and absorbed the Gulf coast line to Brownsville. At the present time it has no other local connection. The section of country that it seeks to develop lies south and west of Houston. A traffic manager makes his headquarters here, and the general offices of the road are in the Binz Building. Its lines entering Houston are the St. Louis, Brownsville and Mexican line, the Frisco

Lines east and the line of the Houston Belt and Terminal Co. The B. F. Yoakum interests are generally considered as controlling these roads.

The Houston Belt and Terminal Railroad Company, owned and controlled by the Gulf, Colorado and Santa Fe, the Frisco lines in Texas, the St. Louis, Brownsville and Mexican and the Trinity and Brazos Valley railroads, was organized in June, 1906. It is strictly a Houston enterprise and all material used in its construction was bought, so far as possible, in Houston. Its new depot is one of the handsomest structures of the kind in the country. It is a three-story, steel-frame building of Doric architecture. Its exterior is faced with St. Louis red brick and its interior is finished in Italian marble. The building fronts on Crawford Street, 250 feet between Texas and Prairie Avenues, and its covered platforms and its sheds extend back 1,000 feet. Its freight depots are almost equally important.

In the foregoing pages is given a brief summary of the railroad history of Houston from the earliest date to the present time, and while it shows in a general way that Houston had much to do with formulating and perfecting nearly all the earlier plans, it does not show how vitally important was the work done by individual Houstonians, nor does it show the clear and intelligent appreciation of the magnitude of the work undertaken, possessed by the pioneer railroad builders in Houston.

Even before the movement for the construction of a railroad towards the North had taken form, and while the whole question had scarcely advanced beyond the stage of intention, Houston men were busy devising means to secure more rapid communication with the interior of the state. On February 7th, 1850, the Brazos Plank Road Company was incorporated. Its incorporators were: E. B. Nichols, Paul Bremond, Wm. J. Hutchins, W. M. Rice, A. S. Ruthven, B. A. Shepherd, Thomas M. Bagby, James H. Stevens, S. L. Allen, William A. Van Alstyne, A. McGowan, T. W. House, Francis Moore, and C. Evans.

On June 23, 1852, a meeting was held at the Capitol Hotel, for the purpose of appointing delegates to a railroad meeting in Washington County. Judge H. F. Allen was chairman and Henry Sampson, secretary, of the Houston meeting. Five delegates, J. C. Massie, T. M. Bagby, C. Ennis, A. S. Ruthven, and Judge Allen were appointed to represent Houston at the convention which was to meet at Chappell Hill on July 3. Paul Bremond, A. J. Burke, W. M. Rice, Abram Groesbeck, and Henry Sampson, were appointed a corresponding committee. The following resolutions were adopted:

"Whereas, the citizens of Houston are duly sensible of the present importance and growing necessity of greatly increasing facilities of communication and transportation with those portions of the state whence the most valuable trade of said city is derived; and

156

"Whereas, the growth of population, production and wealth in the interior already authorized and demand the expenditure of capital in the attainment of that object; it is, therefore

"Resolved:—That the city of Houston will do its part toward any system of internal improvement calculated to advance her interests and facilitate her commerce with the interior, that may be found practical and expedient.

"Resolved:—That this meeting is fully impressed with the conviction that the trade of this city and the interests of the people of the Brazos and Colorado Valleys demand the construction of a railroad from this city to Austin, the capital of the state, and that with proper exertion and the aid within our reach, the construction of such road is entirely practicable.

"Resolved:—That the citizens of Houston will gladly cooperate with the people of Washington County and of other counties, in the proposed mass meeting to be held at Chappell Hill, July 3, proximo, and that delegates be sent to represent this city at that meeting."

The day after that meeting the Telegraph, while strongly advocating the building of a railroad, also urged adhering to the idea of the plank road. The argument it used was that the necessity for better facilities for communication with the interior was a present and pressing need and one that could not be delayed. It stated that the Plank Road Company, chartered two years before, already had about 23 miles graded and that the road could be planked and thus rendered immediately available, at very small cost. It then pointed out that a charter could not be obtained for a railroad under three years, and that the charters then in existence were worse than useless because they were all loaded down with "tapping" privileges which gave outsiders the right to tap the road every few miles with lines only a few miles long, thus enabling them to gain the advantage of facilities which cost the originators millions of dollars, without rendering any return benefit.

However neither the plank road nor the Chappell Hill discussed railroad was ever built, nor advanced further than the stage of agitation and talk. The graded road was used, just as it was, and unquestionably did good service, for the trade of Houston in the early fifties had grown to no mean proportions. Had the merchants of that day been less unselfish, or rather less far-seeing, the actual construction of railroads might have been longer delayed than it was. As to Rome, all roads led to Houston, and the people of the interior had to come here whether they cared to do so or not. The difficulties of transportation were things that concerned those only who had to reach the only market in the state, and relying on her natural advantages, Houston could afford to be dilatory about furnishing rapid transportation to her less fortunate customers. The volume of trade was very great, and very profitable. An idea of the magnitude of the ox-wagon trade, and the number of those engaged in it can be formed from reading the following extract from an editorial published in the Telegraph, May 2, 1855:

"The editor of the Panoplist says, if he were called on to say what was the 'peculiar institution' of Houston, he would say it was ox-teams and teamsters. He spoke the truth. Ox-teams and teamsters have been the pride and glory of this city for many years. Whatever else might have been dispensed with as instruments of its prosperity, they are indispensable, for they form the connecting link between the merchant and the planter, without which both merchant and planter could do nothing. They have a position in this great and growing state second to no other interest, and they stand in the same relation to the general prosperity that railroads, canals and steamboats do in New York and Pennsylvania.

"Not less than 4,000 bales of cotton have arrived in this city in the last two weeks on ox-wagons, giving employment to 4,690 yoke of oxen and 670 wagons and drivers. Besides the above there have been at least 200 arrivals of wagons freighted with other produce than cotton. But let us calculate the amount of capital and industry employed in handling cotton alone.

"Last year, with a short crop, the receipts at this point were in round numbers 38,000 bales. The loads average from 3 to 10 bales, according to the roads, but, say, an average of 6 bales to the wagon, which is probably over the mark, then there were 6,333 trips required for last year's business. Many wagons make from four to six trips per year. At an average of four trips there were 1,566 wagons, giving employment to an army of teamsters twice as large as the number of men engaged in whipping Mexico at San Jacinto.

"Each of these wagons require on an average, seven yoke of oxen, which, with regular teamsters, are changed for fresh cattle several times each year. Wagoners tell us that it requires a fresh team as they are almost exclusively fed by grazing along the road. At this rate it requires, in round numbers, 25,000 yoke of oxen for the year's business. Oxen are worth an average of $50 a yoke. Wagons, complete, $150 each. The capital engaged was as follows:

25,000 yoke of oxen at $50 a yoke	$1,250,000
1,566 wagons at $150 each	234,900
Making a total of	$1,484,900

The expense of a trip will average $40, and the gross amount of freight money about $100, giving the result of the business as follows:

Freight, at $100 per trip on 6,333 trips	$633,300
Less expense, $40 per trip	253,320
Net profit	$380,010

"The cotton transported last year was fully 40 per cent less than the whole transport engaged in the trade. In fact the upfreight from this point required much more than 40 per cent greater transportation than the cotton, to say nothing of the corn, sugar, and molasses, hides, skins, etc., brought to this market. There must be considerably more than two million dollars invested in transportation to and from Houston, two-thirds of which would be unnecessary if we had about 200 miles of railroad; or, in other words, here is $1,300,000 that might be invested in railroads to great advantage.

"We can have no sort of transportation without capital, and delay investment in railroads as we may, a similar investment must be made in wagons and oxen, which means that in about three of four years more instead of 2,000 wagons we will require 8,000, at a cost of about five million dollars. Wagons and oxen last about five years and when worn out are a total loss. Railroads can be constantly repaired, and the cost of repairs in twenty years is only equal to the original investment. These figures are merely estimates, but they are approximately correct and they serve to show what large sums of money are being thrown away each year on present means of transportation.

"We hope the day is near at hand when railroads will be one of the 'peculiar institutions' of this city and of the state, when the ox shall give way to the iron horse which travels with twenty times the speed of the ox and carries a thousand times its burden."

Notwithstanding the fact that the charter of the Houston and Texas Central Railroad was fairly bristling with "tapping" privileges, the handful of live and progressive citizens of Houston determined not to wait until the old charter could be amended or a new one obtained, but to go ahead and begin the construction of the road at once. These pioneer railroad builders were Paul Bremond, Wm. R. Baker, Wm. M. Rice, Cornelius Ennis, Wm. J. Hutchins, A. S. Ruthven, B. A. Shepherd, T. W. House, W. A. Van Alstyne, James H. Stevens, and Dr. Francis Moore. Although these men were the leading merchants, bankers and business men of Houston, not one of them was wealthy, measured by the standard of today, and it is highly improbable that as much capital was invested in the railroad when the first steps were taken towards its construction, as would be required for the construction of a modern skyscraper. They had what proved to be about as powerful as capital, an unlimited supply of grit and determination. Once having put their shoulders to the wheel, all thought of failure or weakness was abandoned.

The first shovel of dirt was thrown up by Mr. Paul Bremond on January 1, 1853, at a point that would be crossed by a line continuing Louisiana Street across the bayou, near where McGowan's Foundry stood. A contract for the construction thus begun had been made, but before the road reached a point about where the old city limits were, the contractor threw up his contract and left town. As soon as he realized the magnitude of his undertaking, he quit.

Mr. Bremond had never had the slightest experience as a contractor, yet he did not hesitate, but promptly took the contract himself. It was not long before every dollar that had been paid into the treasury was gone and Mr. Bremond had spent his own fortune and stretched his credit almost to the breaking point, and yet the actual laborers were not paid. Sub-contractors became disgusted and quit. The laborers became more than disgusted. They armed themselves with clubs and hunted for Mr. Bremond, going in gangs on Saturday nights, and individually on other days of the week. They attacked his home and carried away his fence when they found they could not get him to carry away. No railroad builder ever had so strenuous a time as he. Yet he was not discouraged. He had made up his mind to build that road and he did it. He was not an orator; in fact he was no speaker at all, and yet on the few occasions when he was caught by the outraged laborers, he succeeded in talking himself out of "a bad fix," and convinced the laborers that he was the best friend they had and one who was acting for their best interest. As an illustration of this peculiar gift as a conversationalist in that special line the following story used to be told:

One of the sub-contractors, growing weary of his inability to get a settlement of his account, went to one of the leading lawyers, and after explaining all its details placed his claim in his hands for collection. The lawyer told him he would go over and talk with Mr. Bremond. "No, you keep away from him, for it will do no good and he will convince you that I owe him money before he gets through," said the client. The lawyer insisted on going anyway and told the contractor to wait in his office until he came back. He was gone for quite a time and came back looking worried. In reply to a question as to what he thought of the case, the lawyer blurted out: "I think you have treated Bremond d——d badly and I'll have nothing to do with your case."

"It is pleasant to recount that not a man who ever trusted Mr. Bremond, willingly or through compulsion, ever lost a cent. He paid everything in the end and paid it willingly. The truth is he was an enthusiast, he looked ahead and discounted the future. He knew what he could do if given time and assistance. He had faith enough to invest all of his own fortune, and a large part of the fortune of several of his friends, and he asked only that others should contribute their time and labor to the same end.

It took Paul Bremond five years of actual warfare and concentrated trouble and discord, to build fifty miles of road. But when the road had reached Hempstead, the worst of its troubles were over. The rich and rather densely settled countries near there became at once tributary to the road and it began to be something of what its projectors had claimed it would be. Thirty miles more were built in the next two years, and then the great Civil War broke out and stopped everything. However, the Houston and Texas

Central road had grown to good proportions, had reached about to the, then, center of production and was fairly and safely on its feet.

While the early fifties seem to have brought about a realization on the part of the people of Houston of the fact that the railroads were necessary to bring the products of the state here, railroads were also equally necessary to carry them to tide water. The fact that the facilities afforded by Buffalo Bayou were inadequate and that these must be added to become apparent. With that object in view, a railroad meeting composed of leading citizens of Galveston and Houston, was held at the Capitol Hotel in 1852, for the purpose of discussing the construction of a line of railroad from Houston to Galveston. Hon. Hamilton Stewart, mayor of Galveston was selected as chairman, Messrs. M. B. Menard, Willard Richardson and Hiram Close of Galveston; Col. D. J. Landes, of Washington County; Hon. David G. Burnett, Frances Moore, Jr., and Hon. Ashbel Smith, of Harris County, as vice-presidents, and William R. Baker, of Houston, and H. H. Smith, of Galveston, as secretaries. A committee of thirteen was appointed to outline a plan of campaign, and to take steps towards a thorough organization. Immediately after the adjournment, Houston subscribed $300,000 towards the building of the road, and Galveston did equally as well. However, it was not until two years later that actual construction was begun, and the road was not completed until 1858. This road is now known as the Galveston, Houston and Henderson Railroad and forms part of the Gould system of roads. It is one of the best pieces of railroad in the United States, and one of the best paying railroads in the country as well.

Houston having thus secured a road to the North, one to the South and one to the West, Mr. Bremond, (the same man who built the Houston and Texas Central), conceived the idea of a great east and west line, one that would traverse the richest sections of the state. For a long time he tried to interest outside capitalists as well as those at home, in his plans, but failed. Then, realizing what he had accomplished before, he determined to build the road himself with his own resources. His idea was to build a line from Shreveport to Houston and from Houston to Santa Fe, New Mexico. He concluded to build the Shreveport end first, and accordingly, on July 4, 1876, he threw the first spade of earth for his road at a point near the old Texas and New Orleans depot, in the Fifth ward. Mr. Paul Bremond was president of the road, and his son-in-law, Major S. C. Timpson was secretary and treasurer. Mr. Bremond again had a strenuous time in railroad building, but profiting by his former experience, and above all by the reputation he had earned then of carrying out anything that he undertook, he soon got everything moving along smoothly and built the road to Shreveport and constructed about twenty miles of the line to the west before his death. For some reason the western branch was never completed.

A fact not generally appreciated is that of the seventeen railroads centering at Houston, there is not one that does not make Houston its terminus. There are no through trains entering or leaving Houston. There are through Pullman coaches and passenger cars, but no through freight trains, and all trains leaving here are made up in Houston.

Houston is the greatest railroad center in the Southwest, and there are more railroad employees paid off in Houston every month than at any other point in the Southwest. There are 2,843 trainmen and clerks who are paid off here and in addition to these there are 3,000 men employed in the two great railroad shops here, which brings the total number of employees to 5,843, and the amount of salaries and wages paid them is, in round numbers, $7,000,000 annually.

The International Railroad is preparing to move its general shops to Houston soon, which will greatly increase these figures, but at present only the Houston and Texas Central and the Southern Pacific roads have their shops here. These two roads have invested $1,042,216 in their plants, pay out $1,349,200 in wages and do $2,744,722 worth of repair and construction work each year.

Their shops are equipped with the best and latest machinery, and can turn out at a moment's notice everything needed in car or locomotive construction or repairing. They have machines for making the dainty tacks for the silk curtains in the palace car and machines for making the iron beams and castings that go in the frames of such cars and weigh hundreds and thousands of pounds. As a matter of fact neither shop makes locomotives and yet each has all the facilities for making them and could if it were necessary, turn out one locomotive each day.

The railroads own and operate 450 miles of track in Harris County and the money invested in them is $20,000,000, over one-half of which is invested in Houstonian terminal facilities, shops and offices. An idea of the immensity of the traffic can be formed from the statement that for the fiscal year closed June 31, 1911, 90,000 trains were handled in and out of Houston, and that the freight handled by those trains footed up very nearly half a billion tons. Of the 90,000 trains slightly more than one-half were passenger trains, and, excluding excursions and special occasions, it is estimated that these trains handled over 400,000 regular passengers during the year. Seven roads have their headquarters here, while all the big systems are represented in the city. The newest acquisition is the International and Great Northern, which has just moved its general offices here. These offices include the following departments: General freight and passenger office, auditor's office, treasurer's office, general claims office, general attorney's office, and the offices of the several division superintendents. Judge T. J. Freeman, the new president, during all the time he was receiver of the road maintained general offices in Houston. Judge Freeman's ability has rescued the I. & G. N. from bankruptcy and made it one of the best equipped roads in Texas. Judge Freeman is in the first rank of railroad officials in America and is one of the three great builders Texas had given to the railroad world. The other two are B. F. Yoakum and Judge R. S. Lovett.

The coming of the I. & G. N. and the Frisco to Houston has added about six hundred well-paid employees to Houston's railroad population. The officers of the Frisco that came to Houston in 1911 were those of the vice-president and general manager, auditor, treasurer, car service, purchasing agent and stationer.

Even before the International and Great Northern road moved its general offices to Houston it was doing an immense business here and this point was to all intent and purpose its principal point in Texas. Its coming brings about 250 men and their families and swells the pay roll of the railroads here an additional half million annually. The company owns several desirable places in the city, where their own office building can be constructed for the accommodation of the general offices, but it is likely the building will be on San Jacinto Street, where the freight office of the company is now located. This building was originally constructed with the object in view of adding other stories. At present the offices are located in rented quarters.

The Sunset Central system is the largest railway system under one management in Texas. Thornwell Fay is vice-president and general manager. It operates four companies embracing six lines. These railroad companies have an assessed valuation in Harris County of $5,611,926, of which $2,424,770 is located in the city of Houston. The receipts from the sale of tickets to passengers at the Houston station during the fiscal year closed in June, 1911, were $4,828,053.47. The principal terminal of the company is the Grand Central passenger station on Washington Avenue. Thousands of passenger trains are operated in and out of this depot every year and hundreds of thousands of people pass through its gates.

The freight terminals are north of the passenger depot, near the extensive system of shops. These terminals have thirty-two miles of trackage and enormous sheds and warehouses. Nearly five hundred yard clerks, switchmen and others are employed in these yards, working in two shifts, one night and the other day, in order to keep up with the enormous traffic.

All the Sunset Central general offices are now located in their new nine-story building, corner of Franklin and Travis Street. This building has just been completed at a cost of $512,793 and is one of the finest buildings in the city.

The Missouri, Kansas and Texas Railroad Company of Texas is also making extensive improvements. The company has already spent hundreds of thousands of dollars improving its property and has not yet completed its task. Additions have been made to its terminals in the way of increased warehouse and track facilities, the latter having been doubled, in order to care for its large and rapidly increasing business. A building has been constructed for the locomotive department, another for the car department, artesian wells have been sunk, so as to give the company its own water-supply, and many other improvements have been made. The company now has property in Harris County assessed at $510,710. During the past year the pay rolls were: in local shops, $31,081.90; in offices, $21,901.55; in operating department, $36,963.45.

The San Antonio and Arkansas Pass Railroad runs its trains into the Grand Central depot. The company owns property in Harris County amounting to $593,150. It is one of the most important of Houston's railroads. Its main offices are in San Antonio, but it keeps a good force here. Its local pay rolls for 1910 were: in freight and passenger departments, $19,927.25; shops and roundhouses, $11,326.15; in yards and to train men, $20,312.59; to all others, $9,573.30.

The Gulf, Colorado and Santa Fe road was one of Houston's largest industries but with the advent of the Houston Belt and Terminal Company the road leased all its Houston property to that company and became one of its tenants. The property of the Santa Fe in Houston is valued at $1,300,000. The only employees of the company in Houston are freight and passenger agents. The road has more than a passing interest in the Houston Belt and Terminal Company, since the vice-president of the Santa Fe is also president of the Terminal Company. The Gulf, Colorado and Santa Fe operates about 8,000 passenger and freight trains in and out of Houston each year.

Col. J. G. Tracey and two or three associates organized a Houston Belt and Terminal line in 1882. They had surveys made, obtained some rights of way, and then, for unknown causes, abandoned the enterprise. Nothing further was ever done towards constructing such a line, until in June, 1905, the Houston Belt and Terminal Line was organized. The company began active operations at once and expended more than $5,000,000 for the completion of a system of railroad terminals for both freight and passenger business designed to handle all the terminal business of Houston if necessary.

Four roads, the Santa Fe, the Frisco, the Trinity and Brazos Valley and the Brownsville are joint owners and are now using the terminal facilities. The passenger station, described briefly elsewhere, is very handsome and cost over half a million dollars, the marble used in its interior decoration costing $45,000. The whole system is constructed on scientific, and practical lines so that it is perfectly equipped for the objects for which it was designed. The depot building was dedicated March 1, 1911, and has been in active use since that date.

The Frisco has made many improvements during the last year, the greatest being the establishment of its through line to New Orleans. This is one of the fastest and most thoroughly equipped trains in the United States. It has oil-burning locomotives, steel passenger trains, cars and baggage coaches all equipped with electric lights, fans, etc. The distance between Houston and New Orleans, 360 miles is covered in twelve hours. The Frisco has a network of small and great lines in Texas and Louisiana, all tributary to Houston. All the traffic of the Frisco in Houston is handled by the Terminal Company, but the road has a force of about 300 office employees and their pay roll foots up about $360,000 per year. Mr. W. C. Conner, Jr., the traffic manager, is one of the most brilliant and successful of railroad officers and has shining prospects in the railroad world.

Houston's seventeen railroads are the following: Houston and Texas Central; Galveston, Harrisburg and San Antonio; Texas and New Orleans; Beaumont, Sour Lake and Western; Houston, East and West Texas; International and Great Northern (Ft. Worth Division); International and Great Northern; Trinity and Brazos Valley; San Antonio and Arkansas Pass; Galveston, Harrisburg and San Antonio (Victoria Division); Gulf, Colorado and Santa Fe; Missouri, Kansas and Texas; International and Great Northern (Columbia Division); St. Louis, Brownsville and Mexico; Galveston, Houston and Henderson; Galveston, Harrisburg and San Antonio (Galveston Division); Texas Transportation Company.

It is rather remarkable that with all their enterprise and public spirit the people of Houston made but few efforts to improve the navigation of Buffalo Bayou in the early days. As already noted the Republic had made an appropriation for the improvement of the rivers and harbors of Texas, but no one seems to have thought of making use of any of this appropriation for the improvement of the bayou. Newell, in his history of the Revolution in Texas thus describes the bayou in 1838: "It is a very singular water-course, without any current except as caused by the tides of the sea; very deep, and navigable from its junction with the San Jacinto to its forks at Houston, for boats of any draft of water, though too narrow to admit those of the largest class. The soil upon its banks is generally light and sandy."

The Cayuga, later called the Branch T. Archer, was the name of one of the first steamboats to reach Houston. The Cayuga was brought to Texas by John R. Harris and was under command of Captain Isaac Batterson. It was intended originally to run on the Trinity River but was changed to the bayou trade. Soon after that the Constitution was added to the service. She came up to Houston but was so long she could not be turned around, and had to be backed down to Constitution bend in the bayou. No doubt that is the way this big bend acquired its name.

Another early boat was the San Jacinto, which sank in the bayou near where Clinton now is, and still another was the Henry A. Jones which was burned in Galveston Bay in 1839, with some loss of life. A year or so later the Farmer blew up, killing Captain Webb and Henry Sylvester. The Star State plied on the bayou in the early forties and met with several accidents. Once it caught fire and the passengers escaped with difficulty. Mrs. Peter W. Gray, of Houston jumped overboard and was rescued with difficulty.

The Billow, Capt. James Montgomery, brought to Houston the first locomotive for the Houston and Texas Central Railroad. It was unloaded at the mouth of White Oak Bayou at the foot of Main Street and run onto a temporary track. Capt. Charles Burton, afterwards superintendent of the railroad took charge of the locomotive.

The Charles Fowler had the first calliope ever heard in Houston. On her first trip to Houston she stuck at the G. and H. Railroad bridge over the bayou and some of its piling had to be cut away to admit of her passage. The Silver Cloud, laden with fruit, sank at Harrisburg.

At different times there were in the bayou trade, the Ida Reese, the Desmonia, the Old Reliable, the J. H. Sterrett, the Erie No. 3, a stern-wheeler, the Erie No. 12, also a stern-wheeler, the Wren and the Shreveport. The Diana, Captain Pat Christian, and the Lizzie, Captain A. Connors, two magnificent passenger boats ceased running in 1877. The Diana and the T. M. Bagby were built in Ohio for Captain Sterrett, the best known steamboat man in Texas, in 1870, and arrived here the same year. The Diana was 170 feet long, 32 feet beam and 5 feet hold. She had three boilers, two flues and a full length cabin. Her cost was $33,000 and she and the Bagby were as fine boats as any that ran on the Mississippi, which river was said to have the finest in the world.

It is strange, but true, that the first great assistance Houston had in bringing the question of bayou improvement before the public came from Galveston, its bitterest commercial rival. Four or five years after the close of the war, when the railroads had been reorganized and the commerce of the state had grown to large proportions, the Houston people, naturally, began agitating the question of securing better navigation of Buffalo Bayou so as to add to Houston's facilities for handling the rapidly increasing trade. At first Houston stood alone in making its fight. The people of the interior were indifferent, while those of Galveston ridiculed the idea of Houston ever securing navigation of its crooked bayou for ocean-going vessels. Unfortunately for Galveston there was at that time in that city a wharf company that had an absolute monopoly of the whole city water front, and that company was short-sighted enough to take full advantage of the monopoly. It made its rates very high and acted very arbitrarily. It cost $5 per bale to take cotton from Houston to Galveston by rail and then the Wharf Company took a whack at it and there was a big hole knocked in the farmer's or shipper's profit by the time the cotton got on shipboard after leaving Houston.

Houston was not slow about seizing this strong argument placed in her hands by the Wharf Company and began a campaign of education to teach the people of the interior that they were far more interested in securing deep water at Houston than was Houston itself. They were shown that could vessels come to Houston to discharge their cargoes and take on new ones, the fifty miles haul to and from Galveston, and the excessive charges of the Galveston Wharf Company would be things of the past and millions of dollars would be saved by the interior people annually.

The Houston Direct Navigation Company, for the improvement and navigation of the bayou had been formed in 1869, but by 1870 the campaign of education had so far progressed that the question was no longer a local one, in any sense of the word, but was state-wide. The Navigation Company continued the work of deepening the bayou and began the digging of a channel across Morgan's Point. The city had, through assistance given the Navigation Company, spent about $230,000 on this work, when the Galveston Wharf Company again came to its assistance in the most unexpected way. The assistance was real and of great value, though it was entirely unintentional on the part of the Wharf Company.

Charles Morgan, the president and chief owner of the Morgan Steamship line, that for years controlled the ocean carrying trade between New Orleans and Texas ports, asked the Galveston Wharf Company for better facilities and better rates than were given him at that time. The company turned down his request and treated him with contempt. He threatened to come to Houston with his ships unless they treated him more reasonably. They hooted at the idea and told him to go ahead and do whatever he pleased. He did go ahead. He purchased Houston's stock in the Navigation Company, put his engineers and a big dredging force to work, and completed the canal through Morgan's Point. The great storm of 1875 destroyed his fleet of small vessels and a great many workmen were drowned. But work was resumed within thirty days and continued until the cut-off through Morgan's Point was completed. A railroad was built from Houston to Clinton, a point on Buffalo Bayou about ten miles by land, and for a few years the Morgan steamers gave Galveston the go-by and came directly to Clinton. Then the Wharf Company at Galveston realized the error of its way, repented and gave Morgan whatever he wanted and he discontinued his Houston steamers. However, he had demonstrated what could be done and there was a popular demand on Congress to take charge of and develop this important waterway, which had such brilliant promise for the future.

In the late seventies a bill was introduced in Congress for the purchase of the Buffalo Ship Channel by the United States Government, with the view of opening it as a general highway. A corps of engineers was sent by the Government to inspect the work already done. They reported that twelve feet of water, as an average depth of the channel, to the foot of Main Street in Houston, could be had. The condition of the proposed sale of the channel to the Government by Morgan was that the Government should refund to him the amount expended by him in the work and carry out the general terms of the undertaking as accepted by him when he took over the channel from the Buffalo Bayou Ship Canal Company. One of the conditions of the transfer was that the work would be completed to the foot of Main Street as soon as practicable. The Ship Channel was assumed to extend from Clinton to Red Fish Bar. From Red Fish Bar to Bolliver, the Government had done work under various appropriations, the last of which had been $147,000. From Clinton to Boliver the channel varied in depth from 14 to 30 feet, and an inspection in 1880 showed that the channel through Morgan's Point and Red Fish Bar had deepened and widened through natural causes.

On the old channel the Direct Navigation Company had expended about $200,000 before it had transferred the work to Morgan. After the transfer, Morgan expended about $700,000 more in bringing the work to Clinton, and had expended about $125,000 in making improvements at Clinton. There was a long delay and negotiations were not closed until 1891 and the money was paid to Morgan and the channel through Morgan's Point was thrown open to the public on May 4, 1892.

The work of the Government on the Houston Ship Channel has been continuous since the day it took charge. Each Congress, with one exception when no river and harbor bill was passed, has made a liberal appropriation for the work. The bayou has been made straighter by the removal of sharp curves, the stream has been widened and deepened by dredging and the bayou, always naturally deep, has been put in first class condition. If all the channel were as easy of improvement as the bayou, the problem would have been solved long ago. The main trouble exists at one or two points in Galveston Bay. Red Fish and Morgan's Point, involving a stretch of channel about twelve miles in extent, are the chief points on which the work must be concentrated. At these points the sand is shifting and almost as fast as a channel is deepened it is filled up by the sand. The proper solution of the problem, so the engineers say, is to confine the currents and tides that sweep over the channel at these points, so as to direct them along the channel and thus make them do the work of keeping the channel clear. To do this long and expensive bulk-heading will be required. When this is done there is no reason why the large vessels that enter Galveston Bay cannot come direct to the Houston Turning Basin.

The whole thing is simply a question of money. The Government recognized this when, in 1910, Congress passed a bill appropriating $1,250,000 for the development of the Ship Channel, on condition that Houston would raise a similar amount. So soon as this became known, officially, Mayor Rice of Houston, consulted with the Harris County Commissioners, with the result that the Houston Navigation District was formed. An election was held and the proposition to have the Navigation District issue bonds to the amount of $1,250,000 was carried overwhelmingly in 1911, and Houston's future as a deep-water port was assured.

Because the Government engineers have declared that it will cost two and one-half million dollars to complete the Ship Channel, there seems to be an impression, even in Houston, that a vast amount of work yet remains to be done before ocean-going vessels can make use of the channel regularly. That is a mistaken idea. A big work will have to be done, but its magnitude is more in the way of expense than anything else. There is very little difficulty about it. It is expensive because about twelve miles of the channel will have to be bulk-headed to protect the channel from shifting sands at Morgan's Point and Red Fish Bar, or reef. The bayou itself from Morgan's Point to the Turning Basin, is wide enough and deep enough to admit of the safe passage of large steamships of 18 to 20 feet draught, while the channel in the bay from Red Fish Bar to the end of the jetties in the gulf is equally safe for the same class of vessels. One or two large steamers have already made the trip to the turning basin, safely. The Revenue Cutter Windom, the Steamship Disa and the Steamship Mercator, the latter 250 feet in length, have made successful trips from the Gulf of Mexico to the Houston Turning Basin, thus demonstrating that the Ship Channel is an actual fact and not a theory. It is well known that steamships are the most timid things in the world. They take no chances of getting aground or of being detained in any way, for with them time is literally money. Under these circumstances and conditions it will be difficult to get regular lines of steamers established until the channel is placed in such condition that it will be absolutely safe at all times and under all conditions, as it will be when approved improvements are completed.

The channel in its present condition is used and has been used for years, and an immense traffic goes on over its waters. Numerous small boats ply the channel regularly, while tug-drawn barges carry thousands of bales of cotton and other produce, which swell the value of the commerce to millions of dollars annually. Aside from the actual and tangible profits derived by Houston people from the bayou trade and commerce, there is a greater one, in the fact that having this outlet to the sea gives Houston all the benefits of water rates.

When the S. S. Disa came to the Turning Basin on November 8, 1909, all the newspapers stated that she was the first ocean-going vessel to come up Buffalo Bayou. Such was not the case. In the spring of 1863 a good sized steamship ran the blockade at Galveston and Buffalo Bayou being out of its banks because of a great spring flood, the steamer came directly to Houston and discharged her cargo of arms and ammunition at the foot of Fannin Street. She then took on a cargo of cotton, shipped by T. W. House, Sr., returned to Galveston and ran the blockade again. Unfortunately, the name of this blockade-runner has not been preserved.

The first street railroad company to operate in Houston, was a local concern backed by local capital, which was organized under a charter granted by the Legislature, August 6, 1870, and known as the Houston City Street

Railway Company. A franchise was granted to this company in 1873 by the city council. The stockholders were T. W. House, E. W. Cave, J. T. Brady, and William Brady. About 5½ miles of track was laid by 1874 and the road was operated continuously until 1883. The company had the field all to itself for awhile, but in 1881 the Bayou City Street Car Company was organized and laid a track from the Capitol Hotel to the Union Depot. In 1883 a controlling interest in both these companies was bough by Colonel Sinclair of Galveston who soon sold a half interest in his holdings to H. F. McGregor. The combined trackage of the two lines was about six miles. The lines were rebuilt and extended by Messrs. Sinclair and McGregor until there was a length of about 16 miles all operated by mule power.

The business was so prosperous that others determined to take a hand in it and accordingly, in 1890, a second Bayou City Street Railroad Company was organized. The promoters of the new company, Wm. Boyd and Brother, constructed ten miles of track. Soon after that Sinclair and McGregor sold out their interest to a Chicago syndicate, which had the president of the Chicago City Railroad at its head. This syndicate, in turn, sold its Houston interest to an Omaha syndicate. The new syndicate soon bought a controlling interest in the Boyd Bayou City Company which had been fairly successful. The Omaha people prepared to introduce electricity in operating their cars, and the city council passed an ordinance, October 3, 1890, authorizing them to do so. At the same time the company was given a new franchise for a period of 35 years. The two lines were consolidated and had a total trackage of 28 miles, all being equipped with electric power. The Houston Heights line was constructed in 1892–93. It was purchased by the Omaha people and combined with the other line, thus increasing its mileage to 35 miles. The great financial panic of 1893 was disastrous to the company and in 1895 it passed into the hands of John H. Kirby, as receiver. The company was reorganized in 1896, with A. W. Parlin as president and H. F. McGregor as manager. In 1901, H. B. Rice was entrusted as receiver, with the supervision of all its affairs, and during his control the road passed to the ownership of the Stone and Webster syndicate of Boston, who purchased it at a receivers sale, November 12, 1901.

The new owners placed H. K. Payne in charge as manager and set aside a certain amount of money for rebuilding and improving the property. One of the provisions of the receivers sale was that the new owners should assume all liabilities of the old company. Among these was an indebtedness to the city of Houston for street paving, variously estimated at from $30,000 to $85,000. After long negotiation, the details of which were given to the public, the company agreed to pay to the city $80,000 in full settlement of all claims, and the city agreed to extend the franchise of the road for an additional ten years. The company further agreed to establish a transfer system, vestibule its cars, to build a certain amount of new track within the city limits each year for two years, and to pay to the city one per cent of its gross earnings for 23 years and 2 per cent for the remaining ten years.

The company immediately set about rebuilding the La Branch, Houston Heights, South End, Louisiana, Franklin, San Felipe, Arkansas Pass, Brunner and Washington Street lines, replacing the old, light rails with the heaviest type of rails and substituting grounded girders for "T" rails on all paved streets. The company also began the extension of the Liberty Avenue line, the Montgomery Avenue line, the La Branch line and the Houston Avenue line. New and modern cars and other equipments were supplied, Highland Park was completed, and many improvements were made. Provision was made for the separation of white and negro passengers on the cars in accordance with the provisions of an ordinance of the city, which went into effect October 28, 1903.

The street railroad system of Houston, while far from perfect, has done much in developing and building up the city.

The Houston Electric Company now operates 13 lines in Houston and has a total of 51 miles of track. Several extensions are under way. On the several lines 191 cars are in service and the number of employees of the company is 456. It expends each year on its Houston pay roll $33,839 in salaries and $230,600 for labor. The company has a capital stock of $3,000,000 and is not in any sense a local corporation. It pays large dividends to its Boston owners. David Daly is the local manager.

In September, 1911, the finishing touches were put on the city part of the track of the Houston-Galveston Interurban Railroad. This line is 50.5 miles in length, and is said to be the best piece of track of its kind in the country. It cost $2,500,000 to construct it. The main power station at Clear Creek (half way) cost $275,000 and is fitted with two-fifteen hundred kilowatt generators and three 520-horse power engines.

There are three sub-power stations situated at La Marque, South Houston and at the main station.

Most of the grading was embankment fill, but on Galveston Island and the approach to the causeway, there was a hydraulic fill amounting to about 164,000 cubic yards. Five long bridges were constructed, the longest 612 feet in length, was that over Clear Creek. A passenger station, costing $12,000 has been erected in Galveston and one costing $40,000 is about completed in Houston.

A viaduct 1,900 feet long, built of reinforced concrete, has been constructed over the tracks of the Santa Fe and the Leeland road just beyond the Houston city limits. This road will use the great Galveston causeway, the longest bridge in the world, now almost complete. It will span Galveston Bay from Virginia Point on the mainland to the island. It will be used by all railroads, and other traffic lines of communication entering Galveston.

On account of their intimate connection with transportation matters, there is given here a brief account of Houston's first experience with the telegraph and telephone. The first mention of the telegraph is found in the Houston Telegraph, March 18, 1853. This is the announcement that L. W. Cady & Co., had determined to connect the telegraph line at Alexandria, La., with the Texas and Red River line. A Mr. Preston, who had lately passed through Houston, was then on his way to the eastern counties to arrange for the extension of the line from Alexandria to Houston.

At that time the construction of a line between Houston and Galveston was actually under way, but in 1854 work on it was abandoned, for a time at least, though it was stated that the "gutta percha wire" which was to have been laid under the waters of the bay from Virginia Point to Galveston Island, was in Galveston ready for use. Carelessness in putting up the wires and subsequent neglect of them had caused them to fall down in several place between Houston and Virginia Point. No further effort was made to build the line until in May, 1858. Then a successful movement was inaugurated and the line was built. The plan adopted for raising the necessary money was simple. An appeal was made to the business men, the professional men and to everybody in general, to take stock in the company. The expense of construction was placed at $110 per mile, which made the total cost of the land part $5,500. The submarine cable, warranted to last one year, was to cost $700, thus making the total cost of the line $6,200. Houston was asked to take $3,000 stock which she did. It was stipulated that the stock was not to be paid for until the line was completed and in operation.

In the fall of 1878, Mr. Pendarvis, telegraph operator at Morgan's Transportation Depot, which was over in the Fifth ward near Bonner's Point, installed a telephone plant between his office and the office at Clinton, ten miles away. Because the talking disturbed the clerks in the Clinton office the telephone was removed. Mr. Pendarvis then strung the wires between his office, the Direct Navigation office and the Central Depot. It was found that conversations could be carried on with as much ease as if the talkers were in one room. "When the great convenience growing out of these two connections is ascertained by other railroad men and business men generally," said the Telegram, "there will be, no doubt, a system of telephonic wires several miles in length put up here, connecting not only the depots, but many of the business houses with each other and with private residences."

Mr. Pendarvis was the first man in Houston to use the telephone for practical business purposes, though the telephone had been tested before that, as the following extract from the Houston Telegram of June 18, 1878, shows: "Mr. J. W. Stacey, the efficient manager of the Western Union Telegraph office in this city, has procured a telephone of the latest improved construction which he will put p for use during the military encampment of the volunteers of the state next week. The line will run from the Fair Grounds to Mr. G. W. Baldwin's library room in the Telegram Building and everybody wishing to have the pleasure of conversing with a friend a mile distant will have an opportunity. Our friends from the country and many in the city who are skeptical about the truthful working of the wonderful instrument, will have an opportunity to test it to their satisfaction. To many of them it will be quite a curiosity, and we expect to see its capacity fully tried. Mr. Stacey will make a trial test today and will have the apparatus in perfect working order by the end of the week."

A thorough and practical test of the telephone was made for the first time in a general way in Houston on October 18, 1879, when instruments were established in several railroad offices and in the Telegram office and the editor of the Teleram conversed for over an hour, as he tells us, with Major Swanson, Mr. Dwyer and others at the Central Railway and Sunset depots and offices.

The accounts of these primitive telegraph lines with their "gutta percha wires" for use under water and telephones that enabled one to "talk to a friend a mile away," seem very strange to us of today, when a merchant can go on the floor of the Cotton Exchange and send a message to Liverpool, have it executed and receive a reply before he can make a cigarette and smoke it. Or when one can sit in the library at home, take down the telephone and converse with a friend in Chicago, St. Louis or El Paso, with as much ease and dispatch as one can converse with the next door neighbor. In the newspaper offices in Houston demonstrations have been made of the wireless telephone.

Immediately after the close of the war the "Star State" telegraph line between Houston and Galveston and between Houston and Orange, was absorbed by the Southwestern, the Trans-Mississippi division of the Southwestern Telegraph Company that covered all of the Southern states east of the Mississippi River. The new company was placed under the supervision of Mr. D. P. Shepherd, one of the most expert operators of that or this day, who, his friends claim, was the first telegraph operator in the world to receive a message by ear. In addition to its lines to Galveston and Orange, the company had a line extending to Crockett, where it connected with a line extending to Shreveport. In the latter part of 1867 the Western Union absorbed the Southwestern and this gave the Western Union control of all telegraph lines in the United States.

Mr. Merrit Harris was made manager of the Western Union office in Houston but died soon after of yellow fever, in 1867. Col. Phil. Fall was appointed manager and served for a short time, resigning to take charge of the telegraph department of the Houston and Texas Central Railroad Company.

For over forty years the Western Union remained in full possession of the telegraph field, and then, a few months ago, it was in turn absorbed by the

Southwestern Telegraph and Telephone Company, which is the greatest combination of the kind in the world.

The Houston office is thoroughly equipped. It employs about sixty operators and has over one hundred wires running into it, forming connection with every city and village in this country, Mexico and Canada. It also has connection with deep-sea cables to all parts of the world. Mr. S. P. Jones is manager, succeeding Mr. C. W. Gribble, long the capable manager, and Mr. J. E. Johnson is chief operator. The latter is said to be one of the most skilled electricians in the telegraph service. The Postal Telegraph Company, a rival of the Western Union and its successor, the Southwestern, established its office in Houston, July 5, 1898. By strict attention to business and prompt service it soon built up a good business, and is today a substantial and solid concern. The company employs about thirty operators, and has wire connection with all points on this continent and cable connection with the whole world. On the day the company opened its office here its total receipts were $2.40. Today the daily receipts average between $400 and $500. Not only in Houston but in every office of the company all over the United States, the motto of the Postal is promptness and dispatch, and by adhering to this motto it has succeeded in gaining and holding public confidence. The local manager of the Postal is Mr. John C. Witt.

In 1910, the two telegraph companies handled 3,500,000 messages out of Houston.

The Houston Telephone Exchange was established in Houston by Mr. James A. Stacey, local manager of the Western Union Telegraph Company, in 1880. Mr. G. W. Foster succeeded Mr. Stacey as manager of the telephone company in 1882, the exchange having ninety-four subscribers and no long distance lines. The exchange was first located in the old Fox Building, but Mr. Foster obtained a ten year lease on a room at the top of the market house tower in exchange for ringing the alarm bell in case of fire, the alarms to be turned in by telephone. Only one lineman was employed by the exchange, a negro who divided his time between his duties and preaching.

The first long distance line was built between Houston and Galveston in 1883, and Mr. Foster and his wife, who was as efficient as he, removed to Galveston, where they managed both the Houston and Galveston offices.

The company has just completed an elegant building of its own, a skyscraper, on the corner of Capitol Avenue and San Jacinto Street, which, with its equipments, will cost approximately $1,000,000.

The company had on July 31, this year, 13,874 subscribers, and when it gets in its new quarters it will be able to care for 20,000 subscribers without making further additions to its plant. The work of putting the wires underground was begun in 1896 and nearly all are now in conduits.

The company has a very complete system of long distance wires. There are twelve circuits to Galveston, seven to Beaumont, three to San Antonio, three to Dallas and one each to Fort Worth and Corpus Christi. These are direct circuits and all have branches reaching out over the state in every direction.

It is possible to carry on conversation between Houston and El Paso, New Orleans, St. Louis and even Chicago, and the company does a large commercial business. Plans are now being discussed for the improvement of the service so as to extend it as far as Los Angeles and San Francisco on the west and New York and Boston on the east.

The officers of the company in Houston are: E. G. Pike, division commercial superintendent; G. S. Prentice, district commercial manager; R. E. Hart, division traffic superintendent; Gordon Bell, local cashier. The local service of the company heretofore has been very unsatisfactory and there has been much private and newspaper complaint.

An Automatic telephone company has been preparing for several years to open in Houston. Work has been slow and delays numerous, but there are now several miles of conduit wires and several thousand subscribers. The success of the automatic principle remains to be locally demonstrated. Mr. E. G. Ebersole is the Houston manager. The company is erecting a handsome office building, but has not yet begun to extent service.

In view of the rapid strides that are made almost daily in improving and perfecting the means of telegraphic and telephonic communication, it is but reasonable to presume that methods which we regard as practically perfect today will be regarded as obsolete fifty years from now and will excite as much wonder as the "gutta percha wire" that was used in place of a cable across Galveston Bay, by the first telegraphic company fifty or more years ago, does with us today. There may not be such radical changes in telegraphic methods where wires and cables are used, but where these are discarded and only the wireless used, the advance will be revolutionary.

Two wireless companies operate in Houston. One is a private concern owned and operated by the Texas Company. This company has 2,700 miles of private telegraph wires in Texas, Oklahoma and Kansas. These lines are used by the company only, and the wireless plant is kept always in readiness for instant use, in case the wires should fail from any cause. The company has similar outfits at Beaumont and in Oklahoma.

The Texas Wireless Telegraph-Telephone is the only one engaged in doing a pubic and commercial business. Its location is admirable, being on the 18th floor of the Carter Building and having its wire tentacles spread from a tower forty or fifty feet above the roof of that tall building. This great elevation is very advantageous for it gives the electric waves free play and wide range. Another advantage is that it is as far removed from metal roofs and street wires, which are enemies to the free transmission of electric waves. The company has now in operation a station here, one in Victoria and another in San Antonio. It has thoroughly equipped stations at

Fredericksburg, Waco and Fort Worth, but, for some reason, only the first named are in commission. Probably it is because of the difficulty of securing competent operators, these being scarce. The area in which the Houston plant can do effective work in sending messages is about 500 miles. The instrument is not powerful enough to send a message further than that except under exceptionally favorable conditions, but it is delicate and powerful enough to receive them from an indefinite distance.

The local manager of the company frequently hears the Norfolk Navy yard operator sending messages, and can get messages from Washington. Cape Hatteras and from a station on the southeast coast of Cuba. All these stations are equipped with powerful machines. Three codes are used. The ordinary Morse code is the one in general use. All German vessels use the Continental code, while the United States Navy uses the Navy code. Of course a wireless operator must have all three codes at his finger ends.

The Texas Wireless Company is a Texas company. All its stock is owned in Texas and it is controlled and managed by Texas people. Mr. G. R. Spielhagen is president and general manager with headquarters in Houston, while Mr. E. G. Prince is local manager.

CHAPTER XV - SOCIETIES AND CLUBS

Free Masonry in Texas. Holland Lodge and Texas Grand Lodge Organized. First Lodge of Odd Fellows. Knights of Pythias and Elks. The Houston Turn Verein. The Volksfests. Societies of War Veterans. Terry's Texas Rangers. Second Texas Infantry and Waul's Legion. Hood's Texas Brigade. The Bayou City Guards. Dick Dowling Camp U. C. V. and Post McLennan No. 9, G. A. R. Houston Militia Companies. The Light Guard. Troop A. First Texas Cavalry. Jeff Miller Rifles. The Annual No-Tsu-Oh Carnival. Z. Z. and Thalian Clubs. Country Club. Houston Club. Charitable Societies. Organized Charities, Faith Home, Wesley House, Florence Crittenden Home, Star of Hope Mission. Houston Settlement Association.

It is not generally known that the establishment of Free Masonry in Texas was accomplished not only through the greatest difficulty, owing to the isolated and widely separated condition of those willing to engage in such work, but also that the act itself was one replete with danger to those engaged in it. At that time Texas was a part of Mexico and the people of Mexico looked on all secret societies, and Free Masonry in particular, as tools of the evil one and punished all those who had anything to do with them, as heretics and servants of the devil.

Dr. Anson Jones, the last President of the Republic of Texas, the first master of Holland Lodge No. 1, and also the first Grand Master of Masons in the Republic of Texas, fortunately left a manuscript dairy from which the following facts are taken:

In the winter of 1834–35, five Master Masons, who had exchanged the signs of their order, resolved to establish Masonry in Texas. President Jones says that this was not without peril, for every movement looking towards organization of any kind, was craftily and censoriously watched by Mexican spies in the employ of the government for that specific purpose. However, these very conditions made some kind of organization on the part of the American population an absolute necessity for self-protection, and personal rights and liberty. Accordingly, Anson Jones, John A. Wharton, Asa Bringham, A. E. Phelps and Alexander Russell in association with J. P. Caldwell, banded together as the first Masonic lodge in Texas. Their first place of meeting was in a wild-peach grove on the General John Austin place back of Brazoria. The spot was a family burying ground, and for that reason, as well as on account of its environment, was a secluded place, and deemed safe for the work in hand. Here, at 10 o'clock on a day in March, in 1835, was held the first formal Masonic meeting in Texas. It was determined at that meeting to apply to the Grand Lodge of Louisiana for a dispensation to open and form a lodge to be called Holland Lodge, in honor of the worshipful grand master of that body, J. H. Holland. After some delay the dispensation was granted, and Holland Lodge No. 36 (under dispensation) was instituted at Brazoria, in the second story of the old court house.

The activities of the lodge were interfered with by the struggle for independence by the Texans. At the last meeting of the lodge in Brazoria, in February, 1836, Anson Jones, presided and Fannin, the Texas hero, was senior deacon. Brazoria was abandoned in March, and the Mexicans, under General Urrea destroyed the Masonic records, jewels and other property. The few members of Holland Lodge were scattered in every direction. When, in due time, the Grand Lodge of Louisiana chartered Holland Lodge No. 36, it sent the charter to Texas by John Allen, who delivered it, with other papers, to Anson Jones at a point on the prairie between Groce's and San Jacinto, when Jones was marching with the Texas army. Dr. Jones put the documents in his saddle-bag and took them with him to where the army was camped at Lynchburg on Buffalo Bayou. The result of the battle of San Jacinto saved not only Texas but the charter as well for had the Mexicans triumphed the charter would have shared the fate of the dispensation at Brazoria.

For various reasons, no attempt was made to reestablish the lodge at Brazoria, though the charter was eventually taken to that place, but, in October, 1837, Anson Jones and associates, reestablish it at Houston. About the same time Milam Lodge at Nacogdoches and McFarlane Lodge at San Augustine obtained charters from the Grand Lodge of Louisiana. Delegates from these two lodges and from Holland Lodge, convened in Houston in the winter of 1837–38 and organized the Grand Lodge of the Republic of Texas, and the connection of these three lodges was transferred from the Florida jurisdiction to that of Texas. Holland Lodge No. 36, became Holland Lodge No. 1, of Houston.

For several years the Grand Lodge met at various points in Texas, but in 1866 its permanent home was established in Houston. An appropriation of $50,000 was made towards building a temple and to this the Houston Masons made a handsome donation, so that when the temple was completed, and dedicated in 1871, its cost was $113,000. It was erected under the supervision of Mr. C. J. Grainger, one of the early wealthy citizens of Houston, a past master of Holland Lodge, of 1854, who gave his work as a gift to the Grand Lodge. Some years later, when the population of the state had increased and the center of population had shifted, it was thought advisable to remove the home of the Grand Lodge to a more central point, and Waco was chosen. That city erected a temple at a cost of $150,000 for the lodge. Perhaps one of the most interesting if not important meetings of the Grand Lodge, was the 46th communication, which was convened at Houston, December 8, 1881. Interest was centered in the visit to the lodge, on that occasion, of General Albert Pike, of Washington, D. C., Provincial Grand Master of the Grand Lodge of the Royal order of Scotland in the United States, and said to have been the highest Mason in America, Sovereign Grand Commander of the Supreme Council of the Ancient Accepted Scottish Rite for the Southern Jurisdiction of the United States. He had been elected to that position twenty years before. General Prior was also Provincial Grand Prior of the Great Priory of Canada of the United Military and Religious Orders of the Temple.

It is rather remarkable that the same man who was so largely instrumental in introducing Masonry in Texas should also have played an equally important part in establishing Odd Fellowship. Anson Jones, who may be termed, with truth and justice, the father of Masonry in Texas, was also the father of Odd Fellowship. In 1838, he and four other brothers organized Lone Star Lodge No. 1, I. O. O. F. in Houston, and he was the first Grand Master of the organization in Texas. The progress of Masonry and Odd Fellowship in Houston has always been side by side. Each has had periods of great prosperity and periods of depression, but in all instances the prosperity has predominated, and, today they are two of the most solid and well established orders in the city. Lone Star Lodge No. 1, I. O. O. F. has the distinguished honor, shared equally by Holland Lodge No. 1, of the Masonic order, of having had two of its members fill the high and exalted office of Grand Master of both the Grand Lodge of Masons and Grand Lodge of Odd Fellows. These were President Anson Jones and Henry Perkins, of Houston. In recent years Masonry in Houston has been most furthered by the efforts of Hon. Frank C. Jones, a 33° Mason and the present potentate of El Mina Temple nobles of the mystic shrine.

In 1870 the young men of Houston took great interest in Odd Fellowship, with the result that Lone Star Lodge No. 1, grew rapidly in numbers and influence. This influence was not exerted in Houston alone but extended to other nearby cities. As a result interest in the order increased and it may be said, truthfully, that the present great usefulness and influence of the order in Houston dates from that time. Henry Perkins, who was Grand Master of the Grand Lodge, was a most enthusiastic worker. He is one of the few really worthy and distinguished citizens of Houston of the early days, who has never been given that place in the history and traditions of the city, to which his merits entitled him. One reason for this was the excessive modesty and aversion to publicity, which characterized his life. He was willing to work for the good of the order and always kept himself as far from the lime-light as possible. He was a man of independent means, a great student and lover of books, and as a consequence was known, really, by but few men.

Next to the Masons and Odd Fellows, the Knights of Pythias is the oldest secret organization in Houston. Lone Star Lodge No. 1, was organized in 1872, and is therefore not only the oldest lodge of the order in Houston, but the oldest in the state. The order has always been popular here and is very strong, both numerically and in every other way. There are fourteen primary lodges and subsidiary organizations of the order here, and they are all flourishing and each has a full membership.

Strange to say there is only one lodge of the Elks organization in Houston. It is Houston Lodge No. 151, B. P. O. E. It was organized in January, 1890, and is in a most flourishing condition, numerically. The lodge has over 600 members, and plans for a magnificent building of its own are now under consideration.

The Turn Verein, the first German Society in Houston, was organized January 14, 1854. In its first minute book is recorded the following:

"We, the undersigned, assembled this forenoon in Gable's house, to confer in regard to the institution of a Turn Verein. It was the wish of all to belong to a society where each feels as a brother to the other and lives for him and with him as a brother. We have, therefore, associated ourselves under a brotherly pressure of hands and promised each other to organize a Turn Verein with energy and love in the cause and assure its existence by continued activity."

(Signed) T. Heitmann, F. Reinmann,—Marschall, Louis Pless, John F. Thorade, Robert Voight, E. B. H. Schneider, August Sabath, E. Scheurer, and L. Scheihagen.

Houston,
January 14, 1854.

The young Verein had scarcely seen seven years when the great Civil War broke out. The original ten had grown to about a hundred and almost to a man they volunteered to do battle for their adopted country. A company was formed, under the leadership of Captain E. B. H. Schneider, composed of members of the Turn Verein, and was among the very first troops to leave for the front. That they were not parade soldiers is attested by the frayed and shot-torn company flag which is among the most prized and sacredly guarded treasures of the Verein.

But before the war the Verein had already accomplished a great deal. Under their auspices a gymnastic school for both sexes had been established, for the motto of the Verein was: "only in a healthy body dwells a healthy soul." One of the early volunteer fire companies was recruited from the Turners. When the war closed the Turners were poor in purse, in common with everybody else, but they were rich in hope and energy and it was not long before they had new life and vigor instilled in the Verein. Within two years after the close of the war they had gotten their affairs so well in hand that they were enabled to start a semi-public school, which, according to the testimony of old Houstonians, was the best school of its scope and purpose of the period. Able teachers were employed. Tuitions were insufficient to defray expenses and the Turners made up the deficiency out of the treasury of the association. In the great yellow fever epidemic of 1867 one of the principal teachers died and the school was suspended and never again resumed.

At that time foreign immigrants were settling in the North and West and were avoiding the South because the advantages of the South had never been properly placed before them. The Verein undertook to correct this and had printed at its own expense, pamphlets setting forth the claims of Texas and circulated them in all the large towns of Germany. This work was very effective in building up the state and particularly Houston. The Turn Verein cultivated music and popularized it by means of vocal and instrumental concerts.

With the view of combining all of Houston's citizens and harmonizing their work for the common good, it organized, in 1869, the Volksfest, which was also aided by other German associations. For about twelve years the annual Volksfest was one of the great events of Houston, but gradually interest died out, and by 1880, it was evident that something would have to be done if it were intended to continue the celebration. Then dissentions arose and the affairs of the Volksfest association got into court. At that time (1881) there were 100 members of the Turn Verein. There was also another German Association, known as the German Society, about of the same numerical strength as the Turn Verein. Almost every German citizen of any note was a member of one of these associations. These two associations determined to come to the rescue of the Volksfest Association, and to assume all responsibility for future celebrations. Accordingly, a meeting was held at the city hall on Sunday morning, December 4, 1881, for the purpose of adopting a charter and by-laws for the new association. Hon. E. F. Schmidt was called to the chair and Professor Stereouwitz was made secretary. The charter and by-laws were read and adopted without discussion. By the admission of new members the membership increased to about 250. It was decided that it would not be best for the new organization to take further definite action pending litigation over the Volksfest fund then in the District court. Two months later the two factions of the Volksfest Association effected a compromise of their differences whereby the dignity of each was preserved, and it was decided to give the next festival under the consolidated management.

The announcement was made, March 11, that the charter of the Volksfest Associations—amended to admit of the consolidation of the two associations—had been forwarded to Austin and that so soon as it was legalized and returned, a new and enlarged directory would take up the work that was needed to insure the permanency of the Volksfest. It was planned to make the coming festival the grandest that had ever been undertaken. An interstate military drill was suggested but the idea was abandoned because there would be no time to arrange for more than a State drill. It was decided to do away with the decorated wagons that had always been a feature of previous festivals, and to apply the money thus saved as a fund to be used as prizes for the greatest military and firemen's competitions ever seen in Texas, and to induce the attendance of singing societies from all parts of the state.

Early on the morning of May 4, 1882, a salute of fourteen guns was fired by the Texas Old Guard Artillery announcing the opening of the fourteenth annual Volksfest. There was a grand procession. John D. Usner was Grand Marshal, with J. J. Fant and William Rupersburg as assistants. The Adjutants were: John Morris, A. R. Jones, S. S. Ashe, H. Kleinicke, George Bauss and Ben Keagans. The parade and the festivities that followed were beautiful and enjoyable. Only one or two subsequent annual Volksfests were held and then they were abandoned voluntarily.

Though primarily a child of the Turn Verein the Volksfest had really no official connection with the Turners and its fortunes and misfortunes affected it in no way. The Turners continued to grow in strength and popularity, until today it is one of the strongest and most influential organizations of the kind in the state, and one of which all citizens of Houston are proud. They have recently sold part of their property on Texas Avenue and contemplate erecting one of the finest club houses in the South.

Nearly one hundred of the 300 survivors of Terry's Texas Rangers met in Houston on December 16, 1880, in annual reunion. A committee composed of local survivors of that command had made extensive preparation for the event. That committee was: S. S. Ashe, of Co. B.; W. R. Black, of Co. B.; P. C. Walker, of Co. K.; J. M. Morin, of Co. D.; T. U. Lubbock, of Co. K.; W. H. Albertson, of Co. H.; S. H. Jones, of Co. H.; and M. F. de Bajeligethe, of Co. K.

This was one of the most famous cavalry regiments in the Confederate Army and was the only Texas regiment of cavalry that saw active service on the other side of the Mississippi River during the whole four years of the war. The record it made has perhaps never been surpassed by any cavalry command in the history of the world. It was recruited in 1861, in response to a call made by Benjamin Franklin Terry for recruits who could come armed and equipped to serve in the Confederate Army. The response was so prompt that the regiment was recruited to its full strength at once (1027) and had thirteen supernumeraries, who enlisted for the war as vacancies occurred. The following brief summary of the regiment's record tells better than hundreds of written pages could do, what brilliant service the command rendered the Confederacy:

Full strength of the regiment at the beginning, 1027 men, rank and file. Recruits received during the war, 398. Absent during the war, at times only, 28. Discharged for wounds and disease, 271. Killed in battle, 377. Absent from wounds or disease at the close of the war, 79. Present for duty at the surrender, 317.

The command was mustered into the service on June, 1861, and served until May, 1865, and during that entire time was out of actual service but 21 days. It was in 38 general engagements and 160 skirmishes. The regiment, known officially as the Eighth Texas, had five colonels, seven lieutenant colonels, five majors, three adjutants, three quartermasters, three commissaries, thirty-one captains, twenty-nine first lieutenants, twenty-four second lieutenants and nineteen third lieutenants. The members of the command, living in Houston, who were present at that reunion were:

Col. Gustave Cook, Lieutenant Col. B. A. Botts, Maj. A. L. Steel, Maj. B. F. Weems, Sergeant W. D. Cleveland, Privates S. S. Ashe, T. U. Lubbock, Sam H. Jones, W. R. Black, J. M. Morin, P. C. Walker, W. H. Albertson, and M. F. de Bajeligethy. Of these only four are living today: Major Weems, Sergeant W. D. Cleveland and Privates S. S. Ashe, and T. U. Lubbock.

The Second Texas Infantry and Wauls Legion held their first reunion at Houston, July 4, 1882. There was a business meeting at Gray's Hall during the morning and a banquet at night. Captain J. C. Hutchison delivered the address of welcome and General T. N. Waul, the commander of Waul's Legion, responded with feeling and eloquence. A thorough organization was effected and the following officers were elected:

President, General T. N. Waul, of Waul's Legion. First vice-president, Col. Ashbel Smith, of the Second Texas. Second vice-president, Col. H. P. Timmons, of Waul's Legion. Corresponding secretary, Col. O. Steele, of Waul's Legion. Recording secretary, H. P. Roberts, of the Second Texas. Treasurer, Sam E. Jones, of the Second Texas. Chaplain, Rev. J. J. Clemens.

The following members were enrolled at the business meeting: Second Texas—F. W. L. Fly, Major, Company A.—Captain, William Christian, D. S. Smith, William Cravey, H. Graves, Tom Ewell, Dave Lynch, D. Mahoney, D. Callahan, and Joe Smith. Company B.—Philip Huebner, Daniel Smith, Sam Allen, Henry Hartman, William Harting. Theadore Keller, A. J. Hurtney, H. P. Roberts, and H. Holteamp. Company C.—Dr. S. E. Jones. Company D.—Captain, J. E. Foster. Company G.—A. M. Armstrong, E. S. Parkell, A. J. Horton, P. D. Ring, G. L. Gee, J. W. Daniel, Jack Jones, J. F. Borden, C. A. Hope, William Hunt, J. W. Farmer, J. K. Addison, E. T. Cottingham, P. D. Scott. Company H.—J. B. McArthur, R. E. McArthur, T. D. Sullivan, R. G. Broaddus, H. C. Broaddus, L. L. Stuart, M. J. Houston, E. W. Hudson, H. H. Gilber, J. G. Hill, L. W. Broaddus.

Waul's Legion—E. E. Rice, Sergeant Major; Oliver Steel, Lieutenant Colonel, Second Battalion; S. P. Allen of Company E.; Charles Warneche of Company B.; William Burse of Hogue's Battery; Isaac A. Levy, John Wagner, and Charles Holdermany of Company B.; Captain F. A. Michels, Captain L. Hardie, Jacob Koch, of Company B., Second Battalion; P. Briscoe, A. W. Littig, G. M. Noris, H. G. Hutcheson, S. M. Williams, B. A. Smalley of Company A., Second Battalion; Louis Kosse.

These signed the record as members in attendance and in addition to these names were added the following records which are of the greatest value since both the Second Texas and Waul's Legion had so many men from Houston and Harris County in their ranks.

Second Texas Infantry—Company B.: Captain, W. C. Timmins; J. W. Mangum, first lieutenant; J. D. McCleary, second lieutenant; A. S. Mair, third lieutenant; A. J. Hurley, orderly sergeant; J. B. Cato, second sergeant; D. C. Smith, third sergeant; S. L. Allen, fourth sergeant; O. J. Conklin, fifth sergeant; W. H. Tyson, color sergeant; Phil Huebner, first corporal; H. D. Donnellon, second corporal; privates:—A. F. Amerman, Phil Angus, T. H. Brooks,—Barrow, T. P. Bryan, Wm. Block, William Blanton, John Clark, Mike Callahan, Matt Conklin,—Cogkin, Tom Conway, Tim Grim,—Duncan, N. T. Davis, Henry Drier, Sterling Fisher, B. Foster, Ames N. Alberts, John Bouquet, J. Beutcherger, J. T. Bell, Henry Bitner, Nicholas Castello, George A. Christie, William H. Clark,—Cheeney, Horace Church, A. Cunningham,—Claspell, Phil Duggin, C. S. Doty,—Forney, C. F. Gehrman, Charles Finkleman, M. Gilreath, J. B. Hogan, Henry Hartman, William Hartney, J. C. Hart, Dan. Huebner, Henry Holcamp, W. E. Jones, Theodore Keller, John Kirk,—Klein, Joseph Le Due, James Lamber, William Little, Tom Lillie, Henry Meyer,—McCarthy,—Meeks, Joe Michaels, James Manuel, M. M. McLean,—Northrup, Tom Patterson, William Perry, Peter Rhein, H. P. Roberts, W. G. Spence,—Shaot, Joe Smith, William Tulsen, J. White, William Wharf,—Williams, A. T. McCorkle, Antone Merkle, William Miller, George A. Newell, J. C. Potter, E. Rothman, A. Riter, Alex Senechal, F. D. Shaw, A. B. Seale, E. A. Sprague, Earnest Trinks, William Worgs, Ed H. Wilson and—Hoffman.

Company C.—This was the famous Bayland Guards, a company raised and commanded by Dr. Ashbel Smith, who was afterwards the colonel of the Second Texas Regiment. The roll given is the original roll of the company at its organization:

Asbel Smith, captain; J. R. Harrill, first lieutenant; S. S. Ashe, second lieutenant; M. A. Lea, third lieutenant; R. D. Haden, first sergeant; R. M. Woodhall, second sergeant; W. H. Bryan, third sergeant; E. M. Wasson, fourth sergeant; R. G. Ashe, fifth sergeant; Isham Palmer, first corporal; C. M. Owens, second corporal; J. Hagerman, third corporal; C. E. Jones, fourth corporal; H. Parnell, surgeon; privates:—W. S. Alger, John Alfson, Mosley Baker, J. W. Barnes, G. H. Brown, Amos Barron, Barton Clark, J. V. Dutton, L. J. Ellidge, J. P. Evans, F. M. Fitzgerald, Amos Fisher, J. G. Haden, S. E. Jones, R. V. Tompkins, Wm. White, B. F. Lamson, Henry Love, Daniel Matthews, F. M. Rundill, James A. Rhea, T. J. Armstrong, G. R. Baker, Hiram Bartlett, C. H. Brooks, T. L. Blagreaves, Jesse Brooks, D. Dugat, Daniel Duncan, J. T. Elledge, G. W. Ferrand, Sol Fisher, L. J. Harper, S. A. Hadden, Wm. Evans, Stanley Brown, W. H. Woodhall, Sol Lawrence, J. Murrell,

Henry Ong, P. L. Reeves, Otis Rush, James A. Stewart, J. W. Tompkins, A. J. Thomas, A. G. Voortman, Sol Williams, John Holtz, W. A. Terrell, T. W. Timmins, J. B. Thomas, J. B. Vanhouten, A. J. Woodall, and Sam Houston, Jr., son of General Sam Houston.

This company was organized in Harris County April 27, 1861. The Second Texas Infantry was organized August 17, following. Col. J. C. Moore was its first colonel. When he was promoted to be a Brigadier General, Lieut. Col. William P. Rogers became colonel. Colonel Rogers was killed at Corinth and was succeeded by Col. Ashbel Smith, who commanded it until the surrender. The regiment saw much active service and distinguished itself at Corinth, where, through a blunder, it was ordered to take an impregnable point, and sent to do work that it would have required two or more brigades to accomplish. The Second Texas did not falter, but made the attack and was nearly annihilated, leaving its brave colonel and most of its officers and men on the field. The regiment also sustained heavy losses at Vicksburg and was captured there when the stronghold was surrendered. After its release from the Vicksburg parole the regiment was transferred to this side of the Mississippi and was in the Trans-Mississippi department when the war closed.

Waul's Legion.—This body was organized in Washington County, in the spring of 1862, and was composed of ten companies of infantry, one battalion of cavalry and two batteries of artillery. In the legion was a company of infantry commanded by Captain Sam Carter, all the members of which were from Harris County, and another Houston company, commanded by Captain Otto Natheuesius, who was a trained soldier, having served in the Prussian army. He was promoted early after reaching the other side of the river and Captain Frank A. Michels assumed command of the company. Charles Warnecke, Charles Warner, Louis Kosse, John and William Kersten and John W. Stanfield of Houston were members of this company. Captain Louis Harde of Houston also commanded a company in the legion. With the exception of Edgars' battery, the legion was ordered across the Mississippi in August, 1862, and became a part of Walker's division. Trellis' cavalry battalion was detached and included in Van Dorn's brigade and Forest's cavalry. The infantry under command of General Waul, helped defend Vicksburg, and after the surrender, when that officer was promoted, was divided into two battalions, one commanded by Colonel Timmons, and the other by Colonel Wrigley.

Hood's Texas Brigade Association was organized in the parlor of the Hutchins House, May 24, 1872. At that first meeting there were sixty-five survivors of that famous command present. On motion of General J. B. Robertson, an ex-commander of the Brigade, General J. B. Hood was called to the chair, and Maj. Robert Burns was requested to act as secretary. General Hood made a speech and said that the object of the meeting was to organize the survivors of the old brigade into an association to be called Hood's Texas Brigade Association of the army of Northern Virginia.

Col. Winkler moved that there should be chosen a president, a vice-president, a secretary and a treasurer, who should serve for one year. Also that there should be an executive committee of two members from each regiment whose duty it should be to gather all matter for a correct history of the brigade.

The object of the association, as stated by resolution, is for friendly and social reunions of the survivors of the brigade, and to collect all data for rolls and history and to perpetuate all anecdotes, incidents, and many things connected therewith, and to succor the needy among its members. It was decided to hold a reunion once every year. The officers elected at that first reunion were: president, Col. C. M. Winkler; vice-president, Gen. J. B. Robertson; secretary and treasurer, Maj. J. H. Littlefield. Mrs. M. J. Young, of Houston, who, for all the four years of the war had labored unceasingly for the brigade, and who had raised and sent to Virginia, early in the war, $35,000 in gold, for the purpose of establishing a Texas hospital in Richmond, and who had sent clothing and medicine for them, was present and received an ovation not second to that given the old leader, General Hood. The first act of the association, after its organization, was to elect Mrs. Young "The Mother of Hood's Brigade" by a standing vote.

Houston is directly interested in Hood's Brigade since it furnished one of the companies that formed part of the Fifth Texas Regiment in that famous body of troops. There were but three Texas regiments in the army of northern Virginia. The Houston company was the Bayou City Guards, known officially as Co. A, Fifth Texas Regiment. Nearly every prominent family in Houston had a representative in its ranks. Capt. W. D. Cleveland was one of the company, but after arriving in Virginia he was disabled and incapacitated for the infantry. He did not come home however, but went to Tennessee, joined Terry's Texas Rangers, and remained with that command until the close of the war.

It is a matter of regret that a full roster of the company is unobtainable. There were one hundred men in the company when it left Houston in 1861. In 1862 Lieutenant Chute came back for recruits and secured six. One or two others joined the company in Virginia. The company was in twenty-four great engagements and in a number of heavy skirmishes. The only roster that can be made out is from the partial records in the war department at Washington, giving the killed and wounded in thirteen of the great battles they were engaged in. That list, supplemented by another prepared from memory by one of the company is given here:

A. Angel, killed at Manassas; John Bell, killed at Manasssas; Sam Bailey, wounded at Manassas, wounded at Gettysburg and killed at Spottsylvania; T. P. Bryan, killed at the Wilderness; Lieut. J. E. Clute, killed at Gaines' Mill;

Robt. Campbell, wounded at Manassas, wounded at Chickamauga, wounded at Darby Town; S. Cohn, killed at Gettysburg; Joe Cramer, wounded at Gettysburg; W. H. Clarke, wounded at Gettysburg, wounded at Chickamauga, wounded at the Wilderness; Louis Coleman, wounded at Gettysburg; J. DeLesdernier, killed at Manassas; George DeLesdernier, killed at Gaines' Mill; John DeYoung, killed at Manassas; B. C. Dyer, wounded at Sharpsburg; C. W. Diggs, killed at Gettysburg; J. C. Deloch, wounded at the Wilderness; A. H. Edey, wounded at Gettysburg; Capt. D. C. Farmer, wounded at Gettysburg; Lieut. B. P. Fuller, wounded at the Wilderness; T. W. Fitzgerold, wounded at Gettysburg; E. Fragee, wounded at Gettysburg; J. H. Garrison, wounded at Gettysburg; C. B. Gardner, wounded at Chickamauga; J. Heffrin, killed at Manassas; Sam D. Hews, wounded at Manassas; Frank Kosse, killed at Sharpsburg; J. V. Love, killed at Gettysburg; John Leverton, wounded at Gettysburg; J. E. Landes, wounded at the Wilderness; J. R. McMurtry, killed at Manassas; Wm. McDowell, killed at Gettysburg; J. Massenburg, killed at Manassas; J. Morris, wounded at Gettysburg and at the Wilderness; E. A. Nobles, wounded at Manassas; Geo. Onderdonk, wounded at Gaines' Mill; J. O'Nally, wounded at Manassas; N. Pommery, wounded at Gettysburg and Chickamauga; F. W. Plummer, wounded at Chickamauga; W. Reiley, wounded at Manassas; T. H. Revely, wounded at Gettysburg; G. J. Robinson, wounded at the Wilderness; J. H. Robbins, wounded at Chickamauga; B. C. Simpson, wounded at Manassas and Gettysburg; A. Stewart, wounded at Sharpsburg; H. G. Settle, wounded at Gettysburg, and killed near Richmond a year later; C. F. Settle, wounded and captured at Gettysburg. He made a wonderful escape from Fort Deleware exactly one year after; W. L. Steel, wounded at Chickamauga; J. H. Shepherd, wounded at the Wilderness; S. H. Watkins, wounded at Gettysburg; D. W. Walker, killed at Manassas; A. Wolf, wounded at Seven Pines, killed at Sharpsburg.

The other members were: A. Beasly, Pat Burns, Robt. Burns, afterwards brigade commissary, T. E. Bigbee, J. A. Cameron, I. Elesessor, W. B. Ferrell, W. A. George, Wm. McGowan, afterwards Adjutant of the Fifth Texas Regiment; G. Miller, F. M. Poland, C. Stevens, H. P. Welch, S. O. Young.

Of the entire company there were known to be living only the following in 1911: J. A. Cameron, Houston, Texas; B. L. Dyer, Opelika, Ala.; W. A. George, Houston, Texas; James E. Landes, Chappel Hill, Texas; F. M. Poland, Houston, Texas; N. Pommery, Clark Milstret, County Cork, Ireland; Dr. S. O. Young, Houston, Texas.

As Texas saw but little of the real warfare of the Civil War, the chief part taken by Houston as by other Texas cities was the furnishing of troops for the great battlefields on both sides of the river. The reunions of the larger units have indicated how heroically Houston did her share, like the rest of the South robbing the cradle and the grave to send soldiers to the front.

Hundreds were attached to other organizations and thousands of citizens who came to Houston after the Civil War had participated in the great conflict. A full list of these is of course impossible. The heroic achievements are perpetuated not only by the annual reunions of the commands named but also by the local lodge of United Confederate Veterans. It is certain that those who have been or are now citizens of Houston fought for the South in every battle of the conflict. Also hundreds of Houstonians participated on the other side, moving to this city after the war.

Camp Dick Dowling No. 197, U. C. V. was organized in 1892. The late General C. C. Beavens was largely instrumental in organizing it and creating interest and enthusiasm. The year before, he had organized Camp Magruder at Galveston and was a most enthusiastic worker in all that promised to perpetuate the memory of the Confederate soldier. Camp Dick Dowling is one of the best organized and hardest working camps in the South. Its membership is only about 300, but its meetings are always largely attended and the interest shown today is equal in every way to that shown when the organization was new. Meetings are held twice each month, at which lectures and talks by the comrades are given. The camp looks after the sick and indigent Confederate soldiers, not only among its own members, but all others to whom its attention is called. It buries its dead and no Confederate soldier is ever allowed to occupy a paupers' grave.

The present officers of the Camp are: J. J. Hall, commander; Geo. H. Herman, 1st lieut. commander; J. T. Clower, 2nd lieut. commander; Al Longnaker, 3rd lieut. commander; W. C. Kelly, adjutant; Dr. W. A. Haley, surgeon; Rev. S. H. Blair, chaplain; J. C. Fowler, officer of the day; F. R. Jones, vidette; M. W. McLeod, flag bearer.

During the year 1910, fourteen members of the Camp died.

Post McLennan No. 9, G. A. R. was organized in 1885, and has been in active service ever since. Not having such abundant material from which to draw as the Confederate Veterans had, its membership has necessarily been limited. Still the organization has been kept intact and there is quite as much interest shown today as there was on the day of its organization. It has a ladies' auxiliary, which does an immense amount of good work and cares for the sick and needy of the Post. There are about one hundred active members of the Post and Decoration Day is faithfully observed by them.

Houston has chapters of the Spanish American War Veterans and of the Sons of the American Revolution, both of which are headed by Brigadier General James A. Waties, and has also organizations of the Sons and Daughters of the Confederacy and other patriotic societies.

The Houston Light Guard, the military company most famous in peaceful achievements the country has ever known, was organized on San Jacinto Day, April 21, 1873. Col. Fairfax Gray, who had served in the United States Navy before the war, and who had rendered distinguished service as an officer in the Confederate Army, was the first captain of the Guard. Soon after its organization interest began to flag and the company soon existed in name only.

Late in the fall of the same year some of the most zealous members got together and determined to reorganize the company. Interest among the others was revived and a meeting was called. The attendance was good and a complete reorganization of the company was effected. Captain J. R. Coffin was elected captain. The renewed interest was not allowed to wane, and the new captain put the boys to drilling and did everything possible to make them soldiers. Uniforms were procured, the color being cadet gray, better known as Confederate gray. The company worked so hard and accomplished so much that when the carnival of King Comus occurred in February, 1874, the company took part in the parade, the members wearing their uniforms for the first time. They did even more than that, for three months later, in May, they entered in a competitive drill against four outside companies at the Volkfest celebration. They did not get the prize but they did get experience and the next year, at Austin, under command of Captain Joe Rice, they won a sword valued at $500.

The company acted as a guard of honor and escort to Ex-President Davis of the Confederacy, and has the distinction of having been the first guard of honor Mr. Davis had after the war. The ladies of Houston presented the company with a beautiful flag, in 1875, and the honorary lady members presented it with another in 1882.

In the early eighties the martial spirit was very strong all over the country, particularly in the South. Military companies became all the rage and competition between them on the drill ground was very keen. As a rule the members of these companies bought their own uniforms, paid their own traveling expenses and everything of that sort. The only thing the government furnished them was arms. The Houston Light Guard was ambitious. Its first appearance in an interstate drill outside of Texas was at New Orleans in 1881. It was beaten by three companies, but got fourth prize, $500.

Next year the boys went to the interstate drill at Nashville, Tenn. They were again beaten by three companies, coming out fourth, but had the great satisfaction of beating the Lawrence Light Infantry, a crack company from Boston, Mass. The people of Houston stood by them as closely in their defeats as they did later in their triumphs. From Nashville they came home more determined than ever. The friends of the company, the business men of Houston, determined that they should have another trial. To make the opportunity, they got together and raised the money to offer handsome prizes and to meet the cost of entertaining the visiting companies at an interstate drill in Houston. The fact was advertised far and wide and invitations were sent to all the prominent military organizations in the United States. That was in 1884. A number of the crack companies accepted the invitation. Mr. H. Baldwin Rice was made manager of the drill. The War Department at Washington, appointed three army officers to act as judges and to make an official report of the result to the government. The drill ground was the old fair grounds where now stands the south end "Fair Grounds Addition." Fannin School now stands within a few feet of where the stakes and lines defining the drill field were placed. The drill was the greatest event of the kind that had ever taken place, and all the famous military organizations in the country were here. The drill lasted for a week, a certain number of companies drilling each day in the state or interstate contest. All companies that had ever taken part in an interstate drill were barred from the state drill. The first prize for interstate companies was $5,000. From that the prizes were reduced, so that the last prize was only about one-fourth of that amount. The companies competing in the interstate drill were the Treadway Rifles, of St. Louis; the Columbus Guards, of Columbus, Ga.; the Montgomery Greys, of Montgomery, Ala.; the Washington Guards, of Galveston, and the Houston Light Guard. These were the crack military companies of the United States and most of them had national reputations, and were commanded by the best militia officers in the country.

The Houston Light Guard put up one of the most perfect drills ever witnessed and won the first prize. Omitting the figures grading the several parts of the drill, the totals are given here:

Houston Light Guard, 2.66; Treadway Rifles, 2.55; Columbus Guards, 2.35; Mobile Rifles, 2.29; Montgomery Greys, 2.28; Washington Guards, 1.95. A perfect drill would have given 3.00, the maximum score.

The following memorandum on the drill was submitted by the judges:

"Houston Light Guard.—It is observed that the inspection was nearly perfect. The appearance of the men in their dress, arms and accoutrements, and their neatness, exceeded anything we have seen anywhere—each man like a color man at the United States Military Academy at West Point. Captain Scurry had not proceeded far in the program when, while wheeling his company from column of twos, improperly, the company was placed in a position from which it was almost impossible to extricate it, except as done, exhibiting great presence of mind on the captain's part.

"Captain Scurry's appreciation of the program and its requirements was superior to that of the other commanders.

"The ground was laid out with the view to testing the length and cadence of the step in quick and double time. A company marching as contemplated in the method applied would take the following number of steps in quick and double time, and in the time specified. In quick time, 284 steps in 2 minutes and 35 seconds; in double time, 284 steps in 1 minute and 26 seconds. The Houston Light Guard made the following record: In quick time, 283 steps in 2 minutes and 35 seconds; in double time in 1 minute and 27 seconds. Aside from all practice in this particular, the result was almost phenomenal. Captain Scurry was the only one who marched upon the flags with guide to the left, as directed by the judges."

The Houston Light Guard, having won all it cared for—fame, offered to divide the money prize among the visiting companies, all of whom had been at heavy expense. This offer was refused, with thanks, of course. The next year, 1885, the company, under Captain Scurry, won three first prizes in interstate drills, footing up $12,000. The first was at Mobile, Alabama, in May, and the second, a few days later at New Orleans. The third was in July, at Fairmount Park, Philadelphia. In this drill and encampment all sections of the country were represented, there being seventy-five companies there. Only about one-half of them entered the competitive drill. The Houston Light Guard took first prize, which was a purse of $4,000 and a flag valued at $500.

From Philadelphia the company went to New York, where they were handsomely entertained at the armories of two of the famous New York regiments. It is but a matter of justice to give here the names of the men and officers who made the Houston Light Guards, "World Beaters." They are as follows:

Captain, Thomas Scurry; 1st lieutenant, F. A. Reichardt; 2nd lieutenant, T. H. Franklin; 3rd lieutenant, Spencer Hutchins; quartermaster, W. A. Childress; surgeon, Dr. S. O. Young, at and after the Philadelphia drill; 1st sergeant, George L. Price; 2nd sergeant, R. A. Scurry; 1st corporal, H. D. Taylor; 2nd corporal, W. K. Mendenhall; 3rd corporal, George N. Torrey; privates—Byers, Barnett, Bates, Bull, Byers, Cook, Dealy, Foss, Golihart, Hodgson, Hutchins, Heyer, Reynaud, Swanson, Johnson, Journey, Wilson, R. Kattman, E. Kattman, Lewis, Mahoney, Mitchell, McKeever, Powell, Randolph, Steele, Sawyer, Sharpe, Tyler, Taft, Taylor, Torrey, Wisby; perpetual drummer, John Sessums (colored.)

The next great victory of the Light Guard was at Galveston where it took first prize, a purse of $4,500, over the Montgomery True Blues, San Antonio Rifles, Branch Guards, (St. Louis), Company F, Louisville Legion and Belknapp Rifles of San Antonio. This was perhaps the most perfect drill ever witnessed in the United States, and excited widespread wonder and admiration among military men and the public generally.

The company went to Austin in 1888, and again took first prize, $5,000, in competition with the flower of interstate companies. The next year Galveston wanted to give a great drill, and did so, but the Houston Light Guard was barred, so as not to bluff off other companies from competing. That was the highest honor the company ever had conferred on it. The people of Galveston had the Light Guard as their guests and gave them $500 for an exhibition drill.

The Houston Light Guard showed that they were not merely fancy soldiers when the war with this country and Spain began, for they volunteered promptly, and under the command of Captain George McCormick, went to the front. They served in Florida and Cuba. When peace negotiations began, Captain McCormick returned home and the lamented R. A. Scurry became captain of the company, and in due time returned home with it.

The company owns its armory, the handsomest in the state. It was erected in part with the money the company earned in prizes—about $30,000. Some bonds were issued. These will mature in a few months, but are all provided for.

The names of the Captains of the company since its organization are as follows: Fairfax Gray, John Coffin, Joe S. Rice, George Price, James S. Baker, Jr., Thomas Scurry, F. A. Reichardt, George McCormick, R. A. Scurry, C. Hutchinson, Milby Porter. Dallas J. Matthews is the present capable commander.

For a long time in the Texas National Guard Houston has boasted a crack troop of cavalry. This troop served during the Spanish American war as Troop A, First Texas Cavalry, U. S. V. Major Towles was then captain and C. C. Beavens first lieutenant. Towles was made major and Beavens promoted to be captain. An officer of this troop, James A. Waties, was made colonel of the regiment and afterwards promoted to be a brigadier general. He was succeeded by Luther R. Hare, who subsequently also won a promotion to a brigadiership. Among the Houston citizens who were officers in this regiment are John A. Hulen, Jake Wolters, J. Towles, B. H. Carroll, Jr., and C. C. Beavens.

Troop A. has always been the crack troop of the cavalry branch of the T. N. G.

The Jeff Miller Rifles, which belong to the Second Infantry regiment of the T. N. G. is also a noted Houston company. For some years this company has been commanded by Captain C. C. Breedlove.

The No-Tsu-Oh Association is chartered for the purpose of giving an annual carnival for the entertainment of the people of the state. It is not organized for revenue and is sustained entirely by membership fees and subscriptions made by Houston business men.

The first carnival was held in 1899 and was such a success that it was determined to perpetuate the entertainment so that now it is an incorporated concern and spends about $30,000 each year for fun and frolic. There is a new president, king and queen each year, those who have borne those honors in the past being the following:

PRESIDENTS.

- 1899, Norman S. Meldrum; 1900, B. F. Bonner; 1901, James H. Adair; 1902, John McClellan; 1903, H. T. Keller; 1904, G. J. Palmer; 1905, Charles D. Golding; 1906, George N. Long, Jr.; 1907, W. D.

Cleveland, Jr.; 1908, James A. Radford; 1909, David Daly; 1910, Geo. P. Brown; 1911, David A. Burke.

KINGS.

- 1899, A. C. Allen; 1900, John H. Kirby; 1901, Dennis Call; 1902, Jesse H. Jones; 1903, B. F. Bonner; 1904, Presley K. Ewing; 1905, Jo. S. Rice; 1906, C. K. Dunlap; 1907, H. M. Garwood; 1908, James D. Dawson; 1909, James A. Baker; 1910, W. T. Carter; 1911, Dr. Edgar Odell Lovett.

QUEENS.

- 1899, Miss Annie Quinlan; 1900, Miss Julia Mae Morse; 1901, Miss Aygusta Goodhue; 1902, Miss Clara Robinson; 1903, Miss Bessie Kirby; 1904, Miss Florence Carter; 1905, Miss Sallie Sewall; 1906, Miss Gertrude Paine; 1907, Miss Alice Baker; 1908, Miss Mamie Shearn; 1909, Miss Lillian Neuhans; 1910, Miss Laura Rice; 1911, Miss Annie Vive Carter.

-

A glance at the list of presidents, kings and queens above will show that the best people of the city have constantly co-operated in making the No-Tsu-Oh carnival a success. A week in November of each year is devoted to festivities, parades, and carnival features modeled on the Mardi Gras carnivals of New Orleans and European cities. Large crowds are drawn to Houston during the week. The two great events of the carnival are the annual foot-ball game played between the University of Texas and A. & M. College, and the Queen's Coronation Ball.

An attempt is being made to give the carnival more of an exposition character but so far without great success.

Houston's oldest social organization is the Z. Z. Dancing Club. This was organized over 40 years ago, and its balls and cotillions during each year are of rare beauty. The Z. Z. Club for many years has introduced the debutantes at the opening of each social season with a debutantes' cotillion preceded by a reception at the home of the president of the club.

Spencer Hutchins, the former Ward McAllister of Houston, made the club famous. In recent years Hon. Presley K. Ewing has served several terms as president. He was succeeded in 1910 by J. M. Cary, the present popular president.

Part of the membership of this club in July, 1901, organized the Thalian Club—a regular social organization. Its first president was Major J. F. Dickson. The Thalian Club built a handsome modern club house at the corner of Rusk Avenue and San Jacinto Street in 1907, at a cost of $40,000, and its social functions have been very elaborate. Among its presidents have been numbered the most prominent men of the city in business and social life. Its presidents have been, in the following order: Major John F. Dickson, Mr. R. S. Lovett, Major John F. Dickson, Hon. Frank Andrews, Col. J. S.

Rice, Capt. S. Taliaferro, Hon. H. M. Garwood, Hon. John Charles Harris, and Mr. Joseph Hellen.

The present officers of the club are: E. K. Dillingham, president; J. G. Maillot, vice-president; Murray B. Jones, secretary; J. F. Dickson, Jr., treasurer, and W. L. Thaxton, manager.

The Houston Country Club was organized in 1904 by a number of Houston club men and golf enthusiasts. In 1909 the club purchased grounds near Harrisburg and on Bray's Bayou, aggregating 158 acres of beautiful woodland and lawns. Extensive improvements have been made and a club house of the best bungalow type and containing every modern utility combined with taste and beauty was erected at a cost of $125,000 for house and grounds.

The club has the finest golf links in the South. A course of 18 holes exists with fine natural hazards.

Those instrumental in organizing the club were Joe Rice, E. B. Parker, W. W. Dexter, T. B. Timpson, C. D. Golding and others. The membership is limited to 500.

Its presidents have been, in the order named: Joe Rice, Wm. M. Rice, and Edwin B. Parker, the present president.

A down-town business men's club, known as the Houston Club, was organized in 1894. Most of the business men of the city belong and the entire top floor of the Chronicle Building and the beautiful roof garden are utilized by the club. From 1902 until 1910, for some reason, the club ceased to exist as an active organization, but in 1910, interest was revived, new blood was infused and the Houston Club takes rank as one of the most useful social organizations in the city. Its officers, since its organization have been:

- 1894-95—President, O. T. Holt; Secretary and Treasurer, L. J. Parks.
- 1895-96—The same officers.
- 1896-97—President, J. F. Dickson; Secretary and Treasurer, Ennis Cargill.
- 1897-98—President, Jno. F. Dickson; Secretary and Treasurer, Ennis Cargill, resigned, L. Hoenthal, appointed.
- 1898-99—President, Jno. F. Dickson; Secretary and Treasurer, L. Hoenthal.
- 1899-1900—President, Jos. F. Dickson; Secretary and Treasurer, B. P. Bailey, resigned, Joseph Hellen, appointed.
- 1900-01—President, Jno. F. Dickson; Secretary and Treasurer, Joseph Hellen.
- 1901-02—President and Secretary same as the year before.
-

After 1902 the club was not active until its reorganization in 1910.

In 1910–11 Mr. C. K. Dunlap was elected president and Mr. T. H. Stone secretary-treasurer. Soon after his election Mr. Dunlap resigned and Mr. Stone was chosen to succeed him. The officers of the club are at present: T. H. Stone, president; E. A. Peden, vice-president; Arch. MacDonald, secretary and treasurer.

Houston is fairly well supplied with charitable institutions. While most of the members of these organizations belong to some religious body, many of them are members of no church, but all are influenced by that true spirit of Christianity which finds expression in aiding the poor, relieving suffering and visiting the sick and afflicted.

The central organization is the United Charities. This organization has a modest office in the Binz Building and all its work is carried on in the field. Its objects are to aid the worthy poor and to check the impositions of the unworthy to minister to the sick and destitute, and aid the unemployed to secure work. The association owns no property and is supported entirely by voluntary contributions. The annual sale of "red badges," on the day before Christmas, by the association is one of its chief revenue producers. From this source alone it derives between $3,000 and $4,000 every year.

The ladies of Christ Church established the Sheltering Arms in 1903, and since its opening it has sheltered 140 old and destitute women. It owns its own property and, in addition, has a small endowment. The Catholics maintain St. Anthony's Home. This is a home for old men and old women. The capacity of the home is fifty and it is generally full. The oldest charitable institution is Bayland Orphon's Home. This was originally intended as a home for the orphaned children of Confederate soldiers. It was organized in 1867 and was located at Bayland, on Galveston Bay. In 1888 it was removed to Hereston and now occupies a 34-acre tract of land adjoining Woodland Heights. It cares for about 30 children each year.

A school has been maintained ever since the organization of the home. Since its removal to Houston a teacher has been employed, the sessions of the school corresponding to those of the city school. The county paid to it its proportion of the state tax, but since the extension of the city limits brought the home within the city limits, the city has appointed and paid for a teacher, the amount paid by the city being supplemented by the home. The present managers are: James Bruce, superintendent; R. M. Elgin, William Christian, R. B. Baer, J. V. Dealy, E. W. Taylor, J. F. Meyer and H. J. Dannebaum, board of directors.

The Star of Hope is a mission, under the auspices of the Baptist churches of Houston for the immediate assistance and help of homeless and destitute men. It was founded by Rev. Mordecai F. Ham, an evangelist, and Richard Dowling, a brilliant man who had gone to the gutter through drink and was reclaimed.

The mission is located on Franklin Avenue, near the bayou, and provides beds and meals for unemployed men and helps them to secure employment. Daily religious services are held and a reading room and employment bureau is maintained. It was organized in 1907.

About the same time the Salvation Army in Houston established a free relief and dispensory department and by the furnishing of medicines to the very poor and by the assistance of the local physicians has done a large work.

The Houston Settlement Association is not a charitable institution, but is largely a social one. By whatever name it may be designated it is one of the most useful and helpful organizations of the kind in the city. Its formal organization dates from February 19, 1907, when about a dozen ladies met at the residence of Mrs. James A Baker and banded themselves together for the purpose of extending educational, industrial, social and friendly aid to all those within their reach. That was the formal organization of the association of today, though the nucleus for it had existed for a year or two before then in the sewing class, organized by Mrs. M. M. Archer and several young lady assistants, among the pupils of the Rusk School, in January, 1904. This sewing class met once each week in the Woman's Club free kindergarten room.

The association is non-sectarian, there being representatives of all creeds and beliefs on its board of directors. It has a membership of about two hundred and derives its support from voluntary contributions.

The association has in its charge the free kindergarten of the second ward; a Womans' club; the Alpha club, a social association of young men, and minor organizations. Its greatest work is in coöperation with the school authorities, in establishing and maintaining a domestic science department in the Rusk School.

The officers of the association are: President, Mrs. James A. Baker; first vice-president, Mrs. Frank Andrews, second vice-president, Mrs. John McClelland; treasurer, Mrs. J. E. Crews; corresponding secretary, Mrs. P. B. Simpson, and recording secretary, Mrs. D. C. Glenn.

If ever an institution were properly named it is the DePelchin Faith Home, for it was started entirely on faith, without a cent in its treasury, if it can be said to have had a treasury, and with no visible source of income. Faith in the big-hearted people of Houston was its sole asset. Mrs. E. N. Gray thus tells its story in "The Key to the City of Houston:"

"This is one of the most appealing benevolences of our city, for it has to do with the needs of distressed children. And hard indeed is the heart which is not touched by the cry of a little child.

"This institution owes its inception to the big-heartedness of Mrs. Kenzia DePelchin, who was practically aided in her noble undertaking by some of the ladies of our city.

"Mrs. Kenzia DePelchin's life is an interesting as a story. She spent many years in Houston, an angel of mercy to the sick and destitute. The home which she founded for homeless children stands today as a significant monument to her life of service and devotion to the cause of helpless humanity.

"Born in the Maderia Islands, of English parents, she was left an orphan when very young, but under the care of an aunt she came to Texas, while yet a girl, and then her life of ministry began. She was first a music teacher, and later she was in Drs. Stuart & Boyle's sanitarium as one of its most capable nurses. During the dreadful yellow fever scourge of 1878 she went to Memphis, Tenn., and gave heroic service. When urged to accept the money donated to pay the nurses, she accepted it only to turn it over to a worthy charity of that city.

"The last part of her life was spent as matron of the Bayland Orphans' Home. In the spring of 1892, two homeless little ones were picked up by her and a notice put in the Post announcing that a home would be begun at once. She spent the night in prayer and the next morning a benevolent woman of Houston went to see her. This was Mrs. W. C. Crane.

"With the aid of this lady a small cottage was rented and a lady was found who would loan her furniture and act as matron.

Then the home was a fact, without one dollar ahead and only a crib for possession. On Monday, May 2, Mrs. Crane took out some ice cream and cake and Mrs. DePelchin took the orphans from Bayland Home to the cottage, where they sang their little hymns and with simple ceremony in Mrs. DePelchin's own words, 'they christened Bayland's little sister Faith Home.' The orphans enjoyed the ride and the unwonted feast, and the guests departed with a vivid memory of that May day opening.

"From the small beginning in 1892, the institution has grown and developed, until today it is one of the best equipped of the city's charities, with its own handsome brick building and its many happy-faced little ones, sheltered by its watchful care.

"The Faith Home as it now exists, was organized January 20, 1893, and soon after applied for a charter. It was called 'Faith Home' because the heroic founder of that institution placed her faith in God and the kind hearts of the Houston people.

"This home is not primarily an orphan asylum, but it is a comfortable home, situated on the corner of Chenevert Street and Pierce Avenue, where the father who has lost his wife may place his little ones until he can provide home care for them again; a home where the mother may shelter her helpless children while she earns a living; a home where good care, the best of medical attention, wholesome food and wise, sanitary surroundings are furnished for the helpless children, either orphaned of father's and mother's care or dependent upon the one parent, too burdened to meet their need. The parent who places his child there is supposed to pay three dollars a month, so long as he has work. This is of necessity an uncertain and very limited source of income. Therefore it is incumbent on the general public to see that this institution is fitly supported. There are always some forty children in the home.

"The board of directors consist of the officers and chairmen of the various committees. They are: President, Mrs. T. W. House; vice-president at large, Mrs, M. E. Bryan; treasurer, Mrs. F. A. Reichardt; secretary, Mrs. Jonathan Lane. Mrs. J. W. McKee, Miss H. Levy, Mrs. J. W. Parker, Mrs. Carter Walker, Mrs. Ed. Mackey, Mrs. B. F. Weems, Mrs. W. B. Chew, and Mrs. G. S. Shannon are heads of committees; Mrs. Kerven is the matron."

The Florence Crittendon Rescue Home for Girls was organized November 17, 1896, with the following officers and directors: W. B. Jones, president; I. S. Myer, vice-president; G. W. Heyer, treasurer: A. G. Howell, secretary; Mesdames Belle Blandin, D. R. Cunningham, E. S. Tracy, W. H. Peregoy, S. Beaty, Messrs. E. F. McGowan, W. D. Cleveland, Sr., E. W. Taylor, S. E. Calvitt, Frank W. Fox and George Henrickson, directors. Two and one-half lots, on the corner of Elgin Avenue and Caroline Street were purchased for $700 in February, 1907, and by September, the same year, the home was built and Mrs. Yates installed as matron. On September 16, she reported one girl in the home. Since then the average number of girls in the home has been about seven per month. These girls come from all parts of the state and none is ever refused admission.

The home is not altogether a charitable institution, though it is made as nearly so as possible. So long as a girl is trying to live a decent life and is out of employment the home is open to her and the officials assist her in finding employment. She is charged for board and medical treatment and when she finds employment she must pay to the home one-fifth of her wages until the amount reaches $34. These are the rules for out-of-town girls. During the past 15 years more than 1,000 girls have been helped by the home.

The home is without endowment and is supported by voluntary subscriptions. The present officers and directors are: W. B. Jones, president; Mrs. E. N. Gray, vice-president; A. G. Howell, treasurer; J. C. Harris, recording secretary; Mrs. L. S. Hubbell, corresponding secretary; Mrs. Charles Stewart, I. S. Myer, W. A. Wilson and Rev. Dr. J. L. Gross are directors.

The Wesley House, a Christian center for social educational and religious activities is maintained by the Board of City Missions, an organization composed of representatives from all the Methodist churches in the city. Its departments of work are: A home for self-supporting young women, a kindergarten, night classes for foreigners, a committee for daily visiting, an industrial school, athletic classes for young women, a Sunday school, and preaching in Spanish the first Sunday afternoon of each month. Miss Mattie Wright is the superintendent and Miss Audrey Wade is matron. They have six efficient assistant workers.

The Wesley House Board, in 1907, established the Young Women's Co-operative Home for homeless wage-earning girls. It cares for about 33 girls at a time and an effort is being made to secure $40,000 to erect a home that will accommodate 300 working girls who labor for wages lower than the cost of subsistence. Much good has been accomplished by the home and it seems to be on the threshold of a wider usefulness.

The Young Women's Christian Association, while it has never received loyal support from the citizens has accomplished much for girls and has a comfortable home where many young women board. Gymnasium work and a downtown lunch for working girls in a rest room have also been wholesome features. There is a movement to build a suitable home for the Y. W. C. A., similar to that occupied by the Y. M. C. A.

Among the Jewish people of the city there has been a good work done by the Jewish Charity Home.

CHAPTER XVI - SOCIETIES
AND CLUBS—CONTINUED

First Literary Society. Organization of Houston Lyceum. Early Efforts to Establish a Library. The Houston Lyceum and Carnegie Library. The Ladies Reading Club. Ladies Shakespeare Club. The Two other Shakespeare Clubs. Current Literature Club. Houston Pen Women's Association. Houston Branch of Dickens Fellowship. Lady Washington Chapter. Daughters of the American Revolution. San Jacinto Chapter No. 2, Daughters of the Republic of Texas. Robert E. Lee Chapter 186, United Daughters of the Confederacy. Oran M. Roberts Chapter 440, U. D. C.

While Houston and Galveston have always been bitterly opposed to each other commercially, they have ever been the best friends and have united their efforts to forward and promote all that contributed to intellectual life. As early as 1845–46 there was a literary club, or lyceum, which, while located in Galveston, was loyally supported by Houstonians. Dr. Ashbel Smith, Dr. McCraven and Dr. McAnally were young men at that time and took great interest in the lyceum and contributed regularly to the monthly meetings, lectures, debates and papers on chosen subjects. This was undoubtedly the first literary society organized in Texas and is mentioned here because of the fact that Houstonians took such a leading part in its affairs.

The Galveston institution did not ante-date that of Houston very much, however, for in 1848 the Houston Lyceum was chartered and has been in existence ever since, though at times very quiet and inert. It has had several rather long periods of rest, only to awaken to new life and renewed activity. Soon after it obtained its charter it lapsed into a period of inertia and remained so until 1854 when it was revived for a time and it was thought there would be no further lapses.

The objects and purposes of the Lyceum as outlined in a statement made in 1854 were: "To diffuse knowledge among its members, intelligence and information by a library, by lectures on various subjects and by discussion of such questions as may elicit useful information and produce improvement in the art of public speaking." At that time 382 volumes had been gotten together and a book case was purchased. The Lyceum had no income except that derived from dues and an occasional donation, so its existence was very precarious. During the war it was, of course, in a comatose state, but in 1865 it again became active.

Interest was soon allowed to die out and not until 1877 was an effort made to revive it. In that year its managers raised funds for it by a series of musical and dramatic entertainments, and the reading room was thrown open to the public. The city also came to the assistance of the association and donated the use of a large room in the city hall, known as "The Banquet

Hall." A great mistake that the association had made—that of restricting the membership to males—was corrected in 1888, and from the moment the ladies were admitted, the association took on renewed and permanent life.

For a while Mr. Bonner McCraven acted as secretary without compensation. The ladies made a gallant fight to have the city take over the library, but failed. After a long stretch of adversity it was decided to issue check books at $3 each which would entitle those who bought them to take books from the library. Mrs. M. H. Foster was employed as librarian at a small salary and worked faithfully. The small politicians who hung around the city hall got in the habit of making the library a loafing place and that so disgusted the ladies that they refused to go there. Then, in 1895, Mrs. Looscan, president of the Ladies Reading Club, appealed to that society to come to the assistance of the Lyceum. Every member of the club became a patron of the Lyceum and the books were removed to the Mason Building. The ladies kept up their fight for municipal recognition and, in 1899, they invited the city officials to visit their hall where they made speeches and showed them the empty shelves. Soon after, the city gave official recognition by donating $200 each month for its support. That same year Mr. Carnegie gave $50,000 for a building fund, providing the city would donate a building site, and make an appropriation of $4,000 annually for the support of the institution. A subscription of $7,800 was obtained and the lot, corner of McKinney Avenue and Travis Street was purchased. A contract for the building was let, but the building could not be finished until the city had given $10,000 more for unforeseen expenses and equipments.

The building was formally thrown open to the public in March, 1904. In 1900, the Houston Lyceum and Carnegie Library Association was formed and chartered to take over the effects of the old Houston Lyceum. Mr. N. S. Meldrum also endowed the children's department with $6,000 as a memorial to Norma Meldrum.

The Houston Lyceum had, in 1904, when the transfer was made, about 4,000 volumes which had all been catalogued before the new quarters were ready. Before the actual transfer was made the lyceum library was practically doubled by the gift from a donor, who desired his name to be unknown, of 4,000 volumes. N. S. Meldrum also gave $1,000 for the purchase of special books. This caused a vast amount of work before the library could be put in perfect condition for the use of the public. There were over five thousand volumes to be catalogued. The system of cataloging demanded a complete description of each book, and for each volume a card index and stock card were necessary. Among the 4,000 volumes of the unknown donor were books in Latin and Greek and books that dealt with complicated problems and technical matters. To examine, describe and record them required much time. This work was done by Miss Caroline Wandell, Miss Julia Ideson and Miss Ethel Jones.

It soon became evident that the library needed more books. The demand exceeded the supply.

"The number of books withdrawn from the library for home use," said Miss Julia Ideson, librarian, in her report for 1904, "was 59,751. This seems fairly good for the first year, yet the circulation might have been considerably greater had we had a supply of books anywhere nearly equal to the demand."

"Estimating the population of Houston at 75,000," said Mrs. Henry H. Dickson, president of the board of trustees of the Houston Lyceum and Carnegie Library Association, in a report to the mayor and city council made at the same time, "we are receiving 5½ cents per capita for library purposes. Both Fort Worth and El Paso do much better than that, while San Antonio gave, last year, over $6,000 and received, in addition, gifts from her citizens aggregating over $15,000."

In the seven years of the library's active existence the increase in the number of books has been steady and healthy. In the beginning there were about eight or nine thousand volumes, while in 1911, there are, approximately, thirty-two thousand. In 1904, as already stated, 59,751 books were circulated for home use. According to the report of Miss Ideson, the librarian, for the year ending Feb. 28, 1911, there were 90,877 volumes circulated, which, she states, was an increase over the preceding year. From the same report the following extracts are made:

"The library has shown a substantial growth this year. There were added, during the year, by purchase, 2,542 volumes; by purchase, Meldrum fund, 247; by gift, 355, making total accessions, 3,144 volumes."

"To show the class of people by whom the library is principally used, statistics of occupations were kept. Of those registering their occupations, there were: manufacturers, 9; merchants and business men, 48; bankers and brokers, 4; real estate and insurance men, 32; mechanics, 31; trades, 68; farmers and stockmen, 5; railroad employees (no clerks), 19; engineers, 18; artists and musicians, 15; newspaper men, 8; teachers, 92; physicians, 13; clergymen, 6; lawyers, 9; other professions, 13; stenographers and clerks, 384; salesmen, 28; collectors, 11; miscellaneous, 40."

"The colored branch, for which an appropriation of $500 was made, has had good use. Over 4,000 books, principally children's books, have been loaned."

The "colored branch" spoken of in the report, was the branch for negroes opened at the negro high school in May, 1909. A movement was started by the promoters of this branch to secure for it a permanent building. Mr. Carnegie was asked for a gift and offered $15,000 on his usual terms and conditions, but as these have never been complied with, the negro branch remains as first organized.

The officers of the Houston Lyceum and Carnegie Library Association are: L. S. Denis, president; Mrs. H. F. Ring, vice-president; Mrs. I. S. Meyer, secretary; Mrs. E. N. Gray, treasurer; Mrs. E. Raphael, corresponding secretary; Miss Julia Ideson, librarian.

It will be seen from the foregoing that the ladies deserve the lion's share of the credit for establishing the lyceum and library on a firm basis and the same is true of nearly every literary, artistic and musical movement that has been inaugurated here.

In 1885, the Ladies Reading Club was organized by Mrs. M. Looscan and Mrs. C. M. Lombardi. The first meeting was held at the home of Mrs. Briscoe on Crawford Street and was for the purpose of organizing a society for pleasure and mutual improvement. The movement could not have been in better hands than those of Mrs. Looscan and Mrs. Lombardi.

There were eight ladies at the beginning, namely: Mesdames Looscan, Lombardi, Hill, Perl, Stone and Briscoe, and Misses Allen and Wagley. Mrs. Looscan was chosen temporary chairman and Miss Wagley was chosen secretary. The name adopted by the ladies was the Ladies History Class. The adoption of this name was due to the fact that it was the intention to take up the study of history at once, and to choose the history of Egypt as the first course of study. Just at that time the fate of Gordon at Khartoum was exciting world-wide interest. It was six weeks before a constitution and by-laws were ready for adoption, but during the delay the club was not idle but had taken up a systematic study of that mysterious country and prosecuted it zealously and intelligently. During the six weeks the membership had increased so that it was decided to organize thoroughly and formally, which was done. The constitution and by-laws were adopted and the following named officers were elected: President, Mrs. M. Looscan; first vice-president, Mrs. C. M. Lombardi; second vice-president, Mrs. E. P. Hill; secretary, Miss A. E. Wagley; treasurer, Mrs. M. J. Briscoe.

At that meeting the name of the club was changed to the Ladies Reading Club and plans for future work were outlined.

For the first ten years the club met in the parlors of Mrs. M. G. Howe; afterwards in rented rooms, then at the parish house of the Christ Church, then in the Lyceum library room after that institution had been moved to the Mason Building. Since the opening of the Houston Lyceum and Carnegie Library, meetings have been and are being held on the upper floor on the hall designed for club meetings.

As already noted it was the Ladies' Reading Club that took the first steps towards saving the Houston Lyceum from oblivion and which also led to the establishment of the Carnegie Library here. During the twenty-six years of the club's existence it has been faithful to the objects which it had in view at its organization, namely, the creation of interest in intellectual and social culture and the creation of a common ground on which ladies having a literary taste might meet. It has used its influence in bringing celebrated lecturers to the city, and in behalf of every measure intended to advance educational interest.

A few years ago it was determined to broaden the influence of the club by admitting associate members, not to exceed ten. These associate members pay more dues than regular members, but are excused from contributing to the regular literary exercises. They are treated as regular members except that they cannot hold office.

The membership of the club is fifty, exclusive of associate and honorary members.

The following named ladies have been honored with the presidency of the club since its organization: Mrs. M. Looscan, Mrs. C. M. Lombardi, Mrs. M. E. Cage, Mrs. C. A. McKinney, Mrs. H. F. Ring, Mrs. P. K. Ewing, Mrs. R. M. Hall, Mrs. W. A. DeLaMatyr, Mrs. William Christian, Mrs. B. A. Randolph.

Those who have filled the post of recording secretary are: Miss Annie E. Wagley, Mrs. P. H. Goodwyn, Miss Fannie G. Vincent, Mrs. G. F. Arnold, Mrs. W. B. Slosson, Mrs. H. F. MacGregor, Mrs. C. R. Cummings, Mrs. P. K. Ewing, Mrs. C. F. Beutel, Miss Emilia Celestine Bujac, Mrs. G. A. Taft, Miss Laura Yocum, Mrs. A. L. Metcalf, Mrs. J. P. Carroll and Mrs. March Culmore.

The broad-minded members of the club are thoroughly alive to the best interests of the city and state, and certain days of the year are set aside for discussion of Texas topics.

The officials of the club, in September, 1911, are: President, Mrs. R. M. Hall; vice-president, Mrs. G. A. Taft; second vice-president, Mrs. I. S. Mayer; corresponding secretary, Mrs. J. G. Boyd; recording secretary, Mrs. B. A. Randolph; and treasurer, Mrs. D. C. Glenn.

The Ladies Shakespeare Club was organized November 29, 1890, with Mesdames E. Raphael, I. G. Gersom, I. Blandin, Blanche Booker, and Misses C. R. Redwood, Lydia Adkisson and Mary Light as charter members. The club was formed for the sole purpose of literary study and during the many years of its existence nothing has ever been permitted to divert it from the course marked out by its members at its initial meeting.

The creed of the club has but two articles: First, that Shakespeare's plays were written by Shakespeare and not by Bacon; second, that Shakespeare is the crown and chief glory of English literature.

Until the completion of the Carnegie Library, the club had no permanent home, but met at private houses, public halls and other convenient places. This lack of permanent headquarters was not allowed to interfere in the least with the club work and the course of study for each year has been conscientiously carried out. It has been serious work, too. The club placed itself in close communication with the Chicago University where much valuable study and research work connected with Shakespeare have been done and, in addition, on one or two occasions has been instrumental in having Professor Clark, of that University, come to Houston for the purpose of delivering his famous lectures on Shakespeare.

Of course Shakespeare has been the great trunk of the tree, but it has had many branches which have invited the members to deviate occasionally and follow them up. For instance the study of Henry VI and kindred plays led to historical research while certain of the romantic plays opened the way towards dramatic construction. The members have never hesitated to follow any line that offered to throw light on the hidden mysteries and profound learning of the great bard. Its labors have been great, but they have been pleasant at all times for they were labors of love.

The Study Shakespeare Class is simply a number of ladies who have banded themselves together without official organization for the purpose of studying the plays of Shakespeare. Mrs. Alma McDonnell is the moving spirit and it was through her efforts that the ladies were brought together. She has the well-deserved reputation of being a thorough Shakespearean scholar, and has the ability to impart her knowledge and enthusiasm to others, so the success of the Study Shakespeare Class has been very great.

Another Shakespeare Club was organized October 1, 1904, at the residence of Mrs. A. G. Howell. There were fourteen ladies present and an organization was perfected at that first meeting by the election of Mrs. J. W. Lockett, president; Mrs. J. W. Carter, vice-president, and Mrs. Harry Tyner, recording secretary. Since most of the members were residents of the south end of the city, the name South End Shakespeare Club was chosen, and the membership was limited to twenty-one. As soon as the club was organized the ladies went to work and began the study of the tragedy, Othello. The history of the play was given by Mrs. Howell and why Shakespeare wrote it was explained by Mrs. Carter. Since that initial meeting, the club has been very active and its members have studied and discussed many of the plays and writings of Shakespeare.

One of the most interesting clubs of the city is the Current Literature Club, which was organized in 1899, by Mrs. Si Packard. Her idea was to get a number of congenial women together for the purpose of reading and keeping up with the books of the day. In response to her call about twenty ladies met at her house and the club was organized. Mrs. Packard was elected president and held the office for four years. The character of work done by the club and its methods of work have been thus described by Mrs. J. T. Lockman.

"At first, only the novels of the day were read and discussed. Meetings were held at the different homes and books were carried from place to place by the librarian. It was lots of work but it was lots of fun. After the study hour was over, the hostess of each meeting always had a social feature prepared for us, something so bright and cheery that the memory of our 'good old times' lingers lovingly with all charter members. No one ever dreamed they could stay away from a meeting. But the current novels got to be so trashy that the ladies became disgusted and threw them aside. The library was completed and the club moved into permanent quarters and all fun ceased. The club took up the study of more serious matter and engaged in studying works on travel, history, art, literature and preserves its original intention, in part only, by reading and discussing the current magazines and periodicals. The club has forty active members and twenty-five associate and honorary members."

The officers of the club are: President, Mrs. J. T. Lockman; secretary, Mrs. E. A. Adey; treasurer, Mrs. E. Scheultz.

The first year of the Houston Pen Women's Association was completed March 23, 1907. At the first annual meeting reports were made by Mrs. Elizabeth Strong Tracy, the president, and by Mrs. Florence N. Dancy, the secretary. From those two reports the following facts are taken. The question of organization had long been discussed by the women of Houston who were engaged in writing for the newspapers. Nowhere else in the state were there so many members of the Texas Woman's Press Association. Eighteen women responded to a call to women of the press and to women engaged in literary work, and attended a preliminary meeting at the residence of Mrs. William Christian. Mrs. Christian was made the temporary chairman and Mrs. Dancy, secretary. Mrs. Tracy, Miss Katie Daffan and Mrs. Dancy were appointed a committee on constitution and bylaws. A few days later a permanent organization was effected.

Mrs. Tracy was elected president; Mrs. Abbie N. Smith, vice-president; and Mrs. Dancy, secretary. The membership consists of historians, poets, writers of prose, authors, journalists and newspaper writers. The success of the club has been marked. Its officers are: President, Mrs. J. M. Limbocker; vice-president, Mrs. M. B. Crowe; second vice-president, Miss Abbie N. Smith; recording secretary, Mrs. R. R. Dancy; corresponding secretary, Mrs. Grace Zimmer; treasurer, Mrs. E. S. Tracy.

The Houston Branch of the "Dickens Fellowship" was organized in 1909, at the home of its president, Mrs. E. Raphael, with an enthusiastic membership composed of the following ladies: Mrs. E. W. Luhn, Mrs. A. S. Dyer, Mrs. J. R. Parks, Mrs. T. C. Dunn, Mrs. W. W. Ralston, Mrs. S. C. Robbins, Mrs. J. B. Slack, Mrs. W. Southward, Mrs. Jules Hirsch, Mrs. E. Adey, Mrs. Jas. Breeding, Mrs. E. Raphael. These received the first certificates of membership from the London Branch of the Dickens Fellowship.

This branch is the only off-shoot of the London Fellowship in the South, and the ninth branch of the United States. The object of this organization is to foster the love of Dickens' writings, to emulate his genial kindliness, humanitarian impulses and living interest in all things great and small; and to pass along the philosophy of life so vividly portrayed by the beloved author.

The Fellowship is still in its infancy, but as it grows it hopes to become great in numbers and greater in capacity for betterment of the mind and spirit of its members and those allied to it by the brotherhood of man. The present officers are: Mrs. E. Raphael, president; Mrs. A. S. Dyer, vice-president; Mrs. W. W. Ralston, secretary and treasurer. The membership numbers about twenty active workers.

The club members subscribe to the official magazine, "The Dickensian" published in London, and so keep in touch with the spirit of Dickens' lovers elsewhere. This branch hopes to celebrate in a fitting manner the hundredth anniversary of Dickens' birthday.

A chapter of the Daughters of the American Revolution was organized in Houston, during November, 1899, by Mrs. Seabrook W. Sydnor, who had been appointed regent at Houston for the general organization. The chapter took the name of Lady Washington Chapter and was organized in the parlors of the Rice Hotel. The following named ladies were charter members: Mrs. S. W. Sydnor, Mrs. W. C. Crane, Mrs. J. C. Hutcherson, Mrs. W. L. Lane, Mrs. Thos. Franklin, Mrs. James Journeay, Mrs. Henry Lummis, Mrs. Paul Timpson, Mrs. M. H. Foster, Mrs. H. F. Ring, Mrs. Botts Fitzgerald, Mrs. D. F. Stuart, Mrs. W. R. Robertson, Mrs. C. L. Fitch, Mrs. Susan R. Tempest, Mrs. H. T. Warner, and Mrs. R. F. Dunbar.

The Chapter has been in active existence since its organization and its affairs are in excellent condition. Social functions, in commemoration of national holidays, bazaars and other entertainments, for the purpose of raising money for special purposes, historical research and kindred matters have occupied the attention and interest of the members.

The Chapter has erected a monument to Alexander Hodge in the Sam Houston Park. Hodge was a Revolutionary soldier and served with Marion. He came to Texas and served with the Texas army, thus becoming a veteran of two revolutions, each among the most successful and far-reaching in the history of the world. He died and was buried in Texas. Among his descendants is Mrs. Seybrook Sydnor, who has been State Regent and most active in promoting the interests of the Daughters' organizations in Texas.

San Jacinto Chapter No. 2, Daughters of the Republic of Texas, was organized in 1901. The chapter has accomplished a great deal in the way of perpetrating the memories of the Texas heroes who established the independence of Texas, and has collected many valuable historical data. It has taken under its care. San Jacinto battlefield and has marked, with suitable monuments and tablets, historical points and localities associated with early Texas history.

The chapter has at present fifty active members. Its officers are: Mrs. J. J. McKeer, president; Mrs. E. T. Dumble, first vice-president; Mrs. G. A. Fosgard, second vice-president; Mrs. Geo. Hamman, third vice-president; Mrs. M. B. Urwitz, secretary: Mrs. C. H. Milby, treasurer; Mrs. Rosine Ryan, historian.

Robert E. Lee Chapter, 186, United Daughters of the Confederacy, was organized in 1897. The first officers were: Mrs. J. C. Hutcherson, president; Mrs. M. G. Howe, vice-president; Mrs. T. R. Franklin, vice-president; Mrs. M. H. Foster, secretary. There were fifty charter members.

This chapter is one of the largest and hardest working chapters in the state and has accomplished a great deal since its organization. Its growth has been rapid from the first year of its organization. Its members have contributed generously towards all monument funds, one of the most beautiful of which is that known as the Spirit of the Confederacy, located in the city park, and have done much to preserve the memory of the Confederate soldiers who have passed over the river and to care for and comfort those who are still on this side.

The present officers of the chapter, October, 1911, are: Mrs. M. E. Bryan, president; Mrs. J. F. Burton, Mrs. J. L. Bates, Mrs. Carter Walker, Mrs. G. L. Black, vice-presidents; Mrs. W. A. Rowan, recording secretary; Mrs. W. H. Bailey, corresponding secretary; Mrs. P. H. Fall, treasurer; Mrs. A. G. Henry, registrar; Mrs. J. W. Dittmar, curator.

Oran M. Roberts, Chapter No. 440, United Daughters of the Confederacy was organized in 1901, with sixty charter members. Its first officers were: Miss A. A. Dunovant, president; Mrs. S. F. Carter, first vice-president; Mrs. T. W. House, second vice-president; Mrs. Wharton Bates, third vice-president; Mrs. W. B. King, fourth vice-president; Miss Jennie Criswell, recording secretary; Mrs. Jonathan Lane, corresponding secretary; Mrs. B. M. Stephens, treasurer.

During the first year of the Chapter's life its membership increased to 314. The chapter has made donations towards monuments but its main efforts have been in behalf of indigent and needy Confederate soldiers.

The officers of this chapter, October, 1911, are: President, Mrs. Will Hansen; first vice-president, Mrs. J. M. Gibson; second vice-president, Mrs. Hattie S. Hatch; third vice-president, Mrs. Uvalde Burns; fourth vice-president, Mrs. Sidney Huston; recording secretary, Mrs. E. C. Reichardt; corresponding secretary, Mrs. B. B. Knolle; treasurer, Mrs. W. Worsham; historian, Mrs. S. T. Steele; librarian, Miss Williams; registrar, Mrs. J. Hyndman; custodian, Mrs. Kaufhold.

In all matters relating to culture, patriotism, and civic and municipal improvement, the women of Houston have played a leading role and the story of their efforts and the list of their accomplishments has not been and is not now told. A book of this scope can only indicate the organizations or the principal ones of them and the directions in which their activities tend.

There has been no great religious, literary, patriotic, charitable or civic movement in which the noble women of Houston have not led and in many of these movements they have borne almost the entire burden and are entitled to the largest measure of praise for the successes, many times brilliant ones, that have been achieved along the chosen lines of effort.

CHAPTER XVII - ORGANIZED LABOR

Organized Labor is Prosperous in Houston. Houston Labor Council's Full Report Showing Numbers and Conditions in all the Organized Crafts. Good Wages are Paid and Sweating System is not in Vogue.

The labor associations of Houston are very numerous and very well organized. Each branch of labor has its own organization, and the entire membership of all of them foots up in the thousands. The Stowers Building, corner of Congress Avenue and Caroline Street, was formally dedicated to the use and occupancy of the various labor organizations of Houston on Jan. 14, 1905. This huge building was transformed into a home for the Houston Labor Council with imposing ceremonies. Among the prominent labor organizations taking part were the following:

Amalgamated Sheet Metal Workers' Local No. 54; Bakers' and Confectioners' Union No. 28; Bed Spring and Mattress Makers' Union No. 844; Blacksmiths' Union No. 32; Boiler Makers' Union No. 74; Bookbinders' Union, Local No. 110; Brewery Workers' Union, Local No. 111; Bricklayers' and Masons' International Union No. 7; Carpenters' and Joiners' Union No.—; Carriage and Wagonworkers' International Union No. 109; Houston Typographical Union No. 87; Icemen's Protective Union No. 9254; International Alliance Theatrical Stage Employees', No. 65; International Association of Machinist, No. 12; International Brotherhood of Electrical Workers, No. 66; Iron Moulders' Union of North America, No. 259; Journeymen Barbers' Union No. 74; Journeyman Tailors' Union No. 247; Musicians' Protective Union No. 65; Painters' and Decorators' Union No. 130; Patternmakers' League of America; Plasters' International Protective Union No. 140; Plumbers' and Gasfitters' Union No. 68; Bridge and Structural Iron Workers; Building Laborers International Protective Union; Carriage, Cab and Delivery Wagon Drivers' Union; Cooks and Waiters' Union; Theatrical Mechanical Association; Tile Pipe Layers' Protective Union; Woman's Union Label League; Printing Pressmen's Union No. 71; Retail Clerk's Protective Association No. 165; Shirt Waist and Laundry Workers International Union, Local, No. 38; Soda Water Workers' Union No. 11, 300; Team Drivers No. 489; Texas Association of Steam Engineers, Houston, No. 1; Stenographers' and Typewriters' Association; Railroad Employees' Association. Since then the unions have maintained a common headquarters and parade in strength each labor day.

The following figures, furnished by Mr. Max Andrews, clerk of the Harris County Criminal Court and editor of the Labor Journal, were especially prepared by a committee from the Houston Labor council. They represent the situation as it existed in July, 1911.

The total number of industrial workers in Houston is 25,000, graded as follows: Men, 15,000; women, 6,000; children, 15 years and under, 4,000.

Organized: Men, 55 per cent; women, 2 per cent.

Of the skilled trades, 85 per cent are organized and 15 per cent unorganized.

During the last ten years the hours of labor have been decreased all along the line from ten to eight.

During the past ten years there has been an average increase in wages among the crafts of 25 per cent.

However, during this same period the increased cost of living, ascertained through government authorities, has increased 40 per cent. Thus it will be seen that the increased cost of living far exceeds the increase in pay secured.

The total number of organized men and women in Houston is 8,250.

The best organized crafts are the plumbers, printers, brickmasons, plasterers, stone cutters and marble cutters, about 100 per cent strong.

All trades limit the number of apprentices. This has not worked a hardship on the boys and has had much to do with maintaining a living wage for the journeymen.

The sentiment and general feeling toward union labor in this city and community is good. All important work is performed by union men.

The central labor body (the Houston labor council) consists of delegates from all locals in this jurisdiction that are affiliated with the American Federation of Labor. Thirty-three are affiliated at this time. The meetings are not open to the general public.

The labor council meets over the Hammersmith shoe establishment, 305 ½ Main Street.

Unions care for their sick and dependent and bury their dead. This is due them through membership.

The federated shop men have a committee on conciliation and arbitration, which has been recognized by the Harriman system. The central council has an arbitration committee.

There is no open conflict between the unions of Houston and the Manufacturers Association, Citizens Alliance or Employees Association locally.

The Ministerial Association has no fraternal delegate in the labor council at present.

Some of the working conditions are thus indicated: Packing House; Number employed (men, women and children), 500. Wages, for men, $1.50 to $2.00 per day; for women, 75 cents to $2.00 per day; for children, 50 cents to $1.00 per day. Labor is seasonal. Approximately 12½ per cent unemployed. Married men get living wages. Work ten hours per day. No Sunday work. Wages do not cause dependency. Little opportunity for training or educational advancement. Conditions sanitary and healthful. Employees subject to danger from machinery and occupational diseases. No sweating system exists. Employees are not organized.

In the railroad shops and yards, there are, approximately, 4,000 employed. Working conditions, fair. Labor seasonal. Married men receive living wages; however, not commensurate with the advances in necessities of life. Hours of labor, nine hours per day. About 25 per cent of laborers work Sundays. Conditions are very good for training and educational advancement. Sanitation and health, good. No sweating system exists. Subject to danger from machinery. Ninety per cent of workers organized. Average wage for all employees about $2.50 per day.

In the cotton oil mills and cotton compresses, the number employed will approximate 1,500. Working conditions, fair. Wages, for men, $1.50 to $2.50 per day; for women, $1.00 to $1.25 per day; for children, 50 cents to 75 cents per day. Labor is casual, a majority of the workers being steadily employed during the months of September, October, November, December, January and February, but during the remainder of the year must seek other means of support. Married men receive living wages. Hours of labor from 10 to 12. Employees work every Sunday during operating season. Wages and general conditions are scarcely removed from dependency. No opportunity for training or educational advancement; however, conditions are far in advance of many cities in the Southern States. Sanitary conditions, fairly good. Workers subject to danger from machinery and occupational diseases.

In the saw mills and factories, the number of employees is 500. Working conditions, reasonably fair. Wages for skilled men, $2.50 to $3.00 per day; unskilled men, 75 cents to $1.75 per day; women, 50 cents to $1.00 per day; children, 25 cents to 75 cents per day. Labor is steady; about 10 per cent are unemployed. Majority of men make scant living. Hours of labor, 10 per day. Do not work Sundays. Wages paid barely keep employees above dependency. Little opportunity is afforded for training or educational advancement. Conditions generally are sanitary and healthful. Workers subject to danger from machinery and occupational diseases. No sweating system exists. About 10 per cent are organized.

In the general stores there are approximately 3,000 employed Working conditions are not good. Wages for men, $5 to $18 per week; women, $3.50 to $10; children, $1.50 to $5. Labor seasonal. About 12½ per cent unemployed. Married men do not receive wage consistent with average living conditions. Hours of labor from 10 to 15 per day. Do not work Sundays. Most employees do not receive wage sufficient to relieve them of dependency; especially is this true of the women, girls and children. Not one out of 1,000 has opportunity of advancement along training and educational lines. Unless the general public intercedes conditions in Houston will soon parallel the larger cities of the country and young womanhood will be sacrificed at the altar of greed and avarice. Conditions are now deplorable. In most instances stores and shops are arranged in sanitary condition. Labor is unorganized.

At the Breweries there are approximately 500 employed. Working conditions are exceptionally good. General scale of wages from $2 to $5 per day. Labor seasonal. About 3 per cent unemployed. Married men receive a living wage. Hours of labor, eight per day. Operate 24 hours per day, with three shifts of eight hours. Most of the employees work Sundays. Employees are independent and most of them are home owners. Conditions sanitary and healthful. Employees are subject to danger from machinery and occupational diseases. All are organized. All workmen in breweries, where steadily employed, must join the Brewery Workers' Union; most compact and thoroughly organized of any craft. It pays large sick and death benefits.

As to common labor, there are approximately 5,000 laborers employed. Wages, for men $1.25 to $2 per day; women, 50 cents to $1.25 per day; children, 25 cents to $1 per day. Labor is casual. About 25 per cent are unemployed. About 10 per cent of the workers are organized. Married men do not receive a living wage. Hours of labor from eight to ten per day. Only those employed for elevator service, street cars and emergency men are required to work Sundays. Wages and general conditions increase dependency. No opportunity for training or educational advancement. Conditions generally are sanitary. No sweating system is vogue.

The industrial crafts include carpenters, plumbers, painters, plasterers, sheetmetal workers, brickmasons, machinists, blacksmiths, lathers, typographers, printing pressmen, bookbinders, musicians, electrical workers, bartenders, tailors, coopers, bridge and structural iron workers, boilermakers, marble workers, journeymen barbers, elevator constructors, pattern makers, iron molders, garment workers, horseshoers, stationary engineers.

Of the above crafts there are about 3,000 employed. This is independent of those working in the railroad shops, mills, compresses, etc., elsewhere compiled and accounted for.

Carpenters and Joiners—Approximately 75 per cent organized; wages, union, $4 per day; non-union, $3.50 per day. Conditions good; all large contracts and buildings employ union labor; union provides sick and death benefits for its members. Death benefit grades upward, according to length of membership; carpenters meet in their own home and are in a most prosperous condition; work seasonal; union men are independent and families enjoy training and educational advantages. No Sunday work.

Plasters—Conditions are good; 90 per cent are organized. Wages, union men receive $6 per day; non-union men, $3 per day. Do not work on Sunday.

Sheetmetal Workers—Very good condition; work seasonal, but rather steady. Wages, union men, $3.50 to $4.50 per day; non-union labor, lower. About 90 per cent of craft organized.

Brickmasons—Splendid condition; about 95 per cent organized. Wages, union men receive $6 to $7 per day; non-union men, $3 to $4. Many homeowners among them.

Machinists—Work steady throughout the year and pretty well employed. Wages, union men, $3.80 per day; non-union men, $2.50 per day.

Theatrical Stage Employees—Number about 100; conditions in large playhouses good and all employed therein are organized; wages range from $15 to $25 per week; all theatres give Sunday performances. Picture shows and vaudeville houses are unsafe, unsanitary and unorganized; much work is needed among them; in most instances incompetent and child labor is employed and the general public is subjected to danger through them.

Blacksmiths—Reasonably fair conditions; about 65 per cent organized and union growing. Wages, union men $3.80 per day; non-union men, $2.50 per day.

Lathers—Steadily employed at present; work would not be classed as casual here, but is rather steady throughout the year. Wages, union men receive from $4 to $6 per day; non-union men, $2.50 per day.

Following are the statistics for the printing trade:

Printers—About 225 in membership; organized 100 per cent strong. Wages, from $3.50 to $8 per day, varying according to men and position. Job offices and ad rooms work time scale, eight hours per day. Machine men work on a piece scale, and average from six to seven hours per day. About 75 per cent of the printers are home owners.

Printing Pressmen—One hundred per cent organized; work eight hours per day; wages average $3.50 per day; many home owners among them; sanitary conditions in shops good.

Bookbinders—One hundred per cent organized; hours of work, eight per day; wages, average $4 per day; sanitary conditions exceptionally good.

Other crafts are as follows:

Electrical Workers—Eighty per cent organized; union men work 8 hours; wages from $3.50 to $4.50 per day; all employed.

Bartenders—About 80 per cent organized; hours of labor eight per day; scale of wages, $15 to $21 per week.

Tailors—Poorly organized at present; hours of labor ten per day; wages, from $2 to $3, most work is by piece.

Coopers—One hundred per cent organized; work seasonal to a great extent; hours of work, eight per day; average wages from $2.85 to $4 per day; conditions sanitary.

Bridge and Structural Iron Workers—Organized 100 per cent strong; hours of labor, eight per day; wage scale from $3.50 to $4.50 per day, work exceptionally good here for the past two years and prospects flattering; duties are most hazardous.

Boilermakers—About 90 per cent organized; wages $3.50 to $5 per day for union men; non-union wages lower; work fair.

Marble Workers—Work eight hours per day; wages $4 to $6 per day; organized 100 per cent strong; conditions good.

Journeyman Barbers—White and colored unions are organized; about 80 per cent organized; conditions above the average; no Sunday work.

Elevator Constructors—Organized 100 per cent; work good; all employed at present; no Sunday work; wages $4 per day.

Pattern Makers—Well organized; wages, fifty cents per hour; nine hours; no labor on Sundays.

Garment Workers—Only craft of women organized; have a union of about 200 members; work eight hours; wages from $9 to $18 per week; no Sunday labor; exceptionally good sanitary conditions prevail.

Horseshoers—Good conditions; work eight hours; average wages $2.50 to $3.50 per day; 75 per cent organized.

Stationary Engineers—Work eight hours; conditions good; about 80 per cent organized; average wages $3 to $4 per day.

Painters, Decorators and Paperhangers—Work eight hours; wages, for union men, $3.50 to $4 per day; no way to ascertain wages of non-union men; best mechanics organized; about 80 per cent in union; conditions fairly good and improving.

Plumbers—About 200 in number; 100 per cent organized; work eight hours per day, half holiday on Saturday; scale of wages, for union men, $6 per day; sanitary conditions generally good; union has many educational features to perfect skill of workmen.

CHAPTER XVIII - BOARD OF TRADE AND BANKS

Organization of Board of Trade and Cotton Exchange. The Cotton Exchange Building. Officers of Exchange. Cotton as King. Cotton Compresses and Warehouses. The Houston Business League. The Chamber of Commerce. Houston's Early Banks. Growth Shown by Bank Clearings. Houston's Modern Banks. City's Big Trust Companies. The Houston Clearing House.

The Houston Board of Trade and Cotton Exchange was organized May 16, 1874, in the parlors of the Hutchins House. Captain C. S. Longcope was elected president; Col. W. J. Hutchins, vice-president; Mr. George W. Kidd, who was really the originator of the idea, was elected secretary. On the first board of directors were: B. A. Botts, F. A. Rice, George Porter, S. K. McIlhenny, W. D. Cleveland, Fred Stanley and A. J. Burke.

Perkins Hall, later known as Pillott's Opera House, was leased for a number of years and equipped with only one small bulletin board the Exchange was launched on its career. That single board did duty for a long time and was ample for all the needs of the Exchange, for the telegraph service was meagre in the extreme and a good sized slate would have answered quite as well as the board. Telegraph rates were very high in those days and the Gold and Stock Exchange, the great collecting branch of the telegraph company for commercial news and quotations was in its infancy, so that it cost a great deal of money to secure even the smallest commercial service. Mr. Kidd, who was commercial editor of one of the local newspapers, used to supplement the exchange reports with items that came to his paper. When the market house burned down, the opera house that was located in the City Hall above the market house was destroyed, and Houston was left with only Pillott's Opera House as a theatre. The place was in constant demand, and the Exchange, having a lease on it and only its one little bulletin board to put out of the way, made a nice income by hiring the hall to theatrical companies. This money was devoted to the extension of the telegraph service and soon the Exchange was receiving a fair service, and one that induced other members to join the organization. At that time the Exchange had very few inducements to offer outsiders to become members, but that soon changed. There had been about twenty prominent business men and merchants who had stood by the Exchange from the day of its organization, but it was for the purpose of sustaining the organization and perpetuating it, and not for any immediate benefit they could derive from it. Now, however, the Exchange began to receive much more valuable information and its usefulness became apparent. Quite a number of new members came in, and while the association was far from a safe and secure basis, yet it was well on the way. Secretary Kidd did an immense amount of work and was untiring in his efforts to build up the Exchange. There was one important branch of the work that could be carried on independently, and entirely outside of telegraphic or other sources of information—local statistics could be compiled, and to that important work Secretary Kidd turned his attention. He not only compiled all the early statistics, but laid the ground work for the more elaborate and complicated system that prevails in the Exchange today.

When through-rail connection was made between Houston, St. Louis and the great West, Houston sent a strong delegation of members of the Exchange and other business men, on a missionary expedition to tell the people up there what we were and to find out what they had. This delegation did good work, with the result that a fine trade soon developed between the two sections. One of its most marked benefits, from a local point of view, was its effect upon the Cotton Exchange. It brought out the Board of Trade feature of that organization, and demonstrated how valuable it could be made. Then for the first time the directors of the Exchange went seriously to work. In 1877, they obtained a charter as the Cotton Exchange and Board of Trade. They framed new rules and regulations, increased the initiation fee and the annual dues from members, and made provision for a regular and permanent revenue with which to meet the expenses of the Exchange. The institution was placed on a firm basis and from that time until today its course has been upward.

A general meeting of members of the exchange was held January 15, 1882, for the purpose of discussing the advisability of the Exchange owning its own building. At that meeting it was decided that ground should be purchased and a building should be erected if financial arrangements could be made. Committees were appointed to look into the details of the question. Other meetings were held, and on May 29, 1883, the ground for the building was purchased. The architect's plans were accepted January 4, 1884, and on March 1, of the same year the Exchange borrowed $40,000 for ten years, with which to put up the building. The contract was let March 15, 1884, and the corner-stone was laid by the Masons on June 5, 1884. The building was completed and turned over to the Exchange on November 15, 1884. Since then the building has been completely remodeled to meet the growing needs of the members. Additional stories have been added and today, in addition to being one of the handsomest and best arranged exchanges, the building is one of the most convenient and useful office buildings in the city. It is located at the corner of Franklin Avenue and Travis Street. No cotton exchange in this or any other country gives more information to its members than does the Houston Exchange. There are long distance telephones reaching all over this and adjoining states, where a member can talk to a customer hundreds of miles away with as much ease and without delay, as if he were in the next room. There are two telegraph companies that have special wires on the floor of the exchange, while the Exchange itself is in direct and, what may be termed instantaneous, communication with all the great exchanges in this country and across the water as well. To illustrate the rapidity with which business is transacted through the exchange, it is said that an order can be sent to Liverpool, executed and an answer received back here in Houston in three or four minutes. This is not an extraordinary occurrence.

The Houston Cotton Exchange and Board of Trade has been of incalculable benefit to Houston and has done an immense amount of work looking to the upbuilding of the city. Almost from the day of its formation it has been active in the work of building the ship channel. It has always had a standing committee on the ship channel, and the annual report of this committee has always been one of the leading features of the annual meetings of the Exchange. It has done work in every way and in every direction for the advancement of the material interests of Houston. Today much of that work is in the hands of able, special organizations, but the initial steps in all of them were taken by the Houston Cotton Exchange and Board of Trade.

Perhaps the best way in which the importance and growth of the Exchange may be shown is by calling attention to the fact that when it was organized, and for some years after, a seat on the floor could be purchased for five dollars and the annual dues were twelve dollars, a dollar each month. Today a membership in the Exchange costs $2,000 and there are so few sellers at that figure that it is extremely difficult to buy a certificate of membership. The annual dues are $50, payable in advance. There are fees and other dues, amounting to thousands of dollars which furnish funds for the current expenses.

The following have been the officials of the Exchange:

- 1874-75—C. S. Longcope, president; W. J. Hutchins, first vice-president; B. A. Shepherd, second vice-president; Geo. W. Kidd, secretary.
- 1875-76—W. D. Cleveland, president; Geo. L. Porter, first vice-president; S. K. McIlhenny, second vice-president; T. W. House, Jr., third vice-president; Geo. W. Kidd, secretary.
- 1876-77—Geo. L. Porter, president; J. H. Blake, first vice-president; T. W. House, Jr., second-vice-president; S. K. McIlhenny, third vice-president; Geo. W. Kidd, secretary.
- 1877-78—H. R. Percy, president; Fred A. Rice, treasurer; Geo. W. Kidd, secretary.
- 1878-79—S. K. McIlhenny, president; Wm. V. R. Watson, vice-president; Fred A. Rice, treasurer; Geo. W. Kidd, secretary.
- 1879-80—Wm. V. R. Watson, president; Louis Harde, vice-president; Fred A. Rice, treasurer; Geo. W. Kidd, secretary.
- 1880-81—A. H. Lea, president; T. W. House, vice-president; Fred A. Rice, treasurer; Geo. W. Kidd, secretary.

- 1881-82—S. K. McIlhenny, president; E. L. Dennis, vice-president; Fred A. Rice, treasurer; Geo. W. Kidd, secretary.
- 1882-83—S. A. McAshan, president; H. W. Garrow, vice-president; Fred A. Rice, treasurer; Geo. W. Kidd, secretary.
- 1883-84—S. A. McAshan, president; H. W. Garrow, vice-president; Fred A. Rice, treasurer; Geo. W. Kidd, secretary.
- 1884-85—W. D. Cleveland, president; H. W. Garrow, vice-president; Fred A. Rice, treasurer; Geo. W. Kidd, secretary.
- 1885-86—W. D. Cleveland, president; H. W. Garrow, vice-president; Fred A. Rice, treasurer; Geo. W. Kidd, secretary.
- 1886-87—W. D. Cleveland, president; H. W. Garrow, vice-president; T. W. House, treasurer; Geo. W. Kidd, secretary.
- 1887-88—W. D. Cleveland, president; Wm. M. Read, vice-president; T. W. House, treasurer; Geo. W. Kidd, secretary.
- 1888-89—W. D. Cleveland, president; Wm. M. Read, vice-president; T. W. House, treasurer; Geo. W. Kidd, secretary.
- 1889-90—W. D. Cleveland, president; Wm. M. Read, vice-president; T. W. House, treasurer; Geo. W. Kidd, secretary.
- 1890-91—W. D. Cleveland, president; Wm. M. Read, vice-president; T. W. House, treasurer; Geo. W. Kidd, secretary.
- 1891-92—Wm. M. Read, president; E. W. Sewall, vice-president; T. W. House, treasurer; Geo. W. Kidd, secretary.
- 1892-93—H. W. Garrow, president; Felix Halff, vice-president; T. W. House, treasurer; Geo. W. Kidd, secretary.
- 1893-94—H. W. Garrow, president; Felix Halff, vice-president; T. W. House, treasurer; Geo. W. Kidd, secretary.
- 1894-95—H. W. Garrow, president; Felix Halff, vice-president; T. W. House, treasurer; Geo. W. Kidd, secretary.
- 1895-96—H. W. Garrow, president; Felix Halff, vice-president; T. W. House, treasurer; Geo. W. Kidd, secretary.
- 1896-97—H. W. Garrow, president; Felix Halff, vice-president; T. W. House, treasurer; Geo. W. Kidd, secretary.
- 1897-98—H. W. Garrow, president; Wm. V. R. Watson, vice-president; T. W. House, treasurer; B. W. Martin, secretary.
- 1898-99—H. W. Garrow, president; George W. Neville, vice-president; T. W. House, treasurer; B. R. Warner, secretary.
- 1899-1900—H. W. Garrow, president; George W. Neville, vice-president; T. W. House, treasurer; B. R. Warner, secretary.
- 1900-01—H. W. Garrow, president; George W. Neville, vice-president; T. W. House, treasurer; B. R. Warner, secretary.
- 1901-02—H. W. Garrow, president; George W. Neville, vice-president; T. W. House, treasurer; B. R. Warner, secretary.

- 1902-03—W. D. Cleveland, president; George W. Neville, vice-president; W. B. Chew, treasurer; W. R. Warner, secretary.
- 1903-04—W. D. Cleveland, president; John M. Dorrance, vice-president; W. B. Chew, treasurer; W. J. DeTreville, secretary.
- 1904-05—W. D. Cleveland, president; John M. Dorrance, vice-president; W. B. Chew, treasurer; W. J. DeTreville, secretary.
- 1905-06—M. E. Andrews, president; E. W. Taylor, vice-president; W. B. Chew, treasurer; W. J. DeTreville, secretary.
- 1906-07—W. O. Ansley, president; E. W. Taylor, vice-president; W. B. Chew, treasurer; W. J. DeTreville, secretary.
- 1907-08—E. W. Taylor, president; James H. Adair, vice-president; W. B. Chew, treasurer; W. J. DeTreville, secretary.
- 1908-09—A. L. Nelms, president; James H. Adair, vice-president; W. B. Chew, treasurer; W. J. DeTreville, secretary.
- 1909-10—A. L. Nelms, president; James H. Adair, vice-president; W. B. Chew, treasurer; W. J. DeTreville, secretary.
- 1910-11—A. L. Nelms, president; Jno. W. Sanders, vice-president; W. B. Chew, treasurer; W. J. DeTreville, secretary.*
- 1911-'12—A. L. Nelms, president; A. W. Pollard, vice-president; W. B. Chew, treasurer; J. F. Burwell, secretary.
-

*Secretary DeTreville died June 21, 1910. Mr. J. F. Burwell acted as secretary from June 21 to August 10, at which date he became the regular secretary.

Houston long ago passed that point in her growth as a commercial center, where her supremacy depended on the handling of any single commodity, such as cotton, but from the early ox-wagon days to the present time when the railways bring the produce of Texas, and of the Southwest as well, to the point where rail and water transportation join, cotton has been king, and will always continue to be king. The reasons for this are both natural and artificial. Natural from the geographical position of Houston; artificial because of the energy, fore-sight and business acumen of the men who have had the commercial destiny of the city in their keeping.

During the last ten years the most wonderful and far-reaching changes in the methods of marketing cotton have taken place, and had not Houston adapted herself promptly to meet these changes and the conditions brought about through them, she would have been left high and dry, a mere way-station on the commercial highway.

The greatest of these changes was in the method of buying and selling cotton. Formerly the farmer or interior merchant, who traded with the former for his cotton, shipped it to Houston, or to some other large city, to be sold at once, if prices were favorable, or to be held, subject to his order, for better prices. The commission merchant, or cotton factor, as he is called, would advance part of the value of such cotton to the shipper, so the method was satisfactory to all concerned. However, the big cotton consumers on the other side conceived the idea of establishing their own agencies in this country, with the view to cutting out middlemen, as far as possible. These agencies scattered buyers all over the state. This, at once, caused a radical change in the cotton business and relegated, in a great measure, the old cotton factor with his slow but safe method, to a secondary place. Quick transportation, the telegraph and telephone, assisted materially in bringing about the change, for they enabled the farmer or merchant hundreds of miles away from Houston, to learn as much about the market as the man on the floor of the cotton exchange could learn. Today, under the new system, cotton is bought in every little town and hamlet in the state, directly from first hands, and the seller gets the full market value of the day, too, for there is always sharp competition between buyers.

This had led to the development of what is called the free on board business, which has eliminated about all the army of middlemen of former days. Under it a firm of exporters will contract to ship, let us say, 1,000 bales of cotton of a given grade and weight, at a fixed price. The price covers all charges and expenses up to the time the cotton is placed on board a ship at the port. The seller guarantees the cotton to be according to contract both in class and weight, so the buyer is protected against loss in case the shipment is deficient in any way.

Realizing the probable and possible changes in the methods of handling cotton that this new business would bring about, and knowing that provision must be made for the proper care of the vast number of bales that would necessarily have to be concentrated at some point under its working, Houston began, at the very conception of the business, to develop and care for it. Her old warehouses and compresses were renovated and, in some instances, enlarged, new ones were built and everything was done for facilitating and properly earing for the trade.

A piece of forethought which has been of the greatest advantage was placing every warehouse and compress in the city either on the banks of the ship channel or on some railroad. The advantage of this is that it eliminates the costly item of drayage and this alone gives Houston an advantage of from 10c to 12 1/2c per bale over all competitors. The extent of such an advantage can be appreciated when it is known that frequently a cost of 5c per bale will cause a change in the routing of cotton. Today no place in the country has greater or better facilities for handling and earing for cotton than Houston. This is no idle boast as the following brief description of those facilities show:

The Cleveland Compress is the oldest in years of continuous service of all Houston compresses, but it is old in no other way, for it is strictly modern in all its equipments and absolutely up-to-date in every way. It is located on the north side of the ship channel, and has a frontage of several hundred feet on the channel, where there is every facility for loading directly on ships or barges for the Gulf of Mexico. The company has just completed an addition to its yard and shed room, so that its total capacity is now 55,000 bales. The compress has a capacity of 100 bales per hour. Captain Wm. D. Cleveland is president of the company and Mr. D. Mullaine is superintendent of the press.

The Magnolia Warehouse and Storage Company, formerly known as the Weld-Neville Company, has doubtless the most magnificent and thoroughly equipped warehouse and compress in the United States. This company has recently made extensive additions to its plant, the cost of which was $200,000. The plant has always been considered one of the largest and best equipped institutions of its kind in the South, and this expenditure of so large a sum in the way of additions, shows that its owners have confidence in the growth of Houston's already immense cotton business, and its permanency as a commercial and industrial center. It really goes beyond local faith in such matters, for, in a measure it reflects the sentiment of outsiders, one of the leading members of the firm being a member of the New York Cotton Exchange. The immensity of the plant is shown by the statement that the new brick warehouse has a storage capacity of 75,000 bales and covers an area of 264,000 square feet. The warehouse is as perfect as experience and science can make it, and is as perfectly protected against fire as the ingenuity of man can devise. It is divided into compartments separated from each other by thick brick walls, and each compartment is fitted with Grinnel automatic sprinklers These are ingenious. Should a slight fire occur, so soon as the heat from the burning bale reaches a certain temperature, it melts a wire which forms an electric circuit which opens the sprinklers thus flooding the compartment and at the same time rings a bell in the office showing exactly where the fire is located. The mechanism of these sprinklers is so delicately adjusted that on one occasion the heat caused by the sun set one of the sprinklers going and flooded a compartment. This perfect fire protection and the protection against weather, entitles the warehouse to a very low insurance rate. This alone is a great thing for it will attract large quantities of cotton to Houston where it can be stowed safely and have at the same time the advantage of the lowest insurance rate obtainable. In the storing of cotton the insurance rate is a big factor.

The company's property is located at the juncture of Bray's Bayou and the ship channel and has a frontage of 1,500 feet on the channel and 700 feet on the bayou. A reinforced concrete retaining wall is now being constructed along the whole water front, which will be so constructed as to afford modern shipping piers and ships where vessels may be easily loaded. This wall is now well under way towards completion and will cost $100,000. The tedious and expensive method of trucking cotton from one part of the yard to another is avoided by the construction of overhead trolleys or tramways, whereby half a dozen bales of cotton can be transferred at one time, with as much ease as the packages purchased in a drygoods store are handled. The press is of the very latest and most perfect type and has a capacity of 120 bales per hour. Mr. A. C. Cairns is the company's manager in Houston.

The Merchants Compress Company is another of Houston's big cotton handling concerns. It is located directly on the bank of the ship channel, north side, and has its own wharves, chutes and everything for the rapid loading of cotton directly on ships or barges. It also has rail connection with the Southern Pacific and Terminal system. It has an under-cover storing capacity of 35,000 bales and a total holding capacity of 60,000 bales. Its press is very powerful and has a capacity of 150 bales an hour. Mr. John K. Sanders, who for many years has been prominent in Houston's cotton business, is president of the company.

The Union Compress and Warehouse Company has a storing capacity of about 25,000 bales nearly all under cover, and a compress capacity of between 1,200 and 1,500 bales per day. It has trackage connection with the International and Great Northern Railway, the Southern Pacific and Belt Terminal Company and it also has facilities for loading on ships and barges, Mr. A. Breyer is president of this company.

The Southern Compress and Warehouse Company is a new organization. Its yards and compress have just been completed. It is an expansion of McFadden Bros.' business. It is located on the north side of the ship channel, on the International and Great Northern Road. Its compressing capacity is between 1,200 and 1,500 bales and its storing capacity is 20,000 bales. It has wharves and platforms for loading directly on boats in the channel and expects to handle 150,000 bales this coming season of 1911-12.

The Standard Compress Company is a very active concern. It has a brick warehouse and three large sheds located on twenty acres fronting the ship channel. It also has in addition to its water facilities, rail connections with the International and Great Northern and San Antonio and Aransas Pass roads. It has a press capacity of about 1,000 bales per day and a storing capacity of 26,000 bales, nearly all under cover. Mr. M. E. Andrews is general manager, secretary and treasurer.

There are several warehouses and storing yards, without compresses, which increase Houston's facilities for caring for cotton shipped here. The International and Great Northern platform, which is under shed, has a storing capacity for 50,000 bales.

The Direct Navigation company has platform space for the storage of 26,500 bales; the McIlhenny yards, for 2,000 bales; Henke and Pillot, for 1,200 bales and S. Samuels' warehouse for 1,500 bales. These bring the total storage capacity of Houston's compresses and warehouses up to 325,700 bales, and its compress capacity to 8,700 bales per day of ten hours.

As an indication of the value of water transportation, it may be said here that for the commercial year that ended August 31, 1911, there were shipped down the ship channel from presses and warehouses located on its banks, 392, 684 bales of cotton. There is an object lesson in these figures, for each bale enumerated represents a saving from ten to twelve and one-half cents, in the way of drayage.

The Houston Business League was organized as the result of a meeting held February 26, 1895. Forty citizens were assembled. Col. R. M. Johnson called the meeting to order and explained the object of the call to be the organization of a permanent commercial association, to be composed of citizens of Houston who had at heart the interests of the city of Houston. Temporary organization was effected by the election of Colonel Johnson as chairman and W. W. Dexter as secretary.

At this original meeting, committees were appointed to outline purposes and plans and to solicit members. Among those who took part in the first organization were R. M. Johnson, D. D. Bryan, W. W. Dexter, E. T. Heiner, J. M. Cotton, R. B. Morris, C. E. Jones, H. G. Lidston, Richard Cocke, Gus Schulte, J. H. Bright, Hamp. Cook, D. M. Angel, G. W. Steiff, and D. H. McCullough. Following this meeting much active work was done.

The second business meeting was held March 5, 1895. At that meeting several names were suggested for the association, and at first the name Chamber of Commerce was adopted, but afterwards it was changed to the Houston Business League. The purposes of the association were declared in the constitution, which said:

"The object of the Houston Business League is to promote immigration, to create and extend and foster the trade, commerce and manufacturing interests of the city of Houston; to secure and build up transportation lines; to secure reasonable and equitable transportation rates; to build up and maintain the value of our real estate, progressive, efficient and economical administration of our municipal government, to collect, preserve and disseminate information in relation to our commercial, financial and industrial affairs, and to unite as far as possible our people in one representative body."

The following were the first officers of the Business League after it was thoroughly organized: President, J. M. Cotton; first vice-president, Ed. Kiam; second vice-president, J. C. Bering; third vice-president, E. T. Heiner; secretary, W. W. Dexter, and treasurer, Guy H. Harcourt.

After a short time Mr. Dexter resigned as secretary and Mr. George P. Brown was chosen as his successor. No better man could have been found for the important work, and Mr. Brown, by his enthusiastic energy and executive ability soon placed the Houston Business League in the front rank. During his administration a number of large manufacturing plants and other industries were secured for Houston. The Business League also inspired and aided in organizing the Floral Festival and the No-Tsu-Oh association and in other ways brought the name of Houston prominently before the country. In 1910, the league was reorganized, and the name given to its new organization was the Houston Chamber of Commerce.

Secretary Adolph Boldt of the Chamber of Commerce explains very lucidly, in his annual report for 1910, that the Houston Chamber of Commerce is not here by accident, but is the result of growth, development and expansion of the original idea which led to the primary organizations, whose object was to care for the purely business matters, without reference to their surroundings and relations. The secretary's idea is that the body he has the honor and pleasure of serving so well, is the result of business evolution, and that it represents the very latest and most effective methods of building up and maintaining the city's commercial, financial, and social surpremaey. When one glances at what has been accomplished in the past and what is planned for the future, by the Chamber of Commerce, and studies its means and methods, one feels ready to admit the truth of all that is claimed by and for it. The keynote of the success of this organization is its denial of the proverbial myth that business is business and cold blooded, and its recognition that business has a social side that may be cultivated, often, with great profit to the cultivator.

A Chamber of Commerce was organized in Houston in 1840, but the present body has no historical connection with that old one. The Houston Chamber of Commerce is of today and for today. It is of the present and its efforts are directed to the future and not to the past. It is most thoroughly organized and in consequence a vast amount of work is accomplished without friction or unnecessary delay. There is a general association, which has a responsible head, but all the work of the association is accomplished through special committees while routine matters are handled by bureaus. Thus, there is the Traffic Bureau, to which is referred all matters relating to freights and kindred subjects. This is perhaps the hardest worked bureau in the association, and one, too, that is never through with its labors. Then there is the Convention Bureau, whose duty it is to look after all conventions, wherever held, and to make efforts to secure them for Houston and, if they come, to see that they are properly entertained after they get here, for the Chamber of Commerce believes that a favorable impression made on a visitor is a great asset for the city that entertains. The Bureau of Publicity has assigned to it the arduous duty of keeping Houston constantly in the public eye. The methods employed by this Bureau are so many and so divergent that it is difficult to enumerate them with any degree of accuracy. The newspapers, magazines, circulars, in fact, every known method of advertising is used. The Chamber established what is known as "post card day," and the extent of activity in that direction can be seen, when it stated that on one occasion the public purchased and sent through the mails in every direction, more than 100,000 post cards, each showing a view of some part of the city.

The Industrial Bureau has in charge all matters relating to new manufacturing and commercial enterprises. This bureau has accomplished wonders and during the business year of 1910–11 alone, it secured for Houston nineteen manufacturing concerns and twelve wholesale and distributing houses. In addition to this the bureau is now making arrangements looking to securing both factories and commercial bodies.

The accomplishments of the Chamber of Commerce have been so great and so varied that their simple enumeration would fill pages. Nothing that has about it even the most indirect promise of benefitting the city has been neglected by it and it works hand in hand, and unselfishly, with the city administration and other organizations to accomplish the greatest good for the city.

Its present officers are: President, E. A. Peden; first vice-president, W. C. Munn; second vice-president, Edgar O. Lovett; third vice-president, R. C. Duff; treasurer, Guy M. Bryan; secretary, Adolph Boldt; assistant secretary, G. C. Roussel; traffic manager, C. C. Oden; director of publicity, Jerome H. Farbar. Directors: Jas. L. Autry, A. S. Cleveland, David Daly, F. A. Heitman, E. A. Hudson, Abe M. Levy, J. W. Link, J. W. Neal, J. M. Rockwell, John T. Scott, Thomas H. Stone. Secretary Boldt, by speeches and visits, and publicity director, Jerome Farbar, by widely read articles in periodicals, have given the work of the body wide and favorable publicity.

The Organization of the Cotton Exchange and Board of Trade was for the purpose of bringing cotton, grain and other produce here and the object of the Chamber of Commerce was to upbuild the wholesale trade and to build up the manufacturing interests of the city. Each worked for the prosperity of Houston but on different lines and used different methods. In the earlier stages, in order to handle the immense amount of cotton and produce, and in the second stages in order to care for the large commercial and manufacturing interests that were attracted here, vast sums of money were necessary, and this need gave birth to the large banks and trust companies that Houston boasts of today.

Houston has always had banks, but the really great institutions are of comparatively modern date. As a matter of fact Houston can boast of having had the first bank ever organized in Texas, as she can boast of having had so many other first things.

The Commercial and Agricultural Bank of Texas was chartered by the Congress of Coahuila and Texas to S. M. Williams and associates in 1835. In 1836 the same Congress passed an act for the relief of the incorporators. The bank was not organized until after the convention of 1835. That convention denounced and prohibited banks, but had to recognize vested rights acquired before the independence of Texas. The bank was an ambitious one and had nothing small about it. Its authorized capital was $1,000,000 and $100,000 was paid up. It was a bank of issue. The first president of the bank was S. M. Williams and its first cashier was J. W. McMillan.

For many years this was the only chartered bank operating in the state, for Texas chartered no banks until after the adoption of the constitution in 1870. It was by no means popular and obstacles were placed in its way and efforts made to break it down. It was finally destroyed for good when a decision rendered in the supreme court, in 1859, annulled its charter. Soon after that Mr. Williams died and the affairs of the bank were wound up by Mr. B. A. Shepherd, who had become one of its principal owners. As early as 1850, or about that time, Mr. T. W. House, who had begun business in Houston in 1838, was well established and opened a private bank in connection with his cotton factorage business, and in 1854 Mr. B. A. Shepherd engaged exclusively in the banking business and he was the first man in Texas to do so. Mr. W. J. Hutchins was another early Houstonian who did a mixed factorage and banking business. Until after the war practically all the banking business of the state was done in Houston and Galveston.

The First National Bank of Texas, now known as the First National Bank of Galveston, was the first national bank in the state. It was soon followed by others in the order given here: The First National Bank of Houston, the First National Bank of San Antonio and the First National Bank of Jefferson. The first cashier of a national bank in the state was J. B. Root, father of A. P. Root, who was later cashier and then president of the First National Bank of Houston.

During the early seventies Mr. W. J. Hutchins closed out his banking interests and gave his whole attention to his large wholesale business, but Mr. T. W. House, while not abandoning his factorage business completely, gave it less and less attention and devoted himself to banking. After the death of Mr. T. W. House, about 1881, his oldest son, T. W. House, Jr., bought the interest of his brothers in the bank and devoted his time and attention exclusively to its affairs. For many years this bank stood in the front ranks of responsible financial institutions in the state, but in the panic of 1907, owing to many causes, it made a sensational failure, and its affairs are still undergoing adjustment.

The City Bank of Houston began business under the most favorable auspices on November 1, 1870. Its capital stock was $250,000. Col. B. A. Botts was its president until his death in September, 1885. Mr. W. R. Baker was chosen to succeed him. Over-indulgence to customers of the bank, led to its undoing, and on December 19, 1885, it suspended payment and went into the hands of a receiver. Major B. F. Weems was the receiver. Mr. Baker was the principal loser by the failure, which had little or no effect on the credit of the town.

The Houston Savings Bank, whose officers were F. A. Rice, W. D. Cleveland, J. Waldo, M. G. Howe, W. B. Botts and E. Raphael, after doing business for about twelve years, closed its doors February 26, 1886, and Dr. D. F. Stuart was appointed receiver to wind up its affairs. There was not a great amount of money involved, hence the losses were very small.

The foregoing may be classed as pioneer banks of Houston. They seem very insignificant compared with the gigantic institutions of the present time.

If the true test of a city's growth may be determined by the growth of its banks and financial institutions, then Houston can stand the test in a way that few other cities can. Comparing the figures of today with those of ten years ago would be manifestly unjust for there should be and would be a natural increase shown. But taking the figures for one year and comparing them with those for the preceding year and the year preceding that, gives us a true statement of actual conditions. This is the better test and it is this comparison that Houston stands so well.

The total bank clearings for the twelve months, ending December 31, were, for 1908, $1,063,835,612; for 1909, they were $1,279,764,128; for 1910, they were $1,349,403,095. This statement shows that the clearings for 1909 were $215,928,506 greater than those for the preceding year and that the figures for 1910 showed an increase of $69,639,967 over the remarkable increase of the year before. This is strong evidence of Houston's financial growth.

There are twelve financial institutions in Houston, three of them having a capital stock of $1,000,000 each. The First National Bank, capital $1,000,000. The Union National Bank, capital $1,000,000. The Bankers Trust Company, capital $1,000,000. The Southern Trust Company, capital $800,000. The American Trust Company, capital $500,000. The Commercial National Bank, capital $500,000. The South Texas National Bank, capital $500,000. The Texas Trust Company, capital $500,000. Lumbermens National Bank, capital $400,000. Houston Land and Trust Company, capital $250,000. The Houston National Exchange Bank, capital $200,000. The Guaranty State Bank, capital $20,000. Eight of these do a banking business only and four are exclusively trust companies.

From the little two-story brick building on the corner of Main Street and Congress Avenue, formerly the home of Mr. Shepherd's bank, to the immense skyscraper, the home of the Union National Bank, just across the street from Mr. Shepherd's old bank, is a long step, and yet it is only one of the steps that have been taken by all the banks. The banking institutions have grown so rapidly in the last ten years that nearly all of them have had to enlarge their quarters. Some years ago the First National, the Commercial and the Houston Land and Trust Company erected buildings of their own on the three corners of Main and Franklin. The building of the First National is an imposing structure, being eight stories high and built of stone and marble.

Two years ago the bank added to its building, practically doubling its capacity, and reserving all the ground floor for bank purposes. The South Texas National Bank erected a beautiful building on the east side of Main Street, between Congress and Franklin Avenues. This is an extremely handsome building. It is of Greek architecture and built entirely of marble. The massive columns in front are said to be the largest single pieces of marble in any building in Texas. The Union National Bank, formerly the Union Bank and Trust Company, will soon be in its own building. The building is on the northwest corner of Congress and Main. It is twelve stories high, is of steel frame structure and is modern in every respect. It is practically completed and will be one of the handsomest bank and office buildings in America.

The First National Bank aside from being the oldest is one of the largest and most responsible institutions of the kind in Houston. This bank began business with a capital stock of $100,000, but this was increased from time to time, and in 1909 it was increased to $1,000,000. Its present deposits, June 30, 1911, amount to over $7,600,000 and its capital, surplus and undivided profits are $1,378,473.85, every cent of which, with the exception of $300,000 was earned by the bank. During the last ten years the increase in deposits had been over five and one-quarter million dollars. The officers of this bank are: O. L. Cochran, president; J. T. Scott, first vice-president; H. R. Eldridge, second vice-president; W. S. Cochran, cashier; W. E. Hertford and F. E. Russell, assistant cashiers.

The First National Bank was organized in 1866 by Mr. B. A. Shepherd and Mr. T. M. Bagby. Mr. Bagby was its first president and on his death, Mr. Shepherd succeeded him. When Mr. Shepherd died, Mr. A. S. Root, his son-in-law, became president. A year or two ago Mr. Root died and Mr. O. L. Cochran, another of Mr. Shepherd's sons-in-law became, and still is, president. None of the stock of this bank can be bought, as there is none for sale. It is said, that with the exception of one or two shares, all the stock is held by the Shepherd family, or its connections.

The Commercial National Bank was the second national bank organized in Houston. It received its charter in 1886. The capital stock is $500,000. It does an immense business and on June 30, 1911, its deposits were very nearly four and one-half million dollars. It owns its own building, a modern six-story steel frame structure, on Main and Franklin. The officers of the bank are: W. B. Chew, president; James A. Baker, vice-president; Thornwell Fay, vice-president; Oscar Wells, cashier; P. J. Evershade, assistant cashier. The Houston National Exchange Bank received its original charter, in 1889, as the Houston National Bank, but changed its name in 1909. The name was all that was changed for the original aims and policies of the institution have been adhered to. The growth of this bank during the past three years has been so phenomenal as to excite admiration in commercial circles. In July, 1909, it had deposits amounting to $1,705,298.83, and at the June call in 1910, it had in deposits $2,763,829.28, an increase of $1,058,530.45 in twelve months. Again at the June call in 1911, its deposits were $3,308,078.25, a gain of $534,248.97. This bank has only $200,000 capital and the surplus and undevided profits are this year, $132,997.02. The officers of the bank are: Henry S. Fox, president; Joseph F. Meyer, M. M. Graves and H. S. Fox, Jr., vice-presidents; J. W. Hertford, cashier; F. F. Dearing and W. B. Hilliard, assistant cashiers.

The South Texas National Bank was chartered in 1890, and is a very strong financial institution. Its capital stock is $500,000, and its deposits are very large. On June 30, 1911, when the call was made it had in individual and bank deposits $5,172,376.33. The officers of this bank are: Charles Dillingham, president; B. D. Harris, active vice-president and cashier; J. E. McAshan and O. T. Holt, vice-presidents; August DeZavala, Paul G. Taylor and R. H. Hanna, Jr., assistant cashiers.

The Union National Bank is one of the strongest institutions in the South. It really represents three original banks. The Union Bank and Trust Company was chartered in 1905 under the new banking laws of Texas receiving charter No. 1. In 1908, it effected a consolidation with the Planters and Mechanics Bank and, in 1910, it absorbed the Merchants National Bank. When this was done the institution became a national bank, with a capital stock of $1,000,000. At the same time it took its present name. Its officers are: J. S. Rice, president; T. C. Dunn, George Hamman, W. T. Carter, Abe M. Levy, J. M. Rockwell, Jesse H. Jones and C. G. Pillot, vice-presidents; DeWitt C. Dunn, cashier; D. W. Cooley and H. B. Finch, assistant cashiers.

Jonas Shearn Rice, president of the Union National Bank of Houston, and of the Great Southern Life Insurance Company, and an official in many other banking and financial concerns, has long been the most prominent banker of the city and by virtue of business and social prominence and connection with the pioneer family that has done so much for Houston, would perhaps be almost universally regarded as the first citizen of the city. Mr. Rice was born in Houston on November 25, 1855. His mother was Charlotte M. Baldwin, a daughter of Horace Baldwin, who was Mayor of Houston during the days of the Republic and who was a brother-in-law of A. C. Allen, one of the city's founders. His family is of old revolutionary stock, sprung from the sturdy Scotch-Irish and English pioneers of Colonial days in America. His great grandfather Hall was one of those wounded at the battle of Lexington in 1775, but despite that fact lived in Massachusetts to the age of 102 years.

The father of Jonas Shearn Rice was Frederick A. Rice of Massachusetts, who settled in Houston in 1850. He was one of the builders of the first railroad, the H. & T. C., and died here in 1901 at the age of 71.

J. S. Rice is the oldest of a family of 7 sons and 3 daughters. A younger brother, H. B. Rice, is now and has been for many years Mayor of Houston.

Two other brothers, W. M. and B. B. Rice are prominent business men of Houston. In 1887, J. S. Rice was married at Waco, to Mary J. Ross, daughter of Colonel Pete F. Ross, the "hero of Corinth," the niece of former Governor L. S. Ross and the grand-daughter of General James E. Harrison. Three children were born of this union, Laura F. Rice, who was Queen of the No-Tsu-Oh Carnival in 1910, Kate, married in 1911 to Victor Hugo Neuhaus, and Lottie, at school.

The title of Colonel, always used as a prefix to the name of J. S. Rice was honorably earned. In 1874 he became a member of the Houston Light Guard and was prominent as adjutant in the first regiment of Texas Militia organized after the war. He was Captain of the Light Guard when that company was the crack military company of Texas. He was Adjutant General of the First Brigade on the staff of General F. W. James, and was chief of staff for Governor Lawrence Sullivan Ross.

As a Mason Mr. Rice is a member of the local lodge, Chapter and Commandery and is a Shriner of El Mina Temple of Galveston. He also belongs to the B. P. O. E. and Hoo-Hoo orders. He is an ex-president of the Thalian Club, a member of the Country Club and was appointed by Governor Campbell as one of the San Jacinto Battle Ground Commissioners and has done much toward the beautifying of that historic battlefield. In 1905 he was King of the No-Tsu-Oh carnival.

The business career of J. S. Rice has been uniformly brilliant and successful. Following his graduation at the Texas Military Institute at Austin he became a railroad clerk in the office of the general passenger agent of the H. & T. C. road. In 1879, he became bookkeeper and teller of the National Exchange Bank of Houston. In 1881 he and a brother, William M. Rice who is now a resident of Houston and one of the trustees of the William M. Rice Institute, entered into the saw mill business in Tyler County. In 1895 he was made financial agent of the Texas State Penitentiary which post he held until he was, in 1899, appointed by Governor Sayers as superintendent of the Texas State Penal System. He resigned in 1902 to devote his attention to the banking business in Houston. From 1904 to 1909 he was one of the receivers of the Kirby Lumber Company and was elected vice-president of that company on its reorganization. In August, 1905, he became president of the Union Bank and Trust Company, now the Union National Bank with a capital stock of $1,000,000. He is chairman of the Board of Directors of the Bankers Trust Company, vice-president of the J. S. and W. M. Rice Lumber Company, director of the Guarantee Life Insurance Company, and director of the T. & B. V. Railroad and many other concerns. With all this Mr. Rice is genial, accessible, democratic and popular.

The Lumbermens National Bank is also a combination of other banks. It is the youngest of Houston's banks, but is a very strong and healthy youngster. It was organized in 1907, and, in 1909, it absorbed the National

City Bank. Next year the American National Bank and the Central Bank and Trust Company liquidated and turned over their business to the Lumbermens National Bank. The capital stock of the bank is $400,000. S. F. Carter is president; Guy M. Bryan, active vice-president, and Lynn P. Talley is cashier. Messrs. Carter and Bryan are the largest shareholders.

The Guaranty State Bank was organized under the state laws of Texas governing banks, and began business in January, 1910. Its capital stock is $20,000 and its field of operation is Houston, Brunner, Chaneyville and Houston Heights. A. C. Bell is president; H. E. Detering, vice-president, and R. F. Butts, cashier.

The Harris County Bank and Trust Company, which was organized in 1907, had one-half of its capital stock, $25,000, in the House Bank, which failed. The bank survived until July, 1911, when it failed and its president, F. W. Vaughn, disappeared.

Under ordinary circumstances and conditions banks may be found to meet the financial needs of a community, but when the interests are large, varied, and, in consequence, complex, a third medium is needed, and it is to supply this need that trust companies are formed. No bank, however large, can afford to do the work done by a trust company, simply because it is entirely beyond its sphere. No bank can act as a guardian, conserve and invest to the best advantage funds left in trust to it, and then at a specified time, pay over the money to its legal owners. No bank is willing to act as escrow agent, trustee under contract, and a dozen and one things that modern business developments require shall be done. It is for such things as these that the modern trust companies are formed. The trust company supplies a double need. It not only cares for and conserves estates placed in its charge, but it affords a source from which may be obtained long time loans. Usually these loans are made for the purpose of developing and improving, intrinsically valuable, property, the property itself being taken as security for the payment of the debt. The length of the loan, the rate of interest paid by the borrower and the absolute security afforded by the property held as collateral, make such a transaction a safe investment on the part of the trust company, while the comparatively low rate of interest paid by the borrower and the long time given in which to pay back the loan are very advantageous for the borrower. A bank makes its money by lending money for a short time, thus turning it over and over several times a year, while the trust company makes it by lending its money on long time on gilt-edge real estate and other security. Neither infringes on the domain of the other and each is benefitted, directly and indirectly, by the existence of the other. It may be said that the presence of strong banks in a community is an evidence of its financial and commercial importance, while the presence of trust companies is an evidence of the material growth, expansion and development of that community. The banks make and attract money while the trust companies invest the money directly in permanent improvements or in such things that lead to permanent improvements. The phenomenal growth of Houston during the last ten years, has created a demand for and has led to the formation of trust companies here, and today the city has some of the strongest institutions of the kind in the South. The Houston Land and Trust Company is the parent organization of the kind here, and, unlike its successors, it was organized during the blackest and apparently the most hopeless period of Houston's history—the reconstruction days of 1875. It was originally chartered as a land and trust company without banking privileges. It did only a small and unimportant business for many years, but in 1889, it was reorganized for the purpose of doing a regular trust and mortgage business. Since then it has been an active and potent factor in the growth and development of Houston and the surrounding territory. It receives deposits on time certificates of deposit, lends money on city real estate, bonds and stocks and acts in the capacity of executor, administrator, guardian and trustee in the management of estates. It does a strictly trust business and in no way encroaches on the business done by the banks.

The capital stock of the company is $250,000 and the surplus and undivided profits amounted to $318,614.63 on June 30, 1911, which was an increase of $68,614.63 over the previous twelve months. The company owns a five-story building, occupying the whole lower floor, and devoting the other floors to offices. Its officers are: O. L. Cochran, president; R. E. Paine and P. B. Timpson, vice-presidents; W. S. Patton, secretary and treasurer; O. R. Weyrich, assistant secretary.

The Texas Trust Company was organized under the state banking laws, on July 12, 1909, with a capital stock of $500,000. During the two years of its existence it has been remarkably successful. It has endeavored to establish for itself the reputation of being conservative and has accepted only the most promising propositions to finance. This course has been beneficial both to the company and to those concerns approved by it, for its indorsement of a concern, through its services as trustee or registrar, is a stamp of approval that has weight with the public. The company has made money from the day it opened its doors, and while a 10 per cent dividend has been maintained, the profits now foot up nearly a quarter of a million dollars. The officers of the company are: Jesse H. Jones, president; James A. Baker, J. S. Rice, C. G. Pillot, S. F. Carter, J. M. Rockwell, N. E. Meador, John L. Wortham, vice-presidents; Fred J. Heyne, cashier and secretary; Burke Baker, assistant cashier and bond officer. This trust company is to consolidate with the Bankers Trust Company in September, 1911.

The name of Jesse H. Jones, multi-millionaire, lumberman, banker and capitalist, stands for progress in Houston and Texas, so successful are the many projects of this young financier, and so wide-spread his efforts in behalf of the commonwealth, that he occupies a unique position in public esteem in Houston.

The executive offices held by Mr. Jones indicate to some extent his prominence and activity in the business world. He is president of, and controls many successful corporations, most of them organized and established by him in his short score of business years.

He is president of the Jesse H. Jones Lumber Company, the South Texas Lumber Company and the Southern Loan & Investment Company; is chairman of the board of directors of the Bankers Trust Company, the largest Banking institution in Texas; is vice-president and a member of the executive committee of The Union National Bank; is a director of the Houston & Texas Central Railroad, and the International & Great Northern Railroad, recently reorganized, and has otherwise much to do in the business world.

Mr. Jones is essentially a builder and an organizer; he finances and operates large enterprises; his building activities have been unprecedented, and the sky-line of Houston has been literally changed more by him than any other score of men combined. The Chronicle Building, which is recognized as the finest newspaper and office building in the South, was the first of his undertakings after the 1907 panic; the Texas Company Building and the Bristol Hotel Annex were built the same year; the New Majestic, which is the most beautiful theatre south of New York, and the Gas Company Building followed closely thereafter; the new City Auditorium, the finest building of its kind in the United States, was built under his general direction as chairman of the Citizens Building Committee. The Union National Bank Building, just completed, was also erected under his general charge as chairman of the Building Committee for the bank, and he is now building the new eighteen-story Rice Hotel which will be the finest building of its kind south of Chicago, and will represent an investment, when completed, of two and one-half million dollars.

Jesse H. Jones was born April 5th, 1874, in Robertson County, Tennessee. His father, William H. Jones, was an honored and successful farmer and tobacco exporter, and his mother before her marriage was Miss Ann Holman, of one of the old Tennessee families.

In appearance, Mr. Jones has the unmistakable stamp of one well born and bred, possessing dignity and reserve; his clear grey eyes bespeak the born financier; his personality combines a masterful foresight and business shrewdness, with a kindly consideration for his fellow man. He is also endowed with a generous fund of good nature, and that greatest of blessings—a contented spirit.

At the age of twenty years. Jesse Jones left his father's farm where his boyhood days were spent, and started out to see what was in store for him in the walks of life. He came to Texas, stopping four years in Dallas, where he worked in his uncle's lumber yard. Upon the death of his uncle, M. T. Jones, he came to Houston and assumed the management of the M. T. Jones Lumber Company, which business he managed very successively, and closed up in 1906, agreeable to the will of his deceased uncle.

Since then he has been operating—and very successfully so—on his own account, in real estate, lumber and banking—three very substantial lines of business, any one of which is big enough to occupy the undivided attention of most men, yet Mr. Jones succeeds in all of them.

His friends say he works too hard, but he seems to have time for church and school building, and for all kinds of charity and benevolent work. He goes abroad occasionally, spends much time in New York, and wins a golf trophy once in a while.

He inherited four thousands dollars from his father's estate in 1895, the year he attained his majority, and is worth as many millions now—just sixteen years later.

Mr. Jones is a member of all of the clubs in Houston, and of the Sleepy Hollow Country Club, at Scarboro-on-the-Hudston, just out of New York, said to be the richest and finest country club in America.

The church membership of Mr. Jones is in St. Paul's Methodist Church, Houston, and he contributed liberally to the Southwestern University at Georgetown, in commemoration of the memory of his deceased friend, Bishop Seth Ward.

The Southern Trust Company was also organized in 1909, and began business in January, 1910. Its capital stock is $500,000. The success of this company is most remarkable, and it is doubtful if its record has ever been equalled by any similar institution. It is not two years old, but it has paid 10 per cent dividends since its organization. On July, last year, it increased its capital stock to $800,000. The company has a surplus of $580,274.01, every cent of which it has earned. Of this surplus $205,274 was earned from June 30, 1910 to July 1, 1911. The officers are: R. E. Brooks, president; Travis Holland, vice-president; Earnest Carroll, secretary and treasurer; J. M. Powers, Jr., assistant secretary and treasurer.

The Bankers Trust Company was organized in September, 1909, with a capital stock of $500,000 and a paid in surplus of $25,000. This capital stock has recently been increased to $1,000,000 and the company is one of the strongest in the Southwest. It has a surplus and undivided profits of $416,597.41, and loans and discounts of $1,985,693.71. The time deposits and trust funds amount to $798,070.80, and cash on hand and with banks, $226,246.71. The company occupies offices on the second floor of the Scanlan Building. R. E. Brooks is chairman of the board. J. S. Rice is president, and Tom M. Taylor is the active vice-president; James M. Baker, W. T. Carter, S. F. Carter, C. L. Neuhaus, Abe M. Levy, J. O. Ross, and George A. Rick are vice-presidents; C. M. Malone is secretary and treasurer; P. S. Durham is assistant secretary and treasurer; William Malone is manager of the real estate department; E. L. Crain is assistant manager of the real estate department and W. S. Bailey is counsel.

The American Trust Company is the baby of Houston trusts, being born in 1911. Its capital stock is $500,000. The company is located in quarters formerly occupied by the Tinker Bank and Trust Company, which were originally fitted up for the American National Bank. It is chartered under the banking laws of the state to do a regular trust company business. Monta J. Moore is president, and N. B. Sligh is treasurer.

The foregoing gives, briefly, the history of each of the banks and trust companies of Houston, but a better idea of Houston's importance as a financial center, and what is of the greatest importance and interest, the phenomenal growth of these institutions as a whole, may be formed by studying the following condensation of the statement of the Houston banks and trust companies issued June 30, 1911: Total capital stock, $6,670,000. This was an increase over the stock of the previous year of $950,000. Surplus and undivided profits, $3,772,440.36 which was an increase over the previous year of $969,302.56. Deposits subject to check, $31,613,594.16, which was an increase over the year before of $969,668.19. Cash on hand and with other banks, $13,859,279.64. Showing an increase over the year before of $771,008.46. Loans and discounts, $27,297,166.64, which also was an increase of $2,790,607.47 over the previous year.

The business of the banks is facilitated by the Houston Clearing House. Its methods are identical with clearing houses elsewhere. Its manager for the past twenty-one years has been Mr. E. Raphael, the only male survivor of the Raphael family that came to Houston in 1860. At 13 years of age Mr. Raphael began business life as a telegraph operator at a salary of $10 a month. When he was 14 years old he was the operator at Liberty, Texas, from which point he telegraphed to Houston the news of the celebrated battle of Sabine Pass. It was to Mr. Raphael who has always been interested in school work that William M. Rice first confided his intention to endow an institute for the benefit of Houston and he was the first man named as a life trustee of that school.

CHAPTER XIX HOUSTON'S MANUFACTURERS

Primitive Beginnings. Natural Advantages Offered. The First Mills. Advent of Cotton Compress. Coming of Iron Foundries. Revival of Manufacturing Following the Civil War. First Ice Plants. Packing Plants. Conditions from 1880 to 1890. Car Wheel Shops. Electric Lights. Cotton Seed Products. Textile Mills. Furniture and Other Woodworking Plants. Manufacturing in 1905. Coffee Roasting. Launch Building. Manufacturing Statistics. Fuel and Water. Home Products Banquet.

So fundamental a process is manufacturing that it is hard to say just where it begins. The housewife who sets yeast, raises dough and bakes bread, is a manufacturer. The dairy maid who operates a churn dasher in a cylinder of sweet milk, is also one, and the farmer who swings an axe to cut down a sapling in a forest to make a rail fence is a manufacturer. Manufactured means handmade although by a curious reversal of language it is generally used in the sense of machine made. Even in the latter sense who shall say that a pocket knife, a wheelbarrow or a churn is not machinery.

Manufacturing perhaps began in Houston with the dug out canoe that some Indian made and put in the bayou at the site of the city. The first advertisement of that city, which was the one announcing its existence, promised a water saw mill and manufacturing in the stricter sense began with such a saw mill. It followed the usual course of development.

A saw mill, a corn mill, a blacksmith shop, a butcher's shop, a beef factory, bakers' shops, molasses mills—those enterprises in short that are necessary to turn raw products into food and shelter and clothes—for the old-fashioned spinning wheel in many a home was one of the earliest machines for manufacture—with these manufacturing began.

From such simple beginnings, the city's manufacturing interests have grown until it is possible to supply almost any want from things "made in Houston."

Car wheels or locomotives, automobiles or pianos, wooden legs or bust developers, and hundreds of other things are now made here.

According to the United States census report of 1911, Houston has 249 manufactures, employing 5,338 persons, to whom are paid yearly $3,424,000. These figures are gratifying, in a way, but when one looks over the situation as it exists in and immediately around Houston, one cannot refrain from astonishment on finding that there are comparatively so few manufacturing concerns in such an inviting field. It is no exaggeration to say that few points anywhere have so many inducements to offer the would-be manufacturer as Houston.

Aside from its advantages as a distributing and concentrating point, Houston has at its very door everything that a manufacturer needs except, perhaps, some kinds of raw material. There is an abundance of artesian water and an inexhaustable supply of cheap fuel, Houston being on the border of the great oil fields of Texas. It has both rail and water transportation to and from the outside world. It is already the great railway center of the Southwest and it will unquestionably become in the very near future the great manufacturing center as well. So rich and inviting a field cannot be overlooked. It must not be supposed that the Houstonians are not proud of what they are able to show today in the way of factories and machine shops. Such is not the case by any means. Two hundred and forty-nine manufacturing plants for a city of only 100,000 inhabitants is a fair showing and would be such for a city twice its size. There is, however, a feeling of healthy unrest created when one sees what can and should be done in so great a field. As a matter of fact the figures given in the foregoing statement are, in a way, misleading, for, were the railroad and repair shops of the railroads included in them, they would be increased by over 3,000 employees and wages by the addition of over one and a quarter million dollars.

Unquestionably the earliest large manufactory in Harris County was that of Robert Wilson, father of the late Mayor James T. D. Wilson. Mr. Wilson came to Texas in 1828, and soon after his arrival, he erected at Harrisburg, on Buffalo Bayou, an extensive steam sawmill, gristmill, blacksmith, carpenter, turning and other workshops, and houses for the workmen. When Harrisburg was burned by the Mexicans these were all destroyed. Soon after independence was secured and Texas had become a Republic someone built a sawmill at the junction of Bray's and Buffalo Bayous, and for many years this mill did a large business, turning out much of the timber with which early Houston was built. Some time in the middle forties, a large sawmill was built on the bayou in Houston at a point near where the Milam Street bridge now stands. Its location was admirable, for it was easy to float the logs to the mill, either from up or down the stream. The first cornmill was built in 1844 by Mr. Elim Stockbridge, on the north side of the bayou not far from the ford of that day at the foot of Texas Avenue. The motive power was three oxen that walked on a tread mill. It was considered a wonder and the Morning Star boasted that in a steady days work it could grind fifty bushels of corn. The whole cost of the mill, not counting the motive power, was $400.

The advent of the cotton compress in Houston is thus chronicled by the Morning Star in its issue of March 11, 1844: "A few days ago we visited the cotton press lately erected in this city by Mr. N. T. Davis, and were agreeably surprised to find that the machine used for compressing cotton bales admirably answers the purposes for which it was constructed. With the aid of only two hands, Mr. Davis can compress a bale of 500 pounds into a space only 22 inches square (sic) in 15 minutes. The facility with which this work is done is truly surprising."

Since the best modern compresses turn out a 500 pound bale of cotton containing 22 cubic feet, it is evident that the editor of the Star got his notes mixed and that the size of the early bale was somewhat greater than 22 inches square. It is interesting to note the advance that has been made in the compress since that first one was erected. Mr. Davis could turn out four bales to the hour, or working steadily for ten hours, he could turn out forty bales in a day. Those were what are called today "flat," or uncompressed bales of about three times the size of the modern compressed bales. Houston now has six compresses, each one capable of compressing from 100 to 120 bales per hour, or from 1,000 to 1,200 bales per day and their combined capacity is 8,700 bales per day, and in the height of the busy season, when they are worked night and day, they turn out over 17,000 compressed bales every twenty-four hours.

These are the following named, a more detailed description of each being given elsewhere in these pages:

The Cleveland Compress Company, W. D. Cleveland, Sr., president. This is practically a successor to the Buffalo Bayou Compress Company, organized in 1895, with A. J. Burke, president; W. D. Cleveland, vice-president and F. A. Rice, secretary. Magnolia Warehouse and Storage Company, A. C. Cairns, manager. The Merchants Compress Company, John K. Sanfers, president. Union Compress and Warehouse Company, A. Breyer, president. The Southern Compress and Warehouse Company. W. W. Sellers, manager. The Standard Compress Company, M. E. Andrews, general manager.

Mr. Alexander McGowan established an iron foundry and machine shop on the north side of Buffalo Bayou and on the banks of White Oak Bayou about 1851. These shops were at a point about opposite the foot of Louisiana Street, though two or three blocks on the other side of the bayou. The principal work done here at first was in making boilers and casting kettles for the sugar planters and others who were opening up plantations. In 1854, after the Houston and Texas Central Railroad began operation, McGowan's foundry and machine shop became quite an important concern, and did a great deal of repair work for that road.

Four or five years afterwards, Mr. Cushman established the Cushman Foundry and Machine Shops on the north side of Buffalo Bayou near the Preston Avenue bridge, called in that day the "long bridge." Cushman's foundry and machine shops were quite extensive affairs and covered an acre or two of ground. There was a foundry where castings were made, a pattern shop, a machine shop and everything that went to make a complete establishment of its kind. Mr. Cushman had quite a number of skilled mechanics for each of the departments, and was doing a good business when the war broke out. nearly every man in his employ enlisted in the Confederate Army. This was a terrible blow to him for it left him with a large and expensive plant on his hands and no men to work it. He was a man of fine courage and was not easily discouraged. He made the necessary changes and modifications in his machinery, and changed his plant into one for the manufacture of war materials, which the Confederacy soon began to need badly. He cast bombshells, cannon, grapeshot, and everything of that kind and added to his plant a machine for the manufacture of percussion caps. The commanding general of this military department detailed all the mechanics Mr. Cushman needed and Cushman's Foundry soon became one of the busiest and most important places in the state. After the war, Mr. Cushman converted his plant back to its original purposes. A few years later the firm name was changed to Wiggins, Smith & Simpson, though Mr. Cushman retained and his son still owns and operates a pattern shop and necessary adjuncts on part of the ground occupied by the old plant.

The Hartwell Iron Works, another large concern was organized about 1878–9 and has been in active operation ever since. It is one of the oldest and most efficient concerns of its kind in the city and does a large foundry and machine shop business. It manufactures boilers, makes heavy castings and does a large business in iron work of all kinds.

In 1873, the Bagby Brass Works were established by Mr. William Bagby. These were the first brass works established here. They were owned and operated by Mr. Bagby and did a large business. He was a young man of great energy and had he lived the brass works would unquestionably have been made a big concern. Unfortunately he died while in the prime of life, and for some reason, his family closed the works and they were never reopened. There are two brass works here now, each doing a good business. These are: the Kettler Brass Works, M. F. Kettler, president and manager, and the Southern Brass and Manufacturing and Plating Company, T. C. White, vice-president and general manager.

In addition to the foundries and iron works named in the foregoing there are the following, all established within recent years, but all now on a firm and safe footing: The Grant Locomotive and Car Works, The Houston Structural Steel Works, The Union Iron Works, Bayou City Iron Works, Hewitt Manufacturing Company, Houston Iron Works, Layne and Bolder, Lloyd Metal Company, F. H. Ries. These are engaged in the manufacture of all kinds of iron work, from the delicate wire screen to the most ponderous castings and heaviest machinery.

As a matter of fact, no industry in the city is more thoroughly developed than that of the machine shops and foundries. One large line developed by them is the manufacture of engines and boilers. The development that has taken place in so many industries has created a demand for engines of many and varied types, which demand has been met by local manufacturers. There are ample facilities for all kinds of work, and engines are turned out, from the small gasoline engine to the huge locomotive for railroad use. Recently one piece of machinery, weighing 75,000 pounds, was cast and shipped to Honolulu by one of the Houston foundries. As noted elsewhere in these pages, the two Houston railroad shops, each have facilities for making one complete locomotive each day.

The first artificial ice manufactured in Houston was at an ice plant established by Doctor Pearl, who had as his associates two young Englishmen, both former captains in the English army, but who had sold their commissions and had come to Texas to make their fortunes. One was Captain Kentish, and the other, Captain Spencer, a nephew of Earl Spencer who was Lord Lieutenant of Ireland. The ice plant was not a great success from a financial point of view and in 1871, two years after its establishment it closed down for good. When the plant was first established it was Doctor Pearl's intention to have a meat packery attachment, but that part of the plan was never carried out.

For nine years after the establishment of the Pearl plant no effort was made to establish another factory. Then, in 1880, the Central Ice Company was organized. This company took out a charter under the name of the Houston Ice Company. Mr. Hugh Hamilton was its chief owner and the machinery was an abandoned ice machine. For a number of years it confined its operation to making ice alone but in 1888 it took out a new charter under the name of the Magnolia Ice and Brewing Association, which charter was again changed to the Houston Ice and Brewing Company in 1901, under which name it is now known. Its business is very large, for it manufactures large quantities of beer and ice which are distributed to all parts of the state.

The American Brewing Company, another large concern, manufacturing both beer and ice, was chartered in 1894. Its president and principal owner is A. Busch of St. Louis. It, too, does an immense ice and beer business, shipping its products to all parts of the state.

There are several other ice manufacturers in Houston, the leading ones being the Houston Packing Company, Mr. H. Kirkland, president; the Henry Henke Artesian Ice and Refrigerating Company, Mr. H. Henke, president; the Crystal Ice and Fuel Company, Mr. Charles A. Zilker, president; the Irvin Ice Factory, W. H. Irvin, proprietor.

As noted, an effort was made to establish a packery by the Pearl Ice Manufacturing Company, but without success. After the failure of the ice plant, Mr. E. W. Taylor and associates bought some of the machinery and, in 1875, established a packery here which was soon followed by another conducted by Mr. Geiselman. Both of these establishments did a fairly good business for a year or two and then ceased operation. The failure was due largely to their being somewhat in advance of the times and to lack of transportation facilities and a broad market.

In 1894, the first really great step was taken in that direction by the establishment of the Houston Packing Company's plant in this city. This is the largest independent packing house in the United States, and its plant is an immense one, covering many acres. It is absolutely modern and up-to-date in its every detail. Its output is of the highest standard and its business is approximately $4,00,000 annually. In addition to its regular packing house products, those known as staple, it manufactures numerous by-products, for the disposition of which branch offices are maintained at numerous trade centers throughout the South and West. Mr. W. H. Kirkland is president of this company and Mr. E. W. Grundler is its secretary.

Both the Swift and Armour companies maintained agencies in Houston for a number of years, but the field was so inviting that in 1904 the Swift Company established its own branch here, buying property and putting up a building of its own, where it is doing a large and very satisfactory business under the management of Mr. Thomas W. Johnson.

The Armour Company has just completed the erection of its plant here and is also doing an immense business under the management of Mr. Felix Tachior. Neither the Swift, nor the Armour Company does any slaughtering here, but each does a large business in packing meats, manufacturing lard, refining oil, making soap and other packing house by-products.

There are agencies here for all the great packing houses in the United States, this giving evidence of Houston's importance as a distributing center.

In the early seventies, one of the most useful establishments in the city was the Henry House Sash Factory and Planing Mill. There were several iron foundries and machine shops, those of McGowan, Lord & Richardson, Wiggins, Smith & Simpson and other smaller concerns. There were two or three sheetiron and tinners establishments, two wagon factories, a soda water manufactory, a cigar factory, a furniture factory and other small industrial plants, which have all served as foundations for the greater ones that have been built on them.

By 1885 the manufacturing interests of Houston had grown to rather large proportions, and the business done was of considerable magnitude. There were two extensive brick yards that were turning out millions of bricks annually and the demand was in excess of the supply. There were two iron and brass foundries. These foundries turned out steam engines, boilers, compresses, gins, mill supplies, machinery and all kinds of castings and shipped them to all parts of the state. There were five cotton compresses and a large flour mill with a capacity of 400 barrels of flour per day. This mill failed in 1894 and has never been resumed.

Another large industry was the Howard Oil Company that operated mills at Houston, Palestine and Dallas, with the principal works located at Houston, just beyond the city limits at the crossing of the Central and Southern Pacific lines. At this mill about 100 tons of cotton seed were converted into oil daily. Houston developed a sweet tooth about that time, for the three candy manufacturers turned out 8,000 pounds of candy daily. This was shipped to all parts of the state. The Lone Star Barbed Wire Factory had a large shop in the Fifth ward and its product was shipped to all parts of Texas and of the Southwest.

There were seven planing mills, two ice factories, five carriage and wagon factories, a manufacturing drug house, two soap factories, two artificial stone factories, two soda and mineral water factories, one mattress factory, three tank and barrel factories, cigar factories, broom factories, lathing works, and a large number of smaller industries, representing an investment in factories of $2,000,000.

The year 1887 was a bit of a boom year for Houston manufactories for the contemplated establishment of many new industries was announced early in the year. The following became realities in the course of that and the following year:

Howard Oil Mill plant, addition, $200,000; a large refrigerating plant; a brewery costing $124,000; Southern Pacific Shops, completed at a cost of $250,000; Union Depot to cost $80,000; car wheel factory at a cost of $40,000; a bottling works and a cracker factory.

With the exception of the Southern Pacific Shops, the car wheel shop mentioned in the foregoing, was the most important of the contemplated industries. These works, better known as the Dickson Car Wheel Works, had a most humble start. When Mr. Dickson announced that he intended to establish such an enterprise in Houston he was laughed at and the idea of his seriously contemplating entering into competition with the large and old established concerns of the East was ridiculed even by his friends and best wishers. It was said to him that he could not make wheels equal to those turned out by the old and experienced manufacturers, and admitting that he could do so, then he could never get the railroads to use his wheels. However, Mr. Dickson was not easily discouraged. He had faith in his ability to turn out good wheels and to get the railroads to use them. He started with very little capital, and with a small plant. He made wheels and he made such good wheels that instead of the Eastern concerns running him out of the business, he has sometimes run them out. He got the railroads to try his wheels. They did so and found them so superior to all others that they ordered more and more of them, until today the Dickson car wheel is known all over the country as equal to the best manufactured anywhere and Mr. Dickson has had to add several times to his plant to keep abreast of the demand for his wheels. The plant is a large one and is an honor to its founder and to Houston as well.

The Houston Car Wheel and Machine Company though comparatively a young company, having been established in the fall of 1906, is doing a large business in making car wheels, and various kinds of castings and machinery. The officers and founders of this company are: Jules J. Settegast, Jr., president; George H. Hermann, vice-president; A. J. Binz, secretary-treasurer.

The Houston Electric Light Company was organized in August, 1882, and its first officers were: E. Raphael, president and D. F. Stuart, secretary. The board of trustees were: A. Grosebeck, B. A. Botts, F. A. Rice, E. P. Hill, D. F. Stuart, J. C. Hutcherson, G. L. Porter and E. Raphael. Only the old Brush Carbon lights were used. Mr. Raphael exhibited the first incandescent lamp ever seen in Houston in August, 1883. Incandescent lamps were rare at that time, for the carbon lamps only, were in general use. As soon as the incandescent lamp was seen, its great merits were recognized, and Mr. Raphael secured a contract to put the lights in the Howard Oil Mills. He fitted that plant with incandescent lamps, and it was the first incandescent light plant installed in Texas. After a few years' experience Mr. Raphael and his associates sold their electric plant to the Houston Gas Works. That company, in 1894, organized the present Electric company, which is changed only in name, being the same organization, under a different management, as the Raphael Company.

While Texas is the greatest cotton producing state in the world and, in consequence, the greatest producer of cotton seed and its derivatives also, Houston has the distinction of being the greatest producer of cotton seed products in Texas. The business is very large and is constantly growing, for Houston's position as a receiving and distributing point give her advantages that cannot be overcome, or even approached by rival cities. With seventeen railroads to bring the raw material here and with the same number of roads, supplemented by the ship channel, to distribute the finished products, her position is an enviable one.

The manufacturing of cotton seed products is carried on by six large oil mills. The capital invested in these mills is $2,500,000, and it requires over 700 men to operate them. These mills constitute a very important part of Houston's manufacturing interests. The crushing capacity of the mills is 1,200 tons daily and last season they used more than 82,000 tons of cotton seed for which they paid the farmers of the state about $2,275,000. The finished products of the mill sold for $5,000,000. The Houston mills use Texas cotton seed, which is the best and richest in the world, the cotton seed meal of other states having only 49 per cent of protein and fat combined, while that of Texas has a minimum of 55 per cent. Hence their products are always in demand and command a premium in the markets of the world.

The mills in Houston are the Fidelity Cotton Oil and Fertilizer Company, the Merchants and Planters Oil Company, the Magnolia Cotton Oil Company, the Houston Cotton Oil Company, the South Texas Cotton Oil Company and the Industrial Cotton Oil Company. Three of these mills have each a refinery of from 1,500 to 2,000 barrels per day capacity.

These refineries do a large business, because, in addition to the mills in Houston, there are numerous small mills in the interior of the state that ship crude oil here to have it refined. About 75,000 barrels of crude oil were brought to Houston in 1910 for that purpose. Besides the various departments for manufacturing refined products the Fidelity Cotton Oil and Fertilizer Company operates a fertilizer factory, which, while in competition with twenty other concerns in the state engaged in the same business, did the largest business of them all last season. This company maintains an experimental farm near its plant where its fertilizers are being constantly tested. A scientific study of soils is made and the company makes fertilizers to suit various kinds of soil, and also for various kinds of crops. Their work in this way is practical, scientific and valuable. The company turns out about 60,000 tons of fertilizers each year, which is distributed generally over the state.

The refined products of the cotton seed oil are lubricants, oleomargarine, and lard. These are extensively used throughout the country. Besides these, a food is being made to take the place of meat, while cotton seed flour is expected to become a serious rival of wheat flour. The various uses to which cotton seed products may be put are already great and the number is increasing so rapidly that it is no exaggeration to say that before long they will rival those of the wonderful coal tar products. Only a few years ago cotton seed was a source of annoyance to every cotton raiser who owned a gin, for they were considered as absolutely valueless and their accumulation near the gins was a serious embarrassment. They were burned, carted away, and everything possible was done to get rid of them.

Then some genius discovered that oil could be extracted from them and they became valuable. Then it was discovered that the shells of the seed could be ground into meal and converted into a fine feed for cattle, and they became still more valuable. Other uses for them were found, until today the value of the seed is almost as great as that of the cotton itself.

In order to clean the seed, more refined processes of ginning were devised and by this means a fluffy, no-staple cotton is produced. This is known in the commercial world as "linters" and is used largely to fill car cushions and such rough objects. Its main use, however, is in the manufacture of gun cotton and some other high explosives. Its importance in that direction is shown by the fact that the price of linters is largely regulated by the world's political aspect,—peace prospects depressing and a war cloud sending the market upward.

The City Cotton Mills erected in the Second ward, in 1872, were destroyed by fire August 12, 1875, entailing a loss of $200,000, which was complete as there was no insurance. An effort was made to rebuild the mills, but failed. Afterwards Mr. E. H. Cushing, Mr. James F. Dumble and others started another cotton mill at Eureka on the Central Railway, five miles west of Houston, but abandoned the enterprise after a year or two.

An important factory is that of the Oriental Textile Mills, located here in 1903. These mills do a wonderful business, and, in competition with the

Eastern mills, have extended their territory both to the East and West until now they cover points as far east as the Carolinas and as far west as California. They have secured a firm foothold in Mexico and are constantly extending their field of action. Their success has been phenomenal and today they occupy a strong position in the manufacturing world. This success is largely due to the wise and conservative management, for the mills were started with only limited capital and had much to contend with. There were two problems to be solved. First, how to produce goods in the best and cheapest way, yet of only the highest order of excellence, and next to find a market sufficiently large to warrant the making of them. The first was difficult, owing to limited means, and the second, for a time, seemed almost hopeless. The goods were made but no market could be found for them of sufficient magnitude to warrant a continuance of the business. Finally, finding that the market, would not come to them, they determined to go to the market. They sent one man out seeking orders. Their product was so good and their terms of sale so fair, that this first salesman had small difficulty in selling them. His success showed them that they were on the right track and they sent out other salesmen. Soon they had orders for all the goods they could produce and their plant was enlarged to meet the growing demand. Today the plant is one of the best equipped and most thorough to be found anywhere. The Oriental Textile Works is a veritable village in itself. Its houses for workmen are models. It has a school for the children of its employees, and a church. Many comforts and conveniences for those working at the mills are supplied and the factory seems to enjoy the loyal support and friendship of every man and woman working for it. It is, in many respects, a model plant. These mills manufacture burlap, burlap bags, press cloth, textiles and worsteds.

The manufacture of wagons had never been carried on extensively until the incorporation of the Eller Wagon Works in January, 1910. Mr. Frank Eller, the president, had founded the business about six years ago, before the incorporation of the company. They employ regularly about twenty-five men and turn out about six hundred wagons annually, mostly heavy trucks and oil-tank wagons. The officers besides the president are: J. W. Trimble, vice-president; R. E. Brooks, treasurer, and J. M. Powers, Jr., secretary. The office and factory are at 101–7 Crawford Street.

Not until June, 1904, was the first pronounced step taken towards making Houston a great manufacturing center for furniture and woodwork of every kind. In that year the Myers-Spalti Company established their first plant here. From a modest beginning they have added to their facilities, until now, in place of the small building they occupied at first, they have four or five large three and four-story buildings covering several acres of ground, and their plant is one of the largest and best equipped in the South. The number and variety of their products is wonderful, for they manufacture everything wooden, from a toothpick, to the finest and heaviest furniture and office fixings. Their work is all of the highest order, too, for they employ only the best expert workmen. The business done by this firm is immense, they having branch offices at the leading markets, and shipping their products all over the South and West.

The Houston Show-Case and Manufacturing Company, of which John Guinan is president and R. A. Burge is vice-president and general manager, has built up a large business and a fine reputation in the manufacturing of show cases, bank, bar, drug store and office fixtures and furniture. Its plant is on Washington Avenue, Nos. 3600 to 3618.

Houston has the distinction of possessing the only piano and organ manufactory in the South. This is a new industry, having been established only in 1909, but it is already doing a good business. It is a genuine factory and not merely a shop where the various parts of an organ or piano are assembled and put together in a case made elsewhere. The piano or organ is actually manufactured here, from the pedals to the cases, of walnut, oak or whatever other wood is used, in which they are finished. The instruments turned out by this factory are pronounced to be of the highest order by experts.

By 1905, Houston had taken its place as the chief manufacturing city in Texas, and from the great variety of its manufactured products it held a prominent place in the list of manufacturing cities in the Southwest. It had, as already noted, the finest and best car wheel works in the South, and it had also four of the largest cotton seed oil mills in the South. These mills manufacture thousands of tons of oil cake and cotton seed meal and make both crude and refined oil in large quantities, each year. Their products are shipped to all parts of the world. It had brass and iron foundries whose products were in demand all over the state all the year round. It had two immense breweries. It had fine creosoting works, six cotton compresses, big railroad shops, several sash and blind factories, a big packing house, a large flour mill, two soap factories, several candy factories that supplied not only Texas, but a large part of Mexico with their delicious product, several broom factories, brick and tile works that were constantly increasing their facilities to keep abreast with the demands made on them by the building industries. Wagons and buggies were being made and shipped in large quantities, while Houston made tents and awnings that were in demand over Texas and Mexico.

Houston is a great coffee center, there being five large dealers and roasters here. The Check-Neal Company, J. W. Neal, first vice-president and general manager, and the International Coffee Company, Wm. D. Cleveland and Sons, managers, each established in 1896, have their large plants here and maintain branch houses over the Southwestern and Southern States. They are the largest concerns of the kind in the Southwest. The others are: the

Guatemala Coffee Company, Magnolia Coffee Company, Schumacher Company, and the Southern Tea and Coffee Company.

Facts and statistics in regard to the great lumber, rice, cotton, and mineral oil industries are given in another chapter of this volume.

The development of the Ship Channel gave rise to a rather large industry in Houston. The formation of the Houston Launch Club, organized for the purpose of taking advantage of the superb facilities offered by the channel for aquatic sports of all kinds, created a great demand for boats, and that demand was speedily supplied. There are three regular ship yards and a number of individuals engaged in boat building here. Houston has one of the largest and most flourishing launch clubs in the country. The club has a beautiful club house on the bank of the channel, near Harrisburg, at the terminus of one of the street car lines. There are several large and well equipped launches and a number of smaller pleasure boats owned by the members. There are already over 200 boats belonging to the fleet and in 1911 there were contracts made for others to cost very nearly $50,000. The channel is an ideal place for such sport. In front of the clubhouse there is a width of 200 feet and a depth of 25 feet. The channel widens below the clubhouse to 250 feet, within five miles; then to 300 feet; then to 400 feet, where it merges with San Jacinto River, which in turn enters San Jacinto Bay and then Trinity or Galveston Bay. The banks are high and covered with forest trees and flowers which will stand much closer inspection than the famous banks of the Hudson River.

According to statistics collected by Houston's Chamber of Commerce, the city's manufacturing plants turn out 280 distinct articles. Some of these manufacturing plants are small concerns, it is true, but even the smallest is engaged in the manufacture of useful articles here at home that were formerly bought from outside markets and thus all the money employed in their making and all that is paid to their makers is kept at home, thus adding to the general prosperity of the city.

The United States census figures, made public July 22, 1911, shows percentages of increase for Houston manufactures compared with 1904 as follows:

Increase in cost of material used, 88 per cent; increase in capital invested, 87 per cent; increase in number of salaried officers and clerks, 75 per cent; increase in miscellaneous expenses, 72 per cent; increase in value of products, 70 per cent; increase in value added by manufacture, 46 per cent; increase in salaries and wages, 24 per cent; increase in the number of establishments, 19 per cent; increase in average number of wage earners employed during the year, 6 per cent.

Following are the figures for 1909, when the census was taken: Number of establishments, 249; capital invested, $16,594,000; cost of material used, $14,321,000; salaries and wages, $4,254,000; miscellaneous expenses,

$1,942,000; value of products, $23,016,000; value added by manufacture, $8,695,000; number of salaried officers and clerks, 725; average number of wage earners, 5,338; total number of steam laundries, 9; capital invested in laundries, $270,000; cost of material used, $74,000; salaries and wages, $256,000; miscellaneous expenses, $129,000; value of products, $500,000; number of salaried officers and clerks, 34; average number of wage earners, 422.

The question of fuel and water for manufacturing purposes, is of the greatest importance, and it is in that direction that Houston's advantages are so great. Water of the purest kind and in inexhaustible quantities, is obtained everywhere by sinking artesian wells. All the manufacturing plants in Houston have their own artesian wells and are, thus, independent of all other sources of supply. The chief fuel used is oil, and being located on the very border of the great oil fields, Houston occupies a most advantageous position. The supply of oil is great, the production of the Texas fields in 1910 having been 13,000,000 barrels, all admirably suited for steam making purposes. In addition to oil, there is an unlimited supply of lignite which can be delivered at Houston for $1.50 per ton. With properly constructed grates, lignite makes a very satisfactory fuel and is valuable for that purpose. Recent experiments have shown that lignite made into producers gas for firing purposes, doubles its efficiency as used under the ordinary steam boiler. The manufacture of lignite briquettes is being considered by local capitalists.

At a home products banquet given in Houston, on the evening of October 27, 1911, at which 200 business men were guests, more than 50 articles of food were served, all of which had either been manufactured in Houston or produced on surrounding farms and orchards. That fact in regard to the menu justifies its reproduction here. It was as follows:

Oyster cocktail, celery, tomatoes, roast beef, sweetbread, spaghetti and Red Cross chili, yams, wine cured Jasmine ham, sliced corn, beef, macaroni, cornmeal, grits, veal loaf sandwich, tongue sandwich, hot wieners, boiled rice, cervelat sandwich, rolls, sliced bologna, boneless pickled pig's feet, crackers, Red Cross tamales, liver sausage, string beans, head cheese, beer, sliced ox tongue, cider, calf's head jelly, soda water, figs, stewed pears, preserved figs, pure cane syrup, orange marmalade, ice cream, assorted cakes, candy, pecans, satsuma oranges, coffee, cigars.

CHAPTER XX WHOLESALE TRADE AND BIG BUSINESS

Pioneer Conditions of Trade. Steamboat Element in Houston's Business Prosperity. Natural Advantages Built up Great Industries. Water Competition gives Advantageous Railroad Tariffs. Houston's Trade Territory. How Annual Wholesale Business of $90,000,000 is pro rated. City's 376 Incorporated Companies. Growth of Produce Business. Importation of Fruits. Sugar Jobbing Trade. Packing House Business. Changes in Methods of Marketing Cotton. How Houston was Made a Cotton Buyers' Market. Houston, the Great Selling Market for Lumber. Results of Lumber Panic Prices of 1907, in Concentrated Selling Agencies in Houston. Manufacturing Capacity of Big Lumber Firms. Movement of Curtail Manufacture. Facts and Figures on Lumber Industry. Turpentine Trade. The J. R. Morris Plan for Rice Culture. Houston's Rice Mills. Rice Production and Food Value. Houston's Retail Trade and Wage Earners. Capital Invested in Retail Trade.

Trade in any primitive community always begins with barter. An exchange of commodities between neighbors, each supplying the lacks of the other, oftentimes without any other consideration than friendship and good fellowship is the wholesome and beautiful beginning of trade in any pioneer community. Along with this barter and exchange there is often a community use of many articles.

In most towns that grew up in America as the skirmish lines of civilization were flung out westward it was possibly the blacksmith shop that was the pioneer business establishment. The wagon that had lost a tire and the horse that had flung a shoe as the white topped wagons followed the faint new trail into the wilderness furnished the trade for the shop. The first store was a general merchandise store where everything was sold from ploughshares to shoe strings. Hardware, cutlery, groceries, dry goods, boots and shoes, molasses, oil, candles and rifles and all the articles needed to wage the fight with nature for the reclamation of a virgin forest or an unploughed prairie. Eggs, butter, produce, deer hides and coon skins, oats, corn, hay and cotton or any product of farm or field was taken in exchange by the obliging storekeeper who cheerfully reaped the double profit. In the front end of the store was the post-office and at the rear end a primitive bar where straight "licker" and Jamaica rum was served from the barrel. This part of the store was called by the more pious element of the community the "doggery."

Business in Houston began in much the same way save that from the beginning it was modified by the fact that here was the junction of the land trail and the water route and the steamboat element of society and prosperity entered into the life of the town from the beginning.

Nevertheless, so dependent was the community upon its own resources that early shipments of flour brought $13 a barrel and other goods were in proportion.

The lapse of time and the increase of prosperity slowly differentiated business, and stores were established for the sale of separate commodities. The dry goods store in time, ceased to sell brogans and molasses and rum and sold dry goods. But as prosperity advanced yet farther, there was a reversal to type and the modern huge department store where everything is again sold has justified the pioneer conception as to "store keepin'." The saloon was an institution from the beginning and flourished in tents until it could build houses. The character of trade has remained distinct to a great extent.

Houston's greatest industries have developed as the result of natural advantages. Located on the rim of the great pine forests of Texas and Louisiana it became the metropolis of the lumber industry. Situated in the heart of the alluvial coast plains it became the center of the rice and fruit culture, and being the natural seaport for a great basin that extends thousands of miles north and west and east to the Rocky Mountains and the tributaries of the Mississippi the commerce of that section will more and more sweep down upon it. Good business judgment and fair dealing have combined with advantage of location to make Houston the greatest cotton concentration point in the world, with the sometime exception of New Orleans.

The existence of the ship channel makes Houston the natural and logical basing point for freight rates, for it is here that the water and rail transportation meet. Formerly all, or practically all, the traffic of the state was done through Houston, over the bayou. Then the railroads formed connections with the Northern and Eastern markets, and complications arose. Every line of railroad attempted to make a tariff of its own, and where there was no competition and a road had a territory to itself, it made such a tariff as it chose.

When these lines of railroad reached Houston, the situation changed, for here they found a most formidable obstacle in the form of water competition and they were all forced to reduce their rates to meet this competition. Through its ship channel, Houston has all the advantages of an actual seaport, even if the channel were not actually utilized.

This possible water competition forms the basis upon which Houston rates are fixed and they enable Houston manufacturers and wholesale merchants to compete for trade in a large territory that would be closed to them but for the existence of the low rates secured through water competition. It also permits the concentration and reshipment of materials by the jobbers and permits Houston wholesalers to compete with north Texas jobbers, although the latter are much nearer the source of supply.

As a result of her admirable position, Houston has become the great concentrating and distributing point for nearly the whole state, and for some commodities Houston is the concentrating point for the whole state. This, of course, has made Houston very prominent as a wholesale market and the volume of business done is immense. The greater part of the state and some parts of bordering states look to Houston for their supplies.

Among the remarkable effects of Houston's concentrating and distributing facilities, is the fact that this city has been made a wholesale market for commodities not usually classed among those dealt in as wholesale, notably machinery and heavy engines. As a rule all such things as monster traction engines, well-boring machinery, great pumps and similar articles, are ordered direct from the large factories in the East and sales are made direct to the consumer by the factories. However, Houston's splendid warehouse facilities, her cheap freight rates and her position as a distributing point, all combine to enable her to carry large stocks of such commodities and as a result she has become a great wholesale market for machinery. The machinery dealers of Houston handle all kinds of heavy material, from huge traction engines, threshers, reapers and everything of that kind, to plows, scrapers and small plantation supplies. The business is large and is growing, for each year shows an increase over the preceding one. The business done in machinery by Houston wholesalers in 1910 totaled over $3,000,000, which was an increase of about $250,000 over the year before.

It must not be supposed that special privileges or undue advantages are given the merchants of Houston by the rate making powers, for such is not true. Houston's advantages lie in the fact that having the water rate as a right, she has increased and perfected her local facilities by providing large and suitable warehouses and storerooms and has done everything possible to reduce local charges, thus enabling the largest amount of business to be done on the cheapest basis. These low local charges enable Houston merchants to compete in territory that otherwise would be given over to their rivals who have a slightly lower rail rate, but who are less wide-awake or who have other drawbacks. One fact will illustrate this. Houston has few drays or heavy floats for transporting goods from one point to another. They are not necessary because every warehouse, every compress, every manufacturing plant and every cotton yard in the city is located on the line of one or more of the railroads entering the city or on both the railroad and ship channel. This saving in drayage amounts to hundreds of thousands of dollars annually. On the receipts of cotton alone there is saved $100,000 each year, while on other commodities there is a saving of a much larger amount.

Dallas, Fort Worth and other large trade centers have tributary territories covered by special rates made for the purpose of placing them on a fair and equitable footing with Houston or other competitors. In such territory Houston can enter only through using the advantages she has created at home to their fullest extent. As a matter of fact Houston cannot enter the territory having a radius of about 100 miles around Dallas and Fort Worth, even with her local advantages, but in all the other portions of the state Houston is either on an equal footing with those markets or has a slight advantage over them.

It is estimated that Houston's wholesale business amounts to $90,000,000 annually. The leading articles and the amount of business done in each are estimated as follows: Machinery, $3,000,000; hardware, $4,000,000; lumber, $35,000,000; petroleum products, $1,000,000; drugs and chemicals, $4,000,000; paints and glass, $1,000,000; furniture, $1,400,000; dry goods, $1,750,000; liquors, $1,250,000; beer and ice, $2,500,000; groceries, $8,000,000; produce, $4,600,000; sugar and molasses, $2,000,000; tobacco, $1,250,000; packinghouse products, $3,750,000.

When to these is added the business done in electrical supplies, building materials of various kinds, paving materials and a number of other things on which no figures approaching exactness are obtainable, it will be found that the estimated total of $90,000,000 is rather below than above the actual figures.

In addition to the thousands of individuals and unincorporated firms, there are 376 incorporated companies, excluding railroads, trust companies and banks, doing business in Houston. These have a combined capital of $146,943,900. These companies represent all lines of trade and their number is being increased each year.

In 1902, there were but five wholesale dealers in fruits, produce, butter and eggs in Houston. Of these only one was a large dealer. In 1911, there were seven large establishments and perhaps as many as twenty-five small ones, whose aggregate business amounted to about $5,000,000 annually.

In 1902, the Houston jobbers had but little competition, but today some of the markets that at that time were their best customers, notably Beaumont, Bryan, Eagle Lake and Hempstead, are now competitors.

The opening of the Rio Grande country has added greatly to Houston's business, since practically all of the vegetables, fruits and farm products of that territory are sold in Houston. Then, too, Houston's merchants have become large importers of grapes, bananas, prunes, lemons and other tropical and subtropical fruits which are imported direct.

Houston's proximity to the sugar cane fields and its close connection by rail with the sugar producing territory along the Rio Grande have made the city the sugar center of the state, and over $2,000,000 in sugar alone was the record of the Houston jobbers during the season of 1910, while the season of 1911 will undoubtedly show a large increase over the preceding year, since the 1911 crop is a large one. Since the opening of the Rio Grande territory, Houston's sugar business has doubled. Houston's selling territory is

Arkansas, Oklahoma, New Mexico, Tennessee, Missouri and Mississippi. A great wholesale coffee trade has also been built up here.

Packing house products cut no mean figure in Houston's jobbing trade. The Houston Packing Company owns a large and highly equipped plant and does a large business, while Armour, Swift and other outside companies, maintain branches or agencies here and add considerably to the volume of business. A most conservative estimate places the amount of the local business for the season that closed August 31, 1911, at $4,000,000. Outside capitalists are planning to spend $500,000 in building stock yards on the ship channel.

Some years ago it was the custom of the cotton planter to ship his cotton to a commission merchant, to be sold or held for higher prices as the situation might warrant. The system was an excellent one and was highly satisfactory to both parties to the transaction; to the planter, who received part of the value of his cotton in advance for his immediate needs, and to the merchant, who received interest, storage charges and finally a commission for selling the cotton. The system was safe but it was slow and tedious. It was the best that could be devised when the planter had to seek a market for what he produced. It was a cumbersome system as well, because it required the services of so many middlemen.

Then a change took place. Instead of the planter seeking a market the markets of the world sought him. All the great foreign and domestic houses sent their buyers into the interior to buy cotton, and the commission merchant was largely, though not entirely relegated to the past. Former cotton centers, places that had done an immense business under the old system, were forced to change all their time-honored methods or accept the inevitable. There was a new and very important feature introduced into the cotton trade. It became imperative to have some point at which all the cotton purchased by agents in all parts of the state could be concentrated for inspection and arranging before being finally exported. The cotton men of Houston recognized this necessity almost as soon as it arose and took steps to provide such necessary facilities. Houston had large compresses and large cotton warehouses. Had her merchants been less farsighted they might have attempted to take advantage of the city's natural advantages and gone in to make large, but temporary profit out of these. A wiser plan was followed. Instead of taking that advantage, as they could have done easily, they used their compresses and warehouses just as so much capital and used them to attract cotton to Houston, not as an ultimate market altogether, but as a concentrating point for cotton, where it could be stored and handled. Local charges were cut and made as low as possible, with the result that all the great cotton firms of the world have been attracted to Houston, and most of them have either branch offices or local representatives here.

In interested quarters it has been asserted that the railroads unfairly favor this city and that every facility is given the Houston cotton men to do business. The fact that Houston's local or net receipts of cotton amount to between 700,000 and 800,000 bales each season, has been advanced as an argument that Houston is so favored. Houston has advantages as a cotton market, it is true, but they have been created by her own people and have not been given to her by the railroads or anyone else. The market has been made strictly a buyers market; that is, all the rules of the local cotton exchange favor the buyer and the customs of the cotton factors do the same thing. To illustrate this point the following statement of local charges on a bale of cotton bought from a local merchant, is given:

Compressing	$0.50
Loading	.05
	.55

From this total charge of 55 cents per bale, the following items are deducted:

Returned to buyer, account reclamation	$0.10
Returned to buyer, account inspection	.03
Returned to buyer, account ½ samples	.03
	.16

This leaves Houston's net charges on a bale of cotton, 39c, or only 9c more than it costs to ship the same bale to Galveston. The result is that Houston has about thirty firms and individuals buying cotton, which makes a very broad market.

While the compress charge, 50c, is the same at New Orleans and Galveston as at Houston, there are in those places other local charges, such as drayage, and as nothing is returned to the buyer in those markets, it makes their charges from 35c to 45c higher than those of Houston. On drayage alone Houston saves the buyer and seller of cotton $100,000 annually. Under these conditions it is not surprising that Houston has become the greatest spot cotton market in America.

Additional facts in regard to the relation of Houston to the cotton trade are found in other chapters. The chapter on the cotton exchange gives many of them and the manufacturing chapter deals with both cotton and cottonseed products.

Houston is the greatest lumber center in the country. This does not mean that Houston takes first rank as a manufacturing or producing center, but it does mean that more large lumber companies and organizations have their headquarters here and that more mills and more lumber are controlled and sold through offices in Houston than through those of any two or three cities anywhere in the Southwest. Houston has only one or two mills located within its limits, but it is the home of large companies that operate nearly all the great lumber mills in Texas. Some 250 sawmills in Texas, Louisiana and Arkansas, are represented by offices in Houston.

The proverb: "It is an ill wind that blows no one any good" has proven to be literally true so far as Houston is concerned, for it is said that the great financial panic of 1907 was directly responsible for Houston becoming the leading lumber center that it is today. The methods of conducting and managing the lumber business then were very different from those followed now. Before the panic there was a brisk demand for lumber and the mills sold all they could produce. There was a market right at their doors and their sales-offices and mills were practically one thing. The panic came and found them with large stocks on hand and no market of any kind. There was no demand and the problem that confronted them was to find buyers. They solved it by sending agents over the country, who sought to create a demand and who were successful in their efforts. But another difficulty arose. It became necessary to keep in close touch with both the market and the selling agents scattered over the country, and, as this could not be done from the mill, it became necessary to establish headquarters at some central point, and Houston, having so many advantages as a distributing point, was naturally chosen. A large number of the great firms opened offices and established headquarters here while a number of others established agencies, so that practically every large manufacturing and wholesale firm in Texas and the greater part of Louisiana, is represented in Houston. During the last three years the growth of the business has been phenomenal. The Kirby Lumber Company has expanded wonderfully and is now operating eleven mills, manufacturing annually 400,000,000 feet of lumber. This company, which successfully weathered a federal receivership, ranks among the greatest in the world.

J. M. West and associates have increased their holdings in a remarkable way during the past two years, and before that the expansion was also almost equally as great. They now control the Orange Lumber Company of Orange, the C. L. Smith Lumber Company of Merryville, the Hawthorn Lumber Company of Hawthorn, the W. W. West Lumber Company of Lovelady, the firm of William Carlisle & Company of Oklahoma and have built a new mill at Barham, Texas. The combined output of these mills is 175,000,000 feet.

The big firms of Houston, with the total annual capacity of their plants are: Kirby Lumber Co., manufacturers, 400,000,000 feet; Long-Bell Lumber Company, manufacturers, 500,000,000; West Lumber Company, manufacturers, 175,000,000; W. H. Norris Lumber Company, wholesalers,

100,000,000; Vaughan Lumber Company, wholesalers, 100,000,000; Continental Lumber and Tie Company, wholesalers, 100,000,000; Trinity River Lumber Company, manufacturers; 60,000,000; Central Coal and Coke Company, manufacturers, 50,000,000; W. T. Carter & Brother, manufacturers, 50,000,000; Carter Lumber Company, 40,000,000; W. R. Pickering Lumber Company, manufacturers, 50,000,000; Sabine Lumber Company, manufacturers, 40,000,000; Ray & Mihills, wholesalers, 40,000,000; Carter-Kelley Lumber Company, 30,000,000; Big Tree Lumber Company, manufacturers and wholesalers, 30,000,000; C. R. Cummings & Co., manufacturers, 25,000,000; J. S. and W. M. Rice, manufacturers, 25,000,000; Gebhart-Williams-Fenet, manufacturers, 25,000,000; Bland & Fisher, manufacturers, 25,000,000; J. C. Hill Lumber Company, manufacturers, 20,000,000; L. B. Manefee Lumber Company, manufacturers, 20,000,000; R. W. Wier Lumber Company, manufacturers, 20,00,000; Alf. Bennett Lumber Company, manufacturers and wholesalers, 20,000,000; R. C. Miller Lumber Company, manufacturers, 20,000,000; Bush Bros., manufacturers, 15,000,000; Southern Pinery Tie and Lumber Company, manufacturers and wholesalers, 10,000,000.

The total of the foregoing is 1,990,000,000 feet. There is no way to get the exact figures of actual business done by the Houston firms, but if there were it would be shown that Houston occupies a position very near the head of the list of leading lumber centers of the world.

Some few years ago the yellow pine output was figured at around three billion feet a year. Most of this enormous amount of lumber is handled through firms having headquarters in Houston.

In 1901 there were only seventeen persons and firms in Houston handling lumber. In 1911 there are 90 such concerns. Houston, a decade ago, while laying claim to being a large wholesale distributing point for lumber was still in its infancy as a lumber mart. This city is now recognized as being one of the world's greatest lumber emporiums; in fact, Houston is the greatest clearing house of the Southwest, particularly for yellow pine.

As the lumber business of the Southwest continued to expand it became necessary to create a central market, a kind of clearing house. Transportation and banking facilities had to be taken into consideration. Houston could supply both these requisites, hence this city was selected as the proper location and today Houston contains more great lumber concerns than any section except the Pacific Northwest. In the enormous bank clearings of Houston the lumber business figures largely.

Of late several of the smaller mills have been dropping out of business, unable to meet the competition of the larger manufacturers.

Rarely ever do lumbermen meet without discussing the necessity of curtailing output. They invariably contend that in order to maintain a fair market manufacturers must reduce their output. In 1911 more mills than ever have been closed down. In order to crush out the newly organized Timber Workers' Union, nearly 100 mills in the Southwest have closed down and surplus stocks are being gradually depleted. In the summer of 1911, however, there has also been a slacking off in demand throughout the whole country. Because of this dullness in trade some 200 mills have been forced to suspend work. The mills which have closed down have an average daily capacity of 10,000 to 80,000 feet. These mills, however, are not included in the list of mills which have shut down because of the desire to wipe out unionism in the mills. Somewhere around 10,000 mill hands have been rendered idle by the shutdown and this means a tremendous reduction in the daily output.

The largest saw mill in Texas is the Kirby Mill at Bessmay. It has an hourly capacity of 20,000 feet.

The largest double mill is that at Onalaska. It has a capacity of 300,000 feet in ten hours.

There are about 250 mills in Texas that manufacture yellow pine exclusively.

There are about twenty saw mills in Texas that manufacture hardwoods exclusively.

The original forest area of Texas covered 41,980,000 acres.

The present forest area covers about 30,000,000 acres.

The original stumpage of Texas was about 80,000,000,000 feet.

The present stumpage of Texas is about 27,000,000,000 feet.

The present hardwood stumpage of Texas is about 12,000,000,000 feet.

The man who owns the greatest amount of pine stumpage in Texas is doubtless Mr. W. T. Carter* of Houston, whose largest holdings lie near Camden, Texas, a town built up around his saw mill.

* Houston has no more representative citizen nor one more honored than W. T. Carter, although his personal modesty and his vast business interests have caused him to constantly refuse every offer of official position of any kind.

W. T. Carter is a native son of east Texas and of the land where the yellow pine grows. He loves the pine trees and has massed a great fortune out of the lumber industry. It is a common saying among lumbermen that W. T. Carter could build a saw mill with a pocket knife if necessary, but he and his brother, E. A. Carter, recently startled even the lumbermen by erecting, entirely under their supervision and with their own employed labor, the first steel saw mill ever built in Texas. It was built in record time at a saving of nearly $50,000 of the price quoted by contractors and is as perfectly equipped as any saw mill anywhere. The first logs were cut in the new mill on July 4, 1911.

When, as a boy of seventeen, without funds and without financial assistance, W. T. Carter entered into the saw mill business, he had to trade raw lumber to pay the men and teams that helped him to build his first mill, which was located two miles west of Trinity, and which was operated in 1873 and 1874. The plant was moved several times following the forest. The railroad built from Trinity to Colmesneil in 1881, opened up a vast virgin pine forest and the Carter mill was moved to Barnum in 1882 and remained there until 1897 when the plant was destroyed by fire. The mill was then moved and in the midst of his timber holdings the saw mill town of Camden was built up. This mill was destroyed by fire in 1910 and is the one replaced with the huge steel structure. Near it Mr. Carter has large holdings of pine lands. By the steady purchase of timber lands, even in the years following 1892 when great depression ruled and lumber was at its lowest ebb, Mr. Carter has demonstrated his business judgment and sagacity.

W. T. Carter was born in Tyler, Smith County, Texas, February 4, 1856. He is the third son of J. J. Carter and Jane Carter of Georgia, who came to Texas and settled in Cherokee County in 1849. The family was of the old South and well to do, but the war left them in straightened financial circumstances. Mr. Carter's father was Senior Captain of Hubbard's regiment and made a record for valor during the Civil War. After that struggle he became a school teacher and utilized his classical education in country schools. The subject of this sketch studied under him and later under Professor Steele at Pennington, Texas. One of the boy's heroes was an uncle, George T. Anderson, known as "Old Tige," who served in the war with Mexico, in one campaign against the Indians and in the Confederacy, rising under Lee to the rank of Brigadier. Old Tige's example and grit nerved his nephew to heroic struggles in his youth. Governor Hubbard, of Texas, was also a close relative of the Carter family.

In 1879, at Pennington, W. T. Carter married Miss Maude Holley, which he considers the finest investment he ever made, and out of this happy union five children survive: Lena Lister, wife of J. J. Carroll of Houston; Jessie Gertrude, wife of Dr. Judson L. Taylor of the United States Navy; W. T. Carter, Jr., married to Miss Lillian Neuhaus; Agnese Jayne, Aubrey Leon, and Frankie, the two latter at school.

Earnest A. Carter, a brother, is a member of the firm of W. T. Carter & Brother, and has contributed much to the success of Mr. Carter. Other brothers are Lucian C., and Hon. Clarence L., the last named a prominent member of the Houston bar. A sister, Claudia G., lives with Mr. W. T. Carter at the beautiful Main Street home of the family in Houston.

In 1910, Mr. W. T. Carter was King Nottoc XII at the No-Tsu-Oh Carnival. He is a stockholder and director in the Carter-Kelley Lumber Company of Manning, Angelina County, is vice-president of the Union National Bank of Houston and of the First National Bank of Livingston, is president of the Moscow, Camden and San Augustine railroad, which he built, and director of the H. E. & W. T. railroad. He is a member of the Thalian, B. P. O. E., Country, and Houston Clubs, and of the Chamber of Commerce. The family attends the First Baptist Church.

Mr. Carter is a thoughtful student of economic subjects, has traveled much and possesses a broad culture, and is modest, kind and hospitable.

Mr. Carter has the distinction of being the man who first introduced the use of the mill pond in the saw mill industry in Texas. A mill pond is now part of the plant of every big saw mill.

Conservation of the state's timber resources is constantly being agitated. The beginning of this agitation in Texas is due to Mr. J. Lewis Thompson of Houston, President of the Yellow Pine Manufacturers Association. Mr. Thompson and the editor of this volume first gave the matter publicity. The Yale Forestry Class has twice spent the spring term in the woods in pine forests on Mr. Thompson's holdings. At one of these camps, in 1908, a conservation meeting was held, attended by Gifford Pinchot and many lumber manufacturers. It is estimated that Texas has 25,000,000 acres of pine and a hardwood stumpage of 12,000,000,000 feet. This standing timber is estimated to be worth as it stands $108,000,000. This, of course, does not include between $60,000,000 and $75,000,000 invested in mills and trams operated by large concerns.

Contiguous to Houston are half a dozen turpentine concerns, which report an annual output of 375,000 barrels of turpentine and 65,000 barrels of resin. The value of the output is estimated at $600,000, with a capital invested of $500,000. Employment is given to 550 persons.

To the late Mr. J. R. Morris must be awarded the credit of being the first to recognize the possibility of rice culture near Houston. In 1869 or 1870 he organized a company and obtained a charter for the construction of a broad canal from a point on the San Jacinto River to the mouth of White Oak Bayou at the foot of Main Street. He had a survey made and found that the San Jacinto River, was between twenty-five and twenty-eight feet higher than the banks of the bayou at Houston. His idea was, primarily to use the water for irrigating the intermediate prairie, and then, after it reached Houston, to utilize the twenty-odd feet fall for motive power. He argued that all the land between the river and the bayou was natural rice land and that it could be used as such with great profit. Unfortunately there were difficulties in the way of accomplishing his purpose, the greatest being to get permission from the land owners along the river to divert the stream from its natural bed. There were state, and perhaps, national laws against doing such things, and the scheme never amounted to anything beyond drawing attention to the fact that there were splendid rice lands near Houston.

Mr. Morris did not live to see the correctness of his views relating to rice lands, verified, but they have been in every way. It is now an established fact that Texas has some of the finest rice lands to be found anywhere, and that the coast country is admirably adapted to the raising of rice. In Mr. Morris' day it is doubtful if there were as much as one full acre of land in Harris County planted with rice, but now all that is changed and Harris County has over 30,000 acres in rice, while the country tributary to Houston claims 190,000 of the 253,560 acres devoted to rice culture. The rice crop is the third in point of importance of Texas crops. Of the twenty rice mills in Texas, Houston has five and these five mills are of such size that they represent almost one-third of the milling capacity of the state. The Houston mills are the following: Pritchard Rice Mills, capacity 2,400 bags daily; Standard Milling Company, capacity 2,400 bags daily; Texas Rice Mills, capacity 1,200 bags daily; Industrial Rice Milling Company, capacity 1,000 bags daily, and Southwestern Rice Mills, capacity 600 bags daily.

These mills have a combined capacity of 7,600 bags daily, while the total capacity of all the mills in the state is only 25,200 bags daily.

Owing to its great transportation facilities, Houston became, at once, the natural concentrating and distributing point and has remained such ever since the establishment of the industry.

The production in 1910 was about two and one-quarter million bags, which was valued at $5,789,320, but even this small crop had on its face many features of overproduction. As a matter of fact there was no overproduction, for other elements than quantity entered in the problem, the chief being a lack of appreciation of the great food value of rice by the public, which caused, what someone has described, as under-consumption. The people have not yet learned to eat rice, and as the railroad rates have been most unsatisfactory, the producers have had to look to the home market almost entirely. The home people, who eat rice, demand only fancy grades, and as there are only fifty pounds of fancy in every 162 pound bag of rice, it is readily seen that the producer is left with an undesirably large surplus of lower grade rice on his hands at the end of each season. These lower grades are of just as great food value as the higher grade, and the producers hope to convince the public of that fact. Efforts are now being made to adjust railroad rates, so as to admit of an extension of the market. When that is done and the public, in general realizes the great value of rice, the industry will take on new life and activity. It is said that there is enough land along the coast country to produce the world's supply of rice. The industry is still in its infancy, but before many years it will have become a giant.

Whenever there are periods of financial depression over the country it is a noticeable fact that Houston is rarely affected to any great degree, and that real "hard times" are almost unknown here.

The effect is felt in a general way, of course, but it is not deep seated nor lasting and outside the large financial concerns, where large sums of ready cash are constantly needed, a panic, in the least far-reaching, is unknown in Houston. This seems to be a rather broad and sweeping assertion and yet it is a true one, for Houston's business is based on the most substantial grounds which enables it to meet difficulties and overcome them when other places, less favored, would have to succumb. In the first place those engaged in commercial pursuits here are not dependent on the success or failure of any one line of trade, such as oil, lumber, cotton or anything else, but their interests are diversified and when one of these is depressed or even fails there are others to sustain the general situation.

The cause for Houston's stability is found in the fact that there is the basis for a large retail trade here that can be found nowhere else in the Southwest. Vast sums are paid out weekly, biweekly and monthly, in the form of wages with the result that there is always a great deal of money in circulation. Roughly speaking there is paid wage-earners in Houston, about $8,500,000 annually. With such large sums of money kept constantly in circulation, it is not wonderful that Houston should show life and activity, even during periods when her less favored competitors are plunged into the depths of despondency.

Houston's retail trade is very large and is constantly increasing. The local situation, as just pointed out, is very inviting, but to that must be added the constantly increasing demand from nearby territory, opened up by the railroads and the extension of the electric roads.

Houston has 1200 retail establishments which do a business of nearly forty-one and one-half million dollars annually. The following list shows some of the details of the trade, but is not complete, because of the difficulty of getting anything approaching accurate information about the smaller concerns. It shows the class of trade and the amounts invested: Wagons, carriages, etc., $900,000; groceries, teas, coffee, etc., $5,000,000; paints, oils, etc., $750,000; petroleum and its products, $2,125,000; furniture and upholstering, $1,600,000; sash, doors, blinds, etc., $4,000,000; clothing and men's furnishings, $3,000,000; jewelry and optical goods, $1,100,000; dry goods and millinery, $3,000,000; books, stationery, etc., $700,000; drugs and chemicals, $750,000; hardware, crockery, tinware, etc., $3,600,000; engines, machinists and electrical supplies, $2,200,000; boots and shoes, $750,000; grain, feed and bakery supplies, $1,800,000; cigars and tobacco, $300,000; pianos and musical supplies, $400,000; fuel and ice, $2,005,000; toys and novelties, $100,000; florist's goods and seeds, $140,000; saddlery, harness and trunks, $420,000; automobiles and motor boats, $2,000,000; typewriters, adding machines, etc., $1,800,000; brick, tiling, etc., $1,000,000; unclassified, $2,000,000 total amount invested, $41,440,000.

The building of the many suburbs has extended the retail trade and may account in some measure for its rapid increase. The completion of the belt railroad is already beginning to show its effects in the same direction. The figures given in the foregoing are those for the fiscal year closing June 31, 1911.

The estimate of the Chamber of Commerce in November, 1911, is that the annual aggregate of business is $55,000,000.

In the roar and din that accompanied the rush of oil out of the great well brought in by Lucas at Spindle Top in 1900, was sounded the first note of Houston's greatness as a manufacturing and commercial center. That discovery meant much for Texas and it meant much for Houston also, because this city was just at that stage in its development where it was in position to take advantage of the opportunity presented by the creation of this great and new industry.

There are so many points involved in the history of the development of the Texas oil fields, that it is impossible to discuss them here; suffice it to say that their possibilities were great; that Houston was in position to take advantage of the opportunity presented, and that to day, in consequence of its having done so, it is the recognized leader and center of all that involves the handling, financing and exporting of the product of the Texas oil fields; that it is rapidly assuming control of the Oklahoma and other outside fields and that before the close of 1912, all the output of those fields will probably be handled by Houston companies, either directly or indirectly.

As the center of the oil industry, Houston has been prominent since the first oil well was discovered, and each fresh development since then has added to its importance. The Beaumont, Batson, Sour Lake and Humble fields are so near that it was natural that they should have at once, become tributary to Houston. They formed the nucleus, a great one too, for a business which has steadily increased and yet gives promise of greater things in the future, since now all oil industries logically tend to concentrate here.

But a better idea of Houston's importance can be formed from the statement that there are five large oil refineries here, thirteen oil dealers and thirty-nine producers and exporters, twenty-three of the latter being large corporations. Among the producers and exporters is the Texas Company the largest independent oil company in the United States, having a capital of $36,000,000.

Pipe-lines from all the oil fields, including those of Oklahoma, converge at Houston. The production of oil within the territory near Houston is 13,000,000 barrels annually, an output increased greatly by that of outside fields, all tributary to or controlled by Houston.

The various oil companies have now under construction several hundred miles of additional pipe-lines covering north and east Texas, which are estimated to cost something like $7,000,000.

CHAPTER XXI MUSIC AND ART

Houston's Early Development as Musical Center Due to Cultured German Citizens. High Capacity Demanded by Thursday Morning Club. City's Record on Symphony Concerts. The Treble Clef Club. The Womans Choral Club. The Houston Quartette Society. Federation of English Singing Societies of Texas. The Houston Saengerbund. The Houston Music Festival Association. Symphony Orchestras and Grand Operas. The Japanese Maid. Bands and Orchestras. Co-operative Work. Musical Critics. The Future in Music. But Few Local Artists. Hugo Schoppman. Work of Thusetan Donnellen and Edgar Mitchell. Boris Gordon's Famous Portrait. The Art League.

Houston has always enjoyed fame as a musical center, due in large measure to the fact that among the early settlers were so many intelligent, music-loving Germans. As early as 1847 there was an organized German quartette society here, and it is safe to say that at no time since then has Houston been without a musical society, composed entirely or in part of Germans or of native born German citizens. The early German settlers in Houston were, as a rule, men of refinement, education and culture who brought from the old country that great love for music, and for music of high class, for which they are justly famed. Thus the early Houstonians were brought in contact with and influenced by high-class musicians and music-lovers, and that they availed themselves of this blessing is attested by the record they have made and sustained.

The Houston Saengerbund is the oldest German musical association and also the oldest musical association of any kind in the city. It was organized in 1884, and has been in active existence ever since. This organization was largely interested and instrumental in organizing the State Saengerfest and has contributed in many ways toward creating interest in musical matters. It has a very large membership numbering 340 and holds weekly meetings. During the winter months it gives numerous instrumental and vocal concerts, complimentary to its members and friends. It is one of the most influential bodies in musical circles and has done much for the advancement of the highest order of music in Houston. The present officers are: Albrecht Hellbergi, president; W. J. Kohlhauff, vice-president; Anton Brunner, treasurer, and V. Juenger, secretary. C. C. Leib is the capable director.

The German-American citizens have sustained the high standard which their fathers set, but they no longer have a monopoly in that delightful field, for the native Americans have become dangerous competitors and rivals.

Though the early musicians of Houston had in view no other object than to bring music-loving people together for mutual pleasure and enjoyment, and had no intention or desire to pose as teachers or to do aught that might increase or develop, except incidentally, musical talent as it existed, their successors went a bit further and while they did everything to educate and improve the public taste by giving the best music only, they also organized a society which created a higher and broader appreciation of music among the musicians themselves. This association was called the Thursday Morning Musical Club.

This club was organized by the leading professionals and best amateurs, on May 25, 1908. The objects were the study and practice of music and the promotion of a higher standard of musical taste and culture in Houston. Mrs. Robert L. Cox was elected president; Miss Blanche O'Donnell, vice-president; Mr. Fred Dexter, secretary and treasurer; Miss Mary Elizabeth Rouse, chairman of the program committee; Mrs. E. B. Parker, chairman of the board of examiners.

The course of study selected for the first season will give a fair idea of the high aims of this club and will at the same time indicate in a measure its radical departure from the methods of most musical clubs. It included the study of Early and Modern Italian Composers, Early and Modern French Composers, Celebration of the Birth of Beethoven, December 17, Classic German Period, Slavonic Composers, Grieg, MacDowall, and Famous Women Composers.

A membership in this organization was evidence of high ability as a musician, since each candidate was required to pass an examination, which consists in rendering the following:

Pianists, Beethoven Sonata (two movements); four higher compositions of Chopin and Schumann; four modern classics; Vocalists, two arias from opera (singing in original language); two oratorio; four songs, selected from following composers; Schubert, Schumann, Brahms, Grieg, Strauss, Gounod, Chaminade; four songs by American composers (MacDowell, Chadwick, Mrs. Beach, Buck, Foote, Hawley); Violinists, Sonata (two movements); four classical compositions; four modern classics; Organ, Fugue (Bach preferred); four selections from Guilmant, Lemare, Widor, etc.

The following were the charter members of the Thursday Morning Musical Club: Pianists, Miss Mary Elizabeth Rouse, Miss Mary Pauline Bellinger, Miss Blanche O'Donnell, Mrs. Herbert Roberts, Mrs. E. B. Parker, Mrs. Katherine A. Lively, Mrs. I. S. Meyere, Mr. Horace Clark, Mrs. Edgar Gerhardt; Violinists, Miss Stella Root, Mrs. C. E. Oliver, Miss Grace Lindenberg; Vocalists, Mrs. B. H. Wenzel, Mrs. Baltis Allen, Mrs. Henry Balfour, Mrs. Edna McDonald, Mrs. Turner Williamson, Mrs. Robert L. Cox, Mr. Henry Balfour, Mr. Fred Dexter; Organists, Mrs. George Heinzelman, Mr. Horton Corbett.

Mrs. Robert L. Cox who was one of the originators of this club, laid a foundation for a great musical institution and had the organization been continued it would doubtless have developed into a conservatory such as will one day be established here on similar lines. After some time the organization became dormant, but may yet be revived.

The culture value of music is recognized even by those whose souls are not moved, by "a concord of sweet sounds." Houston easily ranks as the musical center of Texas, for no sister city can show an equal number of flourishing musical organizations or a record of an equal number of fine concerts, presenting celebrated artists.

Sixteen Symphony concerts were given in Houston in the month of April, 1911. This record has not been equaled in the United States.

The absence of factions, the generous spirit and the cordial cooperation of the city's professional musicians have contributed largely to the phenomenal musical growth. The daily papers have given all possible encouragement to musical endeavor. The Sunday issues devoting an entire page to music here and elsewhere.

Mrs. Wille Hutcheson, a musical critic of discrimination, has made the upbuilding of music in Houston her life work. To her, belongs unstinted praise for her loyalty to local musicians, who have found her ever ready to commend worthy effort and "to faults a little blind."

Houston is the possessor of many fine instructors in the various branches of music. The foundation for a solid substantial musical education may be laid here. The students of music, guided by their wisdom have come to know and understand the serious study of music, as an art, and not a shallow accomplishment. The churches pay marked attention to the music whereby their services are enriched and rendered more inspiring. "Musicales" have been a favorite method of entertaining during the social seasons.

Of the many fine music clubs and organizations to promote music, the Treble Clef Club, as the oldest local American Society surviving, points to sixteen years of honest effort, with many discouragements in its pioneer work, and to its growth up to the present time, when the sweet and luscious fruit of success is enjoyed. The following is a sketch of this organization, which is interesting and illuminating as to the musical conditions that have prevailed at various stages of Houstons musical development:

On April 18, 1896, a number of Houston ladies met to discuss the formation of a singing society, to be composed of women's voices, resulting in organization, with the following officers, who promoted the growth of the same: Mrs. J. O. Carr, president; Mrs. Giraud, treasurer; Miss Campbell, secretary; Mr. W. S. Mason, musical director.

The organization was first known as the Ladies' Singing Club, which it was found expedient to change to Treble Clef Club, as complications arose through another club having a similar name.

Under the inspiring direction of Mr. W. S. Mason, the club prospered and concerts of a high artistic standard were given, notwithstanding the difficult environment incident to pioneer musical work.

Mr. Mason's removal from Houston in 1898 called Mr. R. B. Savage to the post of director. After two successful seasons, when the Treble Clef concerts had become the musical events of the city, upon Mr. Savage's departure, Mr. Fred Dexter became director for one season. At the close of his term the club was without a leader for several seasons, suspending active work.

Mrs. W. C. Munger became president in 1898, which office she still fills. Through her indomitable will and energy, the club resumed work the season of 1904, with Mrs. Vina Avery-Beck-with as director, rapidly attaining its former prestige as a choral body. After two seasons of excellent work, Mrs. Beckwith left Houston, succeeded by Mr. Horton Corbett, who resigned the post in January, 1908. Mrs. Robert L. Cox was immediately elected to the vacant office, carrying the club through the interrupted season to a brilliant close at the final concert in April.

In Mrs. Cox the Treble Clef Club has a musical director, whose musicianship and business sagacity seem equally matched.

The singing of the club members, whose number has grown under her leadership from 23 voices to 75, is a popular feature of their concerts. Financially they have attained the enviable position of ending their season with a handsome balance in the treasury. The following artists have appeared as soloists with the Treble Clef Club since Mrs. Cox assumed the directorship: Madame Schumann-Heink, Mme. Jeanne Jomelli, Mme. Mariska Aldrich, Mme. Hissem de Moss, Alexander Petschnikoff, Mme. Charlotte Maconda, Miss Alice Sovereign, Miss Myrtle Elvyn, Mr. Frank La Forge, Mme. Bernice de Pasquali, Mr. Rudolph Ganz, Mr. Oscar Seagle, Mr. Francis MacMillen.

The associate membership numbered six hundred and seventy-two in the season of 1910–11. The closing concert called out an audience of over four thousand people. To the glory of the Treble Clef Club let it be said, no pledge has been unredeemed, no contract broken, during the sixteen years since its organization.

The following are the officers chosen for the season of 1911–12:

Mrs. Robert L. Cox, musical director; Mrs. N. C. Munger, honorary president; Mrs. George W. Heinzelman, president; Mrs. C. H. Dorman, first vice-president; Mrs. W. D. Hume, second vice-president; Mrs. Charles D. Crawford, secretary; Miss Gertrude Rolle, treasurer; Mrs. T. C. Rowe, librarian; Mr. Sam T. Swinford, club accompanist.

The Womans' Choral Club was organized in November, 1901. Mrs. Whille Hutcheson, who is intimately connected with all that is musical in Houston, was its first president, but after organizing and getting the club well on its feet, she was forced to resign because of the demands made on her as a newspaper worker. Miss Mary Carson Kidd was the first musical director, but went abroad for study and was succeeded by Mrs. E. B. Parker.

The club has brought many artists here and has given three concerts each year, the mid-winter concert being the grand affair and the only one, for admission to which tickets are sold, the other two being complimentary to the associate members.

The club has an active membership of fifty. Its present officers are: Mrs. Turner Williamson, president; Mrs. W. M. Abbey, vice-president; Mrs. Horace Booth, secretary, and Mr. Hu T. Huffmaster, director.

The Houston Quartette Society is the oldest surviving English singing society of men in Houston, having been organized by the late D. D. Bryan, Joseph Taylor and James Giraud, in August, 1900. It was the intention of these gentlemen to build up a permanent organization from the remnants of the Houston Glee Club, the Houston Quartette Club and the half dozen or more musical associations and organizations that had been formed from time to time and then had been allowed to die.

Mr. Fred Dexter was chosen as musical director. He entered on the discharge of his onerous duties with energy and zeal and it is largely to his splendid efforts that the great success of the society is due.

It was decided at the first meeting that the organization should use its utmost influence and endeavor to bring the best musical talent to the city, and to that end an associate membership was formed. Many artists of reputation have appeared under the auspices of the society.

To the Society belongs the honor of having created the Federation of English Singing Societies of Texas. This federation was formed in the fall of 1903, by Mr. D. D. Bryan, the president, and Mr. Fred F. Dexter, the musical director of the Quartette Society. In order to gather the presidents and musical directors of the various singing societies of the state, they were invited to attend as guests of the Houston society, a concert of the Houston Quartette Society, at which Mme. Schumann-Heinck was the attraction, and to attend a meeting at the Rice Hotel the next morning to discuss the question of federation. There was a large attendance of English singing societies and the state federation was formed. The two first state festivals were held in Houston, those of 1904 and 1905, the attractions being a grand chorus of 400 voices from over the state, and the Damrosch and Pittsburgh orchestras.

The Quartette Society has done a work of untold value for moral and social life in Houston, and it is principally through its accomplishments that Houston now occupies such a prominent position in the musical world. It has about fifty singers, including the best male voices in Houston.

The first president was Dudley Bryan, and the first musical director was R. B. Savage. Mr. Bryan was the president continuously for several years until his death, when Mr. W. H. Hurley was elected, and he was succeeded by Mr. B. A. Randolph, who, in turn, was followed by Mr. Ward D. Hume, De

E. Clinton Murray, Mr. Hohn Charles Harris, Mr. Nelson C. Munger, and Mr. George W. Hurd, who is the present incumbent.

Mr. Fred T. Dexter succeeded Mr. R. B. Savage as Musical director and held that position for several years. Mr. Hu. T. Huffmaster took up the musical directorship three years ago and is the present conductor.

The Quartette Society was the first local club to establish an associate membership for the purpose of bringing outside artists to Houston, giving a fixed number of concerts during the season.

The following world-renowned artists have appeared with the Houston Quartette Society: Nordica, Gadski, Schumann-Heinck, Ellen Beach Yaw, Companari, Suzanne Adams, Eugene Cowles, Leonora Jackson, Beresford, David Bispham, Charles Clark and Evan Williams. Many other noted artists have also appeared under the club auspices.

The active members are as follows: First Tenors—Joe Brukmuller, E. J. Daly, Lee Dawson, J. C. Dionne, Geo. E. Doscher, James Girand, A. H. Hensch, C. C. Henry, Adair Lockman, D. E. Simmons; Second Tenors—James H. Adair, Jr., A. Alban, H. A. Arnold, Jr., R. T. Giraud, A. W. Hart, H. A. Story, Dr. C. W. Hoeflich, N. C. Munger, Jr., L. E. Norton, E. E. Reed, N. R. Rushmore, Fred L. Toombs, H. J. L. Toombs; First Bassos—L. A. Blanchard, F. S. K. Clemens, R. G. Dawson, John W. Graham, D. R. Hodges, W. H. Hogue, George W. Hurd, John McCleary, C. R. Munger, George B. Meyer, Charles W. Soby, Ira J. Weigle; Second Bassos—C. W. Bocock, H. F. Bohmfolk, A. P. Burr, C. H. Dorman, C. E. Girton, C. Grunewald, J. Kennedy, N. C. Munger, Sr., S. R. Pickens, George M. Woodward, Edwin S. Woodhead, G. B. Hopper, T. Howen and Hohn Bridge.

The officers and directors of the Houston Quartette Society for the season of 1911–12 are as follows: C. W. Hurd, president; Jno. W. Graham, vice-president; H. F. Bohmfalk, treasurer; S. R. Pickens, financial secretary; F. L. Toombs, corresponding secretary; F. S. K. Clemens, librarian; Nelson C. Munger, Ward D. Hume, and H. F. MacGregor.

The Houston Quartette Society and the Womans' Choral Club amalgamated in 1911.

The formation of the Houston Music Festival Association was due to a conference between a few music loving citizens and Mr. Beach, manager of the Chicago Symphony Orchestra in the parlors of the Rice Hotel early in March, 1907. Nothing was done at that meeting, but a few days after, another meeting was held and a permanent organization was effected. The officers chosen were: A. S. Cleveland, president; Dr. Henry Barnstein, first vice-president; W. D. Hume, second vice-president; and S. A. Kincaid, secretary and treasurer. At that meeting the Chicago Orchestra was engaged to come to Houston, April 27, and 28.

Mr. Douglass Powell agreed to act as musical director and undertook to train a chorus of several hundred voices for the occasion, though the time was very short for such an undertaking. Miss Bessie Hughes promised a chorus of five hundred children's voices. Mrs. R. L. Cox personally interviewed representatives of the different singing clubs and, of course, aroused their interest. Mrs. Wille Hutcheson and Miss Arlette Cranford did much to interest the public.

The orchestra was the Chicago Symphony Orchestra, Adolph Rosenbecker, conductor. This orchestra returned for the 1909 festival, when Mr. Jules Albert Jahn conducted the chorus. In 1910 there were orchestral concerts only, furnished by the Damrosch Orchestra. In May, 1911, the Damrosch Orchestra returned, and there was a massed chorus conducted by Hu T. Huffmaster. All of these festival choruses were conducted in a masterful way, and too much cannot be said of the faithful, hard, effective work of the members of the choruses.

The association now has a membership of five hundred. Its officers are: W. D. Hume, president; Dr. H. Barnstein, first vice-president; Dr. E. O. Lovett, second vice-president; J. C. Bering, third vice-president; Guy MacLaughlen, secretary-treasurer; Wm. M. Rice, P. W. Horn, Abe M. Levy, John McClellan, J. C. Harris, David Daly and George Torrey, directors. The able business methods of the secretary, Guy MacLaughlen have done much to give the association an assured place.

In April, 1911, Dr. W. S. Jacobs brought the Russian Symphony Orchestra here for a series of ten concerts, affording the music lovers of Houston the greatest feast of music they have ever had in this city. A repetition is earnestly hoped for.

Other organizations that have helped Houston musically during the past ten years are the Houston Symphony Club, E. Lindenberg, director, which helped to create a demand for orchestral music, and the Girls' Musical Club, which has its strongest life yet to come.

On the night of November 1, 1901, the Metropolitan Grand Opera Company of New York gave a grand performance of "Lohengrin" at the old auditorium. This organization was brought here by D. D. Bryan, James A. Giraud and H. D. Lea. These gentlemen achieved a great success with a large undertaking.

During the succeeding ten years there have been other wonderful operatic performances. The Metropolitan Opera Company has produced "Parsifal," "La Boheme" and others; the Savage Opera Company has given "Madame Butterfly," Wagner and Verdi operas, and others. Musical attractions have appeared under the auspices of the Prince Theatre, and artists have been brought here by individuals. Mr. C. E. Oliver has brought Gabrilowitsch, Sembrich and Bonci. Miss Alice MacFarland has brought Liza Lehmann and her company; also John Barnes Wells, Alexander Russell, Paulo Gruppe, and she has managed other concerts.

One of the most brilliant musical events in Houston was the opera, "The Japanese Maid," that was produced in Houston in October, 1911, by some fifty girls, the pupils of Mrs. Edna McDonald, under the supervision and stage management of Mrs. McDonald, who had constructed the opera out of fragmentary materials, planned the stage setting and pictures, and drilled the girls. Mrs. McDonald has rank as one of the most gifted musicians of Houston and was a pupil of Madame Gadski in Berlin and was at one time under engagement with Henry W. Savage to sing a leading role in one of his operas.

It would be a hopeless task to attempt to recount all that individuals have done for Houston's musical culture as so many club presidents, officials, directors, and business men and women have borne so large a part. Houston has many capable teachers in every branch of music. Mrs. Robert L. Cox, Mrs. Edna McDonald and Mr. Anton Diehl conduct what are in fact conservatories. There are several first-class bands and orchestras prominent among them being the Herb and Lewis band and the Thayers and Beckers Orchestras and the Majestic Orchestra.

Many of the churches have fine pipe organs and paid musical directors of choirs.

The Houston Choral Club and the Houston Quartette Society having amalgamated in 1911, make a strong composite organization for the winter season of 1911–12.

The theatrical managers often present musical attractions of note, usually light opera but occasionally grand opera such as Bessie Abbots engagement in 1911, when La Boheme and Madame Butterfly were sung.

Among those who have accomplished great good by musical criticism are, Mrs. Wille Hutcheson, Miss Arlette Cranford, Mr. Sam T. Swinford, Jr., Mr. James Dow, and Miss Alice McFarlane the last three named being themselves musicians of distinction. There would be an imposing list of those who have once lived in Houston and have gone out from this city to attain distinction in the world of music but these have not done so much for the musical development of the city, which is the real theme of this chapter as have the men and women who have labored at home.

Judged by the appreciation of symphony concerts, by the work of musical directors and massed choruses, by home soloists, concert artists, orchestras and bands, by church singers, by capable teachers, and by the growing demand for the highest order of musical attractions there is every reason to predict a brilliant musical future for Houston.

Houston has produced great physicians, great lawyers, great financiers and great statesmen, but never great artists. There have been one or two rather good painters, but never one who attracted attention beyond the circle of his immediate friends and acquaintances. There might have been an exception to this and Houston might have possessed a great painter, had not fate determined otherwise. There was a young artist who came to Houston in 1856, who, had he lived, would have unquestionably impressed his genius on this community. This was Hugo Schopmann, a young German, who had been graduated at one of the great art schools of Germany. He had artistic talent of the highest order, was a man of independent means and followed art for arts sake alone. He devoted himself to landscape painting, though, simply for the pleasure he took in doing so, he painted one or two portraits of his friends which were justly admired by all who saw them. He was highly educated and a man of great refinement and had he lived, his influence on this community would have certainly been great. Unfortunately he was among the first victims of the yellow fever epidemic of 1858.

The only native Houstonian who ever achieved fame as an artist was Thusetan Donellan. His was a peculiar case. It seems unjust to him to exclude him from the roster of artists and at the same time unjust to art to include him. He was almost without education of any kind; had never seen a picture greater than those produced by scene painters; knew nothing of paints and pigments; in brief, he was as ignorant of art as an Indian. And yet he had moments of inspiration when he would produce wonderful pictures. He would paint picture after picture all so badly drawn, illy proportioned and so badly done that to call them daubs would be flattery, and would then begin and finish a portrait or landscape that would be something of a masterpiece. In his moments of inspiration he would work like a friend, taking time, neither for food, sleep nor rest until his task was accomplished. He was a musical genius also and could play on all instruments, although he knew no more of the science of music than he did of art. He was justly famous for his violin playing, having a wonderful sweet touch. When he was young, the citizens raised a purse and wanted to send him away to be educated, but he had too much vanity to permit him to think that he could be taught anything and he refused the offer. When he was about twenty-three years old he painted one of the finest portraits of Sam Houston that has ever been produced. It was really a work of art and was purchased by the state or one of the departments and is now in Austin. With only a small miniature to guide him, he painted a life-size portrait of the wife of a Houston banker, that was marvelously good and which would have reflected credit on any artist. And yet, with all this, the vast bulk of his work would have been unworthy of a second-class sign painter. He died several years ago.

Another young artist of an entirely different type, was Edgar Mitchell, a young man who came to Houston from Virginia in 1880. He was not a professional artist, but was a very talented amateur. He was about twenty-two years old, but even at that age the grim reaper had marked him for its own and he died of lung trouble a year or two after his arrival here. Had he lived he would have accomplished something in the field of art for he had talent of high order. One or two of his productions are still preserved by his friends. One of his best paintings is owned by the Houston Light Guard and adorns their armory.

Houston is the domicile of a portrait painter of note whose work sometimes reaches up to the standard of genius and always proclaims him a clever and talented artist. He is a Russian by nativity, a pupil of Verestchagin and other world-famed painters, and has made Houston his headquarters since 1906. This artist is Boris Bernhardt Gordon. His most notable portrait is that of Dr. B. H. Carroll, Sr., president of the Southwestern Baptist Theological Seminary, but he has also painted greatly admired portraits of William M. Rice, the donor of the Rice Institute and of Mrs. Rice, both of which will hang in the administration building of the William M. Rice Institute, of Governors Lanham, Campbell and several other chief executives of Texas and a famous portrait of Sam Houston. More than two score of the notable men and women of Texas have been painted by Mr. Gordon, whose work is both artistically praiseworthy in high degree and commercially successful.

The greatest and most promising work, having for its object the creation and development of artistic taste and talent, is that being done by the Art League. This is an association of ladies who have undertaken to instill into the minds of the children of Houston a love and discriminating taste for the artistic and beautiful. Those children who have talent are given facility and encouragement to develop it. At stated periods there are lectures on painting and sculpture; great works of art are described and their beauty pointed out. When possible, good pictures and statuary are shown and described in detail so that the children may learn something of the rudiments of art. Drawing and painting, both in oil and water colors are taught in the school and encouragement is held out to the pupils by assuring them that their best productions will have place in the art exhibit, at which time the best works of the school are shown to the public.

The work being done by the Art League is destined to produce happy results for even though it produce no great artist in the future, it will have instilled into the minds of the rising generation a love for the beautiful and artistic that cannot fail to have a beneficial effect on the community at large.

Houston has two good engraving companies, the Texas Engraving Company and the Star Engraving Company, each of which turns out a high grade of commercial art in designing and engraving. Sam B. Kaiser has achieved success along similar lines and as a cartoonist and Bert Blessington, the Post's cartoonist and artist has made the public fully familiar with his work. H. C. Norfleet does good work on similar lines, and Will Allen, once of Houston, has attained success in New York as a pen and ink artist.

CHAPTER XXII HOUSTON'S PUBLIC BUILDINGS

City's Early Court-Houses and Jails. The New County Court House. Present County and City Jails. A Peripatetic Post Office. The New Federal Building. The Viaduct. The City Market House. The New Auditorium. The City Fire Stations.

A small log cabin for a court house, a couple of tables under an awning for a market, a back room in a small country store for a post office. These were the places where the first affairs of Houston and Harris County were looked after in the early days. The first grand jury met behind a screen of bushes under a big tree. At the same time the Congress of the Republic of Texas was in session in a rough wooden structure on the site of the present Rice Hotel.

It was in 1838, while Harris County was still called Harrisburg County, that the first court house was erected. This court house was located on the corner of Congress Avenue and San Jacinto Street and faced Congress Avenue. It was constructed of pine logs and was in two parts, under one roof, separated by a gallery. Each of the two rooms was about sixteen feet square, and the gallery was ten feet wide. In the rear were two small rooms, about ten feet square, which were used by the county and district clerks.

The first jail as already narrated, was equally as primitive, being constructed of heavy logs, hewn and mortised and was practically a big box, having neither doors nor windows. There was a hole in the roof and a prisoner passed into the jail through the hole, down a ladder and then the ladder was withdrawn. There was no way to escape except by cutting through the thick log walls. The jail was located at the corner of Congress Avenue and Fannin Street and was surrounded by a high board fence. Near the jail was a curfew bell which warned all negroes of the streets at 9 p.m. This bell was also used to sound fire alarms.

The first brick court house was built in 1850, and was located about the middle of the block. It was two stories high and had a cupalo. It had four entrances and was a small and cheap concern, costing only $15,000, but was considered a grand structure in those days.

The second brick court house was erected in 1859 and was built near and fronting Congress Avenue. This building was practically a three-story structure, having a large basement, used to store records and such documents. This house, becoming unsafe, was torn down and a larger one of similar design was built nearly on the same site in 1869. An item of interest connected with the building that was torn down is the fact that much of the brick and other suitable material was purchased by Rev. Father Querat and used in the construction of the Church of the Annunciation on Texas Avenue.

A third brick court house was erected in 1882, and was placed farther back nearer the center of the block than its two predecessors. It was quite an imposing structure, superior in every way to the two that had preceded it. It stood longer, too, but was torn down in 1908 to give place to the present magnificent building.

An election was held April 22, 1907, and the county was authorized to issue $1,000,000 in bonds for the purpose of building a new court house and building county roads. The money was to be divided equally between the roads and court house.

So soon as the necessary legal preliminaries could be taken, the contract for the new court house was let and work was begun. The contract was a large one, and a large sum of money was involved, but at no stage of the movement, from the moment that it was decided to erect the building until it was completed and thrown open to the public, was there a hint of "graft" or other dishonesty, connected with it. The building cost, in round figures, $450,000 unfurnished, and a glance over it will convince anyone that the people got full value for every dollar they paid for it. It is no exaggeration to say that the Harris County court house is a superb building. It is built of Texas granite, St. Louis hydraulic pressed brick, marble, structural steel, bronze and terra cotta, and it is one of the handsomest buildings to be found anywhere. It is almost square, and is two hundred feet high from the base to the dome. It is of beautiful architecture. The large columns are of solid granite and have Corinthian capitals. There are four broad flights of granite stairs, one on each of the sides of the building, leading to the second story, where are located the various county offices. The basement is used as offices for the justices of peace and for other purposes. The higher courts are located on the third floor. Everything is admirably arranged for the comfort and convenience of the occupants. The interior finish is in every way in keeping with the beautiful exterior, and on the whole Harris County has reason to be proud of its court house.

At the unoccupied corners of the block are neatly kept grass plots, and surrounding the whole block is a low granite wall. Rows of beautiful oak trees border all four sides of the block within the granite wall. Those at the four corners are much larger than the others. The reason for this is that they were planted by Mr. J. R. Morris, over a quarter of a century ago. He planted them with his own hands, saying that he put them there to serve as his monument and cause people to think of him some time when they rested under their shade. The entrance which is most used is that on Fannin Street.

The Harris County court house will meet all demands that are likely to be made on it for many years to come.

The court house was formally dedicated on Texas Independence Day, March 2, 1911. The ceremonies were very elaborate and impressive. Judge Wm. P. Hamblen, dean of the Harris County bar, was unable to be present on account of his illness, which terminated in his death three months later. In a letter to the committee on arrangement, he said:

"Allow me to say that it would please me to be able to congratulate our people personally upon the completion of such a handsome structure as we have reared for the accommodation of our courts. At the time of the founding of Houston, 1836, I doubt if there was in the United States a building that would compare in architectural beauty and mechanical embellishments with our court house. So far as I am concerned, having lived in that day, I know of none; and such a building now, in this day, for a community like Houston, is an embellishment of which all citizens should be proud. Moreover and especially have our people a right to congratulate themselves upon the uniform integrity of those who have occupied judicial positions in Harris County since the beginning of our history. There has not been in all this time one suspicion of wrong doing by any of the judicial officers of this county."

When the city built its first market house it erected a two-story building on the Congress Avenue side of the building which was a combination city hall and city jail. This was used by the county for a number of years as a jail. Finally, in the late fifties, the county erected a jail of its own, using for that purpose a lot on the northeast corner of Preston Avenue and Caroline Street opposite where the present police station now stands. This old jail was a small affair. It was built of brick and was two stories high, though the stories were so low that the building had the appearance of being scarcely more than one story high. The small windows and doors were grated but in no other way was it a stronghold. For a time it did very well for the purpose for which it was designed, but crime in Houston soon outgrew it and it became something of an outrage on humanity and decency. It had only six cells, each 10 by 12 feet and a ceiling only 9 1/2 feet high. In 1876 the Telegram denounced this Calcutta black hole and stated that there were thirty-nine prisoners confined in those six little cells. At the same time the Telegram stated that the Harris County Commissioner's Court was trying to get permission from the legislature to build a jail, as it was necessary at that time, for counties to secure authority from the legislature, there being no general law authorizing counties to construct jails, or make similar improvements.

The editorial in the Telegram evidently stirred the commissioners into action, for the construction of a new jail was begun early in 1879, and the building was completed and turned over to the county authorities in March, 1880. It was located just across the street from the old jail on the southeast corner of Preston Avenue and Caroline Street. The architect and superintendent of construction, Eugine T. Heiner, stated in his final report that the construction had cost $33,993. It was two stories high and was more modern and up-to-date than any similar structure in the state at that time. The exterior was of Philadelphia pressed brick. The interior was divided into two sections, the jail proper, containing fourteen iron cells or cages, each 7 by 10 feet, and the annex portion containing departments for women, invalid prisoners and juvenile offenders, jailor's room, sheriff's office, reception chamber and cloak room. These were all in the front part of the building occupying all the ground floor, and also part of the second story. Each room was supplied with gas, water and up-to-that-date conveniences. While the interior of the structure was ornamented with tile flooring and marble mantles, handsome chandeliers, etc., its security of structure with supplementary doors to its massive iron cages, was in striking contrast with the delicacy of its finish. The jail proper was all iron cage work, the floors between the first and second stories around the cages being of perforated iron. The cells could be locked or unlocked singly or simultaneously by a lever device. Besides, each cell door had an independent lock. Water could be thrown through the entire system of cells.

On a frontal tablet was the following inscription: C. Anson Jones, county judge; O. C. Mulligan and James Harrington, commissioners and building committee; Eugine T. Heiner, architect; Campbell & Grainger, builders.

That jail, as large and modern as it was, soon became too small. Then, too, that part of the city where it was located had several residents who objected strenuously to having a jail, where executions took place occasionally, so near them. It may be stated here that the attic of the jail was so arranged that it could be used as a place of execution and that it was actually used for that purpose two or three times. Public opinion was aroused against having the jail in that location and finally, in 1891, the commissioners court determined to purchase a new site and erect a new and yet more modern jail. The block of ground at the foot of Capitol Avenue was purchased and a large jail was constructed on it. The building is nearly twenty years old. For some years the Criminal District Court held its sessions there, a large court room being one of the features of the building. When the new court house was completed the Criminal Court was moved to it and since then the building has been used for jail purposes only. The cost of the ground and building was $150,000. Efforts were begun in 1911 to secure a larger and more adequate building.

Soon after the completion of the present jail, the city purchased the old jail and converted it into police headquarters, and city lock-up. On the second floor is located the city court which holds two sessions each day.

Prior to 1890, the Houston post-office was something of a peripatetic affair being moved here and there to suit the convenience of the postmaster. During the days of the Texas Republic, a man by the name of Snell was postmaster, and he located the post-office on the west side of Main Street, between Preston and Congress Avenues, in a small frame building that was about the middle of the block. After Texas became a state, a new postmaster was appointed and he removed the office down to what was called the

Mansion House, on the northeast corner of Travis and Franklin, where the Southern Pacific Building is now located. The next postmaster moved the office to the corner of Main and Preston, where the Fox Building now stands. The next move was to the northeast corner of Fannin and Congress. The post-office remained there for several years and was finally moved across the street to the northwest corner. From here it was moved to the rear of the Fox Building on Preston Avenue, near the little alley on that block. Its next move was to the Miller Building on the southeast corner of the same block. It remained there only a short time, being removed to the Taylor Building on the southwest corner of Preston and San Jacinto, where it remained until 1890, when it was removed into its own building on the southeast corner of Fannin and Franklin. In 1888, Congress had appropriated $75,000 for the purpose of building a post-office at Houston and later added $15,000. With this a site was purchased and a building erected which was completed and occupied in 1890. In a short time the building was found to be totally inadequate for the needs of the city and substations had to be established. Ten years later Postmaster Strong declared that he needed five times as much space as was at his command. He made strong representation of his pressing need for more facilities, with the result that a commission was sent here from Washington, and, in 1903, a block of ground between Rusk and Capitol Avenues and Caroline and San Jacinto Streets, was purchased for $120,000 for the purpose of erecting a post-office and Federal Court building on it. There were several appropriations made and there were also many changes in plans until finally, in 1908, the appropriation was definitely fixed at $400,000. Advertisements calling for bids for the work were published in May, 1908. The building was to be erected on Federal Square and was to be three stories high, and 170 by 121 feet in area, with quarters not only for the post-office but for the Federal Court and all Federal officials as well. The building was not yet completed in September, 1911, and in the meantime the business of Houston had increased so wonderfully and rapidly that, it is said, when the building is completed, which will be by January, 1912, it will be necessary to retain the substations, there not being room enough in the new building to handle all the mail.

The new building, while not completed, is practically so, needing only the finishing touches. It fronts 167 feet on San Jacinto Street and has a depth of 120 feet. Its architecture is massive, being a compromise of the Doric with more modern forms. It is ornamented with marble balustrades and handsome entrances and at various points are ornaments in harmony with the general construction and design of the structure.

The approaches to the building have been made part of the general design. There are walks and grass-plots in front and a broad driveway in the rear. All of this has been worked out in concrete, the entire block being covered with the same material with the exception of the spaces left for grass plots.

To show the wonderful increase in the post-office business at Houston during the last ten years, the following statement is given:

YEAR	RECEIPTS	INCREASE	PER CENT
1901	$118,180.93		
1902	143,730.92	$25,549.99	22
1903	168,514.78	24,783.86	17
1904	194,102.44	25,587.66	15
1905	210,456.34	16,353.90	08
1906	230,410.13	19,953.79	10
1907	279,513.11	49,102.98	21
1908	302,721.95	23,208.84	08
1909	340,090.54	37,368.59	12
1910	400,880.21	60,789.67	18
1911	454,316.44	53,536.23	13

The building is exclusively for the use of Federal officials, the lower floor being devoted entirely to the use of the post-office department. There is a main corridor on this floor running the entire length of the building, with an electric elevator at each end. This corridor is beautifully finished in oak and marble. The postmaster and his assistants have offices on this floor, where also are located the working departments of the post-office. The judicial departments are located on the second floor. There are several court rooms, and offices, clerks' rooms and a law library. There are also the offices of the several court officials such as attorney and marshal, and the jury rooms.

On the third floor are the railroad mail department, internal revenue, civil service, army and navy recruiting offices and the offices of the attaches of the agricultural department.

From the beginning of construction the government has had a supervising architect here and every detail of work has been carefully inspected.

Another great public work that has just been started, is the viaduct, connecting the south side of the city with the Fifth ward. This is a magnificent piece of engineering work, and when completed its benefits to the whole city, and the Fifth ward, particularly, will be very great. Work has commenced at the south end of the viaduct, at the junction of Main Street and Commerce Avenue. The structure will extend over Buffalo Bayou, and to the west of the mouth of White Oak Bayou and will cross that stream further on and extend far into the Fifth ward to a point on Montgomery Avenue. The length of the viaduct is to be 1,500 feet and its width sixty feet. It is of steel and concrete and when completed it will be one of the finest structures of its kind in the country. Its estimated cost is $600,000. It is the intention of the city to prosecute work rapidly so as to complete the viaduct as quickly as possible, for the need for it is very great. When completed all that part of the city lying north of White Oak Bayou will be brought into rapid and easy communication with the south side.

The story of Houston's market houses has been told elsewhere in these pages. There have been three or four, the two last, preceding the present one, having been destroyed by fire. The present market house is a combination of market house and city hall. It is on the same location as its immediate predecessors but is, in every way, superior to them. The building is an imposing structure and with its two lofty towers has become a familiar landmark of Houston.

The ground floor is given over entirely to market purposes, while the offices of the heads of the various city departments, and the city council chamber are located on the second floor. In the center, facing Travis Street, is the entrance of concrete, below and between the two towers. The second story walls are faced in hydraulic brick with concrete trimmings. The large roof is of slate. In the higher of the two towers is a clock with a dial eight feet in diameter. The bell that strikes the hours and half hours, was cast for the city in 1876, has passed through two fires and consequently has sounded its own downfall on two occasions, and is still as serviceable as when it was placed in the first tower. The interior of the building is finished in natural pine. In the central portion of each tower, stairways rise to halls that lead to a broad hall running parallel with Travis Street and on either side of the main and entrance halls are offices, while at the Preston Avenue end of the building is the large council chamber, whose walls are decorated with pictures of as many of the mayors of Houston as it was possible to get.

The building is heated with steam and has electric lights, it is not only a beautiful building but it is a very useful and convenient one. Messrs. Geo. E. Dickey & Co., were the architects and Thomas Lucas was the contractor who built it.

Houston is proud of her public buildings and has a right to be, for there are none finer in any Southern city and few superior anywhere.

The present city administration has accomplished much good in many ways, but it is doubtful if it could have done more to advertise Houston and bring its name before the country, than by erecting the auditorium. This is an advertising age and cities as well as firms and individuals must do all in their power to keep in the lime-light or be content to occupy a place behind their more progressive competitors. The Houston auditorium stands as the highest type of best advertising, and more than this it is really a fine business investment on the part of the city, for it is evident that one or two great conventions attracted here by it, will leave in the city almost as much money as the enterprise cost. This money is left with the people who are the real owners of the auditorium, for it was built with the city's money.

After 1900 the growth of Houston was so rapid and the city was so often called on to entertain large conventions that it became evident that provision must be made for the proper care of these. Houston's position as the great railroad center of the state made it the natural convention center, and the demands on its hospitality were growing. Recognizing that action must be taken to meet this demand, the citizens determined to enlist the city administration in a movement having in view the erection of a large auditorium, ample enough to accommodate the largest body that might choose to come here. The great importance of the building was recognized by the commissioners, but they were determined that it should be constructed out of current funds of the city; that no bonds or anything of that sort should be issued and that when completed the building should be absolutely free from debt. The attitude of the commission met with public favor and indorsement, and on March 1, 1910, work was commenced on the building and it was nearly completed when it was dedicated to public righteousness by Rev. Dr. R. C. Buckner, November 19, 1910, at the formal opening of the Baptist General Convention of Texas, the first convention to hold its session in the new building.

Mayor Rice was present and explained that the formal dedication would not take place until the building was absolutely completed. The building is one of the largest and finest auditoriums in the Southwest. It cost the city $235,000, and was a cash transaction, not a dollar being owed on it when it was completed and turned over to the city.

The building was planned after a committee of citizens had visited many leading cities and inspected auditoriums and large public balls. All the good features of these were noted, and it was upon the recommendations of this committee that the architects drew their plans. The result was the present superb building which is more perfect and better fitted for its purposes than any similar building in the country. It is located between Milam and Louisiana Streets and Texas and Capitol Avenues, covering the greater part of the block. It is constructed of pressed brick with Bedford stone trimmings. There are entrances on Texas, Louisiana and Capitol Avenues, with a driveway extending underneath the building from Capitol to Texas Avenues. The building fronts 250 feet on Louisiana Street and 150 feet on Texas and Capitol Avenues. In addition to the main entrance there are a number of small entrances, by means of which the building may be emptied in a few moments. In case of a fire, the audience, even if it were large enough to fill the hall, could get out of the building before the fire department could respond to the alarm. There is little danger of fire, however, for the building is as nearly fireproof as it is possible to make it.

The main auditorium room will seat, comfortably, 7,000 persons, and the stage is one of the largest in the country. In addition to the main hall, there are several smaller assembly rooms where small conventions and committees can meet.

The Central Fire Station at the corner of San Jacinto and Texas Avenue is said to be one of the most useful buildings of its kind in the South. It cost only $30,000 but it is almost perfect in detail and admirably suited for the purposes for which it was designed. It is two stories high and, on the lower story, has a floor space of 10,000 square feet. It extends 100 feet on each of the streets named. Since the building was erected for practical use rather than for ornament, there is no particular architectural adornment, yet it is a handsome building, constructed of steel gray brick. There are three broad entrances on each of the streets for the entrance and exit of the fire-fighting machines, while at the rear there is a wagon entrance, so that any machine returning to the building may enter that way and be drawn forward to its usual position. The upper story is given over to offices, a dormitory, a gymnasium and bath rooms. The whole building is steam heated and lighted with electricity. The chief of the fire department and his assistant have offices on the first and second floors. The outlying fire stations are of modern and scientific construction.

CHAPTER XXIII ARCHITECTURE AND BUILDING

Tents and Log Huts Were First Buildings. Primitive American Architecture. The First Brick Houses. The First Three-Story House. The First Four-Story Hotel. The Latin Influence. The First Six-Story Office Building. Effect of Introducing the New Building Materials. Restrictions Placed by Climate on Architecture. First Eleven-Story Building. South Texas National Bank Building. The Carter Building. First National Bank Building. The Union National Bank Building. The Chronicle Building. Southwestern Telephone Building. New Union Station. Southern Pacific Office Building. The Court House and the Federal Building. Apartment Houses. The Bender Hotel. The New Rice Hotel. Architecture of the Churches. Y. M. C. A. Building. Suburban and Country Homes. The Wm. M. Rice Institute. Houston Residences. Building Permits.

The early architecture of Houston was primitive in the extreme, consisting as it did of a few tents, scarcely, if any better than those of the Indians who made their homes in the surrounding country. Then as the early Houstonians became more fixed in their location they became more ambitious and a few log cabins were erected, the first building of that kind whose record has been preserved, being the old log jail. This was merely a box made of hewn logs, and had neither doors nor windows, access to it being possible only through a hole in its top. There were other buildings before that, however, and there were at least two board constructed, single-story buildings in 1837. One was the Indian trading post near the Preston Avenue bridge, mention of which has been made elsewhere, and the other was a one-story, one-room frame house, on the southeast corner of Smith and Preston, which was purchased by Col. Nathan Fuller, and formed the nucleus for the residence he built there.

It is a remarkable fact that the first hotel in Houston, destined to shelter presidents, ministers, senators and congressmen, as well as scores of statesmen and great soldiers, should have been a log cabin, while the first storehouse should have been a pretentious frame building, both erected in 1837. In those early days "jack-leg" carpenters were in greater demand than skilled architects. Renaissance, Gothic Styles, Pompeian effects, Flemish halls and such things were, if not unknown, uncared for. All that was wanted was a house, so the architecture of that day may be described as Primitive American. The tall steel-framed building has come to be known as the distinctive American style of architecture, but it is much truer that the distinctively American style was the log cabin and the box-shaped frame house.

For several years after 1837 there were no other building materials used than hewn logs and poorly dressed planks and boards. Until 1845 there was not a brick house in the city. That year Mr. Geo. Ennis and General Nichols built two small brick houses, one on Main between Franklin and Commerce, and the other also on Main near the corner of Congress Avenue. In 1852, Mr. Paul Bremond erected a two-story brick building on Main Street, and the next year Mr. B. A. Shepherd erected a two-story brick building on the northeast corner of Main and Congress. These two buildings proved to be a little in advance of the city's requirements, however, for the second story of each was vacant for some time. These early, two-story structures established the commercial style of architecture, and for four or five years there were no more ambitious buildings than they.

Following a great fire in the winter of 1858–59, Mr. Wm. Van Alstyne erected the first three-story brick building in Houston, on the southeast corner of Main and Congress. At the same time Mr. J. R. Morris erected the first four-story, iron-front building about in the middle of the block on the east side of Main. There were several other large buildings erected about the same time, the principal one being a two-story brick erected by Mr. J. T. D. Wilson, on the northwest corner of Main and Congress. In 1859, Mr. Hutchins began the construction of the Hutchins House, the large four-story brick hotel that stood on the site of Houston's first hotel.

At this period of Houston's growth, the Latin influence, transmitted from Spain and Southern France throughout Mexico and the French colonies of the Mississippi Valley, began to impress itself on commercial as well as domestic architecture in Houston. There are still examples of this to be found here. The old stories around Market Square have in many instances the double gallery with cast-iron columns and balconies, the high decorated window openings of the old French quarters and there are a few notable examples of the low, heavy arches and undecorated walls of the Spanish type. These, with one or two ornately carved doorways, form some of the most interesting links in Houston's architectural development.

The first approach to the modern office building was in 1894 when the six-story Binz Building was erected on Main and Texas Avenue. It is a connecting link between the old Houston of the Republic of Texas and the modern great commercial and industrial Houston of today. On January 15, 1886, one of the landmarks of Houston was torn down and carted away, in ten hours. This building stood near the corner of Main Street and Texas Avenue, opposite the Rice Hotel, and was erected at the same time that the Capitol was built and served as an adjunct to that building, containing the offices of the Land Commissioner and of some other of the state officials. It was, perhaps, the third building erected in Houston, and was demolished by Mr. Jacob Binz, the owner, to make place for the Binz Building, which marked the first approach to fireproof construction by the introduction of concrete, stone and steel as building materials in Houston. Since then, wonders have been accomplished in the construction of architecturally beautiful and commercially useful buildings.

But a greater and more far-reaching change was wrought by the introduction of these new building materials. The methods of the builders and contractors were revolutionized. Before then, elements of chance and luck entered into every contract. Estimates of probable costs were based on so much material at a roughly estimated, average cost, with an added profit for the contractor. With the introduction of stone, concrete and steel, all that was changed and modern scientific methods of management became supreme. Building materials became staple articles, obtainable when, and in as large quantities, as wanted. Business stability was assured and the contractors were enabled to employ scientific methods in their undertakings. Fluctuations in the value of lumber, brick, cement and even of labor became less marked and the intelligent contractor was enabled to figure his costs on a structure involving millions of dollars, with far more accuracy than could the old contractor have done on one involving only a few thousands. The scientific builder became the successful builder who left scarcely anything to chance. The old "rule of thumb" methods were superseded by scientific planning and the careful working out of details on paper so that the costs could be properly and accurately estimated and the multitude of materials accurately manufactured, some at great distance from the site, and yet all assembled with a degree of accuracy that is the real secret of good and rapid construction.

The changes brought about in architecture were less far-reaching than were those in building, for aside from the greater opportunities for decoration and ornamentation afforded by the new material, there were other things, such as climate, which had great restrictive influence. A building however beautiful and architecturally perfect, suitable for New York or any of the other Northern cities, would be entirely out of place and unsuitable for Houston. The choice of designs has therefore been somewhat limited and excepting one or two of the public buildings, one or two apartment houses and four or five churches, small effort has been made to secure outside architectural beauty except along well known and oft-repeated lines.

The tall buildings belong to a class all their own, a type common to the whole country, but they are peculiarly adapted to a hot climate because they lift their occupants above the heat and dust of the streets, and Houston has been quick to avail herself of the advantages they offer. She now has twenty-five, ranging from six to sixteen stories in height.

The Scanlan Building, the first eleven-story building in Houston was erected on the site of another historical spot. It occupies the site of the President's Mansion when Texas was a Republic, and the Rice Hotel is now being demolished to make room, on the site of the Capitol of the Republic of Texas, for an 18-story hotel, mentioned elsewhere.

The South Texas National Bank Building stands as a monument to the art and skill of the architects and builders of Houston. Hampered and embarrassed by the fact that the proposed building would occupy an inside lot, thus affording but a limited field for accomplishment, it was imperative to employ the best possible design and to use the richest and most attractive materials. The style of architecture adopted is rather hard to describe, being a Grecian Doric with a composite combination. The front is absolutely plain, but is made very attractive by the material used, it all being of white Georgia marble. The cornices and other ornaments are carved out of solid marble, which is an unusual feature.

The four columns supporting the main pediment are turned from solid slabs of marble, the shafts of each, exclusive of base and cap, being twenty-two feet long. Only the best mechanical skill was employed in constructing this front and from the stand-point of masonry it is doubtful if the work has its equal in the South.

The interior of the building is in keeping with the beauty of its exterior. Only the finest imported marble was used in the construction of counters and columns. The ornamental bronze work is especially attractive and blends beautifully and harmoniously with its marble surroundings.

One of the most attractive features of the interior is the arched ceiling over the main lobby, which affords splendid lighting throughout the first and second stories, and at the same time creates a beautiful decorative scheme. The most skillful artists were employed in decorating the building and the results obtained by them is pleasing both in detail and as a whole.

Dallas and Waco each has a taller building than the Carter Building in Houston but neither has so complete an office building as this is. It is one of the strongest buildings in the state and is absolutely fireproof. It is a steel frame structure, sixteen stories in height, and has, in addition, a basement, storage vault floor and roof garden, making it practically a seventeen-story building. The foundation and steel frame are so constructed that five or six additional stories may be put on if desired.

There are four elevators having a speed of 600 feet per minute and provision is made for more elevators should they be needed.

The building has a frontage on Main Street of 102 feet and on Rusk Avenue of 103 feet from grade to top of parapet. The entire base course of the building is of polished Texas granite. Resting on this and extending to the top of the windows of the second story are large Bedford stone columns with architraves around the second story windows at the ends of the building of terra cotta to match the stone. The third and fourth story belts and piers are terra cotta to match the brick and stone. All the window sills and belts are ornamental terra cotta up to the fifteenth story. Kittanning brick, of uniform size and cream color, vitreous and unglazed and strictly waterproof are used on both street fronts of the building, thus giving it the same appearance from either street, and the shade of the terra cotta, stone and brick was made especially to harmonize. The sixteenth story belt course and the drop ornaments between the fifteenth and sixteenth stories are of highly ornamented terra cotta artistically modeled, the chenau to cornice being of copper and illuminated with bull's-eye electric globes.

The main basement entrances are finished with marble and bronze railings. The lobby entrance has ornamental bronze doors, sidelights and transoms, executed in bronze glazed with highly polished French plate glass, and the floor of the lobby is of marble and laid out in elaborate patterns to correspond with the design of the ceiling. The walls of the lobby entrance from the floor to a point twelve feet high are wainscoted with polished Italian and Norwegian marble, and the base, at the floor line, is polished Timos marble, and the pilasters are of green Italian marble. There are fifteen office floors each elegantly finished, having highly polished, pencil-veined Italian marble wainscoting three feet and six inches high and terrazzo and marble floors. All the offices are well lighted and ventilated and provided with electric fans, base plugs, electric lights, illuminating gas and wash basins. There are also numerous drinking fountains supplied with constantly circulating ice water.

There is a complete vacuum cleaning system all over the building. The building has its own water supply which comes from a large artesian well located in the basement and yields 300,000 gallons daily. In addition to its water supply, the building also has its own heating and electric light plants. It is owned by Mr. S. F. Carter, president of the Lumbermens National Bank.

The First National Bank Building, though only eight stories high, is unlike other tall buildings in that it has a great floor space and covers more ground than any of the others. It has a fine frontage on Main Street and extends back over half a block on Franklin Avenue. In addition to that it has an ell that extends back towards the middle of the block, thus making its ground area very great. The building itself is one of the finest in the Southwest. It is eight stories in height, the entire ground floor being devoted to banking purposes, and it is said to be the largest bank home in the South.

The building is of reinforced concrete steel frame construction and is absolutely fireproof. Its exterior is handsome, being of gray brick and terra cotta, with beautiful marble columns and tablets suitably arranged and placed. The halls and corridors are paved with inlaid tiling and marble.

The building has its own water supply, derived from a large artesian well, and also has its own electric light and heating plant. Its office equipments are complete and thorough, there being electric fans, electric lights, gas and hot and cold water in each office, while there are drinking fountains of running ice water in all the halls and corridors. The building is cleaned by the vacuum air process.

The elevator equipment is in keeping with everything in the building and represents a late and high type of electrical machinery in use for elevator service.

The twelve-story, concrete, steel, granite and brick building of the Union National Bank just completed, on the northwest corner of Congress Avenue and Main Street, is one of the most attractive and ornamental structures in the city. It is a skyscraper, but is one in name only, for it is so artistically designed and its architecture is so perfect, that it is free from that indescribable something which attaches to all isolated and excessively high buildings and leaves one with a sense of the incongruous.

The building is twelve stories high, but with the basement it is really a thirteen-story building, while the first story is of almost sufficient height to be counted as two instead of one.

The basement and ground floor are occupied by the bank itself, the basement being fitted up as elegantly as are the other floors of the building. Here are located the safety vaults, waiting rooms, ladies' and gentlemen's private rooms and everything for the comfort and convenience of the patrons of the bank.

The whole of the first or ground floor is devoted to the use of the bank. Its finish is elegant and perfect. Its decorations are of marble, bronze, brass and ornamental iron work so artistically and skillfully combined as to secure a charming effect. There is a lightness and airiness, combined with richness and stability that is very pleasing. A striking feature is the great amount of light—sunlight—that floods the place. There is not a dark corner nor a single place on the whole floor where artificial light is needed. This same thing is true of other portions of the building, for there are two broad and two narrow windows in each office admitting light and fresh air.

There are eleven stories above the ground floor, all devoted to offices, arranged singly and en suite, thus making it one of the most complete and up-to-date bank and office buildings in the country.

The building has its own artesian water supply, its own electric plant, its own heating and ventilating apparatus and is thus rendered independent of outside utilities for everything that tends to the comfort and convenience of its tenants. It is heated by steam in the winter and cooled with chilled air in the summer.

Including the ground the building cost almost exactly $1,000,000.

It is the cost of the ground rather than any desire to get up in the air that is responsible for the high buildings of today.

The Houston Chronicle's skyscraper affords a splendid illustration of the truth of this. The paper needed for its own use a building of at least three stories in height. For its press-room, store-room, composing room, and offices for its various departments such a building was an absolute necessity. A suitable three-story building would cost about $150,000, while the ground on which it was proposed to erect it would cost about $400,000. This was not to be considered seriously for a moment, and to overcome the prohibitive difficulty, the Chronicle built the three stories for itself and then added on seven more stories of attractive offices, as revenue producers. It is true that the building cost nearer $300,000, than the original $150,000, but instead of a purely useful and exceedingly expensive building producing no revenue, the Chronicle now has one of the handsomest combination newspaper and office buildings in the South, over two-thirds of which is revenue producing.

This building deserves more than passing notice. It is fireproof and is ten stories high with a basement story underground. It has a floor space of about 100,000 square feet, or nearly two and one-half acres. Its construction embodies a frame of reinforced concrete with walls of brick. It is a strikingly beautiful building, having a base of polished Texas granite, surrounded by enameled brick of dark green, ending with a projecting course of glazed terra cotta. Above this to the roof line, the building is of pure white enameled brick, ornamented with belt courses.

The interior finish is in every way in keeping with the beauty of the exterior. The halls and corridors have floors of pink Tennessee marble and wainscoting of white Italian marble with black marble base.

The entire building is steam heated, has a system of ice water drinking fountains, electric ceiling fans, electric and gas lights, mail chutes, telegraph and telephone facilities, hot and cold artesian water from its own wells and a vacuum cleaning system. Duplex geared elevators with a speed of 400 feet per minute serve the building.

The building is located on the northwest corner of Travis and Texas Avenue. Work on its construction was begun October 14, 1908, and it was completed and occupied in February, 1910.

The best example of structures designed for special purposes is the seven-story fireproof building of the Southwestern Telephone Company. The design follows the practice recently adopted in Houston, namely the use of light colored material for exterior decoration of office buildings. The first two floors a faced with limestone, while the remaining floors are of light gray brick and terra cotta. A feature, especially noticeable, is the ample window area which insures plenty of light and ventilation for the operators.

The extension of the telephone service has been considered and the building is large enough to care for double the number of subscribers it has at present, and, in addition to this, the steel frame has been made heavy enough to sustain five more stories.

At an expenditure of $1,250,000 the Houston Belt and Terminal Railway Company have given to the city a public benefit most meritorious. The Union Station is commodious. It is bounded on the east and west by Hamilton and Crawford Streets, and on the north and south by Prairie and Texas Avenues.

The appointments are modern. The finishings are expensive and artistic. Thoroughly comfortable, pleasing to the sight, and with every convenience of modern invention, there are larger terminal stations than the Union of

Houston, Texas, but none more replete in the things that make for the ease of the traveling public.

Construction work was begun on the building in September, 9, and the completed station was opened to the public March 1, 1911.

There are eight tracks and four train sheds included in the facilities of the Union Station and 125 passenger coaches can be accommodated at one time.

The structure is fireproof and of stone, brick and concrete with steel supports. It is three stories high, the upper floors being used as general offices.

The owning companies are five and the present tenants of the station of the same number.

Probably the best railroad office building in the Southwest, if not in the entire South, is that of the Southern Pacific Railway Company at the corner of Franklin and Travis Streets. This new structure rears its head nine stories above ground and is erected on a lot that extends 145 feet along Franklin and 14 feet along Travis Street. There is a basement, a sub-basement and still a third basement below the engine room, making in all, 12 stories. The building cost $700,000.

Work was started September 1, 1910, and completed October, 1911.

The building is largely of steel and reinforced construction throughout. All the floors are of reinforced concrete. The steel work is encased in concrete. Fireproof tilling is extensively used. The third and fourth floors will be rented for office purposes, and part of the first floor will be rented for store purposes. The building is equipped with its own refrigerating plant.

The Court House, while one of the most substantially constructed buildings to be found anywhere, still belongs to what is known as court-house architecture. In this instance, however, the architect had much to contend with as is shown by the following extract from the Southern Architectural Review in which the architects explains some of them: "In the development of the architectural scheme for the Harris County Court House, certain requirements were laid down in the program of the competition which led to the choosing of the style of architecture, which had we been free, would perhaps have been developed along different lines. But such specific demands as 'A large dome' and 'Columnated facades' could hardly be disregarded. However, in order to give structural integrity to the building we made them of masonry bearings rather than torture classic columns with steel structural members." The building is very beautiful and is very useful as well. Houston's public buildings are described in a chapter devoted to that purpose.

The new Federal Building is a typical government building, fashioned on classic Roman lines, a style adopted very generally throughout the country for such buildings.

It occupies an entire block of ground and is of white stone with golden oak finish throughout, and cost the government about $450,000. Federal Square is almost in the heart of the city, being bounded by Capitol, San Jacinto, Rusk and Caroline Streets, and only two blocks from Main Street.

The corridors are of marble, the staff work is of the finest, an electric vacuum cleaning system with pipes extending to every part of the building has been installed and the work rooms are light and airy. The building is fireproof throughout and is both impressive and beautiful.

Houston's apartment houses are somewhat in a class by themselves, for they are, in many respects, different from those of other cities. The architects have taken advantage of the tall buildings and arranged the light courts so as to make the most of the prevailing southern breeze. The Rossonian is a fine illustration of the idea; it stands as a perfect type of the apartment house for this climate, and is the most exclusive apartment house in the entire South. In fact, in ranks on even terms with the best afforded by New York, Chicago and other large cities of the East and Middle West. Since its opening in the spring of 1911, the Rossonian has been the scene of many functions. The building stands seven stories and basement high, on Fannin Street, opposite the new Young Men's Christian Association Building, and over $500,000 was expended in its erection. So thoroughly up-to-date is the Rossonian that in each suite of rooms there is an individual, up-to-date ice plant. This is but one of the many novel features and innovations.

There are a total of 74 apartments, together with handsomely appointed reception rooms and hallways. The Rossonian has a private roof garden, which is extensively patronized by the smart set of Texas during the warmer months.

The contractors of the Rossonian were the Fred A. Jones Building Company. The firm of Sanguinet & Staats did the architectural work.

The Savoy Flats, located at Main Street and Pease Avenue, were opened in 1909 and since that time have been exceedingly popular among those who seek modern apartment houses. The building is of seven stories and contains 19 housekeeping apartments, together with four bachelor's apartments. The cost of the land upon which the flats stand and the cost of construction was a trifle less than $200,000, but that is the present valuation of the property.

Throughout the apartments the steel and conduit system of refrigeration is employed, thus affording an individual ice making plant in each apartment.

In the Beaconfield Apartments the people of Houston were given an apartment house par excellence and a building that stands out prominently as one of the best in the city. It is eight stories high and was opened October, 1911. The cost of construction was $150,000.

These apartments stand at the corner of Main Street and Pease Avenue. They are of reinforced concrete and steel construction throughout and fireproof. Lines employed in the most modern buildings of the kind were followed out.

The building contains 16 large suites. In each suite there are six main rooms, two screened balconies, and each suite is supplied with a private bath. The rooms are larger than is usually the case in an up-to-date apartment house and the scheme of ventilation could not be improved upon.

The following is a complete list of Houston's modern apartment houses:

Rossonian, Fannin Street and McKinney Avenue; The Beaconsfield, Main Street and Pease Avenue; The Heisig, San Jacinto Street and Rusk Avenue; The Oxford, Fannin Street and Clay Avenue; The Montrose Apartments, Clay Avenue; The Colonial, Lamar Avenue; The Leona, Walnut Street; The Wilson Apartments, Polk Avenue; The Gables, McKinney Avenue; The Butler Flats, Rusk Avenue and Fannin Streets; The Ivanhoe, La Branch Street and Lamar Avenue; Waverly Terrace, Milam Street and Lamar Avenue; The Warrington, Fannin Street and Bell Avenue; The Archer, Lamar Avenue and Louisiana Street; The McAshan Flats, Main Street; The McAshan Apartments, Main Street and Clay Avenue; The Leeland, Leeland Avenue and Caroline Street; The Sternenberg, Milam Street and Walker Avenue; The Hirsch Flats, Crawford Street and Polk Avenue; The Hirsch Apartments, McGowan Avenue and Fannin Street; The Seigle Flats, La Branch Street, near Congress Avenue; The Levy Flats, Travis Street and Rusk Avenue; The Savoy, Main Street and Pease Avenue; The Corona, Walker Avenue, near Main Street; The Griffin Flats, Louisiana Street, near Polk Avenue; The Ross Flats, Walker Avenue and Louisiana Street; The Cawthon, Main Street and Walker Avenue; The Darlington. Lamar Avenue and Crawford Street.

The past few years have been peculiarly rich in the production of modern buildings, excellent in design, substantial in character and useful to the last degree in their respective fields.

Houston's new ten-story hotel, known as the Hotel Bender, is one of the most elegant and artistically finished buildings in the South. It is ten stories in height with full basement. It is of brick, concrete and steel construction and is fireproof in every way. Its architecture is somewhat different from that usually employed in skyscraper buildings, and an effort has been successfully made to add to the exterior attractions almost as much as to those of the interior. The style adopted for the exterior is Grecian Doric with touches of Italian Renaissance, the whole being commercialized to meet the requirements of local conditions and modern hotel conveniences.

The exterior color scheme is very pleasing, being composed of rich and expensive material, granite base work, columns, terra cotta trimmings and velvet red brick, all of the best of their respective kinds, while the workmanship is of the highest order.

But the interior shows best the skill and good taste of the architect, and the art of the decorator. The main lobby is carried out in the Grecian Doric order correctly. Selected marble and solid bronze ornamental work has been used freely in the decorative scheme, while the Mezzanine balconies overlooking the lobby are very attractive.

The dining room is constructed strictly and correctly in Louis XVI style supplying all the elaborate details required by that style. It is beautifully decorated in French coloring and the sixteen or eighteen panels above the mirror line are hand decorated in oil from French scenes during the time of Louis XVI. This dining room is really a work of art and is one of the most elaborate and expensive rooms of its kind to be found anywhere. The kitchen service is strictly up-to-date in every respect. The large Dutch grill room in the basement is one of the striking features of the building. It is thoroughly lighted, ventilated and beautifully decorated in Dutch design. The furniture is all Dutch. There is a very complete gas grill made entirely of copper, nickel plate, tile and plate glass.

The parlors are located on the second floor, facing the elevators and are furnished in Louis XVI style. On the tenth floor a large banquet and ball room is located, having special reception rooms for ladies and gentlemen. The decorations of the bal room are very elaborate, the decorative scheme being that of Louis XVI. Special furniture and other equipments have been provided, all in keeping with the style of the room. There are two private dining rooms on the tenth floor also, each beautifully finished. There is also dining space on the roof, where there is a charming roof garden.

There are 260 rooms nearly every one having a private bath. In addition there are twelve large sample rooms. The furniture of the rooms is solid mahogany.

Mechanical devices also are strictly up-to-date. The building is equipped with automatic air-washing and cooling and ventilating machines which do away with the use of unsightly electric fans. The heating for winter is equally as effective as the cooling for summer. The elevator service is first class and in keeping with the magnificence of the building. The cost of the building, exclusive of the cost of the ground was $600,000.

In the construction of the new Rice Hotel the architects have been given something of a free hand, and when completed, while its exterior will not differ greatly from the ordinary skyscraper, its interior will be all that the most fastidious taste could demand. Towering eighteen stories above a two-story basement and crowned by a handsome tile roof garden, it will be, to the very last detail, a type of the great modern hotel. The main entrance on Texas Avenue, and the side entrance on Main Street will open into the splendid lobby of white Italian marble surmounted by artistic mural decorations, with a ceiling of picturesque frescoing. Adjoining the office will be the rooms occupied by telephone booths, telegraph offices, a carriage office and well-appointed writing rooms and library, and to the rear of these will be the grill and bar. There are to be four cafes, beautifully decorated and fulfilling all needs, from the gentlemen's grill and breakfast room, to the elegant palm room and dining hall, all arranged and located to best serve the convenience of all classes of patrons. In addition to these there will be the private dining rooms, in size and appointment suitable to the smallest dinner party or to the most elaborate banquet. One of the most marked features will be the great banquet hall and concert room. This will be so arranged that it will serve both for private and public entertainments.

The building will have 525 rooms, 450 of them having private baths. Adequate elevator service will be provided. A new feature will be the establishing of kitchens on every floor for the purpose of serving meals in the rooms.

The roof garden will be a garden in fact and not one alone in name. Situated at a height of about 300 feet above the noise and bustle of the streets, with ornamental lights, flowers, palms and an excellent orchestra it will be a most attractive spot. From basement to top the new hotel will be constructed for the comfort and convenience of its guests, and when completed, will be one of the finest and most beautiful hotel buildings in the South.

The building will front about 175 feet on Texas Avenue and about 125 feet on Main Street. Including the ground, the entire cost will be in the neighborhood of $3,500,000, the construction alone being $2,000,000. Mr. Jesse H. Jones is the moving spirit in this great undertaking, as he has been in so many others that had for their object the upbuilding of this city.

The success of the Houston architects in getting away from the stereotype church architecture has been marked, as is evidenced by the number of original and beautiful edifices they have constructed.

Probably the most interesting group of ecclesiastical buildings in the city is the Christ Church group. This is composed of the church proper, parish house and rectory. The church is of the perpendicular Gothic, executed in red brick and sandstone. The other buildings are of the same general order, modified somewhat to meet the limitations of the brick with which they are built. Incongruous as are their surroundings, the vine-covered church and rectory, with the deep cloister of the parish house between, form an architectural group that has no superior in Houston.

The First Church of Christ, Scientist, is another beautiful building, distinctive in design. Its architecture is Roman Doric, which has been adhered to very closely. It is constructed of stone, terra cotta and gray brick. The setting of the building is fine, for it is surrounded by large trees that lend a color and charm that are very pleasing.

In the St. Paul's Methodist Episcopal Church the architectural lines follow those of the Italian renaissance, though the building, as a whole, is patterned after the Roman temples. The dome is Byzantine.

The First Methodist Church follows the early English Gothic, adhering to that architectural scheme, both within and without, with absolute fidelity.

The Central Christian Church is an adaptation of the Roman.

The Temple Beth Israel is Byzantine though patterned after an Americanized version of that style adopted by many Jewish synagogues over the country.

The First Presbyterian Church, while following the Italian renaissance architecture shows clearly other influences. It is considered one of the most unique structures of its kind in the South, for while the Gothic architecture always calls for the lofty tower, this church has the tower, but instead of employing the Teutonic influence the architect has used that of the very early Roman.

The Church of the Annunciation is strictly Italian Gothic.

With the advent of suburban additions, beautified by landscape effects, an architecture representing a new manner of living and action has come and is gradually transforming the appearance of the city. The country club was the first step in that direction and has served as an example for much that has followed in the movement towards suburban and country homes.

Among the handsome new buildings is the Y. M. C. A., an exclusive association building, on McKinney Avenue and Fannin Street. It is modernly equipped in all its appointments and cost $200,000. It was erected in 1907–08.

The building is five stories in height and includes a magnificent lobby and reading room on the first floor, gymnasium, bowling alleys, swimming pool, handball court, baths, lockers and dressing rooms and a full athletic complement. On the second and part of the third floors are assembly rooms, study and class rooms. A part of the third floor and all of the fourth and fifth are devoted to apartments for men. In all there are ninety-one rooms, providing ample accommodations for about 125 men. All of the rooms are uniform in size and are neatly furnished according to a man's notion of comfort.

Light colored pressed brick and marble were used in its construction. It contains 66,000 square feet of floor space and is the largest Association building in the South.

The question of architecture was one of the first problems that confronted the board of trustees of the Wm. M. Rice Institute. They early decided that the new institution should be housed in architecture worthy of the founder's high aims, and upon this idea they entered with no lower ambition than to establish on the campus of the institution a group of buildings conspicuous alike for their beauty and their usefulness, which should stand not only as a monument to the founder's philanthropy but also as a distinct contribution to the architecture of our country. With this end in view they adopted a general architectural plan embodying the educational program which had been adopted by the institute. Such a general plan, exhibiting in itself the most attractive elements of the architecture of Italy, France and Spain, was adopted by the board in 1910.

Immediately thereafter plans and specifications for an administration building were prepared and the contract awarded. Soon after the contract for the mechanical laboratory, machine shop and power house was let. The architecture of the Administration Building shows borrowings from the best periods of many southern countries. Round Byzantine arches on cloistered walks, exquisite brick work of Dalmation design are features, together with Spanish and Italian elements in profusion; all in a richness of color permissible nowhere save in a climate similar to that of south Texas. The dominant tone is established by the use of a local pink brick, a delicately tinted marble from the Ozark Mountains and Texas granite, though the color scheme undergoes considerable variation by the free use of tiles and foreign marbles. To meet the local climatic conditions there are in the building many windows and loggias and a long, broad cloister open to the prevailing winds.

The Laboratory is to be a two-story, fireproof building 200 feet long and forty feet deep, with a cloistered walk extending its full length on the court side, and will. be built of materials similar to those in the Administration Building. The machine shop, adjoining the Mechanical Laboratory in the rear connects it with the power house. The lofty campanile of this group, visible for miles in every direction, will be the most conspicuous tower of the institute. These with the students' hall are the only buildings under construction at present, but when all are completed, the harmonious architectural effect will be seen to advantage and will form one of the greatest, external attractions of this great institution.

Houston is rapidly becoming a city of beautiful homes, and, judging by the record made within the four years ending July 31, 1911, the growth and expansion in building have just begun. The records of the building inspectors office show that during the fiscal year, ending February 28, 1907, $892,000 was spent on residences in Houston, while the same records show that during the year ending February 28, 1911, $1,200,000 was spent on residences. The records show that during the last decade Houstonians have invested $9,000,000 in homes of all kinds, from the humble cottage to the palatial residence. Of the latter class Houston has some of the most beautiful and expensive in the South. In the fashionable sections of the city are residences that have cost from $50,000 to $75,000 and quite a number of others whose cost was very little below these figures. All styles of architecture and all kinds of building material have been used. There has been a great variety of taste shown, with a result that is really pleasing since it prevents anything like monotony or sameness. During the year closing July 31, 1911, there were 931 permanent permits for buildings and improvements issued at the city hall, classified as follows:

295

One nine-story steel office building, to cost $512,793.00; one twelve-story steel bank and office building, to cost $400,000.00; one ten-story hotel building, to cost $30,000.00; one seven-story telephone building, to cost $150,000.00; one eight-story apartment house, to cost $100,000.00; one six-story reinforced concrete building, to cost $77,850.00; one six-story brick and steel hotel building, to cost $70,000.00; one church (Sacred Heart), to cost $56,000.00; one three-story cold storage plant, to cost $50,000.00; one church (Christian Science), to cost $38,800.00; one two-story telephone building, to cost $33,000.00; one four-story concrete warehouse, to cost $26,000.00; one three-story brick building, to cost $25,000.00; one two-story depot and car shed, to cost $20,000.00; one two-story brick warehouse, to cost $18,000.00; one three-story reinforced concrete wagon factory, to cost $18,000.00; one four-story brick building, to cost $17,000.00; one three-story reinforced concrete coffee plant, to cost $15,000.00; one two-story addition to power plant, to cost $15,000.00; one one-story brick building, to cost $13,000.00; one one- and two-story brick building, to cost $12,000.00; one one-story brick building, to cost $10,000.00; one two-story brick building, to cost $10,000.00; one one-story brick building; to cost $8,000.00; one addition to elevator factory, to cost $6,000.00; five flat buildings, to cost $59,300.00; eight one- and two-story brick buildings, to cost $43,800.00; thirteen one- and two-story frame store buildings, to cost $19,100.00; four remodeling, to cost $12,300.00; one veterinary hospital, to cost $9,725.00; 4 churches, to cost $9,900.00; seventeen warehouses, to cost $18,200.00; four schools, to cost $4,447.00; two factories, to cost $2,575.00; nineteen garages, to cost $2,175.00; four offices, to cost $1,185.00; two club houses, to cost $2,800.00; one machine shop, to cost $1,000.00; one cotton shed, to cost $1,000.00; one foundation, to cost $2,000.00; one blacksmith shop, to cost $250.00; two hundred and twenty-seven two-story residences, to cost $665,105.00; 496 cottages, to cost $472,800.00; ninety-six stables, sheds and miscellaneous, to cost $19,385. As the registration permit fee is increased with each $1,000 of construction cost, the sums given always represent a minimum.

CHAPTER XXIV INSURANCE

Houston Gets Lowest Rate of Fire Insurance Premium. Fire Fighting Apparatus. Early Fire Insurance. Planters Fire Insurance Company. Purchase of Bogus Bonds Destroyed Houston Fire and Marine Insurance Company. Guarantee Life Insurance Company. Remarkable Prosperity of the Great Southern Company.

An insurance company is not a charitable institution going about doing good for the mere pleasure of the thing. It does not sign an agreement to give a person so much money in case his property is destroyed by fire, and then sit down with him and wait for the disaster. The company will sign the agreement, but when it does so it will expect and demand that the person who is to be benefitted and the community in which he resides, shall do all possible to prevent the disaster. The company will protect a person against losses, but will, at the same time, demand that it, itself, be protected.

Wherever a community makes ample provision against the danger of fire, the insurance companies encourage the citizens to insure their property, by giving to such community a low rate of insurance premium, and since Houston has received the lowest rate, it is self-evident that all the requirements of the National Board of Fire Insurance Underwriters, for a city of 100,000 inhabitants, have been complied with.

During the decade from 1901 to 1911, there has been a healthy growth in Houston's facilities for fighting fire. In 1901, Houston had eight stations, twenty pieces of fire-fighting apparatus, 13,000 feet of hose and sixty paid men. In 1911, there are nine stations, thirty pieces of apparatus, 30,000 feet of hose and 104 paid men.

The water supply in 1901, consisted of a pumping capacity of 13,000,000 gallons of water and 579 fire hydrants. In 1911, the pumping capacity is 29,000,000 gallons daily, with 843 fire hydrants and 97.8 miles of water mains in service. There are 156 fire-alarm boxes, and ninety miles of paved streets. Every detail of the fire department is carefully looked after and kept in perfect order. Every fire hydrant is flushed and tested daily by a force of men employed for that work only.

That, in a few words, is the Houston of today, but it has not always been so well equipped, nor has there been a need or demand for such perfection. Fire insurance in Houston is possibly as old as the city itself. There is no record of the fact, however, for the first local agent for any company was Mr. John Dickinson, who began issuing policies about 1858. Before that, all the insurance obtained by local merchants and traders was had direct from agencies or companies located in New Orleans. In those earlier days insurance was on a small scale and kept pace with the accumulation of mercantile stocks, and accumulation of cotton and other products of the farms and plantations.

Soon after the establishment of the local agency by Mr. Dickinson and just about the time that he was doing a good and substantial business, the war occurred, which, of course, rendered all insurance moribund. After the declaration of peace, many agencies were established here and for several years the insurance business was conducted by the following firms and individuals: O. L. Cochran, A. L. Steele & Co., S. O. Cotton & Bro., Childress & Taylor, and Raphael Brothers. All these, with the exception of A. L. Steele & Co., are still in business. Besides these there are about twenty-five insurance agencies doing business in Houston.

Soon after the war, about 1868, the Planters' Fire Insurance Company of Houston was organized, with a capital stock of $100,000 and did business until about 1880 when the company went into voluntary liquidation, following a disastrous cotton fire. Capt. E. M. Longcope was president of this company and among its directors were E. H. Cushing, B. A. Botts, W. R. Baker, S. L. Allen, T. M. Bagby and other old citizens, none of whom survive.

About the year 1895, the Houston Fire and Marine Insurance Company was organized and did business for several years. Through a lot of bogus Austin City bonds which were innocently purchased by this company, it was forced to make a disastrous and rather sensational failure a few years ago.

As no statistics are available as to the volume of insurance premiums received in Houston annually by the various local agencies, who represent about one hundred and twenty fire insurance companies, it cannot be recorded with accuracy what the total sum is. From a comparison of the business done by the leading agencies here, it is thought that the premium receipts will run over $1,000,000 per year.

It is somewhat strange that with so inviting a field as it is, Houston should have had no local life insurance company until 1906. In that year the Guarantee Life Insurance Company was organized with a capital of $100,000 and at once became very prosperous, doing a large business. It is now five years old and in addition to its capital stock it has a surplus of $80,000 and has $13,000,000 insurance in force. Its officers are: Jonathan Lane, president; John H. Thompson, vice-president; Chas. Boedeker, secretary-treasurer.

The Great Southern Life Insurance Company is one of the most remarkable organizations of its kind in existence. It was organized on November 1, 1909, and is therefore only two years old, and yet the amount of business it has already done creates admiration and amazement even in large insurance centers, as nothing like it has ever been seen before. It has a capital stock of $500,000 and a surplus of $500,000 and has $10,000,000 insurance in force. A remarkable feature about it is the large number of those among its patrons who are insured for large amounts. It has over fifty policy holders who are insured for $25,000 or more, and one who is insured for

$100,000. This last is the first and only policy for so large an amount ever written for one person by a Texas company.

The phenomenal growth of this company is shown by the following statement: From its organization, November 1, 1909 to December 31, 1909, the company wrote $1,020,000 new business. During the first half of 1910, the new business amounted to $3,028,000, while during the first half of 1911, it amounted to $4,048,000, showing a gain of 33 per cent.

The "Index," published by the Spectator Company of New York, contains the official reports of 181 American life insurance companies, all being in active operation January 1, 1911. Of this number 106 paid for less business during the entire year of 1910 than the Great Southern wrote during the first half of 1911.

This company is making life insurance history at a rapid rate. Its officers are: J. S. Rice, president; O. S. Carlton, C. G. Pillot, J. S. Cullinan, and P. H. McFadden, of Beaumont, Texas, vice-presidents; J. T. Scott, treasurer; Louis St. J. Thomas, secretary.

All the great insurance companies that are permitted under Texas laws to do business in the state have capable local agents in Houston who write a great amount of business.

CHAPTER XXV THEATRES

Santa Anna Broke up First Theatre Project. The Thompson and Buckley Theatres. The Gray Opera House. Early Amateur Dramatic Clubs. Academy of Music First Local Home of Vaudeville. The Beautiful New Majestic Theatre. The Prince Theatre. The Old Majestic. The New Cozy. Moving Picture Shows and Stock Companies.

Only one month and two days after Texas declared her independence, an enterprising theatrical manager, a Mr. G. L. Lyons declared that he was going to establish the first theatre in the new republic, at Harrisburg, and that he would give the first performance about the first of May, 1836. He issued a long announcement of his intention. Evidently he did not consult Santa Anna, for the sudden appearance of that gentleman on the scene seems to have so disarranged his plans that nothing beyond the announcement of intentions was ever heard of him afterwards. Theatrical performances early got a hold on the people of Houston and the fever has never been allowed to die down.

An account of the theatre in the days of the republic appears in an earlier chapter of this volume. The first really good theatre erected in Houston was located in a building that Mr. James Thompson put up in 1854. Mr. Thompson owned four or five lots in the northeast corner of the block on the south side of Texas Avenue, opposite the old Capital Hotel, and on three of these he erected a large house. It was three stories high in the middle, facing Main Street, and had two stories on each side. The theatre was located on the third floor in the center, and was a large hall with a good stage at one end. Some very good performances were given in this theatre. In 1859, this theatre was destroyed by fire and was never rebuilt, but Colonel Buckley put in a theatre in a brick building that he erected about that time located in the middle of the block on the southwest side of Main Street, between Congress and Franklin Avenues. This place was never popular and was seldom used for the purposes for which it had been planned.

About the same time the Perkins Theatre, or as it was called, Perkins Hall was built. This hall was large and comfortably arranged and proved to be very valuable and useful for those who were giving concerts, fairs and bazaars, for the purpose of raising money for the soldiers during the war. After the war, the Gray Opera house was built in the middle of the block on the west side of Court House Square. Then the pretty little theatre in the Market House was built. There have been others constructed from time to time, important in their time, among them being the Old Majestic described elsewhere, the Houston Theatre, which was the principal theatre of the city when it was destroyed by fire in 1908, and the New Majestic, the Prince and the Cozy theatres all of which are described in this chapter.

Houstonians have had the pleasure of hearing nearly all the great actors and singers of the world, who are native Americans or who have visited America. In 1859, Jenny Lind sang here in the old Academy. Patti, Nielson and scores of other world-famed singers have visited Houston, while Booth, McCullough, Barrett and hundreds of other great actors have played here.

Houston early had an amateur dramatic club as the following letter, printed in the Telegraph of February 17, 1845, shows:

"Houston, February 16, 1845. To the Hon. Francis Moore, Jr., Mayor of the City of Houston. Sir:—In behalf of the Houston Dramatic Society, and in furtherance of a resolution of the corps, we herewith place at your disposal the sum of thirty dollars (which amount exceeds the net proceeds from the performance of the last play) to be appropriated by yourself for the relief of the indigent of the city and county. You will exercise your own judgment in deciding who are worthy to be recipients and to whom charity should be a blessing.

"If we needed any apology for charging you with the disbursement of our inconsiderable donation, we would find it in the industry and humanity evinced in your conduct when similar objects have demanded and received your attention. Respectfully, your obedient servants, Thomas M. Bagby, president; Wm. R. Baker, secretary."

There were other amateur associations formed afterwards in Houston, the most important being the Magnolia Histrionic Club, which had great success in 1878, and for some years after. In the early eighties Judge John Kirlicks and the lamented D. D. Bryan, were leading lights in this club and did much to add to its prominence and success. Mr. Bryan's removal from the city for a few years proved fatal to the club and it soon ceased to be an active body.

About the same time the Young Men's Hebrew Club came into prominence. This club, after a few successful years, was allowed to die out.

Mr. Ed. Bremond, son of the "Texas Railroad King," was the first to establish vaudeville in Houston. In September, 1873, he opened the Academy of Music which was located on the southeast corner of Main Street and Prairie Avenue. He had quite a number of "artists," among them Milt Barlow, who had his start in Houston, under Mr. Bremond, and afterwards became famous as an impersonator of aged negroes. His song "Old Black Joe," became one of the classics of negro minstrelsy.

The Academy was quite successful for a short time but soon degenerated and dropped down to what is known as the variety class, and proved a failure. Another vaudeville, on a somewhat lower plane, was Bell's Theatre, which held forth for years on Texas Avenue across the street from the Rice Hotel. It was afterwards moved to Franklin Avenue, opposite the Hutchin's House. In 1893 it was closed by the city authorities but was reopened at once by an injunction. It was finally closed on the death of the proprietor.

Of the theatres in service in Houston the only one that justifies much local pride is the New Majestic, built on the site of the old Shearn Church on the corner of Texas Avenue and Milam Street and completed in 1910. Its cost of $300,000 will doubtless prohibit its ever becoming a great revenue producer but it is a model of construction and comfort and is a place of amusement that for beauty compares favorably with any theatre of its capacity in any country. The builder was Jesse H. Jones and the structure represents local pride and patriotism for it was meant to give the city a place of amusement second to none.

Actors praise it, for every comfort has been provided for them, both in the modern dressing rooms and on the large fully-equipped stage. The public appreciates it because in the whole house there is no angle, no obstructing pillar, nor column and no seat that does not furnish a good view of the stage.

The numerous exits, ample fire escapes and perfect system of ventilation also commend it. In order that the content of 250,000 cubic feet of air might be changed every three minutes, an elaborate plant was built and the concrete walls were interlaced with hollow ducts. From the floor, walls and ceilings, these converge to carry away the vitiated atmosphere into one large tunnel leading to the fan house on the roof. There a large wheel sucks it up and discharges into the open air 80,000 cubic feet of air each minute. The building is constructed entirely of concrete and stone and is as nearly fireproof as a theatre can be built.

Some of the beautiful features of this theatre worthy of special enumeration are: The Pompeian entrance with its marble walls, the ladies' waiting room of the period of Louis the Magnificent, the drinking fountains and mirrors of the foyer, the marble staircase and ingle nooks, the Flemish smoking room with its beams and tiles, the cantilever balcony with its loggias, the great, dark crimson curtain of asbestos, the gilded and rose-wreathed sounding board, the bacchante heads and scroll ornamentation of the stage boxes, the carefully calculated acoustics, the children's play room with nurse and toys, the elaborate lighting and the great circulation fan, the roomy stage with maple apron and ample scenery, and the delicacy and elaboration of the color scheme.

Among the other places of amusement the following are the leading ones:

The Prince Theatre, built in 1909, on the site of the Sweeny & Combs Opera House, known as the Houston Theatre, which was destroyed by fire in 1908. This is a combination theatre and office building. It is six stories high and covers a plot of ground 100 by 150 feet, located on Fannin Avenue opposite the County Court House. The construction is of brick and concrete and the building is fireproof. The cost of the building was $140,000. The theatre is located on the ground floor and is the home of the legitimate drama in Houston. It is cheaply built and entirely inadequate to the present needs of the city. The dressing rooms are abominable and little has been done for the comfort of the actors and artists. There is comparatively easy egress in case of fire, and much danger in that direction has been eliminated. The seating capacity is 1,200. The lessee of the theatre, Manager Dave A. Weis is a man of large experience as a theatrical manager and constantly tries to improve the character of attractions coming to Houston.

The Old Majestic was erected in 1903 at a cost of $35,000. It is of wood and brick construction and has a seating capacity of 800. When erected and for a few years after, it was Houston's chief vaudeville theatre. Since 1909 it has been given over entirely to stock companies. The building is antiquated.

The Cozy, located on Texas Avenue, "forty-five seconds from Main Street" is a very popular place of amusement, devoted to vaudeville. It is a small but comfortable and well-arranged theatre, and has a seating capacity of 800. The building was erected in 1910 by Mr. M. E. Foster and is 50 by 125 feet. Its cost was $25,000.

Other places of amusement in Houston are: The Theato, pictures and vaudeville; The Star Theatre, moving pictures; The Crystal Theatre, moving pictures; The Princess, moving pictures and vaudeville; The Royal, moving pictures and vaudeville; The Dixe Theatre, moving pictures; The Vaudette Theatre, moving pictures; The Bil-Sol, moving pictures; McDonald & Newcomb, moving pictures; John McTighe, moving pictures, and two moving picture places for negroes only.

It is estimated that between 8,000 and 10,000 persons patronize the moving picture shows in Houston daily. The best of those named is the Dixie. The Plaza and the Lyric are open air, summer theatres arranged for comfort during the hot weather. Each is well patronized.

In 1909, 1910 and 1911, Houston had good stock companies playing in the city. The Players Stock Company under the management of Joseph D. Glass, at the old Majestic, and the William Grew Stock Company, at the Plaza in the summer of 1911, were the best of these.

At present the city has abundance of vaudeville theatres, but the Prince Theatre should be given up to stock company work and a great modern theatre for legitimate drama built that would be to that class of theatrical offerings what the New Majestic is to vaudeville.

CHAPTER XXVI PARKS AND CEMETERIES

Purchase and Development of Sam Houston Park. Highland Park. Cleveland Park.
Elizabeth Baldwin Park. City's need of Plaza Parks. Ruined Condition of City's Earliest
Cemeteries. Episcopal Church and Holland Lodge Cemetery. Glenwood and Catholic
Cemeteries. List of other Cemeteries. Sylvan Beauties of Burying Ground. Land Tenure
of Cemetery Lots.

As early as 1882 there was begun a crusade for a city park. Nothing came
of it, however, and it was not until eighteen years later that anything definite
was accomplished. In 1900, Judge Sam Brashear, at that time mayor of
Houston, desiring to leave a monument to commemorate his administration,
purcha for the city, seventeen acres, the site of the present Sam Houston
Park. This park is located on the south side of Buffalo Bayou in the western
part of the city, and is one of the most beautiful places in Houston. Its natural
advantages are very great, and to these have been added the art and skill of
expert landscape gardeners.

The site was purchased by the city, June 19, 1910, and the cost of the land
and improvements was about $50,000. When first purchased, portions of the
tract were badly cut up by gullies and ravines. Some of these have been filled
while others have been made use of in the scheme of beautifying the park.
At first a zoological garden was started, but after making good headway
towards establishing a really creditable zoo, the idea was abandoned and the
collection was sold to an amusement park in Little Rock, Ark. Mayor
Brashear was anxious to extend the park on the opposite side of the bayou,
but this has not yet been done, although the park is connected with that side
by a good wide bridge, and the approaches are first class. The city owns a
good sized tract on the north side of the bayou, immediately opposite the
park, so that it is possible to enlarge it at any time.

Highland Park, near Beauchamp Springs at the foot of Houston Avenue
on White Oak Bayou, is a natural park, and is a beautiful spot near Houston.
It is located on a tract of about twenty acres, lying north of the city near the
junction of Little White Oak and White Oak Bayous. The ground slopes
towards the bayous and is covered with magnificent oak, magnolia and other
forest trees. This park was inaugurated and improved by the Houston
Electric Company as a private enterprise but became a public park,
apparently, by common consent. It is free to all and has many attractions, the
chief one being an artificial lake filled and fed by artesian wells.

Sam Houston Park seems destined to be eclipsed in the near future by
Cleveland Park, when is located just beyond the west bounds of the city on
Buffalo Bayou. This park, consisting of thirty acres, was a Christmas gift to
the people of Houston in December, 1907, and cost the city $45,000. If no
work in the way of beautifying it were done, it would still be a charming

sylvan retreat, for nature has done wonders for it. It is located in a great bend of the bayou, and the earth slopes gently towards the bayou, with numerous natural, miniature hills breaking the contour. In one of the declivities between these miniature hills, a large artificial lake has been made, fed by an immense artesian well. The place was originally intended for a park, and $15,000 had been spent on it before the city purchased it. Thus far the city has made no improvements, but when it does, Cleveland Park will become one of the handsomest parks in the South.

What was known as the old Lang place in the Third ward, at the end of the LaBranch Street cr line, was purchased some years ago with the legacy left by the late Mrs. W. M. Rice, and was named after her, "Elizabeth Baldwin Park." It was cleared, fenced and opened by the Civic Club, but no improvements were made either by the club or by the city authorities. The only adornment it has is its beautiful trees. The park is small, but could be made very attractive.

Several of the additions that have sprung up around Houston have made provision for parks, yet it is hardly safe to assume that future generations of Houstonians will have ample breathing spaces. At present Houston is too much occupied in developing her material resources to pay much attention to her play grounds, but when the time comes, as it soon will, there is no question but that a large work in that direction should be done. The extension of Sam Houston Park with riverside drives on both sides of the bayou is the improvement nearest in sight. Mr. Harvey T. D. Wilson has outlined a plan of park extension and improvement which he hopes to see the city eventually adopt. The city's greatest need is a number of small parks or plazas of one square block in extent. It is an economic mistake for the city not to purchase a number of vacant squares for this purpose.

When the Allens laid out Houston they set aside a block of ground in the First ward, north of Buffalo Bayou near the banks of White Oak Bayou, as a cemetery, and gave it to the city to be used for that purpose. About the same time another plot of ground out on the San Felipe road was dedicated to the same purpose. These two cemeteries are the oldest in Houston, and for several years they were the only places of burial here. Neither was ever very popular with the early Houstonians, and many of the older families buried their dead in their flower gardens. Still there were numerous burials in the two cemeteries and some of the most prominent citizens of Houston and of Texas are buried in one or the other of these two places. Both have become dreadfully neglected, and have been allowed to go to ruin. This is particularly true of the cemetery in the First ward, which has no fence and is used as a public highway. The San Felipe ground, owing to its more isolated situation is some-what better preserved, but it is badly in need of care and attention. The fact that the Jewish Cemetery adjoins it has acted as a protection and has partially preserved it from the fate that has overtaken the cemetery in the First ward.

About the year 1845, the members of the Episcopal Church and Holland Lodge of Masons joined together and purchased a plot of ground in the western part of the city, near the banks of Buffalo Bayou, and established what was afterwards known as the Episcopal-Masonic burial ground. It was on a sloping hill, was free from many trees, and was, for that day, an ideal spot for the purposes for which it was intended. Many of the prominent families purchased lots there and for many years it was used. In the early seventies, it was gradually abandoned. When Glenwood Cemetery was opened nearly all the bodies were removed to the latter place. It was evident that the cemetery had been placed too near town, for even in 1870 the city had encroached on all sides of it except on the bayou side. When Sam Houston Park was established, the cemetery, which adjoins it, was closed for good, and future burials there were prohibited. It is now closed to the public. The old place has many sacred memories clinging to it as some of the best loved Houstonians still sleep there.

The first effort made to establish a really large and imposing cemetery was in 1872, when Glenwood was begun. The site is a naturally beautiful one, opening on Washington Street, and landscape gardening and art have made it one of the most attractive places of its kind to be found in the South. This is the principal cemetery of the city.

One of the oldest cemeteries is the old Catholic cemetery in the Second ward on Runnels Street. This cemetery was established shortly after the establishment of the Episcopalian cemetery. Only members of the church may be buried there.

The names and locations of the other cemeteries are as follows: The German Society Cemetery, is just west of Glenwood Cemetery on Washington Street. The Hebrew Cemetery is on the San Felipe road, half a mile west of the G. H. & S. A. Railway. Hollywood Cemetery is located on the west side of West Montgomery road, half a mile north of the city limits. It is the second cemetery in importance in the city. Its natural beauties are great and many handsome monuments adorn it. The Holy Cross Cemetery, is on the east side of the west Montgomery Road, two blocks south of Houston Avenue. The Magnolia Cemetery lies on the north side of the San Felipe road, one block west of the G. H. & S. A. Railway. The College Park Cemetery (negro), is south of the San Felipe road, one mile west of the G. H. & S. A. Railway. Olive Wood Cemetery (negro), lies at the north end of the Court in Chaneyville.

Houston's cemeteries combine the beauty of the wildwood with the charm of the tropical and semi-tropical plants and flowers that the climate permits to flourish in great beauty and abundance. For ten months in the year the sylvan charm of the natural forest and indigenous plants, vines and flowers hold their sway. Ferns blow in the open air and only have to be put under cover a few chilly nights in each year.

The patriotic societies and organizations have marked the graves of the honored dead, and many a monument to hero, as well as loved one, rises in the city's beautiful cemeteries.

Wealth, moved by grief, has uttered its sorrow in many costly marbles and towering shafts, and many a marble angel with drooping wings broods over the resting places of the dead.

The cemeteries are open to one criticism that applies at least to several of them, and that is, that lot owners sometimes experience great difficulty in having their lots properly cared for. Under the form of deed given in Glenwood, and other cemeteries, no real ownership in the lot passes and the purchaser only buys the privilege of being perpetually taxed by the cemetery organizations which retain the nominal right, although it is perhaps not often exercised, to cast out the dead and resell the lots if the payments cease. If there is any spot on earth to which title should pass in fee simple it is the plot of ground in a cemetery where the dead rest in their last long sleep. The character of title given, together with the lesson from the neglected cemeteries of the early days, points a moral that is not pleasant to read as to the possible future fate of these wooded and flowered retreats where the dead rest.

CHAPTER XXVII OLD LANDMARKS

The Old Indian Trading Post. The Old City Hotel and Hutchins House. Site of Capitol and Land Office Buildings. Houston's Mansion. Where the First Store Stood. Two Historic Bridges. Sites of Early Railroad Construction. The Old City Wharf. Reminiscences on Destruction of Houston's First Hotel.

There are a number of points in Houston that have historical interest, and as most of them are already forgotten or almost unknown to the present generation and in a few years all of them, with one or two exceptions, will be entirely forgotten, it may be well to place some of the most important on record in these pages.

What was known as the home of Mr. Horace D. Taylor, located on the north side of Preston Avenue, on the south side of Buffalo Bayou, near the Preston Avenue Bridge, was formerly a great Indian trading post. It was owned and conducted by Mr. George Torrey. The post was established early in 1836 and was in active operation for several years. There were one or two tribes of Indians near Houston. They were "tame" Indians and were about as civilized as Indians ever get to be. The largest tribe was the Creek, and another tribe lived farther north on the San Jacinto River. These Indians visited Houston often and were here until in the late fifties, when they were removed to the territory north of Red River.

Houston, or rather the place where Houston was afterwards located, must also have been a favorite home for the wild Indians for there were numerous evidences of them found here in the early days. All that region south of Preston Avenue and west of Louisiana Street, must have been a burial ground for the Indians, for it is a common thing to dig up bones, arrow-heads and such articles all over that vicinity.

The trading post was abandoned early in the forties, and the Indians then transferred their patronage to Mr. John Kennedy, who had a store on the northwest corner of Travis and Congress, and to Mr. Cornelius Ennis, who had a store on Main Street between Franklin and Commerce. The Chief of the Creeks was an Indian named Mingo, who was a rather superior man. He spoke fairly good English and always conducted himself well, even when he was drunk, in which state he was every time he come to town. Mingo died, and was buried somewhere out on the San Jacinto, before his tribe was moved away.

Perhaps there is no place in Houston that has so many memories clinging to it as the northeast corner of Travis and Franklin. Here was built Houston's first hotel, the old City Hotel conducted by Mr. Geo. Wilson, father of Mr. Ed. Wilson, the latter still a citizen of Houston. This first hotel was an insignificant affair, constructed out of logs and stood for many years. It fell down in 1855 and another one-story structure was built on its site which was soon torn down to make way for the Hutchins House, which in its day was the finest hotel structure in Texas. The old Hutchins House was a great meeting place and, as already noted in these pages, nearly all of the leading state societies and organizations had their beginning in its parlors. The building was destroyed by fire and the site, after remaining vacant for several years was finally purchased by the Southern Pacific Railroad, and the present magnificent office-building of that road was erected on it.

Workmen are now engaged in tearing down the Rice Hotel, to make way for one of the largest and finest hotels in the South. The location is on the site of the old Capitol of the Republic of Texas. This locality is too well known to everybody and its history is too familiar to require more than passing notice. Just across Main Street from the hotel site is the Binz Building which stands where the first Land Office of the Republic of Texas stood. There were other government offices in the old frame building which stood there, but the chief one was the Land Office.

If one believed all the stories and traditions connected with President Sam Houston, one would be forced to believe that he was ubiquitous, or that he was largely peripatetic, for there are several places pointed out as "Sam Houston's home" in Houston. There is a house in the Second ward, another in the Fourth ward, and there may be yet others while the friends of Mrs. A. C. Allen claim that he made his home at her residence on the corner of Main and Rusk. Each one of these stories may be true, but the fact remains that the official home of the President of the Republic of Texas was in the President's mansion on the southeast corner of Main and Preston, where the Scanlan Building now stands. It was a "mansion" in name only, for it was a small wooden house that was so badly constructed that it barely kept out the wind and rain. After the Capital was moved to Austin the "mansion" became the shop of a hatter.

There are other points to which interest is attached from a purely commercial point of view. One of the chief of these is the northeast corner of Commerce Avenue and Main Street, where the first store or warehouse was erected in Houston. Aside from being the first warehouse it was the third house of any kind built here. It was a small one-story frame building and was erected in February, 1837. Though it was comparatively small it was at the time the largest building in Houston. Afterwards it was extended back towards the bayou, so that its rear elevation looked like a big two-story house. It was built and occupied by Mr. Thos. Elsberry, but afterwards passed into the hands of Messrs. Allen and Pool who used it as a cotton and hide warehouse. There was a large door cut in the rear of the building and instead of draying or trucking the bales of cotton down to the steamboats, they were dumped bodily out of this door and rolled right on the boats. The fall of twenty or thirty feet often proved disastrous to the bales when the ropes, used as ties, would break. The methods of handling and caring for so valuable an article as cotton were about as crude and wasteful then as they are now. Everything about a bale of cotton has been improved on except handling and protecting it from the weather. A point of interest connected with that old building, which stood until long after the war, was the fact that several of the wealthiest and most influential citizens of Houston began their careers within its walls. Mr. J. T. Doswell who gained a large fortune as a commission merchant and who was afterwards a large cotton exporter in New Orleans, began his commercial life on that site as book-keeper for Allen & Pool and when he resigned to go in business for himself he was succeeded by Mr. Wm. R. Baker, who in turn resigned to engage in business for himself. He began by renting a part of the same warehouse and when he died, he was one of the wealthiest and most successful citizens of Houston. There were several others though none so successful as these two.

There are two bridges that deserve to be placed among the historical locations. One is the Preston Avenue bridge and the other is the small bridge spanning White Oak Bayou not far from where it empties into Buffalo Bayou. Over these two bridges, for many years, practically all the commerce of the state passed. It is impossible to even estimate the value of the products that have passed over these bridges coming into Houston or the value of the goods that passed going out.

There are three points that have historical interest from a railroad point of view. The first is near the west end of the old McGowan Foundry, for it was there that the first shovel of dirt was thrown by Mr. Paul Bremond when the construction of the Houston and Texas Central Railroad was begun. The second is the southwest corner of Polk Avenue and San Jacinto Street, where the first passenger and freight depot of the Buffalo Bayou and Brazos Railroad was located. The third is the southeast corner of McKinney Avenue and San Jacinto Street, where, during the war, the Galveston, Houston and Henderson Railroad had its passenger and freight depot. Thousands of soldiers and hundreds of tons of munitions of war have passed over that spot, for during the four years of the war that road was in constant operation and the military authorities took entire charge of the road.

Of course the old wharf at the foot of Main Street and extending down as far as San Jacinto Street, is historical, but as the only change likely to be made in it will be one of improvement and growth, it is not necessary to speak of it especially here.

On October 1, 1911, workmen began tearing down the Rice Hotel, which stands on the site of the old Capital, to make way for a new hotel which is to cost two million dollars and is to be the finest hotel in the state. In this connection the following extract from the columns of the old Telegraph, will be read with interest, since it tells of the fate of Houston's first hotel and of some of the distinguished men who patronized it. In its issue of May 16, 1855, under the heading, "The Fall of a Historic House," the Telegraph stated that the oldest house that was standing in Houston on the preceding Saturday had been reduced to a mass of ruins. It was the original City Hotel, a log building in the rear of the Telegraph office on Franklin Avenue. After an existence of nearly twenty years it had fallen because of old age and decrepitude. It was built by Maj. Ben Fort Smith, a pioneer in Texas and in Houston, and the Telegraph said: "It had been in its day the hotel par excellence of the Capitol and commercial metropolis of the glorious old Republic of Texas. The President and his cabinet and the senators and representatives and officials of the first and second Congresses had dined there, and so, too, had foreign ministers."

"Rusk, who was a great man before the Republic, was once glorified at its tables with a sacrifice of good things—fowls at $6 a pair, butter at $1 a pound, eggs at $3 a dozen and champagne at a fabulous price per bottle." "It has been said that the dinner was planned to encourage a reconciliation between Rusk and Houston, and that it was so far successful that Rusk, in toasting Houston, his old opponent, said: 'Houston, with all thy faults I love thee still.'"

The fall of the old house evidently put the editor in a reminiscent mood, for he goes on to say: "Texas had great men in that day and their name was legion. It was an insult to take a man for anything but great, brave, chivalrous and even rich. Everybody was rich, or in the army or navy or public service, which was the same thing. The City Hotel had a barroom, one of perhaps twenty that flourished in the town, where steam was kept up at the explosion point, and the collapse of a decanter, pitcher or tumbler, as it came in contact with the brains of some unlucky devotee at the shrine of chivalry or bravado, or of the kindred virtues usually worshiped 'when the wine was red in the cup,' was no uncommon occurrence. Those were the days of duels, bowie knives and pistols, poker, keno and faro, when ten, twenty or fifty thousand dollars would be lost and won in a night. Texas was the prophecy of California, and Houston a very San Francisco. No mines were dug, but gold was plenty and men managed to live without sweating their brows. If a man worked at all, he earned his $8 or $10 a day, but precious few worked at all. Buck Peters and Jeff Wright were the practical jokers. Judge Shelby was on the bench, and was indicted by his own grand jury for playing backgammon with his wife. Gus Tompkins, fertile in expedient, but fractious, with his large brain and small body and lightning impulses, was a terror to evil-doors. Felix Huston commanded the turbulent army, Commodore Moore had not come to Texas then, and the navy was divided with several competent but less ambitious commanders, not least distinguished among whom was our old friend Boots Taylor, a very Chesterfield in manners. Carnes and Teel and Morehouse and Deaf Smith lived in those times with a host of other noble spirits whose lights have long since gone out."

"We notice a few survivors of those glorious days still among us. Col. Frank Johnson, one of the heroes of the storming of San Antonio, and the surrender of the Mexican garrison under Cos, sat with us on a log under the very eaves of the old building the day before it fell, and with him was another survivor, Honest Bob Wilson, who was expelled from the Senate of the old Republic, but was reelected and borne back in triumph upon their shoulders by an indignant people, to the Capitol."

CHAPTER XXVIII HOUSTON'S GROWTH AND PROGRESS

The Several Periods of Houston's History. The Plan Followed in Writing the City's Story. A Chapter of Recapitulation. Characteristics of the Pioneer Builders. Trade Revival Following Annexation. The Days of Ox-Wagon Traffic. Benefits from the First Railroad. The Destructive Early Fires and their Results. A Pen Picture of the City in 1857. Houston During the Civil War. Blockade Running and Trade Conditions. Houston as Military Headquarters. Feverish Gaiety of the War Period. A Dearth of Food and Clothes. Confederate Money and Shin Plasters. Rapid Business Revival When War Closed. Texas on Gold and Silver Basis. City Looted Under Carpet Bag Rule. A Pen Picture of Houston in 1879. A Period of Lethargy and Stagnation. The Years of Growth and Expansion. Rapid Increase in Property Values. City's Population Doubles Each Decade. The Great Skyscraper Era. Synopsis of City's Relation to Big Business Taken from City Directory of 1911. What Houston has Accomplished in the 75 Years of its Life. The Promise of the Future.

Houston's history, if it were divided into periods would be classified somewhat as follows:

- The period of the Republic, from 1836 to 1845.
- The Ante-Bellum period, from 1845 to 1861.
- The Civil War period, from 1861 to 1865.
- The short period of recovery, from 1865 to 1867.
- The Carpet-Bag period, beginning 1867, whose effects lasted until 1882.
- The period of lethargy and slight growth, from 1882 to 1895.
- The decade of rapid growth from 1895 to 1905.
- The skyscraper period, from 1905 to the present time.
-

The early chapters of the present volume describe the earliest period with a good deal of attention to the details of growth and the genesis of the several institutions. As the different kinds of enterprises that go to make up a city do not grow symmetrically nor synchronologically they cannot be foreshortened into a composite picture and hence the several elements and institutions of civic prosperity in fairness to themselves had to be traced severally and so the beginning and progress of each has been indicated in turn.

The municipality and its officials; the public improvements; the law and the lawyers; the physicians and the institutions they founded; the bench and bar; the banks and the bankers; the railroads and public service corporations; the great financial institutions; the builders and architects and the results of their labor in brick and steel and stone; the capitalists and the wage earners;

the preachers and the churches; the public schools and the Rice Institute; the newspapers and the writers; the captains of commerce and of industry and their great business enterprises; trade and manufacture; music and musicians; art and artists; clubs and societies and organizations to better the social welfare; and the several classes of citizenship who have stood for these things; have all been treated in turn.

As these grew, Houston grew from a group of log huts and tents to a busy village on a water course that led to the sea, grew to build railroads, grew to throw out the tentacles of enterprise in all directions, grew out of the village status and the small town ideas and ideals, grew to be a real city with the throbbing complex life of a city and a city's multifold interests, grew to teach the nation something about the problems of city government, grew to be an example in the conduct of public schools, grew to be the home of many beautiful churches, grew into a great buying market for cotton and many other commodities and a great selling market for lumber and many other things, grew into a city of factories, grew into a great port of export and a center of distribution for a great territory, grew to adorn herself with costly public buildings and grew up into the air with great business structures, and is steadily growing into a huge metropolis.

This chapter is one of rapid recapitulation. One that takes a backward glance at the city during its several periods and rethreads the complex story from the days of the pioneers to the present and then summarizes notable elements of very recent growth, grouping them into an avenue of achievement through which opens the vista of a splendid future, for the story of Houston will doubtless ever remain an unfinished story and the sequelae will make eve fairer chapters because the future of Houston should ever be novel in daring and epic in grandeur.

The builders of the future should remember, however, that had their predecessors not chosen wisely and built well the foundations, their own achievements would have been lesser and more circumscribed.

The popular conception of pioneers is that brawn and muscle are their main and distinguishing attributes. In popular estimation, the aesthetic, the refined and the artistic have no place in the composition of a pioneer. He is imagined as being roughly educated, if at all, with a careless disregard for books or for literature in any form, concentrating his interest on his immediate surroundings and having something amounting almost to contempt for everything not directly bearing on his physical comfort.

Now it is a remarkable fact that the pioneer Houstonians resembled such a type of pioneer in no way at all, for among them were many really brilliant and great men. Of course there were also representatives of the rough class, but these were not numerous and had too little weight or influence to stamp their individuality on the community. Society was largely composed of men of education and learning; of professional men, lawyers, doctors, statesmen and soldiers—men whose mental and moral qualifications would have reflected honor on any community. Neither is it surprising that such conditions should have prevailed, for among the early Houstonians were well educated representatives of many of the most prominent families of the older states, while among the foreigners, mostly Germans, were some of the most highly educated and well born men of Europe. Under conditions such as these it is not surprising that Houston was at first, more than in later years, an educational and intellectual, as well as a commercial center. Hon. A. W. Terrell, formerly United States minister to Turkey, once uttered a memorable address in which he showed the great number of highly educated men among the signers of the Texas Declaration of Independence. Such men composed the early citizenship of Houston.

After the establishment of the Texas Republic, Houston became a great social and political center, for here were gathered statesmen, congressmen, foreign ministers and others whose presence added materially to the life and gaiety of the city. Then, too, there was a large influx of professional men, planters, merchants and others who, with their wives and daughters, added largely to the social life of the little town. The means of enjoyment were limited, of course, but there were gatherings, visitings, dinings and other forms of social pleasure.

In December, 1845, the first state election was held. Peter W. Gray and J. N. O. Smith were elected representatives and Isaac W. Brashear was elected Senator. The following February, Texas took her place among the states of the Union. As soon as that occurred, immigration from the South and West began and new life was enthused into the state and particularly into Houston. Trade revived, land values increased and a regular boom set in. There was a brisk demand for all staple goods and the wholesale trade of the city became very great. All these goods were received by water, but their distribution to the interior had to be made by means of ox-wagons and that gave rise to an immense industry. The very difficulties of transportation created this industry and it soon became highly remunerative. It was of great proportions, too, for it is recorded that on one day there were ninety-seven ox-wagons that entered the city over the Long Bridge alone, and that it required 1,164 oxen to haul these wagons. As there was a large business done with the West also, wagons from which section came into the city over the San Felipe road, an idea of the magnitude of the business may be formed. This form of transportation, while very slow and tedious, was very reliable and certain, for while the roads at times were bad, as a rule they were very good. There was danger from attacks by Indians, but the wagoners guarded against that, by keeping together, and traveling in large parties.

The great bulk of Houston's trade with the interior was done by wagons, even as late as 1856, or three years after the Central Railroad had been started. Three years later, or in 1859, the wagon trade with the Northwest became a thing of the past, for by then, the railroad had reached a point where its influence was felt. As soon as this occurred, Houston began to feel the benefits of the change. Her business increased by leaps and bounds. Houston real estate increased in value from the time that the first shovel full of dirt for the construction of the Houston and Texas Central Railroad was thrown, but the increase was most pronounced after that road had reached Hempstead, fifty miles from Houston.

The following extract from the assessment rolls of the city, shows the valuation of Houston real estate for the years named: 1858, $2,127,123; 1859, $2,485,851; 1860, $3,339,285; 1861, $3,386,493; 1862, $3,581,923; 1863, $4,426,571.

The city was visited by two disastrous fires, one in 1858, and the other in 1859, which, while looked on as calamities at the time, were really highly beneficial. Up to that time there had been only two or three small brick buildings erected, and the whole business part of the town was composed of frame buildings. The first fire destroyed the block bounded by Main, Congress, Travis and Preston, and also destroyed the Main Street front of the block opposite. The second fire destroyed the block bounded by Main, Franklin, Congress and Travis. These two fires gave opportunity, of which advantage was taken, to replace the old wooden buildings with brick ones.

Until the beginning of the Civil War, the affairs of the city were administered in an honest and progressive spirit, which was characteristic of the people. Public office was considered a high honor and the very best citizens were chosen to act as public servants, and esteemed it an evidence of the confidence of their fellow citizens.

Just what Houston was before the war is well shown by this extract from the Telegraph of January 21, 1857:

"A gentleman from the States who has just returned from a tour through the principalities of Texas says that of all places he visited in the state, the city of Houston presents the best evidence of wealth and substantial prosperity, and that he has no doubt that it is destined to be by far the largest city in Texas. He based his belief on the advantages possessed by the city in its geographical position, at the head of the principal bay and harbor of the whole coast; upon the start it has already attained in the trade and commerce of the state; upon the energy, and enterprise it exhibited in building the first railroads and extending iron arms to embrace the whole territory of the Lone Star State within their commercial grasp; upon the disposition to be found among the people of the interior to cultivate friendly relations with our city and to secure to themselves the benefits of a market such as no other point in the state can offer them."

This vista of prosperity was rudely blurred by the Civil War.

When the great Civil War began in 1861, Houston had over two hundred miles of railway centering here. The Houston and Texas Central road extended to the north as far as Millican, a distance of 80 miles, the Buffalo Bayou and Brazoria road led to the west as far as Allyton, about 80 miles, and the Texas and New Orleans road to the east as far as Orange, about 80 miles. These made Houston the railroad center of the state, and a point of the greatest military importance. It became at once the great concentration and distributing point for troops and munitions of war, and the resultant activity was very great. Early in 1862 the Federal fleet menaced Galveston so seriously that everybody who could get away left there and came to Houston. Thus the population was increased in a novel way. Military Headquarters for the Trans-Mississippi Department were established at Houston, and it became the military, commercial and social center of the state.

There was, of course, a great show of prosperity and business, but it was all show and had but little that was real and substantial about it. There was some real prosperity, but this was confined to only a few people. Those who had a great deal of money to begin with, and who could keep out of the army, were enabled to add largely to their fortunes by obtaining permits to ship out cotton and bring back a certain amount of arms and ammunition for the use of the soldiers. It is true that a strict blockade was maintained by the Federal ships off Galveston and all other Texas ports, and that there was great risk in blockade-running, and yet one success would more than cover the losses from two or three failures. Cotton could be bought for Confederate money and after it reached a foreign port it could be sold for a dollar a pound in gold. The return cargo of war munitions was scarcely higher in price in foreign markets than during ordinary times, so that the profits on a successful round trip were very great. Most of the blockade runners, those who owned the cargoes and financed the operations, had headquarters in Houston. It would seem that this alone would have added greatly to the general prosperity, but such was not the case. The whole thing was rather a close corporation and only one or two individuals shared in the profits. Besides there were no great numbers employed in the work. One or two small, but very swift vessels, manned by as small a crew for each vessel as possible, a big capitalist at this end to buy the cotton, a salesman who went with the cargo to sell it, eager competitive buyers at the other end, prepared to give gold for the cotton and to sell arms and anything else for a return cargo,— that was all. Less than a dozen men and one small vessel could easily do all that was necessary to make a big fortune by one successful trip, or lose a small one by failure. This is narrated here to show how one-sided was the prosperity brought about by blockade running and how little the general public shared in it.

Houston being military headquarters, army contractors and hundreds of such people flocked here. There was a great deal of money in circulation, but it was Confederate money and it was just about as hard to get hold of as any other kind of money. One had then to earn what he got, as now, and as all avenues of money making were closed, except those opened for the fortunate and favored few, there was real want and great poverty among the masses. About the only things that were plentiful were brass bands and gaudy military uniforms, for there were enough brilliantly plumed staff-officers in Houston during the whole war to have made an entire regiment of Texas troops such as General Lee said he needed and wanted so badly. The chief way in which Houston suffered during the war was in having general business halted, and in having all foundries and workshops closed except those employed in manufacturing war materials. Even those that were open and in operation were operated by soldiers, detailed for that purpose. The Federal troops never were responsible, directly, for any injury to Houston, for they never got closer than fifty miles to it. Yet there was great want and suffering among the people, for even the coarsest food was expensive and hard to get, and clothing was all homemade. Any old style and any old thing was good enough just so it covered nakedness.

A very fair statement of actual conditions in Houston about the middle years of the war would be the following: General Magruder and his staff lived on the fat of the land. Several favored and adventurous merchants grew rich, honorably, by running the blockade. Dozens of army contractors got rich, any old way. The great mass of the real men were off at the front fighting for their country, and their families at home suffered for the absolute necessities of life. That is not a very nice picture but it is a true one.

Yet the city were no funeral trappings. Houston was never so gay and lively as during those war days. It is true, that nearly every week tidings came from the front that plunged some family in deepest grief, or in painful anxiety about the death or painful wounding of a son, brother, father or sweetheart on a distant battle field. Still the gaiety went on. And yet all this round of mirth making was not for the sole purpose of pleasure. Some of it had a higher and nobler motive.

The women of Houston were constantly at work raising funds to supply clothing for the soldiers and to procure hospital supplies for the sick. In order to do this they gave concerts, balls, fairs, oyster suppers, in fact they did any and everything in their power to raise money. And they succeeded too. Public balls and concerts added greatly to the general gaiety of the city, and scarcely any one paused to think of the heartbreaking cause that led to their being given. But the good work of the women was not all so pleasant as giving balls and concerts. They organized as nurses, and took charge of the local hospitals that were established for sick soldiers. When the hospitals became crowded they opened their homes to the sick and wounded soldiers, and they were unceasing in their devotion to the great work they had undertaken.

Coffee, tea and flour became things of the past almost, and were so scarce that they were only within the reach, even when a stray supply showed up, of the very wealthy. There was plenty of sugar in this part of the state, because of the proximity of the sugar plantations, and there was plenty of corn meal and bacon and meat, but beyond that, there was nothing. Many substitutes for tea and coffee were found but there was none for flour. Sweet potatoes roasted to a crisp and then ground in a coffee mill, made a good substitute for coffee. Sassafras root made good tea. As a rule, however, most people drank only hot water.

One of the greatest problems the people had to contend with was securing lights. Every family became its own candle-maker. These candles were wonderful creations made of tallow and having wicks of home-spun cotton. They had to be snuffed about every two minutes, otherwise they gave no light at all.

About the queerest hardships the people had to undergo developed the latter part of 1863. The money gave out. Even Confederate money became so scarce that the people had no medium of exchange. What little Confederate money there was in circulation was in bills of large denomination. There were no small bills at all. In this dilemma each merchant in town constituted himself a bank of issue. At first the plan worked very satisfactorily, but soon it was so overdone that everybody became disgusted, and refused to take any of the notes or bills except those issued by well-known and responsible firms. As the number of these was limited, the confusion soon became almost as great as ever. The older citizens tell of a German druggist, who did not have the best character for honesty, issuing thousands of dollars of these "shin plasters," as they were called. No one would take them, and finally he refused to take them himself, giving as his reason the fact that everybody else refused them, and that he had a right to do what everybody else did.

There was a great deal of both tragedy and comedy in Houston during the four years of the war, but on the whole comedy prevailed, and people went on buying and selling, laughing and weeping, marrying and giving in marriage.

Almost before the echo of the last gun of the war had died away, Houston began to show life and animation. Business became brisk and there was evidence of prosperity on every hand. This was due to several causes. Houston had felt few of the ill effects of the war, except those that were general to the whole country, and certainly none that could be considered more than temporary and transient. But the real reason for the great prosperity lay in the fact that there were large quantities of cotton stowed away on the plantations and farms—the accumulations of four years, which found a ready and ravenous market at fabulous prices. Houston's trade became at once very great, and the prosperity was great also. There was plenty of money and it was easy to get hold of. It was real money too, gold and silver, for Texas was the only state in the Union that was on a gold and silver basis in 1865. Large quantities of foreign gold were shipped here with which to buy cotton, and gold became the currency of the country. This prosperity was somewhat checked in 1866 by the occurrence of the cholera epidemic of that year, but the check was only temporary and before the fall of 1866, everything was booming again. The winter of 1866–1867 was very active in all branches of business. The presence of a large body of troops, the Federal army of occupation, while annoying and exasperating, was possibly beneficial from a commercial point of view, since they had to purchase all their supplies in the local market.

This prosperity was effervescent, however, for after the supply of old cotton had been exhausted, it was found, that owing to the difficulties of securing suitable labor, it was almost impossible to produce more. Then the great yellow fever epidemic of 1867 broke out, accompanied by an equally great disaster, the establishment of carpet-bag rule in Texas and of course, in Houston, and all semblance of prosperity fled.

All the county and city officials in Houston were removed from office by order of E. J. Davis and their places filled by men, who, with few exceptions, were irresponsible rascals or negroes. Then began a struggle for white supremacy, which lasted for several years, during which time the dishonest officials proceeded to loot the country and city.

By 1879 the bonded debt of Houston was very close to $2,000,000 and the affairs of the city were in a desperate condition. A very true picture of the Houston of that day was given by a citizen of Iowa, who visited this city and after his return home wrote the following letter to the Davenport, Iowa, Gazette, in 1879:

"This (Houston) is the great railroad center of Texas, and if railroads make a great city, this is destined to be one. It is the terminus of the Galveston and Houston, the Houston and Texas Central, the Galveston, Harrisburg and San Antonio, the Texas and New Orleans, and the Great Northern railroads, the last named of which also has a branch to Columbia. Besides this it is the harbor of the Morgan line of steamships, running to New Orleans, Havana, Brownsville and Vera Cruz. Is not this a good foundation for a city? * * * * It has a charming climate. Its trees are green and its flowers are beautiful and fragrant. It has some (not many) good buildings, business houses and residences. It has the finest market house in the West and the finest market. It has some good looking stores, dry goods and groceries, and, I am told, a good cotton press. But the city looks shabby. There is not a paved or macadamized street in the town, and but few decent sidewalks, and no system of sewers at all. Wooden troughs are placed in the gutters in some places, and waste water from houses is conducted into them through other wooden troughs. This water does not run off, but stands and emits an unhealthful odor. If such a want of cleanliness does not breed disease it is only because the day of wrath is being put off.

"I was told that the city has an enormous debt, and that some are recommending a surrender of the city charter to avoid payment, but I cannot believe that the better men of Houston will suffer such a stigma to attach to their city.

"She has the recuperative power within herself which needs only to be awakened to impel her to throw off the load by which she is oppressed. The city is beautiful for situation and were it paved, painted and polished up, it would shine like a star."

Most of the evils this writer complained of have been done away with and the bright future he predicted for Houston has become a fact.

When Houston had finally compromised her bonded debt, she was placed in position to turn her attention to those things that have made her great. But the following twelve to fifteen years, or from 1882 to 1895, her progress was slow. The city barely held its own and there was little growth either in commercial importance or in population during that period.

The year 1895 marked the end of the period of lethargy and inaction. There was a recognition of Houston's advantageous position by outside capital and home people began to share in this new born confidence. The growth was not phenomenal, but it was satisfactory and of such character as to attract attention, and was altogether along safe and conservative lines. During the next decade the expansion and growth became wonderful, and at one time it reached such proportions that it created alarm, and predictions were freely made that Houston would be overtaken by the fate of other "boomed" cities. These predictions have proved groundless and what was considered undue inflation in 1900 was considered as ridiculously conservative five years later.

The change of form of municipal government, from the old board of aldermen with a mayor, to the five commissioners, inspired the greatest public confidence, and the city entered on an era of growth, expansion and prosperity that was of such marked proportions as to attract the attention of the outside world. The commission form of government became effective in 1905. In less than a year, the guarantee that it gave of a business-like management of public affairs and the consequent stability of every other form of business, inspired the greatest confidence, and capitalists vied with each other in their efforts to add to the commercial and manufacturing industries of the city. From September, 1906 to September, 1907, there were 146 new enterprises chartered in Houston, with a total capital of $14,836,375, while twenty-eight of Houston's established corporations increased their capital stock $3,340,000.

The assessed valuation of property in Houston, in 1901, was $27,534,271, while the bonded debt was, including the funded debt incurred by the carpet-bag government, $2,995,000.

For the year 1911 the assessed valuation is $77,294,351. (The real value is nearly $200,000,000), while the bonded debt is only $5,919,000 or just twice as great as it was ten years before, while the city has a hundred fold more to show for its debt.

Houston has never redeemed any of the bonds issued, for the simple reason that none, save those funded, have ever fallen due. The oldest outstanding bond issue is that of $524,000 of 30 years funding bonds, bearing 6 per cent interest, issued January 1, 1882, and maturing January 1, 1912. The city will be able to pay these bonds when due and will do so.

The city's charter permits the levying of $2 on every $100 of assessed valuation, but the commission has gradually reduced this rate until now it is only $1.70 on the $100.

The following figures taken from the books of the assessors office do not fairly show the true values, but they do fairly indicate the wonderful ratio of increase in the value of Houston property, not only during each decade, but the remarkable increase of each decade over the preceding one: 1880, assessment $5,502,416; 1890, $12,946,485; 1900, 27,480,898; 1910, $77,294,351. In 1880 the bonded debt represented almost two-fifths of the assessed value of Houston's property, while in 1911, it represented only one-thirteenth.

The original city limits of Houston were nine square miles. During the reconstruction period this was inflated many miles in every direction but was reduced, as has been recounted, back to the original limits. By 1903 it overlapped this area in every direction and the limits were rationally extended to include 16 square miles which is the official area today, but the city again overlaps in every direction.

According to the federal census the population of Houston within its city limits was 27,557 in 1890 and in 1900 it was 44,633, while by the census of 1910 the total was 78,800. Together with Houston Heights, Brunner and other suburbs, however, between which and Houston there exists only the artificial boundary of an imaginary line and which are one with Houston in continuity, growth and development, the population is 105,860, so that Houston is actually the largest city in Texas.

Although practically all the acreage of Harris County is fertile there is only 11 per cent under cultivation and the development of the 89 per cent of the county lands will vastly increase the city's growth. The development of all south Texas will also help this city.

The story of the great building era of recent years has been told but it should be noted that the skyscraper period of building has only been in progress since about 1905 and that 19 of the 28 buildings of six stories or over that Houston boasts have been completed within the two years preceding November 1, 1911.

Permits for the erection of 981 buildings were granted by the city for the year closing February 28, 1911.

A quarter of a century before, in 1885, there were 98 buildings constructed in Houston in the course of a year and their total cost was $286,000 or about half the cost of an ordinary modern skyscraper. Of the 98 buildings of that year, 80 were dwelling houses, and only six were factory buildings.

At any time since January 1, 1909, there has been at least $5,000,000 worth of construction work in progress in Houston, huge new skyscrapers being begun as soon as others were completed. On October 1, 1911, over $7,000,000 worth of construction work was in progress. Houston's latest city directory, issued in the summer of 1911, thus summarizes the advantages of Houston as the home of big business:

"In cotton, lumber, oil and rice, Houston is preeminent. It collects and distributes for export the great bulk of the Texas and Oklahoma cotton crop and much from elsewhere. Here are annually handled 275,000 bales. By concentration facilities and saving on railroad rates Houston saves the cotton trade some $4,000,000 annually. Most of this saving is to the growers and initial shippers. From all over the world, great cotton interests send their representatives here. Manchester, Liverpool and Hamburg are accustomed to send scions of their great trade houses to learn the cotton business in Houston. Even Japan is represented among the cotton factors and brokers of Houston by a native firm. Cotton compresses, cotton oil and cotton seed products have large plants and interests.

"Houston is perhaps the greatest lumber city in America. There are 49 corporations of yellow pine lumber manufacturers here, whose combined capital aggregates $85,000,000. An annual business of $40,000,000 in lumber is transacted by the lumber men in Houston. Some 250 saw mills in Texas, Louisiana and Arkansas are represented here. There are six national banks and four large trust companies, two of the largest of the latter having just consolidated, that have a combined capital stock of $7,000,000. Two of the banks are capitalized for $1,000,000 each. They are the Union National and the First National. The checking deposits of the Houston banks aggregate over $33,000,000 and the saving deposits $3,000,000 more.

"Houston is the second largest primary rice market in the South. It is in the center of a district that annually produces 2,500,000 bags from 282,000 acres planted in rice. Five great rice mills operate here.

"Houston is the market and center of the Texas petroleum district which annually produces 13,000,000 barrels. The largest independent oil company in America, The Texas Company, has headquarters here. It is capitalized for $50,000,000 and owns its own line of oil steamers which traverse nearly all seas.

"Houston is the center of the great sugar growing district of Texas. Near it are 13 sugar mills with a combined capacity of 11,700 tons daily. This district produces 2,350,000 gallons of molasses annually. Every boy and girl in North and South America could have molasses, on his or her bread, grown and made within sixty miles of Houston.

"Some 20 concerns on Houston's produce row do an annual business in the Texas produce market of $5,500,000. The city is the center of the Texas fruit and vegetable trade. The annual wholesale trade of Houston is $130,000,000. The city has over 1,200 retail firms that do an annual business of over $55,000,000. The city has 341 factories, producing 282 different articles. The manufactured products of Houston are annually worth $56,000,000. Over 10,000 wage earners are employed in Houston who receive $9,000,000 annually.

"The tax roll for 1912 will carry an $80,000,000 property valuation.

"The city death rate is 13.5, one of the lowest in the country. The death rate among the white population is under 10. These figures are to each 1,000 inhabitants.

"The city has the largest scholastic population and the best public school system of any city in Texas.

"Houston has 64 churches worth over $3,500,000. They are supported by 30,000 communicants at an annual cost of $275,000.

"The railroad shops of Houston employ over 5,000 men who draw an annual aggregate wage of over $3,000,000.

"Houston is the home of splendid newspapers, thoroughly equipped and magnificently housed.

"Harris County has over 300 miles of shell road and is a paradise for automobilists.

"The altitude of Houston is 64 feet and the terrain is everywhere level.

"At Houston 17 lines of railroad meet the sea, and here they have absolute terminals.

"The Houston ship channel, now 18 feet deep for its entire length, carries an annual traffic of 1,500,000 tons valued at a sum in excess of $50,000,000.

"On July 18, 1907, Houston was made a port of entry and has doubled its receipts each year since that time.

"On February 7, 1910, the federal congress authorized the expenditure of $2,500,000 under government direction on the Houston ship channel to straighten it and increase the depth to 25 feet, conditioned that Houston pay half of the amount. On January 10, 1911, Houston, by almost unanimous vote, decided to issue bonds for her one-half of the sum named. The bonds have just been issued and are now open to bids. (These bonds were purchased en bloc by the Houston banks and trust companies and were not put on the outside market at all.)

"At the same time that Houston voted the ship channel bonds it voted the expenditure of $500,000 for the building of a viaduct over the bayou to more closely connect the several sections of the city. These bonds have been sold and work will soon commence on the splendid viaduct. (The bonds were purchased by the South Texas National Bank of Houston and work is now under way on the viaduct.)

"The city has recently voted $500,000 in school bonds for the erection of new schools.

"The figures and statistics quoted are largely taken directly from the city reports and the reports of firms and corporations, the rest are those collated by Houston's active chamber of commerce.

"Socially, religiously, educationally and most of all in business life Houston is the metropolis of Texas and stands on the threshold of yet larger and more splendid growth."

This summary taken from the directory was written by the editor of this volume, and where larger figures are used than those in the body of the text, in the chapters referring to the several industries the larger figures are those of the city's chamber of commerce collated at a later date than the chapters were written.

Houston as a city is 75 years old. It has demonstrated many remarkable things in city building. Within one year from the time that John Allen cut the coffee weeds with a bowie knife down a muddy slope that led to a slowly flowing bayou, the new town became the capital city of the new Republic whose area was 52,000 square miles greater than that of France. In a few years Houston lost the political capital, which sought a spot nearer the geographical center of the state, but it retained the commercial supremacy and is today the financial capital of the state. Its population has practically doubled every decade, but the last doubling actually occurred within a period of some five years. Will it double again within the next five or the next decade? Few students of business conditions will doubt it.

Out of the Houston-Galveston shipping district more goods are sent abroad than from anywhere else in the United States save New York City alone. The opening of the Panama Canal will make this district the great shipping point to South America and the Orient and will also develop it as a great port of entry for foreign goods. One must look to Manchester and to Hamburg to be able even to presage the future commercial supremacy of Houston.

Built in a wilderness Houston has become a metropolis.

Built on an almost sea level plain it has lifted itself into the air. It has disappointed no promoter's faith and has made sober and trite reality of many a promise that seemed but the extravaganza of rhapsody and has then passed beyond the prophecies that were made for it until one almost sneers at the seers of its future for their shortness of vision. In view of that fact who shall dare to paint its future or count the heaven kissing shafts and towers shown in the mirage of the days to come overarched by the rainbows of promise. The arithmetic of the future is of little value, for Houston grows in a geometrical progression. One thing at least is certain. Great Texas will have one great metropolis. It will be a sea-port. It will be Houston!

Made in the USA
Las Vegas, NV
15 July 2023

74767057R00181